IN DEBT TO SHAYS

The Bicentennial of an Agrarian Rebellion

IN DEBT TO SHAYS

The Bicentennial of an Agrarian Rebellion

EDITED BY ROBERT A. GROSS

UNIVERSITY PRESS OF VIRGINIA | *Charlottesville and London*

Publications of the Colonial Society of Massachusetts, Volume 65
Selections from conferences held at the Colonial Society of
Massachusetts on October 3 and 4, 1986, and Historic Deerfield,
Inc., on November 13, 14, and 15, 1986

THE UNIVERSITY PRESS OF VIRGINIA
Copyright © 1993 by the Colonial Society of Massachusetts
First published 1993

LIBRARY OF CONGRESS CATALOGING-IN-PUBLICATION DATA
In debt to Shays: the bicentennial of an agrarian rebellion / edited
by Robert A. Gross.
    p. cm. —(Publications of the Colonial Society of Massachusetts: v. 65)
"Selections from conferences held at the Colonial Society of Massachusetts on
October 3 and 4, 1986, and Historic Deerfield, Inc., on November 13, 14, and
15, 1986"—T.p. verso.
  Includes bibliographical references and index.
    ISBN 0-8139-1353-5 (cloth). — ISBN 0-8139-1354-3 (paper)
    1. Shays' Rebellion, 1786–1787—Congresses. I. Gross, Robert A.,
1945– . II. Colonial Society of Massachusetts. III. Historic Deerfield,
inc. IV. Series.
F61.C71 vol. 65
[F69]
974.4'02 s—dc20
[974.4'03]
                                      92-10332
                                            CIP

Printed in the United States of America

CONTENTS

Foreword   FREDERICK S. ALLIS, JR.   ix
Editor's Acknowledgments   xiii

Introduction
The Uninvited Guest: Daniel Shays and the Constitution
    ROBERT A. GROSS   1

Part One: Merchants and Magistrates
1. The Public Creditor Interest in Massachusetts
    Politics, 1780–86   RICHARD BUEL, JR.   47
2. Shays's Rebellion in Long Perspective:
    The Merchants and the "Money Question"
    JOSEPH A. ERNST   57
3. Debt Litigation and Shays's Rebellion
    JONATHAN M. CHU   81
4. The Federalist Reaction to Shays's Rebellion
    STEPHEN E. PATTERSON   101

Part Two: Political Cultures in Conflict
5. "The Fine Theoretic Government of Massachusetts Is
    Prostrated to the Earth": The Response to Shays's
    Rebellion Reconsidered   WILLIAM PENCAK   121
6. Regulators and White Indians: Forms of
    Agrarian Resistance in Post-Revolutionary
    New England   ALAN TAYLOR   145
7. Reinterpreting Rebellion: The Influence of Shays's
    Rebellion on American Political Thought
    MICHAEL LIENESCH   161

Part Three: A Splintered Society
8. Shays's Neighbors: The Context of Rebellion
    in Pelham, Massachusetts
    GREGORY H. NOBLES   185

9. A Deacon's Orthodoxy: Religion, Class,
and the Moral Economy of Shays's Rebellion
JOHN L. BROOKE   205

10. The Religious World of Daniel Shays
STEPHEN A. MARINI   239

Part Four: Consolidating the Republic

11. In Shays's Shadow: Separation and Ratification
of the Constitution in Maine
JAMES LEAMON   281

12. The Confidence Man and the Preacher:
The Cultural Politics of Shays's Rebellion
ROBERT A. GROSS   297

Notes   323
Contributors   391
Index   393

ILLUSTRATIONS

1. *Veterans of 1776 Returning from the War* by
   William T. Ranney (1848)   23
2. Map of Massachusetts in the new republic by
   Samuel Lewis (1795)   24
3. Petition of the Inhabitants of the Town of Methuen
   to the Hon. Senate and Hon. House of Representatives
   of the Commonwealth of Massachusetts,
   Oct. 2, 1786   26
4. "REPRESENTATION of a COUNTY-CONVENTION for
   REDRESS of GRIEVANCES of COURTS," engraving
   for *Bickerstaff's Boston Almanack* for 1787   28
5. "The Sons of COKE and LITTLETON, returning from
   a rich Feast at Concord-Court," engraving for
   Bickerstaff's Boston Almanack for 1787   29
6. AN ADDRESS, *To the good People of the Commonwealth,
   By His Excellency* JAMES BOWDOIN, *Esquire, Governour
   of the Commonwealth of Massachusetts*. Broadside
   (Boston, 1787)   30
7. "Gen. DANIEL SHAYS, Col. JOB SHATTUCK," engraving
   for *Bickerstaff's Boston Almanack* for 1787   31
8. Portrait of Samuel Adams by John Singleton Copley
   (1770–72)   32
9. Portrait of James Bowdoin II by Robert Feke
   (1748)   33
10. The Manse, Joseph Barnard house,
    Deerfield, Mass.   34

11. House on the site of the Daniel Shays farmstead, Pelham, Mass.   35
12. The events of Shays's Rebellion: a map of strategic sites   36
13. Map of southwestern Worcester County in the era of the Regulation   37
14. List of Persons Subscribing to Oath of Allegiance, February 27, 1787   38
15. Black List for Hampshire County   40
16. Christopher Babbitt, *To His Excellency* JOHN HANCOCK, *Esquire, Governor of the State of Massachusetts*. Broadside (Boston, 1787)   42

FOREWORD

Since neither the form nor the content of this volume follows a conventional pattern, an explanation of its provenance is in order. In the late 1960s the Colonial Society of Massachusetts adopted a policy of holding conferences on various aspects of colonial history and then publishing the papers delivered at these sessions. The first gathering, held in 1971, focused on Boston Prints and Printmakers and was followed by a volume with that title. Since then conferences have been held on diverse themes, including Boston Furniture of the Eighteenth Century, Seafaring in Colonial Massachusetts, Law in Colonial Massachusetts, and Seventeenth-Century New England. Equally varied has been the geographical scope, confined in some cases to Boston, extending in others to Massachusetts, widening out in still others to the New England region as a whole.

In the early 1980s, Ralph J. Crandall, Director of the New England Historic-Genealogical Society and at that time Recording Secretary of the Colonial Society, and James O'Toole, then Archivist of the Boston Archdiocese and presently Professor of History at the University of Massachusetts, Boston, proposed to the Colonial Society Council that a conference be convened on Shays's Rebellion to commemorate the bicentennial of that event. The Council approved the project, and as a result, the Colonial Society invited ten scholars to deliver papers, followed by "Final Reflections" from Harvard Professor Oscar Handlin. Messrs. Crandall and O'Toole staged the meeting, held October 3 and 4, 1986. In due course, it was assumed, the Colonial Society would publish the essays in a volume of its own, as part of the series of volumes from its conferences. An initial step toward the realization of this aim was taken when Robert J. Taylor, a member of the Society, the former editor of the Adams Papers project at the Massachusetts Historical Society, and the author of *Western Massachusetts in the Revolution*, read all the papers delivered at the conference and made a number of useful suggestions on each.

A little over a month later a second bicentennial conference, entitled "Shays's Rebellion and the Constitution," gathered in western Massachusetts. Held on November 13–15, 1986, the meeting was hosted by Historic Deerfield, in cooperation with Amherst College. The program grew out of the efforts of many people in the Connecticut Valley, who were anxious to conduct a commemoration of Shays's Rebellion in the very region where the farmers' uprising had gained its greatest support and taken its most dramatic turns. Several people at Historic Deerfield played key roles in bringing the conference into being. Donald R. Friary, Executive Director of Historic Deerfield, sustained the project from its inception. J. Ritchie Garrison, then Director of Education at Historic Deerfield, helped to initiate the gathering; his successor, Robert J. Wilson, saw to the details of organizing the meeting; Kevin Sweeney, in turn, carried the conference to a successful conclusion. Joining the Historic Deerfield staff throughout this effort was Robert A. Gross, then Professor of History and American Studies at Amherst College. The conference was supported in part by a grant from the Division of Research Programs at the National Endowment for the Humanities. Further assistance was provided by Amherst College, the Baybank Valley Trust Company, Deerfield Academy, the Peter Pan Bus Lines, the Southworth Company, the Strathmore Paper Company, the Hammermill Foundation, the Monarch Life Insurance Company, and the following individuals: Mr. and Mrs. Robert F. Dalzell, Jr.; Mr. and Mrs. Irving N. Esleeck, Jr.; Mrs. Francis McInnerney; Janet A. Riesman; and Joseph Hill Torras.

Where the Colonial Society conference had been a relatively small gathering, attended by some fifty invited participants, the Historic Deerfield conference was much larger, drawing several hundred people to most of its sessions at Amherst College and Deerfield Academy. The conference opened with a keynote address by Professor Garry Wills; in the next two days thirteen papers were delivered, with commentaries by distinguished scholars, musical performances in the evenings, and a screening of a new documentary film on Shays's Rebellion. Professors Michael Zuckerman of the University of Pennsylvania and Carol Berkin of Baruch College delivered summary reflections on the conference as a whole.

At the close of its sessions, the organizers of the Deerfield conference began to contemplate publication of the papers. They were thus amenable to a proposal from the Colonial Society to combine the conference proceedings. Through such cooperation, all the latest scholarship produced by the bicentennial of Shays's Rebellion would be available in a single volume. Accordingly, a formal agreement was drawn up between the two institutions to pool their resources.

Professor Robert A. Gross agreed to edit the volume, and both institutions must consider themselves fortunate to have acquired his service for this project. Not only did he do an outstanding job in editing the work of the individual contributors; he also wrote a splendid introduction to the whole, as well as contributing a delightful paper that he had delivered as the keynote to the Colonial Society conference. The editorial work and the original writing involved a tremendous amount of labor for which all those interested in Shays's Rebellion must be forever in his debt. In a very real sense, this volume is Bob Gross's book.

Frederick S. Allis, Jr.
Editor of Publications
Colonial Society of Massachusetts

87 Mount Vernon Street
Boston, Massachusetts

EDITOR'S ACKNOWLEDGMENTS

Several years after the bicentennial of Shays's Rebellion and five hundred miles or so southwest of the Connecticut Valley of Massachusetts, I continue to owe outstanding debts to numerous individuals who have contributed their energies and talents to the publication of this volume.

The first payments should be made to the individuals who welcomed and supported the idea of a bicentennial tribute to Shays's Rebellion. Donald Friary of Historic Deerfield backed the original plan. Ritchie Garrison, Bob Wilson, Kevin Sweeney, and Mary Metcalf were splendid compatriots in organizing the conference. President Peter Pouncey of Amherst College gave warm encouragement to the effort, as did my colleagues in the American Studies Department, who collaborated in teaching a course on "Shays's Rebellion and the Making of the Constitution" in 1986 and 1987. Students and faculty in that course were active participants in the conference. So, too, were the dozen hardened but still enthusiastic veterans of a summer institute on this subject, sponsored by the Five College–Western Massachusetts Partnership for the Schools. All of these students and colleagues helped to shape my thinking about the events in western Massachusetts during 1786–87 and the larger social and political crisis they dramatized for the new republic. I am particularly grateful to Hugh Hawkins, N. Gordon Levin, Mary Alice Wilson, and to the students in my sections of American Studies 11.

To the scholars who have patiently awaited the appearance of this work, I am immensely grateful. They have been obliged to show greater forbearance than Daniel Shays back in 1787, as he vainly awaited the arrival of Captain Luke Day with his troops for the assault on the federal armory in Springfield, Massachusetts. Despite his promise, Day and his men never showed; Daniel Shays led the march into disaster and into history on his own. At times, in preparing this manuscript for publication, I have anticipated the ignominy of Luke Day, ready in arms but not in action. My rescuers have been many. Fritz Allis of the Colonial Society deserves enormous credit for sustaining this project. His good cheer, wise counsel, and unstinting enthusiasm, kept up amidst severe trials of his own, have inspired my own morale. Steve Nissenbaum, as always, heard me out and read my drafts with his shrewd sense of argument and language. John Brooke, Richard Brown, Steve Innes, Steve Marini, and Alan Taylor persuaded a reluctant author to sharpen his statement and condense his prose.

Several assistants were indispensable to the production of the book. In Amherst, Kathryn Abbott, a graduate student in history at the University of Massachusetts at Amherst, gathered an essential bibliography. A year and a half later, two graduate students in American Studies at William and Mary made possible the final delivery of the manuscript. Kimberly Lankford performed necessary copyediting; Phyllis Hunter researched and discovered the illustrations. In the process, I gained enormous respect for their several skills and their common dedication to scholarship.

Ann Gross kept faith with this project in Amherst, Williamsburg, and numerous other venues; my debts to her as sympathetic listener, critical editor, and emotional ally are now over a quarter century old and will never be repaid. Matthew and Stevie Gross, skeptical teenagers, harbored more doubts; Nellie Gross at age eight showed none. Her trust is as yet unchallenged by experience. To all of them and to the members of their rising generation, I am pleased to present this volume, in hopes that they may sustain together the struggle for social justice and the quest for historical truth.

                                          Robert A. Gross
                                    College of William and Mary

INTRODUCTION

THE UNINVITED GUEST:
Daniel Shays and the Constitution

Robert A. Gross

From August 1824 to September 1825, the marquis de Lafayette made a triumphal tour of the United States to commemorate the fiftieth anniversary of the American Revolution. In his late sixties, the aging hero of the War for Independence traveled up and down the land as "the Nation's Guest," greeting old comrades-in-arms and receiving tributes from a grateful people. Everywhere Americans flocked to see the onetime companion and "adopted son" of George Washington; everywhere they hastened to proclaim thanks to the French aristocrat who had so selflessly helped to create a free nation. Never let it be said of them, one speaker vowed, "as [it had been] of Rome and of Athens, that ingratitude is the common vice of republics." The American people acknowledged their debts.[1]

One veteran of the Revolution was absent from these celebrations, though he had once served as an officer under Lafayette and gained notice for that connection. Daniel Shays lay dying, in obscurity and poverty, in the little town of Sparta in western New York. Back in 1780 Captain Shays had received an ornamental sword from General Lafayette as a mark of personal esteem. But in a moment of need, the Continental officer had sold that "pledge of affection" for a few measly dollars and in the process earned the condemnation of his peers. Denounced as an ingrate without "honour and spirit," a bitter Shays quit the army in disgust, returning home to western Massachusetts, where he would shortly obtain notoriety as the "Generalissimo" of a debtors' revolt. The movement was prompted by the program of hard money and heavy taxes imposed by the state government in Boston to pay the costs of the Revolutionary War. It started with popular protests at town meetings

I

and county conventions, escalated into resistance to the courts, and culminated in a military assault on the federal arsenal at Springfield in late January 1787. For a brief moment Daniel Shays and his army of angry farmers seemed to threaten the Commonwealth of Massachusetts and the future of the American republic. In fact, the uprising that came to be known as Shays's Rebellion was easily suppressed, and its eponymous leader quickly forgotten. Despite a pardon from the state, Shays spent the rest of his life in exile, moving from town to town along the Vermont and New York frontiers. By 1825, as Lafayette was wending his way across the country, few traces remained of the figure who had once commanded a "horrid and unnatural rebellion." Shays had declined into a poor, garrulous old man who drank too much, dependent for a living on a few acres of land and on a pension from the national government he had unwittingly hastened into being.[2]

It is no wonder, then, that Daniel Shays was never invited to the festivities for Lafayette. To Americans of the 1820s, intent on celebrating the unity and virtue of the Revolutionary generation, his presence might have been an unwelcome reminder of conflict and injustice at the nation's start. But surprisingly, contemporaries had little to say when, a few weeks after Lafayette's departure for France, Shays's death was reported in the press. In a list of recent deaths, the *New York Evening Post* carried this laconic item: "In Sparta, on the 29th ult. Gen. Daniel Shays, aged 84; he was an officer of the revolution, and subsequently the leader of a party in Massachusetts called Shays' men." The notice was remarkably benign. Posthumously awarded a generalship he never claimed, Shays was remembered, vaguely, as a political figure from Massachusetts's past. The details of his rebellion forgotten, he was just another of the old men of the Revolution, whose steadily dwindling ranks marked the end of America's "heroic age."[3]

Massachusetts, however, remembered. Newspapers in Boston, Concord, and Northampton were quick to report the death of Shays, whom they identified unfailingly as the military leader of the insurrection against the Commonwealth. But their comments were without asperity. To the *Boston Commercial Gazette,* whose long obituary set the tone for the press, Shays had been a reluctant and repentant rebel. Passing glancingly over his Continental service—

he had quit the army for "reasons quite problematical"—the paper attributed Shays's leadership of the "disaffected" to "the extreme pressure of the times." Even in revolt, he had remained a true republican. Shays was no aspiring Caesar, bent upon military dictatorship: instead, as commander of the insurgency, he had readily taken orders from a committee of civilians, submitting every decision to a "vote of the whole." Early on, Shays "got sick of his enterprise" and would have quit the affair on "perfect assurance of a pardon." That promise never came. But after the rebellion was crushed and Shays had taken refuge in Vermont, he submitted "a humble petition" to the Massachusetts General Court "acknowledging [his] errors and imploring forgiveness." Prompted by "good sense," the legislature pardoned him and everybody else concerned in the disorders and put Shays's Rebellion behind it. Thanks to that act, the Boston paper noted, Shays was able to secure a reward for his military services in the Revolution. Indeed, the grant of a pension to a former rebel against government drew considerable comment. It attested to the final reconciliation of all parties to the Massachusetts conflict. True, the *Concord Gazette and Middlesex Yeoman* could not resist the jibe that Shays had ended up poor and needy, as a result of his "crooked path and errors of former days." But no one questioned his right to the annuity. And through the wisdom of the state, added the *Commercial Gazette,* the insurgents and their descendants had become loyal, respectable, even conservative citizens, prominent "amongst are [our] most exemplary yeomanry." Generous government, reformed rebels: the bitterness of 1786–87 was gone. Daniel Shays, as well as Lafayette, could be admitted into America's "Era of Good Feelings."[4]

That brief moment of acceptance in 1825 was one of the few times in our history when Daniel Shays proved an uncontroversial figure. Before and since, both the man and the rebellion he led have occasioned intense debate. Naturally so, for they are bound up with the very meanings of the American Revolution and the Constitution. In 1786–87 Shays's Rebellion exposed a fundamental crisis of republicanism in the new nation. To discontented farmers in Massachusetts and beyond, the insurgency expressed popular fury at the unresponsiveness and the elitism of the new state governments in the face of widespread economic distress. But many others, especially Patriot leaders who had long been striving for a powerful, central government, took the uprising as the symbol of a republic in peril. In their view, an unruly people, easily misled and manipulated by ambitious demagogues like Shays, was jeopardizing the very liberty for which the Revolution had been fought. It was to end such threats from below and to preserve the American venture in self-government that nationalists in the states launched the movement to replace the Articles of Confederation with a more effective, energetic government. As delegates gathered in Philadelphia during the spring of 1787 to accomplish this end, the "late disturbances" in Massachusetts were still reverberating throughout the land. Shays's Rebellion and the Constitution have been closely linked ever since.[5]

Not every opponent of Shays's Rebellion endorsed the plan of government to emerge from the Philadelphia convention; a few even became leading Antifederalists in the contest over ratification. But over the course of the nineteenth century, ideological lines hardened. Shays's Rebellion became a litmus test of political belief. Nationalist historians applauded the Fathers of the Constitution for rescuing the republic from the anarchy portended by Shays. By contrast, scholars on the Left, especially in the twentieth century, have seen in the Massachusetts protests the true democratic spirit of the common folk; for them, the Constitution was the Revolution betrayed, the American Thermidor. Such have been the terms in which discussions of Shays's Rebellion and the Constitution have been fixed, for nearly two hundred years, in our histories and popular culture.

Half-forgotten at his death, Daniel Shays has become a folk hero. His rebellion has inspired novels, plays, ballads, murals, films, even the name of a folksinging group. For many activists, the insurrection is a cherished symbol of popular unrest: a signal moment in our history when working people rose up in arms against the forces of capitalism and elitism that dominate the nation. Preserving the memory of Shays helps to keep the spirit of protest alive. But one need not be on the Left to recall the protests of 1786–87. Local pride counts, too. Having officially forgiven Shays, the Commonwealth of Massachusetts dedicated a highway in his honor; the road leads through the hills and woods of the west into his old town of Pelham, which proudly announces to passersby that it is "the home of Shays's

Rebellion." Even doctrinaires of the Right now adopt Shays's cause. On the eve of its bicentennial, President Reagan celebrated the rebellion as a taxpayers' revolt which altered the balance between government and people, making future insurrections unnecessary. "Shays' protest was put down forcefully," Reagan declared, "but it helped lead to the adoption of the United States constitution, a blueprint for freedom giving each of us the right to help direct the course of our government to fight against injustice, if you will, without having to lead an armed revolution." No longer was Shays an uninvited guest at official commemorations of the Constitution. Two hundred years after the rebellion, Americans of every political opinion pay "homage to Daniel Shays."[6]

This cheerful consensus is, however, an evasion of history. To bring Shays on board the Federalist ship of state is to deny the purposes of the contending parties in the contest over the Constitution. Back in 1787–88, some nationalists were quite open about their goal of erecting a government capable of curbing the disorderly "democracies" in the states. Soon after ratification, the *Massachusetts Centinel* took a detached view of the successful movement for the Constitution. "In investigating the causes which gave life to the happy form of government which we shall ere long be under," observed editor Benjamin Russell, "the Historian will not forget the era of the late insurrections in this Commonwealth. The insurrections . . . must be considered as the causes of bringing in existence, at a much earlier period than would otherwise have been, the [Federal] government." Safeguarding the republic against a future Shays was hardly the sole object of the Federalists, but it was one the insurgents and their sympathizers readily detected. Overwhelmingly, representatives from Shaysite territory opposed the new government, on the grounds that it threatened to fasten upon the nation the same system of corruption and tyranny that its local sponsors had already attempted in Massachusetts. We need not endorse this position to acknowledge the antagonisms in the fight over the Constitution. But making this admission does complicate celebration of our origins as a democratic nation. For how can we simultaneously fete the Constitution and Shays, if the one was intended to suppress the other?[7]

To break free of that contradiction, it is essential to face up to the social-political conflicts and ideological struggles of the Revolutionary age from which the United States was born. For too long, discussion of Shays's Rebellion and the Constitution has been locked into a narrow, anachronistic frame. Americans have presumed too easily that the contending parties in the 1780s were fighting their battles on modern ground, with political ideas and language that remain vital today. The age of Shays is more distant than we care to admit. But its significance is larger, as well. Restored to historical context, Shays's Rebellion challenges existing understandings of the late eighteenth-century world. The uprising tested the commitment of Massachusetts citizens to republican institutions, revealing the diversity of ideas and allegiances that flourished in the state. It played upon long-standing divisions in the population, even as it provoked new coalitions and remade the political landscape. It was entangled with the coming of markets and capitalism to the countryside, in a far-ranging process that transformed an entire way of life. It exposed the social ferment of the backcountry, intensified religious upheavals, stimulated the founding of newspapers, and brought forth an outpouring of cosmopolitan satire and verse. Shays's Rebellion was, in short, an epoch of a society in dramatic transition.

As event and symbol, the agrarian protests of 1786–87 naturally drew attention in Massachusetts during the recent commemorations of the Bicentennial of the Constitution. Shays's Rebellion, after all, represents the unique contribution of the Commonwealth to the making of the national government. Virginia gave James Madison, the "father of the Constitution," who was joined by the New Yorkers Alexander Hamilton and John Jay in composing the classic *Federalist* essays. At the Philadelphia convention, New Jersey and Virginia offered competing plans of government, while Connecticut devised the successful compromise between the two. Massachusetts produced Daniel Shays. To mark the significance of his insurgency for state and nation, the Colonial Society of Massachusetts, based in Boston, and two institutions in the west, Amherst College and Historic Deerfield, Inc., held major conferences in the fall of 1986. The Boston meeting was a small, invitational gathering of historians, hosted at the society's headquarters on Mount Vernon Street. The conference in western Massachusetts, supported by the National Endowment for the Humanities, linked public commemoration of the bicentennial in Hampshire County, the citadel of the rebellion, with presentations of the latest research. Altogether, some two dozen Shays scholars—a veritable cottage industry of students of agrarian rebellion, political economy, social history, and the Constitution—delivered and commented on papers on the two occasions. A selection of their efforts is assembled here, in an anthology that, in contrast to the circumstances of Massachusetts two centuries ago, constitutes a happy collaboration between east and west.

As readers will quickly discover, the essays herein arrive at no consensus on the insurgency or its consequences. Shays's Rebellion remains as contested today as ever. The contributors to this collection are branded by two centuries of debate and discussion. No more than the Progressives escaped the hold of the nationalist historians they meant to reject do the current authors throw off the weight of their predecessors. They inquire into familiar themes. Predictably, they probe the motives and conduct of the governing elite, reexamine the grievances of the farmers, and explore the politics and culture of the backcountry. They also consider the larger implications of the Massachusetts insurgency for the making of the Constitution. As always, Shays's Rebellion remains an event of both local and national significance.

Nonetheless, this collection marks a turning point in our scholarship. Drawing on work in literature, political science, religion, and social history, it highlights the numerous aspects of eighteenth-century life on which the events of 1786–87 touched. Most important, it enables us to move beyond the polemics that have framed the historiography since 1788 and to place all parties to the conflict within the confines of their own world. Notwithstanding their enmities and their differences of power and wealth, all sides in Shays's Rebellion shared far more with one another than with us. Even so, viewed with empathy across the distance of two hundred years, they continue to speak compellingly about the ambitions and anxieties that people experienced as they struggled to cope with the unsettlement of Revolutionary change.

Shays's Rebellion was, first and foremost, a conflict over debts and taxes, prompted by the fiscal policies of Massachusetts during the severe depression of the mid-1780s. As Richard Buel, Jr., notes in "The Public Creditor Interest in Massachusetts Politics, 1780–86," the uprising was triggered by the decision of the General Court in early 1786 to lay the heaviest direct tax in specie ever imposed on the citizens of the Commonwealth. Why that choice? In addressing the issue, Buel enters a long-standing controversy over the motives of the governing elite, the coalition of merchants and magistrates who held sway during the crisis. Were these lawmakers high-minded men of principle, dedicated to the survival of the republic, as nationalist historians once claimed? Or were they attending principally to their own economic self-interest, as twentieth-century scholars on the Left have charged? Buel advances a fresh case for the government through close analysis of the immediate circumstances behind the 1786 tax. The levy was prompted by an event outside Massachusetts: a federal requisition of money from the states to support payment of the foreign debt. Under the Articles of Confederation, states were honor bound to meet such claims. But heeding the call proved no easy matter in the straitened postwar era. It required legislatures to tax inhabitants for national needs even as the states pressed for funds to pay their own debts. In the competition for money, state obligations often came first. But not in Massachusetts. Faced with congressional demands, the "Public Creditors" of the Commonwealth risked their own investments and supported new taxes, in what amounted to the highest levies in the country.

As Buel sees it, the leaders of trade and finance selflessly subordinated immediate interests to the imperatives of national independence. They rightly recognized the necessity of maintaining public credit. Without prompt payment of the debt, the new republic would never command support from men of property, at home and abroad. In a world of contending nations, its survival would thus remain in doubt. But the "most compelling" consideration was a matter of morals. If popular governments broke their pledges to creditor minorities, then the essence of republicanism, its integrity as a "sovereignty of justice," would be lost. To forestall that calamity, Buel insists, the commercial elite put principle ahead of profit, pressed the taxpayers beyond their limits, and brought a rebellion upon themselves. It was a conscientious display of public virtue, not the sordid pursuit of private gain, that lay behind the crisis of the state.

Where Buel stresses the contingent choices of patriotic policymakers in the mid-1780s, Joseph A. Ernst traces the long-term strategies of Massachusetts merchants in the pursuit of financial gain. That approach, presented in "Shays's Rebellion in Long Perspective: The Merchants and the 'Money Question,'" produces an opposing scenario. Seeking to understand why merchants resisted the emission of paper money so adamantly in the 1780s, Ernst delves into the monetary history of Massachusetts from the 1690s on. From this survey emerges a story of cold, calculating, self-interest, pursued unswervingly over the decades.

Starting in the 1690s, Ernst argues, the "great merchants" of Massachusetts Bay opposed all general issues of paper currency, insisted that government notes be redeemable in specie, and preferred funding schemes that would enrich themselves. Such views put the great merchants at odds with populist forces in the legislature, with whom they fought continuing battles over paper money from the 1720s on. Eventually, in alliance with the crown, the lords of trade got their way. Massachusetts established its own equivalent of the English funding system. Issuing public notes in exchange for private loans and supplies, government endowed merchants with a commercial medium of exchange, while paying them interest in specie—financed by taxes on the population at large. On the eve of the Revolution, great merchants and magistrates cheerfully serviced one another's needs.

It was to restore this "era of public credit," Ernst argues, that the General Court adopted the monetary policies of the 1780s that precipitated Shays's Rebellion. Repudiating the paper schemes by which the Revolution had been financed, enacting new consolidating and funding plans, the legislature reverted to its familiar alliance with the great merchants. Once again, the trading interest enjoyed a medium of exchange that was safe, stable, and securely under its control. No wonder, then, that the masters of commerce, who saw the money question "in ways that squared with a self-seeking ideology of profit making," refused to compromise with the backcountry.

While Buel and Ernst disagree about the conduct of the mercantile elite, they retain the assumption, common among historians of the subject, that the leaders in government and trade acted rationally and deliberately in pursuit of their goals and exercised considerable control over the course of events. Two other essays in this collection implicitly challenge that notion. In "Debt Litigation and Shays's Rebellion," Jonathan M. Chu reconsiders the role of courts and lawyers in precipitating the rural insurgency. From the 1780s on, Shaysites and their sympathizers have indicted the judicial system of Massachusetts for exacerbating the economic crisis by favoring the oppressive demands of creditors. But Chu radically challenges this view of a callous, class-biased legal system. Through a detailed investigation of the cases before the Supreme Judicial Court at its Worcester sitting on April 19, 1785—ironically, the tenth anniversary of the Battle of Lexington and Concord—Chu turns the conventional wisdom upside down. Far from oppressing people in dire straits, he argues, the civil courts of Massachusetts actually aided debtors in the effort to stave off disaster. Such service was hardly intentional, but so inefficient proved the system in the swirling economic crisis that it could be as readily exploited by the weak as by the strong. Opportunities for delay were rampant. The common strategy of debtors was to default—that is, fail to appear—in cases at the county Court of Common Pleas, then appeal judgments to the Supreme Judicial Court. The issues in dispute hardly mattered; the point was to buy time, in hopes that somehow, something would turn up. Perhaps an importunate creditor might settle on favorable terms, rather than wait for a final judgment; alternatively, a lucky defendant might be able to collect his own debts. Admittedly, appeals cost money, but as Chu documents, lawyers were happy to post bonds for debtors and represent their case. To a miserable man on the verge of bankruptcy, why worry about the additional expense? At worst, court costs were only another bill that would go unpaid.

In this legal setting, Chu suggests, merchants, especially traders in middling circumstances, were at a serious disadvantage. Men of vast fortune could grant relief to their debtors and still ride out the economic crisis. But modest creditors faced an anxious effort to stay afloat. If they pressed too hard, too soon for repayment, they might set off a chain reaction of insolvencies; but if they waited too long to sue, they might lose claim to the assets of delinquent debtors.

Exacerbating this dilemma were the costs and delays of the courts. Frustrated by a system that left them equally exposed to the claims of big creditors and the wiles of small debtors, middling merchants pushed for fundamental reform of the courts. Ironically, though their demands merged with the populist outcry against lawyers and courts, they were trying to ease the prosecution and collection of small debts. Had they obtained their way, the plight of debt-ridden farmers and laborers would only have gotten worse.

Chu's essay opens up a new perspective on the Massachusetts court system in an age of Revolution: rather than a handy instrument of upper-class rule, it represented a fundamental arena of struggle between contending social groups. Under the firm control of no single class, the courts may well have served the interests of none.[8]

But then, as Stephen E. Patterson suggests in "The Federalist Reaction to Shays's Rebellion," the merchants in eastern Massachusetts were no more secure in their countinghouses than in the courts. They came under challenge from two directions at once. With the coming of peace, British factors—agents of export firms at home—began setting up shop in New England ports and competing with established American merchants for the custom of the countryside. In the face of this stiff, unprecedented rivalry, the wholesalers in Boston scrambled to expand their business. They aggressively promoted the latest consumer goods and offered liberal terms to retailers and farmers, only to get caught short in the credit crunch of the mid-1780s. Anxious to protect their positions, merchants clung for safety to the legislature and the courts. But in the depression of the 1780s, the commercial elite had now to contend against rural demands for paper money, tender laws, and suspension of the courts. Challenged from without by British interests, the magnates of Massachusetts were equally beset by hostile farmers from within.

In this setting, the embattled elite discovered unexpected benefits from the developing uprising. Leading merchants and politicians seized upon the disorders in the countryside to galvanize support for a strong, national government, armed with the power to protect American trade. This crusade was carefully calculated: "Shays's Rebellion . . . was less a cause of Federalism than it was an opportunity to expand and popularize it." Indeed, Patterson concludes, "if Shays's Rebellion had not occurred, the Federalists would have had to invent it."

However much they exaggerated the radicalism of the farmers, merchants and magistrates correctly perceived a fundamental gap between the backcountry and their own commercial-cosmopolitan sphere. As several essays in this anthology make clear, Massachusetts was indeed riven into opposing worlds of thought and action. In "Reinterpreting Rebellion: The Influence of Shays's Rebellion on American Political Thought," a close reading of the polemical literature of 1786–88, political scientist Michael Lienesch finds that the rival parties spoke different languages of politics. Champions of the backcountry affirmed a radical republicanism that was at odds with the developing political faith of the cosmopolitan elite. In their own eyes, the insurgents were rational, patient, long-suffering citizens, driven by principle to resist arbitrary government. When such protests failed to stop the advance of tyrants, there was no alternative but revolution, which meant, to Shaysites, a happy return to a state of nature and a restoration of liberty in public life.

By contrast, the "Friends of Government" regarded the disorders in the backcountry as the very antithesis of rational liberty. Popular protests were nothing more than the irrational outpouring of violent passion on the part of an unruly mob. In an elective government based on consent, they insisted, jealousy of rulers was obsolete; indeed, to question authority too harshly was to subvert the regime. Revolution was now illegitimate: it threatened a descent into anarchy, which would end inevitably in brutal despotism. In this elitist brand of republicanism, the duty of citizens was simply to vote in elections and then to obey the laws. "Real liberty," remarks Lienesch, "consisted in being 'good subjects.'"

In "'The Fine Theoretic Government of Massachusetts Is Prostrated to the Earth': The Response to Shays's Rebellion Reconsidered," William Pencak also depicts a polarization between town and backcountry. But his appraisal of the two sides offers a dramatic contrast to Lienesch. In Pencak's view, it was not the backcountry rebels but rather the leaders of eastern Massachusetts who proved the authentic defenders of the Revolution. Pencak bases his judgment on the public conduct of the antagonists. Although the insurgents claimed to be acting on the defensive, in order to obtain limited reforms, they pursued aggressive, antirepublican ends. In their collective actions, they went well beyond the restrained practices of pre-Revolutionary crowds and conventions. Forming themselves into a full-scale army, converting county conventions into a counterregime, Shaysites were waging "a revolution against the Revolution."

Actually, according to Pencak, the inhabitants of western Massachusetts had never displayed much enthusiasm for the Patriot cause. They had hardly suffered in the war, unlike beleaguered Boston; they had profited on high farm prices and spent their new wealth on luxuries; they had done little to establish the Commonwealth of Massachusetts, whose Constitution of 1780 they had generally opposed. Indeed, for all the sprigs of hemlock in their hats, few of Shays's troops had even served in the War for Independence.

In the face of this challenge, Pencak maintains, the Friends of Government proved loyal sons of the Revolution. Self-disciplined veterans of the Continental and state forces, they fought in the General Court and in General Lincoln's army for the same principles that had animated their sacrifices in the conflict with Britain: an ideal of the republic as a commonwealth, "a moral whole," devoted to justice and enlisting the active engagement of virtuous citizens. In this spirit, they tried valiantly to ease popular grievances and to avoid bloodshed. Even after the clash of arms, the constant aim was reconciliation, not retribution. In the end, Pencak maintains, the leaders of Massachusetts made an important contribution to the theory and practice of republicanism. Through a disciplined but firm defense of principle, they devised republican remedies for popular rebellion and helped to secure the future of self-government in the new nation.

Although Pencak echoes the progovernment apology of George Richards Minot two centuries ago, his essay is best read as an inquiry into the political cultures of town and backcountry. Indeed, his view of the insurgents as inveterate localists, hostile to the cosmopolitan world of Boston, is supported by other contributors to this collection. In "Shays's Neighbors: The Context of Rebellion in Pelham, Massachusetts," Gregory H. Nobles investigates society and politics in Shays's own town as a case study of the insurgency.

Far more sympathetic to the protests than Pencak, Nobles nonetheless offers a similar picture of the rural *mentalité*. In 1786 Pelham was an insular farming community of a thousand souls. Founded by feisty Scotch-Irish Presbyterians in 1740, the place had passed beyond the frontier stage and emerged as a typical hill town, producing little for market and supporting only a few mills and shops. This subsistence-oriented economy, argues Nobles, sustained a distinctive political culture, through which people responded to public policies in 1786–87.

Shays's neighbors had a long tradition of egalitarian localism. Hostile to outside authorities not only from Boston but from the more developed towns in the Connecticut Valley, Pelhamites went on the offensive whenever their community was threatened. In the Revolutionary crisis they were quick to denounce British taxes and to lead mobs against supporters of the crown. Determined to keep government close to home, they opposed the Massachusetts Constitution of 1780 with equal firmness. It was out of this heritage of proud parochialism that the people of Pelham set forth to "regulate" the state government in the fall and winter of 1786–87. Contrary to Pencak, Nobles believes the protesters were merely resuming the extralegal practices of the Revolutionary crowds. But times were changing; to the new magistrates of Massachusetts, the only legitimate way to conduct politics lay in the authorized forms of citizenship under the state constitution. Repudiating the political culture of the colonial era, the commercial-cosmopolitan elite demanded conformity to the new regime. As the Pelhamites forcibly learned, republicanism was now the norm.

The changing methods and meanings of collective action also constitute the subject of Alan Taylor's essay, "Regulators and White Indians: Forms of Agrarian Resistance in Post-Revolutionary New England." Taylor contrasts the rapid collapse of rural rebellion in Massachusetts and New Hampshire in 1786–87 with the longer-lasting and more successful resistance by the squatters of central Maine to the claims of the great land companies. Organizing themselves as "White Indians," the determined yeomen of Maine avoided large-scale confrontations with the state and obliged the landlords to compromise their demands.

Why the different outcomes in the two cases? As Taylor sees it, the backcountry rebels of New England subscribed to a complex of political and social assumptions that simultaneously inspired their protests and limited their gains. Their political culture was more traditional, more hierarchical than the *mentalité* Nobles detects in Pelham. Accepting an inherited society of ranks and orders, these rural people had no intention to displace their betters in the seats of power. Common folk intruded into affairs of state only when the rulers let them down. In the face of betrayal by their superiors, they might rise up in protest, denouncing public policies from a distance and threatening violence in bloodcurdling terms. The point, however, was to reclaim rulers to the public trust, not to seize power, nor to upset the social order.

Unfortunately for the dissidents, in the postwar republican era the governing class no longer accepted this "protection covenant."[9] In Shays's Rebellion, the elite confidently stood its ground and quickly dispersed the insurgents. Easily intimidated by the gentlemen, the protesters cut and ran, for they had never expected to fight at all. They soon relapsed into familiar patterns of deference. By contrast, the "White Indians" learned from the defeat of the Shaysites to confine protests to their own turf and established an effective cordon around the backcountry. Like the Shaysites of Massachusetts, they were suspending the execution of the laws in hopes that the legislature would honor its obligations to the people. But the world of rulers and subjects was no more. The squatters and tenants of Maine were obliged to turn to politics to win their ends. Unable to secure justice from the traditional elite, they got their way—part of it, at least—by voting for Jeffersonians. In that shift of loyalties from the "Fathers" to the "Friends of the People," Taylor discerns the disappearance of the backcountry's eighteenth-century political culture.

These several forays into the political cultures of the opposing parties differ in key respects. Where Pencak hails the civic republicanism of the magistrates, Lienesch, Nobles, and Taylor detect a class-conscious elitism that only deepened in the course of suppressing the popular protests. But the republicanism of rural folk is equally at issue. To Lienesch and Nobles, the people of the backcountry are radical republicans, hostile to distant rulers, and tenacious in defense of their own rights. By contrast, the rebels in Pencak's and

Taylor's studies prefer the protection covenant, with its culture of localism, to the demands of active citizenship. Whatever their inclinations—egalitarian or hierarchical, participatory or submissive—the inhabitants of rural New England emerge from all these essays with one thing in common: a fierce commitment to the ideal of local community as an organic whole.

But how homogeneous were the settlers in the backcountry? Were they any more united than their adversaries in the towns or any better at directing their own affairs? The essays by John L. Brooke and Stephen A. Marini reveal a countryside in dramatic transition, moving to new, pluralistic patterns of social, economic, and religious life. These were no static "peaceable kingdoms" invaded by a hostile, outside world. Rather, the rural communities that were caught up in the insurrection felt the direct upheaval of revolution and social change from within.

John Brooke maps the social landscape of central and western Massachusetts in "A Deacon's Orthodoxy: Religion, Class, and the Moral Economy of Shays's Rebellion." From this survey, the backcountry takes on a new, more complex configuration. By the 1780s, it had ceased to be a tight, uniform world of subsistence farms, whose pious inhabitants, descendants of the Puritans, centered their lives around town and church. The countryside was splintering into discrete, differentiated communities, owing to the combined forces of commercial capitalism and religious dissent. The old orthodox, yeoman towns, which had once typified the New England Way, now had to compete with other models of community. In some places a cosmpolitan gentry actively linked the population into the markets and culture of the wider world. In others, evangelical sects rose up to compete for converts and to demand the separation of church from state. Surrounded by these alternative communities, the orthodox, yeoman towns struggled to preserve a familiar way of life. Theirs was an embattled, declining world, beset by the relentless incursions of modernity.

The great power of Brooke's perspective is that he supplies the fullest social analysis of Shays's Rebellion to date. Through collective profiles of insurgents, Friends of Government, and neutrals in six communities in Worcester County, he upsets the conventional wisdom that invariably debtors were Regulators, while creditors demanded law and order. In fact, in the gentry citadel of Brookfield, many debtors joined the militia and were "pillars of the government cause," while in the orthodox, yeoman towns of Spencer and Oakham, half of the creditors enlisted in the insurrection. It was thus not financial standing alone but rather the interplay of religion and social structure that shaped popular responses to the widespread economic distress.

Shays's Rebellion took place, then, in a divided countryside, where the advancing forces of capitalism and voluntarism were driving the old corporate world into retreat. Only in small, insular farming towns, according to Brooke, did the ancient ways of New England survive, but in a grim, reactionary mood, akin to the aggrieved spirit of the Puritan settlers of Salem Village a century before when they set forth to do battle against the devils and witches of modern life.[10]

It may be an illusion, however, to treat the Shaysite communities as the remaining bastions of tradition, waging "custom's last stand."[11] In "The Religious World of Daniel Shays," Stephen Marini suggests that even in these places, the Standing Order was in disarray. Marini provides a sustained survey of relgous life among all churches and sects—Congregationalists, Baptists, Shakers, Universalists, and numerous others—in the principal Regulator towns during the 1770s and 1780s. The result is a stunning picture of a far-ranging revolution in religion, penetrating even the most isolated parishes in the countryside. The majority Congregationalists were troubled not only by vacancies in the pulpit but also by conflicts and contradictions of their own making. For decades, they had been fighting over everything from ministerial salaries and parish taxes to theology and church admissions.[12] In a fractured world, Congregationalism could no longer carry out its central mission: providing "sacred legitimation" for the social order.

Then again, many New Englanders were indifferent to the tradition; they had long since deserted the Standing Order for the new evangelical sects, whose numbers were increasing rapidly in the 1780s. Yet the dissenters were also struggling with their own internal divisions. Baptist and Separate congregations rose and fell in short order; competing sects raided one another's members; personal rivalries, doctrinal differences, institutional weaknesses hobbled the formation of stable churches. In 1786–87 some sects were anticipating an apocalyptic end to history; others, like the Shakers, disdained public affairs as "the spirit of the world" and offered a refuge from political choice. "Shays's Rebellion, the first major episode of political dissent in post-Revolutionary New England," Marini concludes, "occurred at precisely the same moment that Congregationalism lost its religious hegemony in rural Massachusetts and a new world of religious pluralism commenced in the New England hinterland." Religious disorder thus accentuated the crisis of civil authority.

Marini's survey of religion, together with the work of Brooke, Nobles, Taylor, and others, produces a powerful impression of a society in profound upheaval. New England was experiencing revolution in every aspect of its life. Population was pouring beyond the limits of settlement and scattering into the vast north country of the region. There newcomers scrambled to create communities overnight, with little guidance or interference from the eastern elite. But in long-settled districts, society was also fluid. With the departure of Loyalists, new men rushed into positions of wealth and power. Social mobility was abetted by the fluctuations of the wartime economy, as well as by the Revolutionary erosion of hierarchy and deference. The merchant class, many of whom were recent entrants into trade, had to compete in an unfamiliar world in which old markets were closed and new ones were yet to be gained. Clergymen struggled to sustain their livings, cope with competition, and keep up their status. Lawyers increased their ranks and gained a new public visibility. So, too, did printers, who established a growing number of newspapers. There was, in short, an unsettling of New England society, as people and institutions pressed beyond existing limits, in a process that expanded aspirations and stirred anxieties at the same time.

Challenged by this explosion of energies, many New Englanders, especially in the elite, hastened to stop change and to secure the social order. Seen in this perspective, Shays's Rebellion crystallized the consolidation of politics and society. The essays in this anthology testify to this campaign to contain the forces of revolution in the 1780s. Along with Nobles and Taylor, Lienesch suggests that the defeat of Shays's Rebellion was a turning point in American political thought; it prompted conservatives to jettison forever the old Whig heritage of resistance to unjust rulers. It also checked secessionist movements from Massachusetts and other states. As James Leamon documents in his essay, "In Shays's Shadow: Separation and Ratification of the Constitution in Maine," a bid to win statehood for the District of Maine was gathering momentum among merchants and professionals in the commercial towns "down East" when the protests against taxes and debts escalated in central and western Massachusetts. Frightened by the spectacle of popular "anarchy," the leading gentlemen in Maine backed away from the independence movement. On the other hand, the campaign for Maine statehood equally undercut the Regulation. It drained off energies that might have gone into forging an alliance between farmers in Massachusetts and squatters and distressed yeomen in Maine. Far from weakening established authority, the three movements of the 1780s—Shaysism, separatism, and Antifederalism—simply got in each other's way. In the process, government was consolidated on the level of the state as well as the nation.[13]

Shays's Rebellion was an epoch in culture as well as politics. The popular protests brought the refined, enlightened gentlemen of the towns into stark encounter with the unpolished, vernacular world of the backcountry. In my essay, "The Confidence Man and the Preacher: The Cultural Politics of Shays's Rebellion," the efforts of two aspirants to literary fame—Stephen Burroughs, the notorious "rogue," and Royall Tyler, the author of *The Contrast* (1787), the first American play to be produced on the professional stage—can be seen as contributions to the consolidation of elite culture. In 1786–87 neither figure held a secure status in society: Tyler, a rakish young lawyer, was perched on the edge of bankruptcy before he remade his career by serving as an officer in General Lincoln's army; Burroughs, a Dartmouth dropout, had been drummed out of Pelham for impersonating a minister and then sentenced to prison for counterfeiting. Despite their questionable credentials, the two writers emerged from their experiences to produce comical portraits of the backcountry that endure to the present day. Their versions of Shaysite territory are as revealing, however, of the narrow-mindedness of so-called cosmopolitans as they are of the parochialism of the farmers. Like the framers of the Constitution, the eighteenth-century creators of a national literature were determined to keep their distance from rural folk, even as they absorbed the irreverent language and wit of the rural "Jonathans" into their texts.[14]

In Shays's Rebellion, we may discern a model of revolution and reaction for the new nation. The growth and spread of population, the churning up of the social order, the weakening of old hierarchies and the establishment of new, voluntary associations, the shifting loyalties of citizens to state and federal entities: this expansion of society beyond its traditional confines, this explosive challenge to inherited limits of class and space gave the early republic the same distended quality that Robert Wiebe discerns in the reckless abandon of the United States in the Gilded Age. And it was to produce the same efforts at consolidation, at ordering and containing a society seemingly out of control, that scholars have identified in that later period. In this context, the contemporaries of Samuel Adams and Daniel Shays may well represent the first generation of Americans to have experienced acutely the relentless dialectic between expansion and consolidation that has marked the social history of the United States from the late eighteenth century on.[15]

This perspective releases us from the assumptions and stereotypes that have framed the historiography of Shays's Rebellion for two centuries. In the Revolutionary era both backcountry and commercial society were equally wracked by disorienting, disordering change, which provoked powerful, political reactions and intensified ideological struggles. The adversaries in 1786–87 did not inhabit mutually exclusive worlds, nor were they engaged in deliberate conspiracies against one another. In fact, so diverse had Massachusetts become, so fractured into competing groups with separate interests of their own, that it is an illusion to polarize the society into two hostile camps. Many rural people shared the grievances of the Shaysites but declined to close courts or to take up arms. Baptists and other dissenters were seldom willing to make common cause with neighbors who were still forcing them to pay taxes to the established church. A few souls fled the hard choices of politics entirely for the comforts of "unworldly" religious sects. In the seaports and country towns, not everyone was a hard-liner, nor were the Friends of Government propelled by a single motive. The townspeople of Concord, Massachusetts, for example, disdained paper money but endorsed rural complaints against the distant government in Boston. When insurgents in Middlesex County marched on Concord to close the courts, town leaders desperately maneuvered to avoid a clash of arms. In the end, the town that prided itself on its resistance to Britain on April 19, 1775, came down on the side of law and order. It sent a company of soldiers to aid General Lincoln's army; nobody joined the insurgents. Even so, Concord refused to support the Bowdoin administration's Draconian measures against the rebellion. Instead, in the spring elections of 1787, an upsurge of voters decisively repudiated the government that had so maladroitly provoked and then crushed the insurrection. Such vacillation between compromise and repression was common in the crisis of 1786–87. It surely reflected the ambivalence of many people in commercial towns, as well as the contrary positions of rival groups in local and state governments.[16]

Still, scholars can no more escape the ultimate confrontation between the government and the Shaysites than could contemporaries at the time. For all their hesitations, thousands of people took sides in an escalating series of episodes that briefly threatened a descent into civil war. At the peak of the crisis, the leading actors—Governor Bowdoin and his allies, on one hand; Daniel Shays and his followers, on the other—enlisted in opposing crusades to defeat the enemies of liberty. What brought them to their fateful encounter at Springfield armory in late January 1787? The answer, I would suggest, lies in a common social process, played out on the arena of Massachusetts politics at a time of severe economic depression and reinforced by the self-propelling dynamic of events. Amidst the unsettlement and uncertainties of the mid-1780s, challenged from without and within, neither side could understand its situation in historical perspective or view its antagonists outside the eighteenth-century categories of conspiracy. Lacking intellectual and social flexibility, both Friends of Government and Shaysites hardened their familiar worldviews: the former, unsure of their own authority and never enthusiasts of popular power, became ever more determined to impose an elitist design on state and nation; the latter asserted with equivalent, counterrevolutionary fervor the ideology of the corporate, Puritan town even as that world was fast disintegrating before their eyes. In the tumultuous effort to come to terms with the collapse of inherited ways, both groups saw themselves as the object of dangerous, illegitimate force. But in the perspective of social history, we may view them as fellow travelers in an unexpected, unwelcome journey toward a destination no one could foresee.

The participants embarked upon this trip with different advantages, derived from their distinctive social locations. Naturally, the elite went first-class, empowered by wealth, office, and culture to impress its claims upon the recalcitrant passengers crowded into the steerage. However sympathetically we may see the different parties in Shays's Rebellion, the fact remains that in Massachusetts, a new republican elite did consolidate power, and the backcountry protests against the advancing modern, capitalist order were silenced for a generation. Admittedly, the governing class was not entirely united, before or after the decision to end the disorders, and the new legislature, elected in the "revolution of 1787," was prepared to conciliate the disaffected, though it declined to issue paper money or to offer more than temporary relief from taxes and debts. It is equally the case that many in the backcountry—farmers profiting on wartime markets, consumers eager for fashionable goods, local politicians ambitious to shine on a larger stage—had readily entered into the economy and politics of the wider world.

Notwithstanding these concessions, the outcome of the conflict was to impose new rules for political and economic action upon all the inhabitants of the state. Although Massachusetts had hardly moved toward laissez-faire, it would sustain the legal structure of capitalism against populist attacks. And it would insist upon conformity to the Constitution of 1780. In later years, politicians and scholars alike might hail the opportunities of the new order—the liberty of trade in the market, the right to vote in the state—as central to the liberal tradition. But the republican regime of Massachusetts closely circumscribed the freedoms it meant to protect. Dragged as well as drawn into the marketplace, coerced as well as induced into the Commonwealth, ordinary people were obliged to comply with terms to which they had never agreed—or be utterly without influence in the larger world. In the construction of the republican citizen, the people of the backcountry were forced to be free.[17]

Veterans of 1776 Returning from the War by William T. Ranney (1848). American writers and artists invariably interpret the Revolution in light of contemporary concerns. This painting of Continental soldiers returning home victorious from the War for Independence reflects the nationalist fervor of 1848, stirred by the American triumph over Mexico. Ranney's Continentals stride home with hopeful spirits and a jaunty step, accompanied by a fiddler's tune—a far cry from the image of dispirited veterans, arriving home to a depressed countryside, that has colored the literature on Shays's Rebellion. (*Courtesy of the Dallas Museum of Art, the Art Museum League Fund, Special Contributors, and General Acquisitions Fund*)

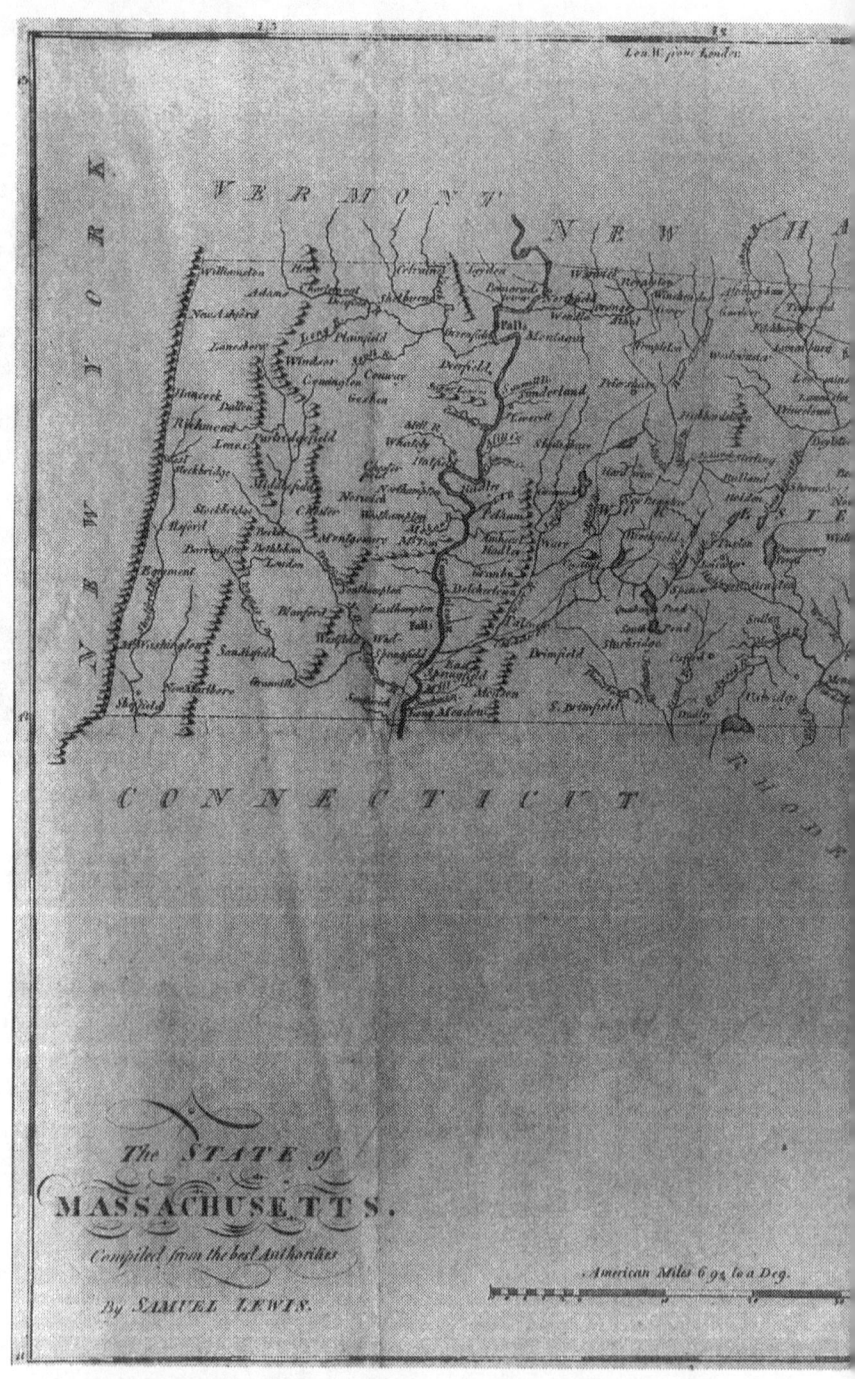

Map of Massachusetts in the new republic by Samuel Lewis (1795). Though this map was produced a decade after Shays's Rebellion, it displays the extensive settlement of towns and filling in of the backcountry of post-Revolutionary Massachusetts. With rapid growth over, the Commonwealth

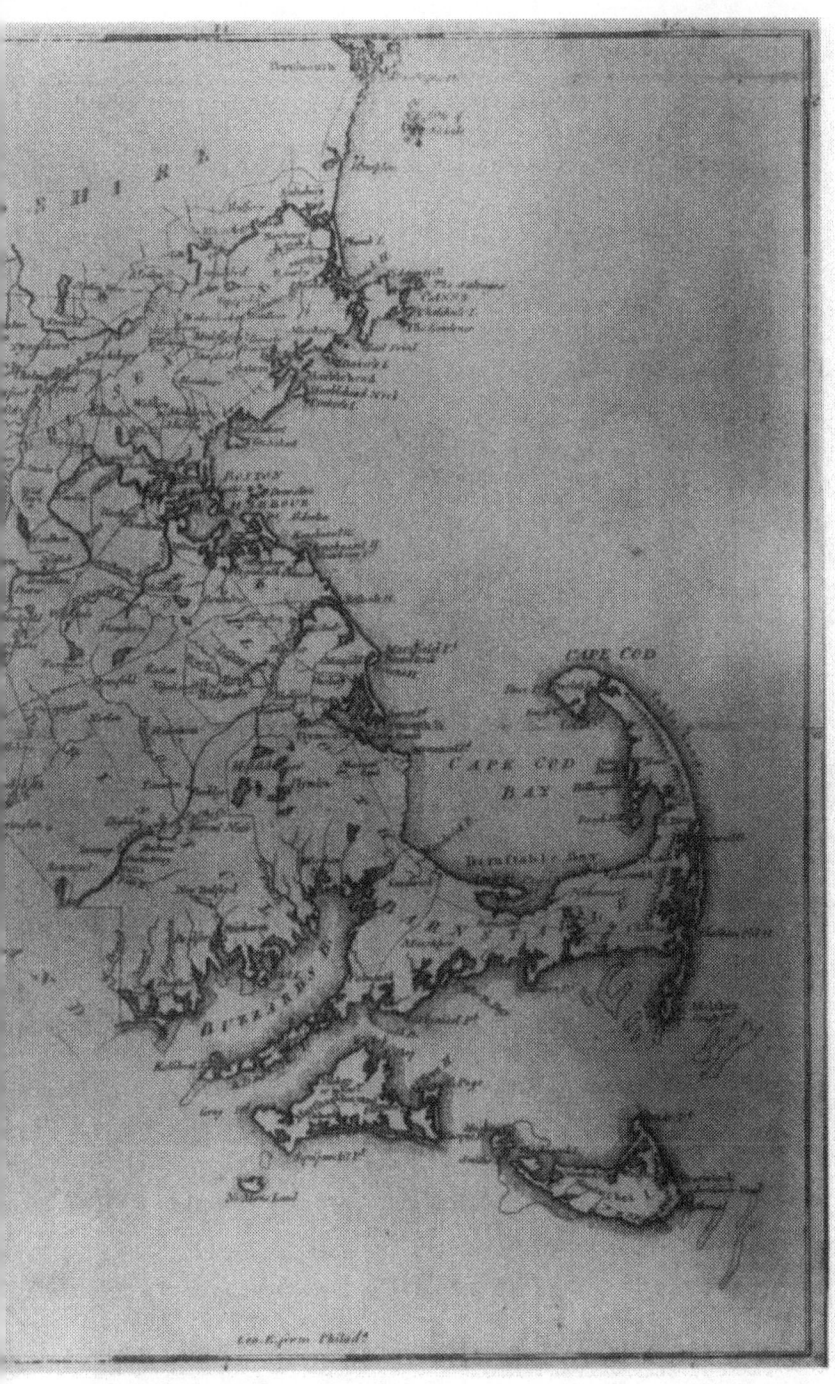

had become a mature agricultural and commercial society, and many of its sons and daughters would move in succeeding decades to northern New England and to the western frontier in search of land. (*Courtesy of the American Antiquarian Society*)

To the Hon Senate & Hon House of Representatives
in General Court of the Commonwealth of Massachusetts –
The petition of the Inhabitants of the town of Pelham Humbly
Sheweth –

Whereas we have a Constitutional Right to Assemble at all
times in an Orderly & peaceable Manner, to Consult upon the Common
good; and Request of the Legislative Body, by way of Remonstrance, Redress of
wrongs done us, or Grievances we Suffer – And as we Conceive by the
Operation of many of the Laws made since the ____ this Commonwealth
and for the want of Some others, the grievances we Suffer are become
too obvious to Escape the Notice of the Lowest Capacity – And has tended
to Introduce mutiny, discord and Confusion thro' the Commonwealth
We therefore think it our duty freely to express our Minds, Respecting
the grievances, and in Some Instances to point out a Remedy and
Request a Relief –

First   We Consider the Sitting of the General Court in the Town of
          Boston a Grievance, we Conceive the Expense of their Sitting
          in Boston to be Nearly double to what it would be were they to
          Sit in Some Country Town Near the Center of the Commonwealth

Secondly The want of a Circulating Medium has So Stagnated buying,
          of all kind among us, that unless Speedily Remedied will
          involve the Greater part of the people among us in a State of
          Bankruptcy

Thirdly   We Consider the County Courts of Common pleas & quarter Sessions
          in their present mode of Administration, a Grievance – for we
          find by Experience that the County Tax for this Town before
          the late war usually amounted to about fifty or sixty pounds
          yearly; But Since the war it has usually amounted to more
          than Six times that Sum; this we Conceive is Occasioned by an
          Extravagant Fee Table, or by an Unnecessary Number of Justices
          who Compose the Court of Sessions; or both –

Fourthly The Salaries of the Several publick Officers are higher
          than the Abilities of the people _____ will admit
          of, therefore we Esteem it a Grievance; We Conceive that Three
          Hundred pounds per annum is a Sum more than adequate to

Petition of the Inhabitants of the Town of Methuen to the Hon. Senate and Hon. House of Representatives of the Commonwealth of Massachusetts, Oct. 2, 1786. This petition from the Essex County town of Methuen is typical of the numerous remonstrances submitted to the General Court from rural towns throughout Massachusetts during the crisis of the 1780s. Invoking the right to assemble and to consult upon public measures, guaranteed by the Massachusetts Constitution of 1780, the people of Methuen lamented the heavy costs of government, the extreme scarcity of money, and the severity of the courts in deciding suits for debt. Though framed as a deferential appeal to the "honorable" authorities of the Commonwealth, the petition expresses the mounting frustration of the backcountry. It pointedly notes that "the grievances we Suffer are become too obvious to Escape the Notice of the Lowest Capacity"—even the members of the legislature. (*Courtesy of the American Antiquarian Society*)

"REPRESENTATION of a COUNTY-CONVENTION for REDRESS of GRIEVANCES of COURTS," engraving for *Bickerstaff's Boston Almanack* for 1787. An instrument of popular mobilization against the British in 1774–75, county conventions gathered again in rural Massachusetts during 1786–87 to protest the financial policies of the General Court and the constitutional arrangements of the state government. To their supporters, the conventions were legitimate means to express popular grievances. But as this illustration from *Bickerstaff's Almanack* attests, conservatives saw them as illegal forums, dominated by demagogues and rogues at the expense of the people. The engraving depicts a robed figure—presumably, a lawyer or a judge—seated at the head of the table; behind him a delegate displays a resolution demanding "No Courts nor Lawyers." Heedless of the contradiction, the other members of the convention enjoy the conviviality of the punch bowls, conveniently placed beside them. (*Courtesy of the American Antiquarian Society*)

"The Sons of COKE and LITTLETON, returning from a rich Feast at Concord-Court. Engraved for *Bickerstaff's* ALMANACK, *1787*. 3d Ed." This engraving in *Bickerstaff's Boston Almanack* for 1787 conveys the common disdain for the legal profession amidst the economic depression of the mid-1780s. Grown fat from a "feast" of litigation at Concord court, the "Sons of Coke and Littleton" show the effects of their excess. In the middle of the picture, a lawyer holds forth in full dignity, but the scenes to the sides tell a different story. On the right, one lawyer supports a full belly, while his associate lies drunk on the ground. On the left, an attorney whips a goat—a symbol of the countryside—while his fellows cheer him on. (*Courtesy of the American Antiquarian Society*)

Commonwealth of Massachusetts.

By His Excellency

JAMES BOWDOIN, *Esquire*,

Governour of the Commonwealth of Massachusetts.

AN ADDRESS,

To the good People of the Commonwealth.

A Spirit of discontent, originating in supposed grievances, having, in the course of the last fall, stimulated many of the citizens in several of the Counties of this Commonwealth, to the commission of acts subversive of government, and of that peace and security derived from it, I thought it expedient to assemble, and accordingly did assemble, the General Court for the special purpose of considering those grievances, and all complaints whatever, and if possibly removing the causes of them. A patient and candid attention was paid to the business of the Session, and every relief given, consistent with the evidence of government, and the principles of equal justice. These the Legislature could not in safety, without bringing upon themselves the detestation of mankind, and the frowns of Heaven.

But relief was not the only object, upon which the General Court bestowed their attention. In tenderness to the misguided, and in hopes of reclaiming the obstinate, an Act of Indemnity was passed for all the outrages, which had been committed against law, and the officers of it, upon this mild condition alone, that the perpetrators should return to a due submission to Lawful authority; and, as a test of their sincerity, should, before the first day of January following, take and subscribe the oath of allegiance, required by the Constitution.

In addition to these measures, the state of the Treasury, the expenditure of monies received, the situation of our foreign and domestic debt, and other important matters, were, in particular detail, communicated to the people, by an address from the Legislature. In that address they were also informed, of the dangerous and destructive tendency of popular insurrections; and the Insurgents were conjured, in the most serious and persuasive manner, to desist from their lawless conduct, lest they should involve themselves and their country in ruin. But, what have been the consequences?—These measures intended for giving them satisfaction and indemnity have been spurned at: And *since* the publication of those measures, the same Insurgents have frequently embodied, and with a military force, repeatedly interrupted the Judicial Courts in the Counties of Hampshire and Worcester; which demonstrates, that the Government is held by them in open defiance; and that the laws are, in those Counties, laid prostrate.

By a resolve of the 24th of October, the Legislature expressed their full confidence, that the Governour would persevere in the exercise of the powers, vested in him by the Constitution, for enforcing due obedience to the authority and laws of government, and for preventing any attempts to interrupt the administration of law and justice; upon which the peace and safety of the Commonwealth so essentially depend.

In the present dangerous and critical situation of affairs, I feel myself constrained, by the most sacred obligations of duty, and for the purposes intended by the Legislature, to call forth powers into immediate exercise, for the protection of the Commonwealth, against the attempts of all persons who shall enterprize its destruction, invasion, detriment or annoyance: And I have accordingly, pursuant to my own ideas of duty, as well as the expostulations of the General Court, ordered a part of the Militia to assemble in arms, for the purpose of protecting the Judicial Courts next to be holden in the County of Worcester; of aiding the Civil Magistrate to execute the laws; of repelling all Insurgents against the Government; and of apprehending all disturbers of the public peace.

It is now become evident, that the object of the Insurgents is to annihilate our present happy constitution, or to force the General Court into measures repugnant to every idea of justice, good faith, and national policy;

And those who encourage, or in any way assist them, either individually, or in a corporate capacity, do partake of their guilt; and will be legally responsible for it. Success, on the part of the Insurgents, in either of those views, must be destructive of civil liberty, and of the important blessings derived from it; and as it would be the result of force, undirected by any moral principle, it must finally terminate in despotism—despotism in the worst of its forms.

Is then the goodly fabric of freedom, which cost us so much blood and treasure, so soon to be thrown into ruins?—Is it to stand but just long enough, and for no other purpose than, to flatter the tyrants of the earth in their darling maxim, *that mankind are not made to be free?*

The present is certainly a most interesting period; and if we wish to support that goodly fabric, and to avoid domestic slavery, men of principle, the friends of justice and the Constitution, must now take their stations, and, uniting under the Government in every effort for suppressing the present commotions and all insurrections whatever, or be infamously accessary to their own and their country's ruin. But in such an union, should they prove as firm in the support of justice and the Constitution, as the Insurgents have been obstinate in trampling them under their feet, the force of government will have so decided a superiority as to put an end to the present convulsions, and restore a regular administration of law, without the horrors of bloodshed, and a civil war: which I most ardently deprecate; and will strenuously endeavour to prevent.

But unless such a force appears, those, which indeed are the greatest of national evils, seem inevitable.

If the Constitution is to be destroyed, and insurrection stalk unopposed by authority, it behooves us, as they regard their own happiness and freedom, will, from necessity, combine for defence, and meet force with force; or voluntarily and ingloriously relinquish the blessings, without which life would cease to be desirable; and which, by the laws of God and Nature ought never to be tamely surrendered.

What would be the end of such events, is known only to Him, who can open the volumes and read the pages of futurity.

Strongly impressed with the truth of these ideas, I must conjure the good people of the Commonwealth, as they value life and the enjoyments of it, as they regard their own characters, and the dignity of human nature, to summon up every virtuous principle within them, and to co-operate with Government in every necessary exertion, for restoring to the Commonwealth that order, harmony and peace, upon which its happiness and character do essentially depend.

GIVEN at the COUNCIL-CHAMBER, in BOSTON, the 12th day of JANUARY, 1787; and in the eleventh year of the INDEPENDENCE of the CONFEDERATED STATES OF AMERICA.

James Bowdoin.

By his Excellency's command.

John Avery, jun. Sec.

[Published by Authority.]

"*Gen.* DANIEL SHAYS, *Col.* JOB SHATTUCK." As the popular insurgency in Massachusetts gathered momentum in the winter of 1786–87, Friends of Government used every means of communication—newspapers, almanacs, broadsides, and sermons—to blast the character of the insurgents. This woodcut from *Bickerstaff's Boston Almanack* for 1787 accompanied editorial attacks on Shays as an upstart and demagogue, scheming for power at the expense of liberty. Ironically, the illustration depicts "General" Shays and Middlesex County Regulator Colonel Job Shattuck as officers and gentlemen, dressed according to rank and equipped with swords. (*Courtesy of the National Portrait Gallery, Smithsonian Institution, Washington, D.C.*)

At left: James Bowdoin, Esquire, Governour of the Commonwealth of Massachusetts, AN ADDRESS, *To the good People of the Commonwealth* (1787). In the face of continuing protests against the courts, Governor James Bowdoin decided on a showdown with the Regulators in mid-January 1787. Ordering the militia to defend the Worcester County courts at their next scheduled session, Bowdoin provoked the escalation of the insurgency into a military confrontation with the government at Springfield armory. In this official proclamation, the governor summons "the good People of the Commonwealth" to support the cause of law and order. His call to arms invokes the rhetoric of the American Revolution as fully as do the Shaysite petitions. For Bowdoin, the stakes of the conflict were no less than the survival of the American experiment in self-government. (*Courtesy of the American Antiquarian Society*)

Portrait of Samuel Adams by John Singleton Copley (1770–72). Excoriated by the British as the arch-revolutionary of Massachusetts, Samuel Adams (1722–1803) rose to prominence in Boston as a spokesman for popular sentiment from the mid-1760s through the War for Independence. But by the 1780s, when he served as state senator and lieutenant governor of the Commonwealth, Adams had moved away from the politics of protest. In the face of agrarian insurgency in 1786–87, Adams invoked the sanctity of republican laws and urged harsh punishment of the rebels. Copley's portrait captures the public image Adams sought to project throughout his career: the staunch tribune of liberty and of constitutional rights. (*Deposited by the City of Boston: courtesy of the Museum of Fine Arts, Boston*)

Portrait of James Bowdoin II by Robert Feke (1748). Son of a Boston merchant prince, James Bowdoin inherited one of the largest fortunes in New England just as he was graduating from Harvard College in 1747 at age twenty-one. He soon thrived in the countinghouse on his own and embarked upon a long career in provincial politics. A fixture on the Massachusetts Council during the pre-Revolutionary period, Bowdoin played a critical part in leading the upper chamber to side with the popular party in the House of Representatives. He was, however, a moderate Patriot, closely identified with conservative, mercantile interests and active in the establishment of the Massachusetts and federal constitutions. This portrait of Bowdoin, painted at the time of his marriage to Elizabeth Irving, presents a cosmopolitan young man, at ease with his wealth and determined to appear a British gentleman in the provinces. (*Courtesy of the Bowdoin College Museum of Art, Brunswick, Maine, Bequest of Sarah Bowdoin Dearborn*)

The Manse, Joseph Barnard house, Deerfield, Massachusetts. Built over the years 1769–72 by the wealthy merchant Joseph Barnard, this large, double-square house expressed the aspirations of a new generation of leaders in the Connecticut Valley. With its elaborate style and elegant furnishings, the structure surpassed in sophistication the country houses of the River Gods, the traditional governing elite in the region. Its owner became an active Patriot in the Revolution and later a strong opponent of Shays's Rebellion. His house symbolizes in the landscape the shift in power wrought during the long struggle for Independence. (*Courtesy of Historic Deerfield, Inc.*)

House on the site of the Daniel Shays farmstead, Pelham, Mass. After paying a call upon Daniel Shays in mid-January 1787, an anonymous gentleman derided the house of the insurgent leader as "a *stye*, it having much more the appearance of a den for brutes than a habitation for men." In a world where houses served as metaphors of government, the plain construction of Shays's vernacular farmhouse attested to his lack of qualifications for leadership. Such was the judgment of many in the elite. But this house, which stood on the Shays homestead in the nineteenth century, was built in the modest Cape style, preferred by the yeomanry of the neighborhood. (*From C. O. Parmenter's History of Pelham, Massachusetts, 1898. Courtesy of the Jones Library, Inc., Special Collections, Amherst, Mass.*)

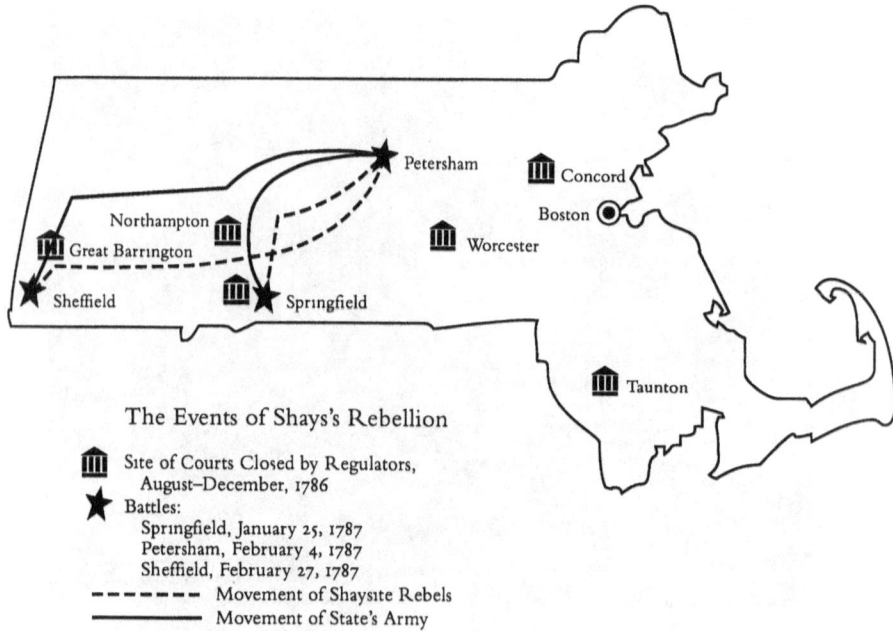

The events of Shays's Rebellion: a map of strategic sites. This map displays the location of the major incidents of the Regulation during the turbulent months from the summer of 1786 through the winter of 1787. Protesters succeeded in closing the courts in many parts of the state, from Taunton in Bristol County to Great Barrington in Berkshire County. But the military skirmishes between government and rebel soldiers took place only in the west. Note that the capital in Boston, located in Suffolk County, and neighboring Essex and Norfolk counties were free from disturbances. (*Courtesy of the Commonwealth Museum, Office of the Massachusetts Secretary of State*)

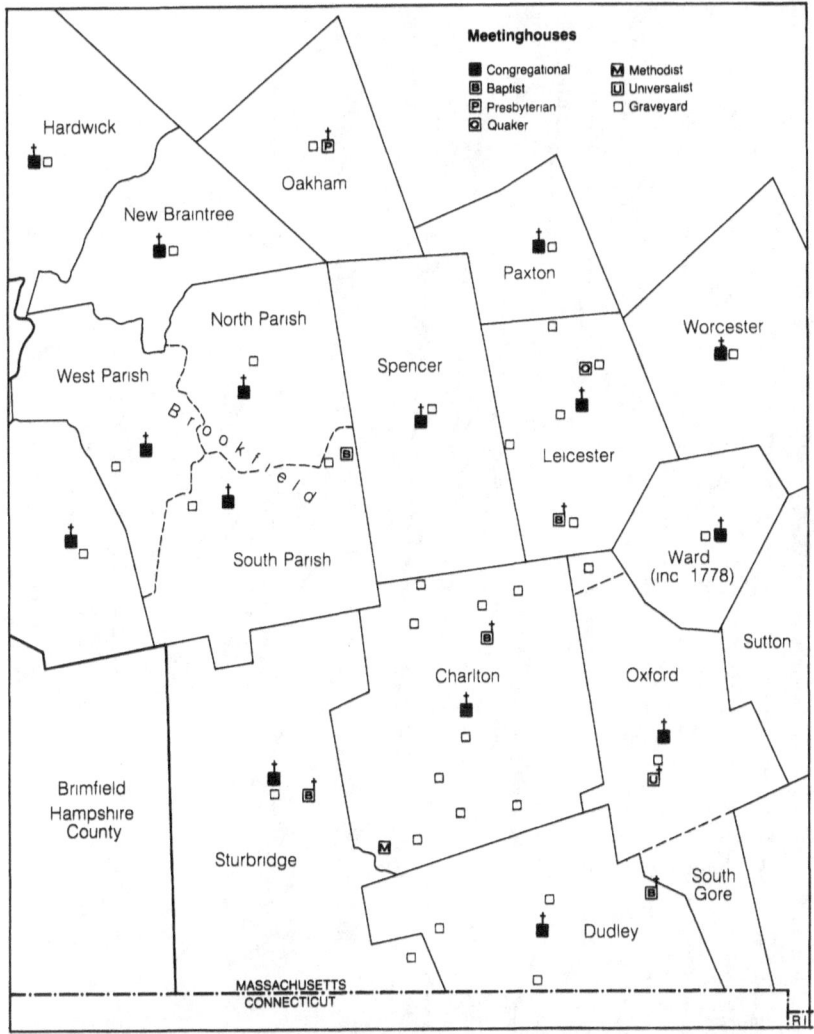

Southwestern Worcester County in the era of the Regulation. Two broad religious regimes met in this south-central region of Massachusetts. To the north and west, the towns supported one established church, typically Congregational, though occasionally Presbyterian. Older and larger towns like Brookfield were divided into orthodox parishes. To the south and east, towns such as Leicester and Charlton supported a number of competing societies, both established Congregational churches and dissenting meetings of Baptists, Quakers, and Universalists. In general, the circumstances of the towns to the north and west, gentry and yeoman towns maintaining a corporate orthodoxy, were quite similar to those prevailing in Hampshire County to the west, while the proliferation of religious dissent to the south and east was an extension of the dynamic impact of the Great Awakening in the Blackstone Valley and southeastern New England more generally. (*Map by John L. Brooke and Lori Wall*)

I _____ ly __ sincerely acknowledge, profess, testify and declare, That the Commonwealth of Mass. __ achusetts is, & of right ought to be a free, Sovereign, and independent State, and do swear, That I will bear truth faith and allegiance to the said Commonwealth, and that I will defend the same against traiterous conspiracies and all hostile attempts whatsoever, And that I do renounce and abjure all allegiance, subjection and obedience to the King, Queen or Sovereign of Great Britain (as the case may be) and every other foreign power whatsoever; and that no foreign Prince, Person, Prelate, State or Potentate hath, or ought to have, any jurisdiction, superiority, preeminence, authority, dispensing or other power, in any matter, civil, ecclesiastical or spiritual—within this Commonwealth—except the authority and power which is or may be vested by their Constituents in the Congress of the United States—And I do further testify and declare, that no man or body of men hath or can have any right to absolve or discharge me from the obligation of this Oath, Declaration or Affirmation—and that I do make this acknowledgement, profession, testimony, Declaration, Renunciation and abjuration, heartily and truly, according to the common meaning and acceptation of the foregoing words—without any Equivocation, mental evasion or secret Reservation whatsoever. So help me God. _____

Pelham Feby 24th 1779

John Markum } Samuel Baker
Daniel _____ } Stephen _____
John _____ } Stephen Lothrop
_____ _____

Tho. _____ } _____
_____ James Lothrop
Isaac E. _____ Shirley
T. _____ Georgiatt _____
Henr. _____ Taylor __ Lynn
Frank _____
William Bispell _____
Thom__ Frank __
Nathan Boston B
Eleazer White Sr

George Winder jun _____ jun
_____
Josiah Southworth jun
JOSEPH Pinkham
William _____
John Cole —
Jos. St. _____
Logan _____

16th of April 1779 by _____
Hans _____ Sworn

List of Persons Subscribing to Oath of Allegiance, February 27, 1787. Once fighting had broken out between Regulators and government troops, the General Court moved to crush the insurgency through a combination of leniency and force. It promised pardons to all rebels who laid down arms and took an oath of allegiance to the Commonwealth—the same oath prescribed by the Massachusetts Constitution of 1780. In response to this offer, hundreds of defeated Shaysites affirmed their loyalty to the government and signed documents like the one represented here. This list contains the names of several of Daniel Shays's neighbors in Pelham. Despite their submission to the state, the signers were barred for three years from exercising political privileges, such as holding office and voting, and from performing other public functions, including teaching school and running a tavern. (*Courtesy of the Massachusetts State Archives, Boston*)

A portion of the "Black List" for Hampshire County. Though the state aimed to reconcile the disaffected, it limited the offer of pardons to ordinary foot soldiers in the Shaysite ranks. The leadership of the rebellion was singled out for punishment, in the belief that it had stirred up the lower orders for selfish purposes. Attorney General Robert Treat Paine accordingly drew up this "Black List" of Hampshire County Regulators for the purposes of prosecution. He was careful to identify Captain Daniel Shays as the "Generalissimo" of the rebellion and to highlight such other leaders as Elijah and Luke Day of West Springfield and Hampshire County convention chairman Daniel Gray. Committed to a deferential society of ranks and orders, the Bowdoin administration believed that common folk would obey the law unless led astray by their betters.   (*Courtesy of the Massachusetts Historical Society*)

Debts gone from
N Salem ———
T'b Col⁰. William Smith
T'b Capt. Jacob Hampson
T'b Peter Hampson (£32)
T'b Jesse Peirce

from Pelham
T'b Capt. Daniel Gray (second time)
T'b Capt. John Conkey
Capt. John Thompson
T'b Capt. David Cowden
T'b Dea⁰. Daniel Gray
T'b ——— ——— (3 time)
T'b ——— ———
T'b² Timothy Packard
————
T'b ——— Dickinson (Capt of ——)

from Whitingsbury
T'b Capt. John Powers
T'b Lt. Simon Reuchard
——— ———
——— ———
T'b Joseph ———
T'b Benjamin Trucker
T'b ——— ———
T'b ——— ———
T'b ——— ———

from Wendell

from Whately
T'b Edward Brown
T'b Ebenezer Bardwell (p s)
T'b Moses Dickinson Jun. (p s)
T'b Abner Nash (p s)
T'b Aaron Ellis (p s)
T'b ——— Morton (p s)

Witnesses
Sam¹ Kendal
Capt. Jon⁰. Meacham
Col⁰. W™. Stacy

Witnesses
Lieut Wilds
Jeremiah Cady
——— Sturtevant
Joseph Lyon

from Hadley
T'b Jeremiah ——— (p s)
——— ———

Conway
T'b Capt. Abel Dinsmore
T'b Lt. James Gilmore
T'b Deacon Sam¹ Hill
T'b ——— Gates — (Capt)

Whatelworth
T'b Salter ———
T'b Samuel Hill (Capt)

Ashfield
T'b M. Ormill Allen   Witnesses
T'b Mililiel Phillips   ——— ———
                              ——— ———

Buckland
T'b Nathan ———

Williamsburg
T'b D'. John Williams
T'b Lieut. Paul ———
T'b George Morrison Lt.

Colerain
T'b Ashbel Mason

Christopher Babbitt, *To His Excellency* JOHN HANCOCK, *Esquire, Governor of the State of Massachusetts* (1787). This broadside appeal to Governor John Hancock reveals the religious excitement and social unsettlement in Massachusetts during the era of Shays's Rebellion. Christopher Babbitt, an inhabitant of Lanesborough in Berkshire County, claimed to have been set free by the "spirit of GOD" and empowered to "run to the Rulers of the State, to do the will of my Heavenly Father." Like an Old Testament prophet, Babbitt denounced the republican leaders of the state—notably, John Hancock and Samuel Adams—as agents of the devil in overturning one government and tyrannizing over another. He was equally adamant against the supporters of Shays "for taking up the gun." In this outright repudiation of the American Revolution, Babbitt affirmed a radical Christian pacifism that was the spiritual refuge of some ordinary New Englanders amid the political turmoil of the age. (*Courtesy of the American Antiquarian Society*)

To his Excellency JOHN HANCOCK, Esquire, Governor of the State of MASSACHUSETTS.

BEING impressed upon the mind, being a beggar, under the divine operation of the spirit of GOD; a man that was made free, 'whom the Son made free, was free indeed;' so free it took all my bodily strength away; vowed to be for God, and no other; longing for the welfare of the children of men; feeling it my mind to running to the Rulers of the State, to do the will of my Heavenly Father, to say to the Rulers, repeal your bloody laws, for they are offensive against God; for the cries of the oppressed have reached the ears of the Lord; ' For vengeance is mine, I will repay, saith the Lord.'

The man that went to General Lincoln, at Pittsfield, to say to General Lincoln, Govern the government for my Heavenly Father, for I am a pilgrim in the world; the man who went to Williamstown, to General Lincoln, asked General Lincoln the reason of his hope, as the scripture saith, 'and he answered not a word;' a man that hath his ears bore to discipline; and we want some Rulers to know the mind of God. How is it with you, Governor Hancock? was you never born again, they say you and Mr. Adams, who first began the great difficulty, began the grand adversary, which is the Devil that deceived Eve, saying, that ' we should be as God, knowing good and evil, he gave her of the fruit, and she did eat.' Neglecting the Scripture for your rule, the Devil deceived you, and you the people. ' The axe is laid to the root of the tree that bringeth forth evil fruits, shall be hewn down and cast into the fire,' as the scripture saith. ' Give us this day our daily bread, and lead us not into temptation, &c.' saying, the King was going to bring in popery amongst us; and lo the great difficulty began, brought in great cost to the government, and slain thousands; they say, ' thou art the man.' They getting the government in their hands, giving a Governor fifteen hundred pounds a year. Having so many rulers, oppressed the people, took away all the cow that a poor man hath, to pay the Governor's salary? Think you can appear before God in peace for so doing? Pray Consider, ' A rich man in hell lift up his eyes in hell torment.' Being faithful to my Heavenly Father, I declare it unto you rulers, ruling with tyrannical power, oppressing the oppressed, refusing to hear their cries, slain a number of men, neglecting to take the scripture for your rule, saying, the second fire to maintain your bloody laws, you first saying, to hold good government, breaking good government, destroying the tea that belonged to the King, or the government, saying, you are excusable. Did you ever know God's penetrating eye, that looks through the secrets of the hearts of the children of men? Robbing men of their arms by violence, to maintain your bloody laws, condemning and hanging men, advising the same things yourselves, yet think ye be excused. A man that discerns betwixt truth and error a man that is for peace in the world, ' blessed are the peace makers!' I would to God that we had such men now; but the Devil has been let loose for a little season, deceiving the children of men. ' The love of money is the root of all evil,' to bind all the base in the world with their tyrannical power, still oppressing the people, swearing the people by their tyrannical power, saying this is for peace; taking the people's hearts against the rulers, yet keeping soldiers oppressing the people by their tyrannical power, saying, this is for peace; and when you have blinded all truths by your tyrannical power, think how you will appear before God in so doing. Pray consider, we'll declare unto you, what is proclaimed in the dark, shall be proclaimed upon the house top. You will call to the rocks and the mountains to fall on you, to hide you from the wrath of the Lamb. And as for Shays, I condemn them for taking up the gun. Was any of you born again? ' except you be born again, you cannot see God in peace.'

Being faithful to my Heavenly Father, I declare unto you Rulers, getting the government in your hands, going to the French, hiring money, not taking the scripture for your rule, as Christ saith in the gospel; enlisting soldiers, and cheating them with your States notes, giving your officers half pay for five years, to maintain your laws by tyrannical power. ' When the wicked bear rule, the people mourn,' Pray consider what you have been doing, where it says, ' in the morn-

ing sow thy seed, and in the evening withholding not thy hand,' longing for the welfare of the children of men, ' and by the fruit ye shall know them,' Exod. 18, 19. ' Hearken now to my voice, and I will give the counsel, and God shall be with thee; and thou for the people.' God's word—mayest bring the causes unto God; and, ' thou shalt teach them ordinances and laws, and shalt shew them the way wherein they must walk, and the work that they must do. Moreover thou shalt provide out of all the people able men, such as fear God, men of truth, hating covetousness, and place such over them, to be rulers of thousands, and rulers of hundreds, and rulers of fifties, and rulers of tens, and let them judge the people at all seasons.' ' Thou shalt not follow a multitude, neither shalt thou speak in any cause to decline after many to wrest judgment.' Levit. 19. 17. Thou shalt not hate thy brother in thine heart; thou shalt in any wise rebuke thy neighbour, and not suffer sin upon him. Ye shall do no unrighteousness in judgment. Thou shalt respect the person of the poor, nor honor the person of the mighty; but in righteousness shalt thou judge thy neighbour.' Deut. 1, 15. So I took the chiefs of your tribes, wise men and known, and made them heads over you, captains over thousands, and captains over hundreds, captains over fifties, and captains over tens, and officers among your tribes; and I charged your judges at that time, saying, Hear the case between your brethren, and judge righteousness between every man and his brother, and the stranger that is within him; he shall not respect persons in judgment, but you shall hear the small and the great; you shall not be afraid of the face of man, for the judgment is God's, and the cause that is too hard for you, bring it to me, and I will hear it, for the Lord your God is God of Gods and Lord of Lords, great God, mighty and terrible, which regardeth not persons, nor taketh rewards. Judges and officers shalt thou make thee in all thy gates which the Lord thy God giveth thee, throughout thy tribe; and they shall judge the people with just judgment. ' Thou shalt not wrest judgment, thou shalt not respect persons, neither take a gift; for a gift doth blind the eyes of the wise, and pervert the words of the righteous.' ' That which is altogether just, thou follow, that thou live and inherit the land which the Lord thy God giveth thee.'— Now these be the last words of David the son of Jesse, who was raised up on high, the anointed of the God of Jacob, and his servant, the Psalmist. ' The spirit of the Lord spake by me, and his word was in my tongue, the God of Israel said, the Rock of Israel spake to me, He that ruleth over men, must be just, ruling in the fear of God; he shall be as the light of the morning, when the sun riseth, even in a morning without clouds; as the tender grass springing out of the earth by clear shining after rain.' And he set judges in the land, throughout all the fenced cities of Judah, city by city, and said to the judges, ' Take heed what ye do; for ye judge not for man, but for the Lord, who is with you in judgment.'

From these scriptures you may see what manner of men judges ought to be, and with such the Lord will be in judging the people; my heart's desire in praying to God for the rulers is, that they may be saved, and if you would your fine must be set in order before you, you must exercise repentance toward God, and make restitution to your fellow creatures; you must go to the owners of the tea and confess your fault; and like Zacheus, restore our fold, without which, doing with all the heart, you may never expect forgiveness of God, nor admission into the kingdom of Heaven; and be sure no man is fit to govern men, who doth not submit to the government of God; and now I will forewarn you whom you should fear, even him who is able to destroy both soul and body in hell, I say fear him; and I desire all christian people to further this advice to all the rulers of State, and remember God hath said of his faithful servants, ' He that toucheth you, toucheth the apple of my eye.'

CHRISTOPHER BARRITT.

Of Lanesborough, in the county of Berkshire.——If I am worthy of death, I refuse not to die.

PART ONE
Merchants and Magistrates

I

THE PUBLIC CREDITOR INTEREST IN MASSACHUSETTS POLITICS, 1780–86

Richard Buel, Jr.

All the states had widely divergent experiences during the Revolutionary War, yet all emerged facing a common problem, that of the Revolutionary War debt. This essay examines the various possibilities that existed for dealing with the debt and the reasons that impelled the government of Massachusetts to embark on a fiscal policy that led directly to Shays's Rebellion. It focuses on the "creditor" interest, which is generally thought to have provoked the rebellion.[1] It argues that the creditors were not entirely homogeneous and that the dominant element among them had more in mind than lining their pockets at the expense of their fellow citizens; that they were also concerned with the larger end of securing Revolutionary achievements; and that in pursuing their larger objective they, as the state's most favored group of creditors, actually placed their personal financial interests in jeopardy by agreeing to hitch their fortunes to those of creditors less favored by state policies as well as to those of federal creditors.

The Revolutionary debt quickly became the key problem of the 1780s. The war had reduced the finances of the Confederation to chaos. The initial mobilization had been financed by having the states most directly involved in the fighting issue paper bills of credit. Soon, however, Congress stepped in with its own bills in

From a paper presented at the Bicentennial Conference on Shays's Rebellion and the Constitution, 1986, sponsored by Historic Deerfield, Inc.

an attempt to establish centralized control over the war effort.[2] This money held its value for about a year but then progressively depreciated until, by the early 1780s, it had ceased to circulate. As a result, Congress increasingly lost control over the continent's resources, and after 1779 direction of the war devolved largely upon the individual states. The French maintained the illusion that Congress was still in charge by subsidizing Robert Morris's operations as financier general during the last year of the fighting, but it was an illusion. The Articles of Confederation, in fact, gave the central government no power to raise a revenue beyond calling on the states for requisitions, which they were slow and reluctant in meeting, if indeed they met them at all.

In 1782 Morris tried to address the problem by "liquidating" part of the federal debt to equitable specie values and by asking the states to fund it, principally with an impost of 5 percent, but his efforts came to naught.[3] The proposal, amounting to an amendment of the Articles of Confederation, required the unanimous consent of the states.[4] Outside his small nationalist clique, Morris was regarded with deep suspicion, and the debt he proposed to fund was that owing only to individuals, not to states.[5] Those states that felt they had given far more than their share to the war effort feared that their interests would be sacrificed to those of individual creditors.[6] They recognized that the impost, as an indirect tax, seemed to be the most eligible way of paying the foreign debt, which was due in hard coin, and therefore more of them endorsed it than might otherwise have done so. Nevertheless, it proved impossible to procure the consent of all. As a consequence, the Confederation remained dependent on an inadequate requisition system for what little revenue it had.

Massachusetts eventually endorsed the impost, but reluctantly.[7] On the grass-roots level it remained unpopular. Many people believed that the revenue from it would be used to pay for commuting the half-pay for life, granted to Continental officers in 1780, into five years' full pay at the end of the war.[8] Commutation, which increased the army debt by 50 percent, was particularly resented in Massachusetts because the state had gone to extraordinary lengths during the war to protect both officers and men from the effects of depreciation. Early in 1779 the legislature had guaranteed to the army the full value of the wages originally stipulated by Congress, and a year later it authorized the issuance of £8 million in treasurer's or depreciation notes to make good its pledge.[9] Though these, like the currency, also depreciated, many regarded commutation as an attempt by the officers to compensate themselves twice over for losses in which the entire population had shared as a result of the war.[10]

The citizens of Massachusetts also felt that the states had been victimized by the collapse of the old Continental money. At the beginning of 1781 these bills had passed at a higher value in Massachusetts than anywhere else in the Confederation. This had led to an enormous influx of them into the state, followed shortly afterwards by a precipitate decline in value that halted their circulation, leaving the treasury and many citizens holding assets that were virtually worthless.[11] One possible explanation for the higher price of Continental money within Massachusetts was the faster tempo of trade enjoyed there after Rochambeau's expeditionary force arrived at Newport.[12] The leadership, however, saw it as the result of their patriotic zeal in taxing the people at the rate specified by Congress's requisitions.[13] They saw themselves as the victims of their own willingness to participate in a national fiscal scheme, and this experience, together with Congress's initial reluctance to grant the state credit for the huge cost of the abortive Penobscot expedition, enhanced the suspicions of centralized authority that lingered on in Massachusetts from the era of imperial rule.[14]

At the same time, Massachusetts had shown a strong disposition to establish its own public credit from the moment the Constitution of 1780 had been ratified. One of the first acts of the new government was to move up the date on which the state would begin repaying its debt from 1788 to 1785. To this end, it invited the state's creditors to subscribe their certificates of indebtedness at fair specie value to newly scheduled loans.[15] The revival of commercial activity accompanying the French presence nearby, together with the opening of a trade with Cuba earning large remittances in bullion, also emboldened the General Court to try paying interest on the principal in specie.[16] It was hoped that this would give the consolidated debt a sufficiently stable value so that it could pass as an asset as well as a liability.[17] During the summer of 1781 the state treasurer had hastily abandoned an attempt to pay interest in specie on the £1.46 million new emission currency Massachusetts had issued at

Congress's behest.[18] But in the following autumn the legislature experimented successfully with an excise as a device for raising hard coin. The initial results of indirect taxation encouraged them to expand the number of dutied articles and appropriate the revenue to paying interest on a major part of the state's consolidated debt.[19]

Nonetheless, more debt remained than there was ever specie enough with which to pay interest on it. The government attempted to cope with the situation in a variety of ways. When a creditor applied to the treasurer for payment of interest, he was given an order on a local collector rather than actual money in payment. The treasurer retained considerable discretion as to when these orders were issued.[20] He also controlled to whom they were directed. This allowed him to exploit the original distinction between that part of the consolidated debt that had been exchanged for the depreciation notes issued to the army (the so-called army notes) and had been funded by an annual direct tax and the rest of the consolidated debt, which had been funded by the excise and impost. An order on an excise or impost collector in a thriving seaport could be a readily negotiable asset.[21] An order on the collector of a rural town, on the other hand, was not likely to be worth much, particularly if no execution had been issued against the official involved, as no local figure was going to risk the wrath of his fellow townsmen if he could possibly avoid it.[22] By occasional procrastination and by a judicious matching of collectors to creditors, the treasurer was able to stretch out his limited supply of specie so as to meet the demands of those creditors living in the seacoast areas, where most of the revenue was raised. This expedient had the advantage of ensuring that the revenue would continue to come in, but the state paid a price for it. Its consolidated notes sold at anywhere from five to eight shillings on the pound, a good deal more than the two to three shillings a creditor could get for the liquidated federal debt but not enough to prevent a development that posed a serious threat to public credit.[23]

I am referring, of course, to the speculation in the debt that the depreciated value of the principal invited. As long as unfunded debts circulated below par, there were incentives on both sides for selling and buying at bargain prices. The seller might be in desperate need of money; the buyer could always hope that the debt would eventually be completely funded and would appreciate in value.[24]

This led progressively to the concentration of the debt in fewer and fewer hands.[25] And in a popular political system, such a process had dangerous implications. What was to stop the majority of public debtors from ganging up on the minority of public creditors?[26] One could argue that the public, having already received the full value of the debt, was therefore bound to honor it on the same terms; one could say that if the state failed to do this, it would forfeit all public credit; and one could point to the acute embarrassments that the lack of public credit had inflicted on the patriots during the Revolutionary War.[27] But these arguments lost much of their force in peacetime. For one thing, the usefulness of public credit was less in evidence than the immediate burden of the public debt; for another, the debtor majority could with apparent reason claim that because much of the debt had been alienated at vastly depreciated prices by the original holders, it should be paid at no more than its current market price, and possibly at less.[28] Such devaluation amounted in effect to a disguised form of repudiation, and its attractiveness increased as people found themselves laboring under a growing burden of private debts in addition to public ones.[29]

To my knowledge, no commentator on Shays's Rebellion, then or since, has denied that a classic postwar recession, stimulated by low consumption during the war, by the rapid expansion of personal debt immediately afterwards, and by the subsequent difficulty of paying those debts, laid the groundwork for the upheaval.[30] In levying a heavy specie tax just when most of the specie that had entered the economy during the war had drained out again, the Massachusetts General Court acted with about as much finesse as had Parliament when it provoked the Stamp Act riots in 1765. Both had perpetrated measures that were clumsy and ill-timed, coinciding as they did with moments when people were scrambling frantically to pay their private debts. Parliament at least had the excuse that distance from the scene had caused its ignorance of local circumstances. The Massachusetts legislature of 1785–86 had no such excuse. Why, then, did it act the way it did?

Congress's requisition of September 27, 1785, to pay one year's interest on its foreign and domestic debts precipitated the crisis.[31] Of the two, the foreign debt posed the more urgent problem. Under the supplemental Franco-American Treaty signed in 1782, the United States had agreed to begin repaying the principal of a Dutch loan guaranteed by the French at the end of 1787 and to begin repaying the interest and principal of the French loan at the end of 1788.[32] Since 1783 the nation's foreign credit had depended on advances made by Dutch bankers, who might also help in refinancing the entire foreign debt. But Congress had reason to fear that the good offices of the Dutch would soon cease if the nation failed to make some headway in raising specie to meet its first formally scheduled payments.[33] The legislature computed that Massachusetts's share of the amount due on the foreign debt, together with interest on the federal domestic debt, came to £145,655, only one-third of which had to be raised in specie.[34] Complying with the requisition, however, far from enriching the public creditors of the state, posed a serious dilemma for them.

The immediate interest of the dominant group of creditors lay in preserving the arrangements that had permitted at least a partial funding of the state's consolidated debt. Unfortunately, because of an adverse balance of trade that had developed after 1783, the yield on indirect taxes had declined to less than £60,000, an amount that placed even a partial funding in jeopardy.[35] Nor was the yield likely to increase, given the trade war with Britain that Massachusetts had embarked upon in 1785. Enraged by a series of British orders-in-council that crippled the state's trade, by the dumping of cheap British manufactures in the American market, and by the appearance of British factors in Boston, the Massachusetts legislature had struck back with protective duties.[36] At first it was thought that raising the duties would increase the revenue, but by early 1786 it had become apparent that yields were continuing to decline.[37] As a result, the holders of the consolidated notes serviced by the excise and impost had a wholly new interest in raising specie through direct taxation.

In order to do so, however, they had to ally themselves with those public creditors who held less favored forms of the state debt, such as the "army notes," and with the federal creditors. Alliance with the federal creditors was a necessity because, despite the reduced yields from the excise and impost, the most eligible way to raise the specie requisitioned by Congress was to divert to this purpose the funds appropriated for paying interest on the consolidated notes. An attempt to divert them had been made early in 1786 and only narrowly defeated, despite the popularity of partial funding in the eastern towns and the political power these towns enjoyed under the Constitution of 1780 because of the provision it made for proportional representation of the population.[38] The precarious political situation the most favored state creditors found themselves in likewise made it expedient for them to try to meet the claims of those holding "army notes."

The incremental cost of satisfying all the specie claims of respective creditors, both state and federal, together with the annual expenses of the government, came to just over £125,000 out of a total tax of £300,000. But before a direct tax for that amount, bearing on all the towns, could be put into effect, some kind of equitable valuation of assets had to be undertaken. The valuations that had been done during the war had been unsystematic at best.[39] The General Court had begun to address the problem of reform in 1784 and in 1785 had delegated the job to a grand committee of unprecedented size. Instead of adhering to fixed proportions for the various counties and allowing them to divide up their quota among themselves, each town had its assets appraised systematically.[40] Though polls continued to account for approximately a third of the valuation,[41] care was taken to have unmovable assets assessed according to the income they might generate, thus preserving a measure of equity between the newer, poorer settlements and the richer, commercial towns.[42] The process was slowed down by considerable foot-dragging, and the final allocations were not entirely free of political string pulling. Nevertheless, the legislature had reason to think the valuation adopted in February 1786 was fairer than any that had preceded it.[43]

The adoption of the new valuation opened the way to the assessment of the largest direct tax for specie the Commonwealth had ever laid. Petitions in favor of paper money or tender laws as alternatives to this measure were rejected by the legislature on the grounds that the experience of the war had shown that they would drive money of real value out of circulation and thus exacerbate the Commonwealth's problems.⁴⁴ Though the creditors could not have been oblivious to the risks they were taking—they must have realized that a people who had lived through a revolution that had started as a tax rebellion would be sensitive to such dramatic increases in taxation—most of the state's leadership felt that private inclinations had already been overindulged, that the time had come to put urgent public needs first, and that a modicum of virtue and restraint would lead to a speedy retirement of the Revolutionary debt.⁴⁵

The creditors were also guilty of what we would call "vanguardism." Massachusetts remained the second largest state in the Confederation and still thought of itself as having been far and away the foremost in initiating and prosecuting the Revolution. It had been the first to mobilize its forces for battle, and it had pioneered what was widely regarded as the most republican constitution on the continent, one to which the people had explicitly consented after an initial series of rejections.⁴⁶ Now, surely, it was time for Massachusetts to lead the way once more by showing the other states how to extricate themselves from the morass of the postwar debt.⁴⁷ And some suspected that if the state did not assert itself in this way, government under the Articles would break down over the issue of public credit. This was a disturbing prospect because the Articles gave the commercial states of the North more protection against dominance by the agrarian states of the South than they were likely to have in a consolidated union.⁴⁸

Yet all of these facts do not fully explain why the majority of the Massachusetts legislature attached so much importance to establishing public credit as to risk their separate "interests" for it. There were undeniable instrumental considerations, going well beyond the wooing of influential support through the enrichment of individuals, or even the potential economic benefits to all of successfully funding the debt. The war had shown that no single nation could long survive in competition with others unless it could command the voluntary support of people of substance: in other words, unless it had public credit. What had enabled Britain to continue the struggle against hopeless odds was its command of credit, as opposed to America's loss of it.⁴⁹ The war had also shown that because of persistent imbalances in the American economy, the nation needed foreign credit as well. Such considerations undoubtedly played a part in influencing the Massachusetts legislature to respond as it did to the requisition of 1785.

But the most compelling influence touched on a larger question, raised with particular urgency in the immediate aftermath of the war, whether it would be possible to establish a stable government based on the consent of the people if one part of the populace violated its pledge to another; that is, if the public debtors inflicted injustice on public creditors. It was in response to a debtor majority in Pennsylvania that Thomas Paine had written that "a Republic, properly understood, is a sovereignty of justice, in contradistinction to a sovereignty of will."[50] By this he meant that it was essential for a republican government to adhere to principles that all could and should espouse. In accordance with this view, many argued that whatever else might be desirable, an unswerving commitment to public credit was the sine qua non for the firm and lasting establishment of a republican government.[51]

As we all know, the legislature's policies provoked a series of court closings culminating in a widespread rebellion, an expensive military repression of it that increased the debt rather than retiring it, and a bitter public reaction to these events that made it impossible to take further action on behalf of public credit at the state level.[52] Other states also suffered court closings, and New Hampshire, too, was briefly confronted with an armed rebellion.[53] But Shays's Rebellion alone took on national significance because it showed what could happen when a public creditor minority, enjoying the benefit of the most legitimate constitution on the continent, imposed more than routine taxes on the debtor majority in the name of establishing public credit. In other words, it showed the futility of the states' trying by their own exertions to save the credit of the nation. In most states in the Union, a minority of public creditors stood opposed in their interests to a debtor majority, and presumably creditors in other states, too, would face uprisings if these states tried to pay their debts.[54] Few who did not enjoy special fiscal advantages were so unwise as to try.[55]

The sole remaining possibility for a solution to the problem of the war debt seemed to be the development of a new form of polity capable both of organizing the total resources of the nation, as the separate states were not, and gathering them in without provoking popular rebellion. That polity would have to be a national one, capable of countering the hostile economic policies of foreign powers and of maximizing domestic revenues from such taxes as the impost. Its precise structure, however, would remain in doubt until after the Philadelphia convention. In the immediate wake of Shays's Rebellion, one thing only was clear: a radically new departure was necessary if public credit, the absolute prerequisite for the founding of an enduring republic, was ever to be established on a national scale.[56]

2

SHAYS'S REBELLION IN LONG PERSPECTIVE:
The Merchants and the "Money Question"

Joseph A. Ernst

This essay interprets Shays's Rebellion as a symbolic moment in a century-long conflict over the "money question"—matters of currency, finance, credit, and prices—in the colony and the Commonwealth of Massachusetts. These closely related issues were at the core of a series of struggles, both political-economic and ideological in dimension, by which the great-merchant class of Massachusetts sought to effect monetary and fiscal policy in its own interest. By the middle of the eighteenth century the great merchants had achieved that goal. But the system of money and finance favored by merchants collapsed with the coming of war in 1775, and it would take a concerted effort to reestablish it, under new political circumstances, by the early 1780s. This revived system underlay the conditions responsible for Shays's Rebellion.

Specifically, this chapter argues that from the 1690s through the 1780s the great merchants opposed monetary and fiscal plans not under their control or to their liking. They advocated that public and private currency issues should be limited in volume and in duration, and wherever possible be redeemable in specie. These concerns in the decades after Queen Anne's War led to a seesaw battle with populist political forces, which viewed paper money schemes as a way of generating growth and development and of realizing a vision

From a paper presented at the Bicentennial Conference on Shays's Rebellion, 1986, sponsored by the Colonial Society of Massachusetts.

of entrepreneurial egalitarianism. But by mid-century the leading merchants, in alliance with crown authorities and English creditors, had regained the upper hand, ushering in "the era of public credit." From this time until the onset of the Revolutionary War, public finance in the Bay Colony approximated the English funding system created in the 1690s. Secure government paper in the form of treasury notes payable by general taxes became available to the great-merchant class as an investment earning interest in specie and as a limited commercial medium of exchange.

After the Treaty of Paris in 1763, all aspects of the money question in Massachusetts were overshadowed by a succession of political-economic crises and Revolutionary disorders. Yet the Revolution opened up the possibility that the great merchants might extend their dominance over money to other areas of the economy, increasing their power to direct growth and development in their own interest. To this end merchants sympathetic to the Revolution joined with other groups to form a "Merchantile Interest," which John Adams identified as "comprehending merchants, mechanics, laborers" and "complicated with the landed interest." With a return to "currency finance" during the Revolutionary War, however, the era of public credit came to an abrupt close, and the "Merchantile Interest" splintered.[1]

The era of public credit that ended with Independence offered the model that a new commercial elite of Patriot merchants strived to re-create in the turbulent early years of the war. Their first move was against the state's paper money system. Pushed to its limits by rising military demands, currency finance had already led to inflation and popular cries for price controls by 1776, threatening both profits and commercial freedom of action. The merchants were relentless therefore in pressing for funding the state's paper currency and returning to a system of public loans and heavy taxes. The triumph of the merchants' policies by late 1777 was remarkable; their extension to Continental dollars four years later was no less so.

Another dimension to this century-long conflict over the money question in Massachusetts was ideological. From the outset matters of currency, finance, credit, and prices were addressed in the broad ideological languages of "Puritanism," "interest," and "virtue." Anti–paper money forces urged a return to the Puritan work ethic as the best way of reducing imports and bringing specie back into circulation. They saw it as only human that man, however capable of virtue and sacrifice of self to the public good, was mainly concerned with the pursuit of selfish interests and the protection of property. Hence, the marketplace could be seen as an instrument both of economic growth and of social order. The proponents of this position were by no means liberal apostles of free trade. Rather, they appraised the state's role in economic life according to the specific situations they faced. The inflow and outflow of specie during periods of changing trade balances was considered as "natural"; consequently, legislators were expected to endorse the mechanism of the marketplace. On the other hand, it was often necessary to reconcile private interests and the public good through laws protecting property and natural liberty. As it happened, the proper course to pursue would depend on the perceived interests of the great-merchant class.[2]

Supporters of paper money adopted the language of virtue, or "oppositionist" ideology. Hammered out in the struggle against the "Financial Revolution" in England, this rhetoric condemned selling the public debt in order to attach the "monied" interest to a corrupt "Court Party." Spokesmen for Massachusetts's popular forces likewise stigmatized hard money sympathizers as "monied men," minions of a Court faction bent upon destroying paper and with it the people's virtue, well-being, and liberty.[3]

The rival ideologies, articulated after Independence, reflected the same contest between social groups and the same competing visions of political economy that had shaped public action on money and finance before the Revolution. Thus it was that the General Court, in its *Address to the People* in 1786, expressed the great merchants' long-standing perspective and repudiated the "old" system of currency finance as a species of fraud that cheated widows and orphans. Instead, the legislators offered a "new" conventional wisdom that the commercial interests could now put into place: wars could no longer be fought without sound money, a funded debt, and loans from foreign and domestic investors; and governments could not renege on obligations to their creditors without endangering liberty's future.[4]

In sum, in the new republic as in the former Bay Colony, the great-merchant class sought to implement monetary and fiscal policies suitable to its interests and its ideological outlook. By the end of the Revolutionary War these goals had been achieved. With political power firmly in the hands of the merchants and a reunited "Mercantile Interest," the response to the Shaysite "Insurgents" seemed a foregone conclusion.

AN INABILITY TO MEET military expenses in the usual way forced governments in England and New England in the 1690s to initiate financial revolutions. The mother country created history's first funded debt and the Bank of England, innovations that made monied wealth more accessible than ever to the state. Here, said some, was a "standing miracle in politics"; said others, a speculative triumph at the expense of virtue and honest trade and a source of corruption.[5]

Massachusetts faced similar demands. An empty treasury and the difficulty of borrowing money forced the government late in 1690 to turn to currency finance. Merchants discounted the new paper notes, squeezing "poor soldiers and seamen" and raising such a storm that everyone finally agreed to take the money at face value. The General Court, in order to make the notes good for public debts, pledged future taxes as a redemption fund. By 1712, when the practice of accepting paper for private debts was made law, nearly £170,000 in currency was outstanding.[6]

In reaction to an imbalanced trade and to currency finance, and in anticipation of continuing and heavy paper issues, merchants began rapidly remitting any coin that came to hand to British creditors. By 1714 specie had drained away, not to return to general circulation before mid-century. At the end of Queen Anne's War therefore, when the Bay Colony struck an additional £100,000 in currency, the de facto convertibility of silver coin broke down. Silver soared in price, undermining views that paper merely replaced coin swept off in sterling debt payments and causing fears of "the currency of silver and gold entirely ceasing" and the depreciation of paper going on forever. Some voices called for fewer, or no, bills and a return to industry and frugality as a way of cutting luxury imports, redressing trade imbalances, and returning "real" money to circulation. Others cried out for more bills as a medium of trade, or for a private land bank as a means of stimulating agriculture, manufacturing, and commerce and thereby replenishing depleted specie stocks.[7]

In this new situation following Queen Anne's War, the great merchants began groping for a solution to the money question. It would be forty years before developments, which included parliamentary control over New England currency, a monetary, trade, and fiscal crisis, and new wartime demands, came together to resolve the merchants' problems. Along the way four major considerations stand out: the initial political failure of the great merchants to limit public currency issues; their ideological response to paper money and that of their critics; the division in ranks caused by Rhode Island's "monetary imperialism" and the reunion of the great merchants when faced with the creation of a private land bank; and above all the merchants' growing dependence on royal governors and imperial authorities for intervention on their behalf.

In 1714 promoters came forward with a plan for a private "Bank of Credit." The bank was the brainchild of several smaller Boston merchant-entrepreneurs and the leaders of Boston's "Popular Party" interested in an expanding role in New England's foreign and domestic trade as well as in local manufacturing, shipping, shipbuilding, and fishing and in land speculation in Maine and western Massachusetts. But when the promoters appeared before a joint legislative committee dominated by wealthy merchants and Council members, they found support lined up in favor of a small public bank, which would both produce a revenue and restrict the currency. The promoters answered with a prospectus for a private scheme similar to their own that had surfaced in London in 1688 and called for subscribers. In October proposals for the private bank, capitalized at £300,000, and for a modest £50,000 public loan came before the legislature. The private bank lost in its bid for approval, and when subsequent lobbying efforts for a royal charter also failed, the matter became a dead issue and remained so for a quarter century.[8]

Defeat of the Bank of Credit only ended up subverting the great merchants' control over the currency. The bank's supporters quickly joined in a populist coalition, expanding the paper money constituency to include agrarians, fishermen, shopkeepers, artisans, and debtors. The coalition supporters in the lower house then made the public bank their own by voting a £100,000 loan issue in the fall of 1716. As the outstanding local currency supply rose to £230,000, and in the common currency area of New England to £310,000, silver and the sterling exchange rate moved to new highs. But in a few years paper fell in volume, leading to cries for another government loan to ease what some saw as a general monetary stringency hampering economic activity.[9]

At this point an additional consideration, the nature of money and its relation to the workings of the economy and to morality—that is, to "political economy," that "branch of the science of a statesman" linking moral philosophy with individual well-being and the wealth and development of state and society—occupied center stage. Between 1719 and 1721 publishers turned out pamphlet after pamphlet debating these matters.[10]

The position of commercial opponents of "printed money" and their spokesmen was simple. Specie alone had "intrinsic" value; and no law could make men think "a piece of paper is a piece of money," especially when the "low esteem of bills" had banished silver and so "raised the price of necessaries" that laborers had to move out of Boston. A drastic reduction of paper money to induce a specie inflow and to make possible a return to hard money was the best of all solutions, they argued; and industry and frugality were the only effective means of creating a favorable trade balance and earning specie abroad. That paper alone could usefully serve as a local means of exchange seemed dubious, but currency issues should in any event be limited to commercial demands.

Propagandists for paper currency located the root problem in a stringency of money, which—however defined—dampened all economic undertakings. They labeled enemies of another public loan as usurers or worse. John Colman, an old Bank of Credit promoter, went further, dismissing the view that specie was the only real money. It had no more "inherent" worth than iron, tin, brass, or paper; only specie's "common acceptance" as a medium of exchange by "men in trade" gave it special value. Moreover, like all commodities, gold and silver fluctuated in price according to supply and demand. Here Colman adopted balance of trade reasoning with a vengeance: as long as trade was unbalanced, hard money would remain scarce. Nor would laws banning specie exports and pegging silver prices do any good. They violated the axiom that fair traders should be as free as possible in their dealings; besides, he added, nothing should be done which "may seem to bear hard" on British trade.[11]

This ideological debate continued on into 1721, lending support to the political cause of paper. Silver threatened liberty, inclining men to "extortion, dissembling, and other moral evils," avowed John Wise; paper, the workingman's friend, seemed less apt to "corrupt the mind." More whimsical was the claim that those upholding "no bank at all but the clam bank" were exploiting a dearth of money to "make 15 or 20 percent, though it be by grinding the poor and trampling on all positive laws of morality." Independent men who knew paper to be the "best medium," not usurers and "screwing misers," should be sent to the assembly. They were; and the new legislature voted yet another loan issue. By then some £300,000 currency was outstanding in New England, the very amount of specie one pamphleteer reckoned had been shipped away in the prior twenty years.[12]

Gradual economic recovery and an additional public loan ended this round in a pamphlet war that wore on for a quarter century. At the moment efforts by the mother country to extend its power over the popular house eclipsed the money question. Matters changed only after Rhode Island's venture into monetary imperialism divided the great-merchant class. A few years later a far greater threat, the creation of the first private land bank in Massachusetts, reunited the merchants.[13]

Crown officials by the late 1720s aimed at returning currency values in the Bay Colony to those of lawful coin and restoring silver to circulation. The new governor, Jonathan Belcher, was directed to limit issues in support of government to £30,000 annually and to rid the province of loan office bills in just over a decade. But when he presented his instructions to the General Court early in 1729, the assembly came forward with a plan for a £50,000 loan with a proviso aimed at stabilizing silver at its highest price in 1721. Belcher sent the scheme to London—minus his signature—requesting permission to sign. The Board of Trade demurred, and an angry governor shot back that royal orders were useless anyway so long as Rhode Island flooded New England with cheap paper.[14]

Rhode Island's monetary practice broadly paralleled that of Massachusetts. The first treasury issues in 1710 covered wartime expenditures; public loans for growth and development followed. The loans had support until 1731, when depreciation drove Newport's merchant elite, backed by the governor and the customs collector, to protest to London. Imperial authorities proved helpless. Rhode Island's charter provided the governor with no veto, nor the crown with any power, over local laws. The province promptly enacted a £100,000 twenty-year loan.[15]

Rhode Island's banks had already caused outcries against that "handful of people who now supply" the Bay Colony "with many things," including "the greatest part of the medium of exchange." But word of the latest and largest loan arrived in the midst of depression and after news of the rejection of Massachusetts's smaller loan designed to stabilize silver. With the government tied down by instructions restricting new currency issues and calling for the liquidation of all loan office bills by 1741, several of Boston's merchant leaders decided to act. Led by James Bowdoin, Sr., Edward Bromfield, Jr., Thomas Cushing, Jr., William Foye, Edward Hutchinson, John Osborne, Samuel Sewall, Jr., Samuel Wells, Jacob Wendell, and Joshua Winslow, a number of the great merchants joined in a private venture, creating a kind of "Merchants Bank of Credit." It offered on loan against good security £110,000 in "Merchants' Notes" redeemable for silver at 19s. per ounce—just under the current price—in three installments between 1736 and 1743. The principal aim was to drive out Rhode Island paper and gradually replenish hard money stocks. The bank failed in its objectives, however, and Rhode Island bills remained in local use until 1750. Silver, meanwhile, rose 5s. by 1736 in response, said some, to recent treasury issues; said others, to the added weight of the merchants' notes.[16]

The Merchants Bank alienated several leading importers and Governor Belcher. As colonial creditors but sterling debtors, men like Thomas Hutchinson, Sr., for instance, never doubted the wisdom of hard money policies and strict legal limits on paper money. The governor began working with these people, considering a range of solutions from banning the merchants' notes and other New England currencies to issuing short-lived provincial bills, sinking them as scheduled, and even redeeming them in specie at, or near, the proclamation rate of 6s. 8d. Little was done, however, until the price of silver dipped in 1736–37, allowing Belcher to connive at supporting a banking plan of the Hutchinsons, father and son, for emitting £60,000 currency convertible in ten years in silver at the 6s. 8d. rate. But when the assembly balked at including a suspending clause, the governor would not sign.

The Board of Trade, meanwhile, had tightened monetary controls: new bank measures were to provide for redeeming bills in coin at proclamation rates and to exempt private debts owing in hard money from payment in paper. Notes issued in anticipation of taxes fell under like restrictions. They were not to exceed £30,000 annually, while currency struck before 1727 was to be sunk by 1741.[17]

Rhode Island's monetary imperialism, the Merchants Bank's failure, tougher British policies, and a "dread" of "drawing in all the paper money without a substitution" led the assembly in mid-1739 to call for ideas for "furnishing" a medium of trade. John Colman promptly offered a private "Land Bank" scheme; eighteen months later five-sixths of the towns boasted land bankers. Critics at the time damned the bankers as "insolvents," freeholders "much in debt," and "plebeians" of "small estates." But scholars have uncovered others: rising Boston merchants; artisans; tradesmen; farmers with "sizeable landholdings"; major businessmen; community leaders; professionals such as "doctors, lawyers, and clergymen"; prominent politicians; land speculators; and new landholders in the interior—in short, many of the same interests that had backed public banks and the populist coalition. Like these earlier banks, this bank promised to capitalize land, stop a ruinous contraction, and provide cheap loans for growth and development.[18]

Opposed to the Land Bank stood the "Silver Bank." Put before the government by Hutchinson, Jr., as a public scheme but rejected, the Silver Bank had come under the control of hard money men and directors of the old Merchants Bank who united in a grand coalition of great merchants to defeat the land bankers. But destruction of the Land Bank came about only after the merchants turned to their London creditors for help in pressuring the government at home to intervene. In 1741 an obliging Parliament extended the "South Sea Bubble Act" to America, eliminating all private banks of issue and requiring the land and silver banks to pay their debts in full.[19]

In London, where Parliament was becoming embroiled in King George's War, the money question was sidetracked for the rest of the decade. In Massachusetts, however, it became the very center of things as the General Court undertook the "resumption" of silver. Resumption is another well-worn tale. By the end of the war, Governor William Shirley, Belcher's replacement, had come to favor fundamental monetary reform. Hutchinson as always had a plan. He proposed abolishing currency by exchanging bills for coin from the promised parliamentary reimbursement covering the Cape Breton campaign and other wartime expenditures. Silver was to be made lawful at the proclamation rate, and remaining paper taxed away; a later act banned other currencies from circulation. Shirley gave his blessing, and after much politicking Hutchinson got "as good" a law "as could be expected." Despite misgivings about redeeming bills at speculative values, the Board of Trade agreed to the need to "suppress an evil."[20]

Shirley's next move was to press for parliamentary regulation putting an end to all New England paper money. The crown paid no heed until leading Newport merchants petitioned in 1751 against the threat of another Rhode Island land bank. Their memorial harped upon currency's crippling effect on America's commercial-creditor class, and the Board of Trade quickly turned to Parliament. The outcome was the Currency Act of 1751.[21]

Resumption and the Currency Act of 1751 did not settle the money question. Yet Hutchinson appears to have thought otherwise, going on about those who had foolishly condemned sinking the currency as a "*shock* to trade" and about a "good currency" having been "insensibly substituted" in place of a "bad one, and every branch of business . . . carried on to greater advantage than before." In fact, the funding operation dragged on for years, coinciding with a severe commercial setback after King George's War and the hoarding of specie. Early in 1750 Thomas Hancock blamed the "d———d" resumption for turning "all trade out of doors, making it impossible to get debts in either dollars or province bills." Indeed, three years later the legislature acted to inflate the value of what little paper remained in circulation.[22]

In the end the postwar trade crisis, a monetary muddle, and the coming of a new war with France caused Massachusetts to turn to a funded debt, a system highly favorable to great-merchant, or monied, interests. Thus in 1750–54 the province undertook to pay its creditors in treasury, or promissory, notes carrying 6 percent interest and redeemable in two or three years in silver at the current legal rate for Spanish dollars. Its reason: with paper "all exchanged by the silver imported from England, and provision made by law that no bills of credit should ever after pass" as legal tender, "there was difficulty in providing money for the immediate service of government, until it could be raised by a tax."

Initial amounts were negligible. The French and Indian War changed that, calling forth £500,000 in certificates of indebtedness, or bonds. In the peak year 1761 the value, in silver, of outstanding treasury notes was virtually double that of the paper money in circulation at the time resumption began. If not fiat money, the new paper instruments were negotiable, receivable at the treasury, and at some point convertible in silver. Moreover, as merchant John Rowe noted, "treasury notes will do as well as money"; the notes in fact came to be called "merchants' money."[23]

The great-merchant class looked favorably upon another fiscal innovation connected with the treasury notes. Starting in 1756, the Massachusetts government sold 6 percent "war bonds," or treasury notes of large denomination, to merchants for specie and certificates of earlier issue. It then turned around and paid hard money for provisions often bought with paper instruments. The treasury notes, of course, were also payable in specie, as was yearly interest, so that from time to time merchants supported delaying the redemption of their bonds.[24]

These policies ushered in the era of public credit, bringing the Bay Colony closer than it had ever been to the British system of funding the debt. And they set the pattern for the merchants' approach to the money question during both the War for Independence and Shays's Rebellion.[25]

THE SECOND PROVINCIAL CONGRESS of Massachusetts slammed the door on the era of public credit in May 1775 and returned to currency finance. Early that month the congress voted a £26,000 issue of the kind the Bay Colony had relied upon, and fought over, in the half century before resumption. The bills were redeemable in a year at 6 percent, or without interest if paid sooner. Another £4,000 followed; and after the transfer of power to the General Court in July, the embattled province authorized more and more paper, in all some £200,000 by year's end. This new money was interest-free and was to be taxed away in the distant years 1778 to 1783. All the money, along with the bills of the other rebellious colonies, was made legal tender.[26]

Depreciation began late in 1775, and in February 1776 the General Court ordered the arrest of anyone even suspected of undermining the currency. But when the agrarian-controlled House of Representatives went further and called for price controls, the Council, where the merchant interest prevailed, took exception. The issue would not go away. That March petitions from farm communities in Bristol, Suffolk, and Essex counties and the coastal towns Newbury and Newburyport condemned the "extravagant" prices of English goods and domestic commodities. The government, however, did no more than impose a £20 fine on sales made for less money in gold and silver; double that for passing bills at less than face value. Other legislation, meanwhile, aggravated inflation by making Continental dollars, which flooded into the state in support of the war, lawful for all payments, including specie debts.[27]

Events moved swiftly. The British evacuated Boston in March 1776, and in April the Continental Congress opened American ports to the world. Economic opportunity was fast returning to commercial areas, leading some observers to remark upon the "rampant" new spirit of commerce; others, upon the danger of "public virtue" being "swallowed up in a desire of possessing paper currency." The coming of summer brought more practical matters to light, from a doubling of costs the past year to the sharp dealings of merchants and farmers alike. By fall newspapers carried one complaint after another against monopolizers and forestallers, who held goods back from market until prices rose. Nothing was done, however, as the legislature set to work arranging a quid pro quo between rival interests.[28]

State elections during the spring of 1776, in the words of one scholar, "reversed the short-lived social revolution that had swung control of government" in the previous two years to "agrarian reformers." The merchants, who by mid-1775 already dominated the Council, led a major faction within the House as well. A deal between interests was not impossible. Agrarians opposed heavy, regressive poll and land taxes; they favored currency finance and price controls. Commercial interests opposed fiat money and price-fixing; they supported taxing as heavily as possible to limit depreciation and boost public credit. They also sought a return of the era of public credit, of the treasury note system of the 1750s and 1760s and the use of paper instruments that, while bearing interest and intended for investment, remained negotiable. The General Court struck a balance: it voted £300,000 in lawful bills redeemable as late as 1784 and £250,000 in treasury notes, in one to three years. Action on prices, taxes, and market control was deferred until late in the year.[29]

By the fall of 1776 consideration of shortages of food, goods, and labor seemed imperative. Reports of "unrighteous" commerce, inflation, depreciation, and a threat of "tumults, disorders, and even a disunion and backwardness in, or defection from, the common cause of America" poured in on the assembly. In November the House designated three great merchants—Thomas Cushing of Boston, Azor Orne of Marblehead, and Tristan Dalton of Newburyport—to meet with delegates from Connecticut, New Hampshire, and Rhode Island in Providence, late in December. At issue were the support of currency values and prevention of "monopoly and high prices of goods and necessaries of life, regulation of vendues, embargo on shipping and such other matters as are of general concern to the New England States." The merchant-dominated conference called for ending currency finance in favor of government borrowing and taxation.[30]

The matter of price-fixing produced a double standard. Farmers got a freeze on the price of cheap stockings, work shoes, flannels, and so on. But for domestic and West Indian produce, ceiling prices were set at or near existing levels—an obvious advantage to seaports and inland commercial centers. European imports could be marked up as much as 275 percent sterling above price cost when sold wholesale. Any markup based upon sterling as opposed to currency values allowed merchants to adjust for inflation and still make a "fair" 275 percent profit. Double standard or no, the conference proceedings were "received, believed and submitted to like the doctrines of holy writ": the General Court stopped issuing bills of credit, enacted a wartime tax, and passed the "First Regulating Act." Designed to "prevent monopoly and oppression," the Regulating Act gave the force of law to the Providence resolves concerning price-fixing.[31]

By early spring when the mysteries of the Regulating Act were revealed, popular leader James Warren was in despair. The legislation was "constantly violated" in Boston, and in broad daylight. In the meantime "bitterness and wrath," in Warren's words, were tearing apart "town and country," the country "endeavoring to starve the town in return for what they consider ill usage from them." The farmers had succeeded, Boston's situation being "little superior to what it was in the siege." "Impracticable" was Warren's final judgment on a law that "would end in bringing the authority of government into contempt."[32]

Warren was not far wrong. The Regulating Act split the "Merchantile Interest" into warring factions. "Joyce Junior," for instance, symbolic executioner of Charles I and leader in the Boston protests by mechanics and day laborers against the tea consignees in 1774, was busy again in the streets and the press during March and April, railing against and escorting from town "Tory" traders and shopkeepers. Their crimes: refusing paper money, offering goods "lower for silver than for paper," and buying up articles "at a dear rate" and then not parting with them for paper. In the west, meanwhile, spring elections had helped swing support in the new House in favor of agrarian interests, which amended the Regulating Act to death, coming up with a radically different measure—the so-called Second Regulating Act. Equally important, the assembly restricted legal tender privileges to Massachusetts and Continental currency.

The Second Regulating Act revised upward the commodity price ceiling and charged selectmen and committees of correspondence with readjusting prices for such things as flour, smithwork, and labor every few months. Selling practices were also tightened up: trading in any manner that has not been "commonly practiced between buyer and seller" in the last several years could bring prosecution; goods sold in violation of the act were open to confiscation and sale in small quantities to retailers and the "needy." The merchants acted to quash the law before it could be enforced and then moved against the state's currency.[33]

Late in May 1777 Boston's town meeting, under merchant direction, went to the core of commercial and money problems. "Trade must always regulate itself," the town instructed its representatives: a "coy mistress," it could only be "ruined by force." The Regulating Acts, with their "innumerable evils directly opposed to the idea of liberty," were to be dropped in favor of free and open commerce and presumably fairer prices. Likewise fiat money was to be eliminated—exchanged for interest-bearing treasury certificates in order to prop up the Continental dollar, the only remaining lawful currency. That returning to the era of public credit and creation of a bonded debt would reward the great-merchant and monied class received no mention. But westerners and the landed interest controlled the House, which on June 1, after much debate, rejected repeal of the Regulating Acts by a thumping 122 to 31. The currency question never arose. As one observer said of the "great dissensions," while the merchants were "warm against" the regulating laws, the House was "determined" to support them.[34]

Seeming "not to know how to go forward or backward," the assembly decided to sidestep matters. A few days after the vote against repeal, the House appointed a committee, which included several Council members, to review the Regulating Acts. It successfully recommended submitting the problem to a conference of delegates from New York, Connecticut, Massachusetts, New Hampshire, and Rhode Island set for late July in Springfield, Massachusetts. Local representatives, merchants Thomas Cushing from the Council and Azor Orne from the House, had attended the earlier Providence conference. The third member, also from the House, was conservative lawyer Robert Treat Paine.[35]

As at Providence, the proposals arriving in Springfield proved easily acceptable to the merchant class. Most important were the repeal of price controls—that is, the Regulating Acts—and the sinking of the state currencies by conversion into treasury bonds and by taxes. By the time the Massachusetts legislature met again in late summer, many western representatives, doubtless busy with the harvest, stayed away. The Springfield resolutions became the law of the land, and on September 26 the assembly renounced in principle currency finance. A fortnight later it voted to repeal the Regulating Acts and to sink all bills of public credit in exchange for treasury notes bearing 6 percent interest. There was also another tax and compensation payment for families of Continental soldiers. Mobs in the meantime still protested commercial hoarding and high prices.

In sum, the Revolutionary War had pressed the older policies of currency finance to their limits, provoking the leading merchants into a desperate fight to reinstate the era of public credit and the system of war finance favored by their class during the French and Indian War. That system was now on the books. The government had legislated the conversion of bills of credit of a dollar or more into a £400,000 treasury note issue. Available in denominations of not less than £10, the notes were funded, or secured, by taxes payable in the spring of 1780 and 1781. They would be redeemed when the time came in the lawful money of the day. As for any bills of credit still in circulation after November 1777, they would be void.[36]

By late 1777 the merchants had succeeded in their scheme for war loans. The full implications of their victory only became known after the war—after specie was lawful money and heavy taxation was in full force. The financial system, however, still had to be defended against sharp-eyed criticism by the few who saw into the future and then had to be restored when the Continental dollar's collapse forced a momentary return to currency finance.

Amidst noisy assertions in 1777 of a need for price controls, the merchants had preached the wisdom of bringing inflation to heel by sinking the currency and of depending upon borrowing and taxation as the twin pillars of sound fiscal policy. Yet in Massachusetts as everywhere in America "square dollars" remained the "sinews of war." With Congress issuing millions every month, inflation was bound to go on. But the conversion and taxation of state currency late in the year sent prices tumbling for the moment. Forty towns, nearly all agrarian, protested. Most significant was their reaction to funding the state debt—and to the possibility that "what little of our estates will be left at the end of the war must go to pay the principal and interest" on the debt to monopolists, monied men, extortionists, and Court merchants. Some towns said simply that instead of impoverishing common people, the government should have taxed the money away at depreciated rates or punished speculators by calling in the bills without redeeming them.[37]

The legislature made two trifling concessions. First, it extended to April 1, 1778, the date for turning in bills of credit, giving westerners more time for the costly trek to the treasury office in Boston. Second, it empowered towns to take advantage of the funding scheme by granting a right to levy additional taxes payable in bills, exchange bills for treasury notes, and apply the notes—which would arguably rise in value—against future taxes. The assembly also appointed a committee, headed by Robert Treat Paine, to explain funding.[38]

On New Year's Day, 1778, newspapers carried an address to the "Inhabitants of the State of Massachusetts Bay." The "alarming" situation of the currency and commerce, readers learned, had led the government to send delegates to the Providence and Springfield conventions, which had produced several proposals. These were duly rehearsed, along with would-be reasons for the funding law: the counterfeiting of the state currency; the advantage of the Continental dollar as the only lawful paper money; the impossibility of taxing away local bills of credit when the need to supply Congress imposed its own tax burdens; and the expectation and benefits for all ranks of lower prices. Most revealing was the justification that the funding would bring to the "American interest" monied men and speculators, especially those of "newly acquired property." A rhetorical question summed up the case: "Hath it not been the universal sentiment since the war broke out, that this generation must fight, and the next pay what we are not able to? How can that be done without loaning the debt?"[39]

"Loaning the debt" meant that the government issued its creditors promissory notes, that is, exacted loans. From 1775 through 1777 the legislature had, in fact, at times borrowed money from individuals on a voluntary basis. But in February 1778 it reverted to forced loans to pay drafts of the Board of War, an agency created in 1776 to provision the state's armed forces and meet Continental obligations.

Within four months the treasury had redeemed £120,000 in notes then maturing by converting them and extending the term of the original loan. Controversy over funding dropped from sight at this point as attacks on "fraudulent" money picked up, triggered by renewed complaints about higher prices and the Continental dollar's depreciation. Port towns, meanwhile, suffered from an interruption of trade and privateering; in the west the combined pressure of taxes and debts kept courts closed.[40]

Recrimination over paper money and prices had returned. Commercial farmers, "forestallers," and middlemen living in a twenty-mile radius of Boston and other ports were condemned for selling "extravagantly dear" produce to townsfolk or to buyers for American and French forces. In June, House members spoke openly of bringing back price controls, a proposal apparently killed by timely advice from Congress against any talk of capping commodity prices as ineffectual and productive of "evil consequences" for the public service and oppressive to individuals.[41]

Commerce improved toward the end of 1778, but commodity prices remained high and foodstuffs scarce. More important, depreciation of the Continental dollar had resumed, forcing Congress to spend more time on currency reform and new ways of financing the war. Massachusetts's fiscal policies were as successful as any in arresting the dollar's slide, yet at year's end a silver dollar cost twice as much in Continental currency as it had at the start. Before long, it was being said, a "cart-load" of paper would hardly buy a "bushel of turnips."[42]

Congress voided $41 million in January 1779, ostensibly because of counterfeiting, offering to exchange the money for other bills or for interest-bearing loan certificates. At the same time the "amazing depreciation" led Congress to implore the states to begin sinking quantities of Continental dollars. In Massachusetts the General Court, "without much debate," voted a £2.8 million levy as part of the $6 million Congress had asked the state to redeem by January 1780. Nothing helped. When Congress renewed its plea in June, the dollar's value had been halved again. A few voices pressed for a return to specie, especially when hard money came into limited circulation after the arrival of the French fleet and soldiery. Some tradesmen even refused to take paper in common payment, but the dollar had its supporters who branded coin a "Tory" device that destroyed free elections and promoted bribery and corruption. No less urgent an issue was rising prices.[43]

Defenders of Continental currency and price control had taken to Boston's streets by mid-June. Handbills appeared threatening destruction upon the property and persons of monopolizers and extortioners—unless they left town—for refusing dollars and thus turning them into "waste paper." They announced that "reliable" merchants and others concerned with trade had recently agreed to reduce merchandise prices, beginning July 15, to May 1 levels, pending similar action by other towns. At issue were the shortage and high cost of bread and other provisions and the government's failure to do little more than enact yet another law against monopoly and forestalling. A continentwide movement in favor of money and trade controls had spread to Boston.[44]

The merchants moved quickly to protect their interests. On June 17, the day following the handbills' appearance, a meeting of Boston's inhabitants took place at Faneuil Hall. After "sharp discussion," delegates left for the Court House across the square to confer with the merchants, who were also looking into inflation. This joint conference agreed to set prices on West Indian foodstuffs and a few other imports, to support the law against monopoly and forestalling, and to use Continental currency in all ordinary transactions. At the end a call went out for towns to gather at Concord on July 14 to consider the *"present distressed* situation of the people" and the advanced price of all articles of consumption. Delegates from 140 towns came and elected Azor Orne presiding officer.[45]

No easy consensus was achieved at Concord. Nearly half of the towns did agree to relatively high price ceilings for a range of Caribbean and country produce and to a need for local meetings to fix wages and prices for tanning, teaming work, domestic manufacturing, and so on, all "in proportion" to the established "rates of the necessaries of life." The towns also had power over European imports. On this issue of importance to the great-merchant class, the Boston Town Meeting met early in November—only to accept as "impracticable" efforts to "affix particular prices to the various articles of European merchandise, or to do anything more than the late convention in Concord had done."

In sum, the new price-fixing arrangements, unlike the old Regulating Acts of 1776–77, were not enacted into law or unanimously supported. Having set the controls "at so high a rate" that they seemed ineffectual, the conference felt a need to explain itself. As Warren slyly commented to John Adams, the Concord convention doubtless did no more than expected; he sent Adams a copy of the proceedings to judge for himself as to whether measures came from fear, fortitude, self-interest, or patriotism.

As for the problem of paper money and price regulation, the twin "causes of our distress," the Concord delegates cited the continuing depreciation of Continental paper and the sharp practices of "jobbers, harpies, and forestallers" at the expense of a "fair merchant" and "honest farmer." The setting of price ceilings aimed at stabilizing the currency and defeating inflation by slow and easy adjustments. And if anyone asked, the delegates huffed, "why we have fixed the articles of consumption and commerce at so high a rate, we answer, that a sudden appreciation of money is not only more difficult, but would in its operation be productive of those insupportable evils which have attended its contrary course." This melancholy analysis—and forecast of events surrounding the Shaysite insurrection when agrarian and debtor interests were being milked by the merchants and public creditors in large part through just such a contraction of the currency—seemed a perfectly reasonable defense of monetary policies in 1779. Later it would be scorned or ignored.

Since the conventional wisdom that summer of 1779 held the excessive quantity of money and the consequent "want of confidence" in Continental dollars to be the root cause of inflation, the agreed-upon remedy was to draw the currency out of circulation. The Concord delegates urged citizens to pay taxes quickly and subscribe liberally to a recent treasury note, or bond, issue aimed at sinking £200,000 by means of public borrowing. In short, price regulation was a stopgap; and the convention's "Address" to the people offered a ringing endorsement of the new financial system based upon public loans and taxation, features dear to the merchants' interest.[46]

Massachusetts held more price-fixing conventions during 1779, while regional conferences took place a year later in Hartford, Connecticut, and soon after, with Congress's support, in Philadelphia. Little came of them. Commodity shortages, high prices, and depreciation continued, unaffected by price controls, until good harvests took care of the first problem and the final gasp of the Continental currency the last. By then the struggle over the money question had led to the entrenchment and consolidation of the system of war finance established in 1777.[47]

Unable to halt the dollar's collapse or to take heart from the current round of conferences over prices and money, Congress pledged early in September 1779 to limit the paper flow to $200 million. The presses shut down within weeks. The next move was to squash the rumor that "as the Congress made the money, they can also destroy it; and that it will exist no longer than they find it convenient to permit it." Such an "execrable deed" seemed unthinkable—until six months later Congress repudiated $195 million by revaluing the dollar at forty to one of specie. States were called upon to tax away the "old" notes within a year and to exchange them for "new tenor notes" at a rate of forty old to every two of the new. Thus did Congress salvage $10 million from its losses. Printed in Philadelphia, the new tenor bore the imprint of a state on one side, the central government on the other. This reflected a desire to share the money on a forty-sixty basis, benefiting both the states and Congress while providing an incentive for redeeming the old currency.

Massachusetts authorized an issue not to exceed £460,000, its share of the new notes. More to the point and consistent with the larger policy of eliminating currency finance, the government also enacted the necessary taxes to sink the old paper dollars plus an annual levy over seven years of £72,000 in hard money to provide new tenor bills with a "gilt-edged" redemption fund. Lawful for all except specie debts, the new currency paid 5 percent interest and was convertible in Spanish milled dollars on December 31, 1786.[48]

Congress's revaluation scheme stabilized the dollar at around sixty to one, where it remained throughout the spring and summer of 1780. But faith in "square" dollars, like the money itself, soon resumed a downward course, taking with it the latest Continental issue. Critics were quick to point out that government both in the states and Philadelphia had already tried, to no avail, issuing bills bearing upon their face "a solemn promise" of redemption in silver and gold. Paying an annual interest in hard money would not help; as long as the new tenor notes were lawful for private debts, anyone receiving them would pass them along. More disquieting was knowing that with old and new bills in circulation, they would "mutually" reduce each other's value.

Newspapers carried numerous ingenious suggestions aimed at saving a currency system on the brink of collapse. None was simpler than the proposal to "release" all Continental paper to find its own value by eliminating it as lawful for private debts. That such action would also eliminate the vestiges of currency finance, restore the state to a specie standard, and strengthen creditor interests and the fiscal policy of government borrowing and heavy taxation adopted in 1777 went without saying. In a move toward this goal, the assembly in September 1780 repealed early wartime measures making Continental dollars a legal tender and created a scale of depreciation for determining the lawful specie value of all debts contracted during the fiat money years after 1777. Receivable now only for the taxes levied to remove them from circulation, the dollar slipped past seventy-five to one of hard money in a headlong fall until virtually passing out of existence a year or so later.[49]

Anti–paper money voices lashed out, too, against the tender provisions of new tenor notes, which had begun their own ruinous depreciation, as "pernicious" to public credit and "unjust" to widows, orphans, clergymen, and all honest, industrious people. After a bitter contest in January 1781, the reunited "Merchantile Interest" drove through a measure empowering the "impartial" state supreme court judges to fix from time to time currency's real worth. Opposition sprang up everywhere: in government, the press, and popular conventions. But by late spring the old emission had failed, and new tenor was going "fast downhill." The notes were soon refused, and in July the assembly canceled their use as legal tender in private payments and set their value at seventy-five to one for taxes. Paper dollars, meanwhile, no longer passed at the treasury. Fiat money was gone; coin was back—coin from war prize sales, resident French troops, and "foreign parts."[50]

The General Assembly in the interim moved to entrench and extend its system of war finance established in 1777 at the time of the conversion of the state currency. This "Consolidation and Refunding" of the debt in 1781–83 has received careful study by historians and is correctly viewed as a major cause of Shays's Rebellion.

At the very moment in January 1781 that the "Merchantile Interest" was making its penultimate move against fiat money, the government enacted legislation liquidating all state securities—that is, treasury notes—according to an official scale of depreciation. This form of debt, then, was to be recalculated on the basis of the securities' would-be specie value at the time of their issue, not at current, depreciated rates of around forty to one. In May and October additional measures, implementing and amplifying the original law, provided for exchanging the old notes and all other certificates of public debt for new "Consolidated Notes" in an amount not to exceed £800,000. A supplemental act in March 1783 authorized another £300,000 to complete the refunding, which dragged on until mid-1785. The notes were redeemable in specie in four installments between 1784 and 1788.[51]

Such in brief is the story of consolidation and refunding. The government seemed willing enough to risk bringing rebellion down upon itself by dealing with treasury securities like any other part of the state debt. Treasury notes bore interest and came in large denominations; and they represented money lent to the state, forcibly or voluntarily. They were negotiable instruments intended for investment, not legal tender, however they were used. Yet as some historians have pointed out, the notes, if not precisely modern money, still formed a part of the total currency supply. And as this chapter has shown, treasury certificates had a place in the financial system ever since the "era of public credit" in the 1750s and 1760s.

Treasury notes, in other words, did circulate during the Revolution as money and did depreciate in the hands of users and holders who bore the cost. The monied men, on the other hand—the wealthy merchants or speculators acquiring the securities on the eve of redemption and hoarding them before cashing them in—stood to gain a great deal from refunding.[52]

STUDENTS OF SHAYS'S REBELLION, beginning with George Richard Minot, have tended to view that event in terms of short-run factors and in a particular economic context: the "hard years" after the Revolutionary War. Only during this century have historians, starting with the Progressives, considered viewing the hard times of the 1780s and the insurrections that followed in a broader class context and in long perspective. And only in the last score of years have scholars, writing largely out of a New Left tradition, explored any aspect of that larger viewpoint and attempted to integrate short- and long-term "causes" of Shays's Rebellion.[53]

The present "neo-Progressive" interpretation focuses on the great-merchant class and its century-long involvement in the money question. From the 1690s on the leading merchants pursued financial and monetary policies that reflected a careful regard for their own interest, a belief in the intrinsic superiority of specie over paper currency, and an ideological approach to virtue, the public good, and social justice shaped more and more by the principles of the marketplace. Motivated in these ways, the merchants were instrumental in abolishing currency finance and banks of issue by the mid-eighteenth century and in substituting a specie currency and a system of funded debt akin to the English funding system established some sixty years earlier.

But the War for Independence caused Massachusetts to restore currency finance. Again the great-merchant class was engaged in a fight over the money question. And again the merchants were instrumental in bringing about a return to hard money, public loans, and heavy taxes—thus setting the stage for the Massachusetts insurrections in 1786.

3

DEBT LITIGATION AND SHAYS'S REBELLION

Jonathan M. Chu

> Annual income twenty pounds, annual expenditure nineteen nineteen six, result happiness. Annual income twenty pounds, annual expenditure twenty pounds ought and six, result misery.
>
> —Mr. Micawber

On April 19, 1785, ten years to the day after Concord and Lexington, William Cushing and four associate justices convened the Worcester session of the Supreme Judicial Court. Collectively, the details of the cases provide a window into the very human circumstances precipitating the events of 1786–87 and foreshadowing the growing crisis within post-Revolutionary legal institutions. The court's list of cases on appeal from the Worcester Court of Common Pleas illustrated profoundly the impact of economic recession and monetary deflation: virtually all the civil cases considered by the court were for problems associated with debt.[1]

The increase in litigation over private and public debt has long been cited as a major cause of Shays's Rebellion. Historians have taken at face value the statements that creditors used the courts to suppress poor agrarian debtors. In this view creditors, usually eastern monied men, ruthlessly pursued small debtors in court, causing the additional burden of fees that frequently exceeded the actual debt. When the burdens became excessive, the exploited debtors attempted to obtain debt relief by shutting down the courts.[2] Yet the

From a paper presented at the Bicentennial Conference on Shays's Rebellion, 1986, sponsored by the Colonial Society of Massachusetts.

court session presided over by Justice Cushing does not illustrate a legal system that was a tool of creditor interests. Quite the contrary. As any observant creditor in Worcester that April of 1785 probably would have realized, the courts were all too easily being manipulated to delay the repossession of assets. Moreover, the debtors were not a weak yeomanry driven to the wall by the commercial classes. Rather they were a special class of debtors who on paper may have had adequate assets to meet their obligations but who had guessed wrong on the twin forces of recession and deflation and found themselves without enough specie to pay their bills. Indeed, the pattern of litigation, the relationships of the parties involved, and the institutional structure of the courts indicate the evolution of a legal system that by 1785 seemed to favor not creditors but debtors.

Massachusetts's historic difficulties in sustaining a positive balance of trade meant a continual shortage of specie that encouraged the use of credit, first predominantly in the form of book debt and then increasingly in promissory notes. Book debts were simply the delineation of a series of mutual promises and obligations rendered in precise economic terms and carried in a merchant's account book. The process by which book debt was accumulated denoted a constant pattern of interaction and a constant ebb and flow of credit and debit. Payable on demand, book debt was a legally enforceable economic obligation, but it might go years without settlement or collection since it also represented ties of social relationships. Under these circumstances repayment rested upon the trust of the creditor and the ability of the debtor to provide labor or goods when the occasion arose over a lifetime. Gradually, however, promissory notes replaced book debt. Like book debt, these notes also reflected the actual transaction of goods and services.[3] Yet promissory notes also intimated that a different legal and commercial reality was in the offing. Written debt instruments created the basis for more impersonal relations between debtor and creditor. They reduced debt to specific transactions that could be assigned and transferred as assets or the equivalent of cash. Once created, promissory notes in lieu of cash could change hands at a dazzling and confusing rate. On the reverse of a January 15, 1785, note from Jonathan Lynde for £18.4.8, Edward Bangs wrote, "Rec'd £11 by your note against John Parker, I sold to Nathan Patch." Whatever the final obligation, it was due Stephen Salisbury, the possessor of the note. Further, by making possible the assigning of assets to third parties, promissory notes facilitated economic transactions; but in so doing, they also eliminated the moderating effects of multifaceted social relationships when hard times struck.[4]

Deflation and recession undermined the equilibrium of the money supply in post-Revolutionary Massachusetts and further helped to depersonalize debt relationships. The state's return to a hard money policy in the aftermath of the war and its insistence on a high level of taxation to redeem the state's war debt severely deflated the money supply and placed a premium upon specie. Generally, deflation of this sort would have meant the transfer of real wealth to creditors and retarding the calling of notes. With the customary 6 percent interest assessed, creditors would have compounded their rate of return the longer the debtor delayed repayment. A wise investor preparing for bad times, however, would have tried to sell notes payable to him, used the proceeds to pay off debts, and converted as much as possible to hard money.

The twin forces of deflation and recession furthermore accelerated the calling of notes by leading creditors who questioned the ability of debtors to meet their obligations. As notes entered the stream of commerce and as economic conditions worsened, the ability of writers to satisfy their obligations in cash increasingly depended upon the impersonal criteria of a market in which the relative value of notes declined. Simply too much money in the form of promissory notes was chasing a limited amount of specie, and, as a result, the worth of the former shrank relative to the latter.[5] All too quickly, the solvency of the holders of notes came to rest upon the economic worth of men with whom they had only a secondary or tertiary relationship and about whom they knew little. In the search for greater liquidity, promissory notes doubtless became the bad money that drove out good. Where a creditor might allow a neighbor or relation to defer payment, he could not afford to hesitate when his own solvency was in jeopardy. And to save himself, the creditor had to use the law as a collection agency.

While creditors theoretically had extensive remedies for the collection of debts, these were to be tested fully in the economic crisis of post-Revolutionary Massachusetts.[6] Before the Revolution the particularistic nature of communities tended to ameliorate the harsher attributes of the system. Smaller debtors were more likely to be exempt from the most punitive attributes of insolvency. When bringing suit, plaintiffs had to prove their claim in the county where the debtor resided or the debt contracted. While colonies varied in their specific terms, in general there were limitations on creditor remedies. Some colonies provided immunity from subsequent prosecution for debts if the debtor took a bankruptcy oath, substituted indentured servitude for imprisonment, and limited the range of goods that could be attached. Before the Revolution the Massachusetts General Court had passed a number of bankruptcy laws only to have them disallowed by the Privy Council. Some of these provided for restrictions on the rights of creditors. Innkeepers, for example, would not have been able to pursue debts of ten shillings or less owed by local residents and would have been barred from enforcing sailors' debts for wine or liquor that had been incurred without the consent of their captains.[7]

Moreover the punishment of insolvency reflected a similar pattern of weakening creditor remedies. Although debtors in post-Revolutionary Massachusetts were subject to imprisonment for debt and to sale into servitude, these measures were increasingly anachronistic. Imprisonment, the ultimate sanction upon debtors, failed to achieve two general objectives of bankruptcy law: protection of other creditors and the prevention of actions that might be detrimental to their interests. The point of jailing someone for debt rested upon the presumption that the alleged insolvent was hiding assets or that relatives could be induced to satisfy the obligation.[8] Indeed, the failure to pay one's legitimate debts denoted fraud. It destroyed the creditor's faith in his debtor and made possible the vision of a smiling bankrupt with money in his pocket. Advising Stephen Salisbury to have Jon Bellows imprisoned, Stephen Sewall declared: "The particular circumstances of the Creditor make it absolutely necessary that Bellows the Debtor should be taken by his body and be obliged to pay immediately, or be committed. I am informed he is a man of considerable Estate—and presume there will be no difficulty in obtaining the money."[9]

Once, however, the insolvent took an oath attesting to his economic circumstances, as he could in Massachusetts, the cost to the creditor of continuing imprisonment dictated release. Significantly, the burdens of pursuing the debt fell upon the creditor after the first fifty days of imprisonment, the 1763 statutory limit. Thereafter, the individual debtor could swear to the fact of his insolvency. Then the creditor could keep him imprisoned if he were willing to pay the jail fees, sell him, if he were single, into servitude, or release him and hope for better days.[10]

The personal circumstances of the small debtor could preclude imprisonment. The smaller the debt, the greater the likelihood the debtor was judgment-proof. Nathaniel Jennison owed Stephen Salisbury three pounds in April 1785. The pursuit of the debt by attaching his body, Jennison pointed out to Salisbury, would not secure payment.[11] Furthermore the incarceration of a debtor cost communities in another way: towns were expected to assume the cost of subsidizing families or individuals because a presumably able individual was rendered unproductive. Unless there was a mean-spirited desire for punishment or a strong presumption of hidden assets, imprisonment for debt in Massachusetts or elsewhere made little sense.[12]

The imprisonment for debt that in fact took place in eighteenth-century Massachusetts was relatively infrequent and mild. Debtors were segregated from other criminals. In Worcester, debtors had one cell on the main floor while criminals were relegated to another and, in special cases, to the dungeon on the lower level. The debtors' accommodations were supposed to have ample space and light and the prisoners themselves to have access to the exercise yard. Some debtors could post bond allowing them to rent rooms next to the jail. Throughout the eighteenth century relatively few persons were imprisoned for extended periods. According to Robert Feer, between 1785 and 1800 only 35 out of 1,905 debtors remained imprisoned longer than one year. Most were released within two weeks; some, within a day.[13]

The sanction of jail in Worcester County became impossible to sustain as large numbers of debtors were incarcerated during 1785–86. On December 6, 1785, there were nineteen in the debtors' cell in the county jail. The next day an additional four were added to the fourteen- or fifteen-square-foot cell designed for eight or nine prisoners. So crowded were conditions, the jailer placed some of the debtors in the lower dungeon and contemplated using the room reserved for women. Nor had conditions improved by March 16, 1786; on that day twenty-five prisoners were in custody.[14] As the prison became overcrowded, its capacity was increased by permitting some debtors to be confined to their homes.[15] Yet, neither jail nor house arrest could produce cash that did not exist.

Reasons for long-term incarceration were self-evident. Public institutions, state and town governments, were generally responsible for those inmates with the longest periods of imprisonment. Joseph Wiser was kept for about a year under the authority of the town of Southborough. His circumstances also illustrate the way in which individuals were vulnerable to the vagaries of local experience. Wiser's term may well have been the result of his sizable debt to the town; he owed £3,121.11.3. One possible explanation for Wiser's plight is that he somehow had become personally liable for uncollected town taxes probably dating back a number of years.[16]

Similarly, the town of Sterling had ordered the holding of Tilly Richardson beyond the statutory limit. His case, however, may well have reflected his jailers' conviction that he had hidden assets. Jailed on March 5, 1785, he was still there a year later, but the reason for his commitment was a debt of only £14.2.4. That their respective towns were prepared to keep Wiser and Richardson in jail also indicates that any costs incurred by their imprisonment were thought to be outweighed by real prospects of financial return.[17]

More significantly, private creditors appeared less forgiving of their debtors in 1785 than were state and local governments. If state and local authorities were prepared to absorb the costs of extended jail terms, private creditors had to weigh more carefully the benefit of the additional charges over the likelihood of eventual collection. At the same time, they had to use whatever sanctions existed to preserve their own solvency. As the premium placed upon specie aggravated the problems of private debt, private creditors began to keep their debtors in jail longer.[18] Of the 101 persons imprisoned for private debts, forty served terms in excess of the statutory requirement. Asa Danforth, a Westminster blacksmith, was kept for nearly two years; John May, Jr., for over a year. The sums owed by the two men were not large in comparison with others similarly detained. Danforth owed £156.5.3; May, £98.4.[19]

Creditors increasingly put their debtors in jail either to apply added incentive to pay or to prove to their own creditors that they were making every effort to remain solvent. When they did, insolvency moved like ripples through a pond. Benjamin Cogswell, a Sutton trader, disputed a debt claimed by Timothy Rawson, another trader from neighboring Uxbridge. The cause of the dispute was a note of uncertain value. In light of the confusion surrounding the assignability of different notes between the two men, there was some question as to whether the note had been discharged. The original note dated back to April 5, 1781, when Thomas Bicknell gave Rawson a note for twenty-eight hundred new emission dollars. Rawson endorsed the note to Cogswell who promised to deliver cash or goods. Cogswell presumed he had satisfied his part of the bargain when he recovered payment from one Daniel Warren, who had another note with Rawson's endorsement to Cogswell on it. Although the Worcester Court of Common Pleas held for Cogswell, the Supreme Judicial Court reversed the decision and granted Rawson the judgment for £520. In the process Cogswell became responsible for an additional £37.8.10 in court costs. When Cogswell was unable to pay, Rawson had him placed in the Worcester County jail for 104 days.[20]

Cogswell's legal defeat had further repercussions. Had he won his case, he might have been able to use the award of court costs in the Rawson action to satisfy another outstanding debt. At the December Worcester session of Common Pleas, he had lost a judgment of £13.13.10 to another creditor, Samuel Read, Jr. Cogswell had appealed but seemed to have had little hope of winning. Indeed, when the case was called before the Supreme Judicial Court, Cogswell made no effort to defend himself. He did not appear, and a default judgment was entered against him.[21]

Cogswell's highly problematic situation also placed Rawson, himself in striatened circumstances, in financial peril. Rawson had had to have Cogswell jailed because he was trying desperately to come up with enough cash to satisfy his own creditors and avoid imprisonment. In addition to the Cogswell action, he was involved in six other pieces of litigation. Besides Cogswell, Rawson had to contend with David Thayer's pro forma appeal to the Supreme Judicial Court of an £829.17 judgment. Thayer had not appeared when the case was called in the lower court, and a default judgment had also been entered against him. Thayer, like Cogswell, chose to appeal the judgment after it was entered. When the case was called in April, Thayer once again defaulted, and the Supreme Judicial Court entered an affirmation of the lower court's judgment and added court costs and interest. The total owed Rawson just from these two actions exceeded £1,370.[22] Rawson also had three individual judgments against him and was the codefendant in two other debt actions. In all five actions Rawson had little expectation of avoiding legal responsibility for his debts. All five were appeals of default judgments, and in four of the cases, the appeals again were not prosecuted.[23] In the fifth, Rawson was named as a codefendant with Aaron Taft, Jr., who had received a note from Rawson and passed it to Elijah Alexander. When Taft could not pay the note and accumulated interest, Alexander sued. Although Taft and Rawson had defaulted at the lower court, Alexander settled out of court for an additional note and payment of court costs by Taft when the case came up on appeal. While the settlement absolved Rawson of any further liability, he had provided the major surety for the appeal and thus could have borne some responsibility for the costs in the event Taft proved to be insolvent.[24] If one assumes Rawson had no financial responsibility in the Taft case and a half interest in the other action in which he was a codefendant, he would have been liable for £61.16.7.[25] By July 22, 1785, Rawson had secured executions on the debts owed him, yet the assets available were clearly insufficient to meet his outstanding obligations. On August 1 Joseph Sibley and others had him committed to the Worcester jail for debts totaling £480. Eleven days later, Rawson had Benjamin Cogswell committed for his outstanding obligations.[26]

Rawson's inability to find the cash to avoid jail forced another of his creditors, John Weson, Jr., to accelerate the collection of a relatively small note, creating in the process new channels of economic distress. Weson had obtained a promissory note written by Rawson to David Sherman on May 24, 1784. Sherman had passed the note to Weson, and Weson demanded payment almost immediately. When Rawson refused, Weson filed suit at the next available opportunity, the September 1784 session of the Worcester Court of Common Pleas. Weson agreed to a continuance to the December session. When Rawson did not appear, a default judgment was entered in Weson's favor. Rawson further sought to delay judgment by appealing to the Supreme Judicial Court even if it meant additional court costs. At the appeal he again failed to appear when the case was called.[27]

The search for money to satisfy obligations and keep these men solvent soon affected others. Although he had won this small judgment, Weson found himself unable to help his father, who would subsequently be jailed in January 1786 by Elijah Dix.[28] Dix, like Weson and Rawson, was afflicted with non- or slow-paying debtors. In addition to Weson's father, Dix was pressing Daniel Road and William Jennison Stearns for payment. Road owed him slightly over six pounds; Stearns £29.6.[29] Dix was an apothecary and had a practice as a physician. He also needed the funds to remain solvent. On the nineteenth, he was also being sued by Daniel Heywood, Jr., for nearly eighty pounds. Heywood had taken Dix to the December common pleas court. Like many others, Dix did not appear, had a default judgment entered against him, and then appealed to the Supreme Judicial Court. Not contesting the appeal, Dix managed to postpone his day of reckoning with Heywood until May 12, the day the writ of execution was returned. While the delay was not long enough for him to be able to use the proceeds from his small judgment against Road, he had shortened the period of his embarrassment.[30]

Dix's other debtor, William Jennison Stearns, was, it would seem, the kind of debtor who stretched the terms of payment beyond tolerable limits even while he was apparently solvent. Stearns may have had difficulties in managing his flow of cash; he also may have chosen to delay payments to maximize his economic advantages. Stearns participated in one of the few appeals actually to be contested during the April Supreme Judicial Court session. This was not surprising since he was the creditor in the action and the lower court had found against him. When the Supreme Judicial Court heard the case, it reversed the lower court's judgment, awarded him £10.12.6, and levied costs upon his opponent.[31] Still, when Stearns was unable or unwilling to come up with the £29.6 he owed, Dix had him committed to jail for nearly two weeks. Stearns, though, probably had sufficient resources to avoid continued imprisonment.

On August 10, the day after he was imprisoned, he and two other Worcester residents joined to give Dix a bond for over three times the amount owed—in essence providing, at three times the value, assets to secure the bond. One of the guarantors of Stearns's bond was Nathan Patch. Patch was one of Worcester's solvent citizens. An innkeeper, he had four cases before the April session, the most by any single plaintiff, collected over £140 in judgments, and most significant, had no creditors suing him. Stearns, moreover, was a cosurety of Benjamin Cogswell's prisoner's bond to Timothy Rawson.[32] Whatever his difficulties were in August 1785, Stearns was sufficiently creditworthy to pay his annual bill with Stephen Salisbury the next March with a combination of cash and a promissory note. Salisbury's acceptance of the note in light of his other collection problems of 1785–87 is ample evidence of Stearns's ability to pay.[33]

With all their problems Dix, Stearns, Rawson, Cogswell, and the other debtors in court on April 19, 1785, looked to the solution Mr. Micawber knew so well: if one could hold out a little longer, something might turn up. Delay, though, was costly once one allowed debts to be litigated. Since costs in Massachusetts were allocated to the loser, the number of default judgments entered against debtors meant an increase in the burden of debt. Still, debtors used the court system to postpone what they recognized to be their obligations. Nearly two of every seven debt cases heard at the December session of the Worcester Court of Common Pleas were subsequently appealed and heard at the April session of the Supreme Judicial Court.[34] Of the 194 debt-related cases heard by the Supreme Judicial Court, 165 were simply affirmations of lower court default judgments. That is, the debtors involved had not contested their obligations at the Court of Common Pleas; they did not even appear in court. Yet they still chose to prolong the contest and refused to prosecute their appeals when called before the Supreme Judicial Court. To do this created additional costs: interest, computed at 6 percent, new writs, appeal bonds, and lawyers' fees would be assessed against the losing litigant, in this case the defaulting debtor. Average court costs for April 1785 were nearly £5.[35]

Costs, however, were unrelated to the size of judgments. The payment schedule rested upon flat-rate assessments such as the filing of writs, judges' and clerks' fees, and lawyers' per diem and litigation charges. A default judgment might save an individual the lawyer's twelve-shilling litigation fee, but it still required the payment of a one shilling sixpence per diem for travel and attendance at the court session. The other charges would have to be paid or guaranteed if the appeal was to be placed on the docket.[36] As a result, the ratio of costs to judgment varied considerably. In the two cases in which Timothy Rawson was a codefendant, *White* v. *Trask* and *Alexander* v. *Taft,* itemized court costs were £4.6.10 and £4.5.2, respectively. The figures were 26.6 and 5.7 percent of the respective judgments. Daniel Road's appeal of the *Dix* case cost him £3.7.7, but the judgment against him was only £7.4.3. Moreover, the costs in the court records understate the actual cost of litigation that would ultimately be borne by the loser since only the winner would have to itemize his costs when the fees became part of the judgment. Thus, it would not be inconceivable, in light of the functional symmetry of legal process, that Road's costs, including his need to file answers to complaints and to secure appeal bonds, equaled his debt judgment.[37]

Despite the eccentricity and burden of legal cost, appeal was one means of coping with insolvency. Appeal was the eighteenth-century equivalent of telling a creditor that a check was in the mail. It provided the debtor an invaluable commodity at no immediate cost: time. Defaulting indicated that the debtor was fully aware of his legal obligation to pay his debts. Defaulting and appealing meant postponing the reckoning beyond the day of judgment to the point when the creditor secured the return on his writ of execution. On June 7, 1783, John Keith issued a note promising to pay Jonathan Livermore £7 on demand with interest. Keith made no payments on the note, and in September 1784 Livermore took him to court. Keith convinced Livermore, the court, or both to grant him a continuance. At the next session in December, Keith defaulted and then like Cogswell, Rawson, and the others, he appealed the lower court's judgment against him. In April he again defaulted. By the time Livermore was able to secure his writ of execution, it was May 16, 1785.[38]

The procedural mechanisms of the Massachusetts legal system and the nature of the relationship between creditor and debtor provided Livermore, Stearns, and others with a distinct advantage. In possession of the goods and cash that may already have been consumed or spent, these debtors forced their creditors to find and regain assets that would make them whole again. Although Massachusetts courts ultimately levied the costs of legal action against the evading, delinquent debtor, the creditor still had to initiate the action. He had to advance the sums necessary to file the writs, copy the papers, and retain the lawyer to pursue the debt. Delay might not be to his advantage. If he failed to act, the debtor retained the cash or goods—or worse, consumed them in the meantime. Alternatively, some other creditor might obtain judgment against the debtor and seize what assets remained or establish a priority against future earnings or acquisitions of property. Indeed, once the creditor obtained judgment against his debtor, he had an indefinite period of time to proceed against person or property in any Massachusetts county.[39]

Popular opposition to the hard money policies of the state portended still more dangers for the anxious creditor: the passage of a new tender law and the spread of cheap money. If a creditor did not act quickly enough, he might have to accept payment in inflated currency. The prospects for the passage of measures to increase the money supply were, however, slim. George Minot estimated that about 19 out of 118 in the House and 35 of 120 in the Senate favored inflating the currency. The problem was that too many looked upon an inflated currency as a salve for "male contents [who] must look to themselves, to their idleness, their dissipation and extravagance, for their grievances."[40] In regions where the absence of specie was most noticeable, some could still hope that legislative adjustments might be made to enable debtors to make payments in tender other than specie, relieve the shortage of money, and provide relief.[41]

Litigation was one, albeit desperate, way to extend one's payments. All the appellant had to do was post a bond for six pounds to cover court costs in the event the case were lost. The bond required one major surety for six pounds and two secondary sureties for three pounds each. Defendants secured bonds with relative ease; one's defense counsel usually provided it. Levi Lincoln provided bonds for twenty-nine appellants, twenty-two of whom had been clients. Two of Lincoln's clients were Daniel Road and a codefendant of

Timothy Rawson, Nicholas Trask. In addition, lawyers were frequently subsidiary sureties for nonclients. Lincoln, who tended to be a plaintiff's counsel, provided secondary sureties for thirty-nine defendants; Edward Bangs was the primary surety for twenty-one clients and gave secondary sureties for eighty-nine other litigants.[42] Indeed, one could prevail upon plaintiff's counsel to be a secondary surety for his appeal. Lincoln also was the secondary surety in six other actions in which he had been the attorney for the opposition, and he was not the only lawyer to provide sureties for the opposing party in a legal action. In eleven other cases, four different lawyers cosigned bonds for their opposition.[43]

The ease with which debtors received help from lawyers in pursuing appeals that were unlikely to be prosecuted raises a question about their supposed antipathy. Even if, as L. Kinvin Wroth and Hiller Zobel believe, the appeal bonds were a mere formality, their presence in such large numbers of default judgments during the April court session argues for a symbiotic relationship between debtor and lawyer that prolonged the appeal process. Assistance to opposing clients even went beyond the provision of a surety bond. Levi Lincoln defended Asaph Sherman when he attacked the deputy sheriff attempting to execute a judgment upon his property. Sherman had been committed to debtor's prison by Lincoln and a number of other frustrated creditors in September 1785.[44]

Defendants may not have objected to lawyers' fees because of the specific charges in their individual cases. It would be a rare defendant-debtor who was sufficiently naive to presume that the offering of sureties on an appeal bond amounted to an act of friendship or kindness. Lawyers who offered themselves as sureties were obviously self-interested.[45] Resentments may well have originated in the debtor's recognition of his dependence upon a group that was everywhere. The multitude of bonds or cases and the sustaining of litigation meant the accumulation of small fees that made for large incomes. Bangs had relatively few clients for whom he was the primary counsel. In 1785 he had twenty-six, of whom twenty-one were defendants and for whom he provided the major surety bond. In one instance, his client was involved in two actions. However, with 89 appeal bonds in which he participated, Bangs had a hand in 116 of 194 actions. Levi Lincoln was the most active attorney representing litigants at the April court. In ninety actions he represented eighty-three litigants.[46] Debtors could easily have allowed the lower court's judgment to stand and thereby have saved themselves Bangs's and Lincoln's fees and the other appellate costs, but they chose not to. That debtors could sustain their actions meant that lawyers were willing to provide services at costs that, for the moment, were acceptable or, in economic terms, cheap relative to the situation.

But the purchase of such services did not have to lead to any love or respect for the legal profession. The pervasiveness of Bangs's practice was not unusual. Eight lawyers handled virtually all the litigation on April 19; of 392 possible parties in litigation, the 8 represented 334. Lawyers like Edward Bangs were young men on the make. After spending the war at Harvard College and then in legal studies at Newburyport, Bangs arrived in Worcester in 1780 to begin his practice.[47] He was part of a young group of newly arrived artisans, merchants, and lawyers who almost immediately tried to change the religious and political institutions of the town. The peak of the divisions occurred in 1785–86 as the town debated the separation of the church into two parishes and its response to the county conventions.[48] These developments and the rapid growth of lawyer's practices did not diminish long-standing antilawyer sentiment. Indeed, lawyers came to be seen as symptomatic, if not the cause, of hard times. Even if lawyers had not produced the distress, it was readily apparent to all that they had done nothing to alleviate it. More significant, they grew fat off creditor and debtor alike.[49]

Since debtors in court could sustain legal costs relatively cheaply, the incentives favored doing anything that might avoid bringing the litigation to an end, for then the additional court costs would come due. As debtors dragged the legal process on, a number of fortuitous events might make possible the redemption of their obligations. Circumstances might arise that would allow the debtor to defer payment. Daniel Bigelow had to sue Jonas Gibbs for payment of legal fees to the deceased William Stearns.[50] The fees due Stearns had begun to accrue as early as March 1781 and ran until January 1783. Stearns's death gave Gibbs a breathing spell of nearly two years. Legal action was initiated in 1783, but it was not until April 1785 that final judgment was rendered for Stearns's estate.[51]

It could also be in the interest of creditors to delay the trial of cases. The creditor might conclude that the effort required to collect the debt was greater than the potential return, or he might make some technical error that would imperil the suit. There was the possibility that the creditor could be compelled to settle for a lesser amount or even lose. In 1781 Ephraim Butler agreed to serve in the Continental army as a substitute for Elisha Clary, Jeremiah Woodbury, John Hammond, and William Bowman. Clary and the others in return promised to give Butler £90 in silver money, along with any produce and necessaries Butler's family might need; the value of the goods was to be set at common prices and subtracted from the total obligation. The sum of £30 was to be given upon Butler's passing muster, and the remaining spread out in monthly payments. Clary and the others further agreed that if they did not make the payments, they would incur an additional £180 penalty. Monthly payments of £2.10 were made until Butler died in February or March 1782, about a year after he concluded the agreement. After his death the family filed suit to recover the remainder of the money and the penalty. At the appeal trial, the family withdrew its suit and was assessed court costs. Arguably, the Butlers may not have had grounds to sue. The agreement conceivably died with Butler, and no further obligation might be seen to exist. The lower court, however, had held for the creditor interest, the Butlers, and still the defendants were able to appeal and pass the costs on to the family. In all likelihood, the defendant debtors offered the Butlers an out-of-court settlement and thereby reduced their obligation below the judgment granted in the lower courts.[52]

For the cash-poor debtor unable to make reduced settlements, delay allowed something to turn up. Clearly, so many debtors would not have routinely appealed their default judgments if they felt the costs outweighed the benefits. Even if judgment was a foregone conclusion, as it was in 165 out of 194 cases, the additional costs might have been negligible at any price. As any bankrupt would have known, a shilling one cannot pay might as well be a thousand.

Stephen Salisbury seemed to realize the perils of the legal process, and debtors seemed to be able to get him to avoid courts on a number of occasions. In January 1786 Thomas Andrews of Leicester acknowledged Salisbury's patience with him, yet when Salisbury appeared at his home, Andrews refused to answer the door. Salisbury, in fact, seemed prepared to accept notes, but Andrews wanted to hold out until the spring, when he could raise cash by selling his farm. Keeping his doors shut on Salisbury, Andrews explained, gave him the opportunity "to settle with my Creditors justly." The next month Andrews again wrote Salisbury that he was trying to arrange with his creditors some resolution of his problems and again begged for time that he might "have an opportunity of transacting some business and disposing of [his] farm."[53]

Deferring legal action under the right circumstances might also have been good business. Salisbury's bluster could have been used to exact more profitable payments in kind. With his brother, Salisbury maintained two stores, one in Worcester, the other in Boston. Trade between the two branches accounted for much of the business's success, and any goods received in kind could be valued at wholesale prices and sold at a profit. Debtors sought to put Salisbury's need for goods to their own advantage. One Ephraim Wetmore advised Salisbury, "I have been informed that you have said that you would have my Body Dead or a Live in case I did not pay you." Nonetheless, if Salisbury was prepared to wait, Wetmore would send him a ton of potash in May in compensation for about half the debt, have enough of a breathing spell to stay in business, and be able to forward the final installment. If Salisbury sued, Wetmore assured him it would only cause him time and trouble.[54]

Stephen Sewall also preferred to pressure his debtors rather than seek legal judgments. Sewall's efforts, however, may have initiated a chain of circumstances that resulted in the imprisonment of other debtors. By March 1786 William Jennison was under heavy pressure to pay his obligations to Sewall. While ostensibly solvent, Jennison had been seriously affected by deflation and was unable to raise the cash needed to settle with Sewall. Unfortunately, Jennison had not been able to get, as he put it, a shilling on the pound from his own debtors and had initiated a number of suits to get the money to discharge his debts. Jennison asked Sewall not to put his note into suit, for "it would be Expensive and disagreeable to me, and I apprehend, no advantage to you."[55]

The dilemma of Salisbury and Sewall, as well as that of other creditors, was to find the process that promoted the maximum return from delinquent debtors. But finding a strategy that curbed the ability of debtors to manipulate the legal system and postpone further payment was most difficult. There were dangers in waiting too long if the debtor became insolvent and other creditors had established priority on his assets. But acting too soon might precipitate a wave of insolvencies affecting the ability of other debtors to pay their obligations. Salisbury and Sewall could avoid legal action since they obviously commanded sufficient influence and resources to compel debtors to give them primacy and thus security. For litigants in difficulty like Timothy Rawson, William Jennison Stearns, and Nathaniel Jennison, legal action was an uncertain process resorted to only if one were also in imminent danger of being declared insolvent. Judicial process made one's solvency dependent not only upon a debtor's willingness to pay his due but also upon the timing of court sessions and the prompt cooperation of local authorities.[56] The commitment to legal action for the creditor implied a kind of despair, a sense that the debtor probably could or would not satisfy his obligations. For the debtors who appealed, their presence before the Supreme Judicial Court expressed an analogous kind of despair—the final attempts to stave off an insolvency brought on by bad bets on the money supply, economic activity, or the reliability of their own debtors.

The actions of debtors at the April 19, 1785, session of the Supreme Judicial Court provide important insights into the legal system. They suggest the need to reconsider the traditional account of the movement for court reform in post-Revolutionary Massachusetts. The assumption that debtors necessarily disliked courts and that creditors liked them misreads the dynamics of the tension between the two and overlooks the specific role courts played in solving their respective problems. If, as current historical wisdom asserts, debtors found the legal system burdensome, creditors also did not find the system to their advantage. The call for the reduction of court fees, the enlargement of the jurisdiction of justices of the peace, and the elimination of the Court of Common Pleas advocated by Benjamin Austin and others ought not to be seen as reforms indiscriminately favorable to debtors.[57] Despite his obvious hostility to lawyers, Austin's suggestions for reform would not have been an unqualified benefit for debtors. His bitter attack upon lawyers' sophistry addressed not the interest of the hopelessly indebted but the claims of those who had been penalized most by drawn-out legal actions, creditors. It was, after all, Austin who argued in March 1786 for the elimination of an order of men "*who are practising the greatest art in order to delay every process . . . who are taking advantage of every accidental circumstance which an unprincipled person might have by the lenity and indulgence of an honest creditor.*"[58]

Austin's calls for the use of binding arbitration and the reduction of fees would have facilitated, not hindered, the collection of debts. Reducing fees lowered the threshold creditors had to cross before initiating action. Smaller amounts would have to be placed at risk in starting litigation, thereby making the action less of a gamble. Binding arbitration would have foreclosed the appeal process that had been so effective in delaying payment. With reforms like these, creditors would be able to initiate action more quickly, they might be more inclined to bring small debtors to court, and they could obtain judgment and collect their money faster. Indeed, the lower fees coupled with the expansion of the jurisdiction of the justices of the peace would have greatly facilitated bringing small, relatively solvent debtors to judgment more rapidly.[59]

The reduction of fees and the changes in court structure would have favored a particular kind of debtor, one who was caught between his own creditors and debtors and was being pressured by larger, more powerful creditors, who had guessed right on the twin forces of recession and deflation or who had far greater resources to weather economic adversity. This intermediate speculator had the most to gain from reform: he could pursue debts owed him that previously were too small to be litigated, while further postponing his other obligations. The expansion of the jurisdiction of the justices of the peace and the elimination of the Court of Common Pleas would give him the best of both worlds. It eliminated an intermediate layer of the system, thereby reducing costs, while it postponed larger judgments to the more infrequent sessions of the Supreme Judicial Court.[60]

Ironically, the apologist for the General Court, George Minot, recognized how delay provided advantages for debtors and how "their perplexities might lead them to an undue use of any advantage." He may also have seen the ways in which the legal system could be used for very selective interests. That, indeed, may ultimately have been the basis of his brief against Shaysites like Timothy Rawson. Minot's sense that the distinction between those who sought to stop specific executions of judgment and those who wanted the complete elimination of courts was being blurred touches upon what may have been the real fear for men like him. If, as the events of the April 1785 court session suggest, reform appealed to a narrow interest that was already manipulating the structure quite well and was being "blended incautiously" with general discontent to promote a more deep-seated animosity to all authority, then anarchy loomed. Advancing a self-interest born of extravagance and indulgence, some men were using recession and deflation as excuses to save themselves from bad bets and bargains. The danger to the republic and to society ought to have been all too obvious: this particular expression of private interest and vice attacked the institutions and public virtue that were vital to sustaining republican governments.[61]

4

THE FEDERALIST REACTION TO SHAYS'S REBELLION

Stephen E. Patterson

Early in this century, Massachusetts judge Jonathan Smith wisely remarked to his fellow amateur historians at the Clinton Historical Society that their understanding of Shays's Rebellion was laden with bias. For over a century, he said, the story had been told by men who had no sympathy with rebellious farmers. They were conservatives who had taken part in suppression of the rebellion or who, subsequently in the nineteenth century, were never able to rise above the limitations of the original conservative analysis. What was needed, he concluded—quite disingenuously—was an impartial examination of both sides.

Yet before this reasonable entreaty had scarcely passed his lips, Smith went on to propose that the first and presumably chief cause of the rebellion was "the absence of a strong national government, commanding the confidence and the obedience of the people." With the best will in the world, he obviously could not escape from the Federalist frame of reference: the structure of government under the Confederation was the problem. Congress and the states had issued "worthless and hopelessly irredeemable paper currency," and the economy was in a shambles characterized by a ruined commerce and "the crushing burdens of public and private indebtedness."[1]

What Smith illustrated, even better than he knew, was the very considerable difficulty in separating Shays's Rebellion from the Federalist analysis of it. This Federalist analysis merits examination. Granted, it tells us more about the men who suppressed the Shays-

---

From a paper presented at the Bicentennial Conference on Shays's Rebellion and the Constitution, 1986, sponsored by Historic Deerfield, Inc.

ites than about the Shaysites themselves. But on the other hand, there are important questions about the Shaysites that can never really be abstracted from the perceptions of their opponents. Were the Shaysites a serious threat to the government and constitution of Massachusetts? Was the rebellion a significant cause of the movement for a federal constitution? Massachusetts Federalists thought so. In fact, many of them agreed with Henry Knox, who later said that the Massachusetts Antifederalists were all Shaysites; in his mind the rebellion, the subsequent Philadelphia convention, and the ratification struggle were of a piece, one long continuous story. This view is what Judge Smith confronted ninety or so years ago. The mistake he made was in assuming he could get a clear picture of a farmer uprising through this Federalist lens. He would have done better to settle for the interesting reflected image of the Federalists themselves.

To get at the farmers' side, Smith should have focused on the changing scene in the rural west, noting that the American Revolutionary War had made western Massachusetts a much different place from what it had once been. From 1775 to 1780 farmers had a tremendous opportunity to sell their surplus production to feed the Continental army. Men who had once been subsistence farmers were encouraged to grow vegetables, grain, and livestock for commercial purposes and with the cash they received in return, even if it was paper, to invest in more agricultural land to expand production. Paper money was so plentiful down to 1780 that even those who might still be called subsistence farmers got used to having cash to pay taxes and to buy consumer items. The demand for French and West Indian imports was intense.[2]

The period after 1780 was not nearly so good for farmers. The vigorous deflationary program of the commercially dominated legislature drastically reduced the available money supply. The state began to exercise a much stronger centralizing pull on the lives of its people through commercial regulation, high taxes, and an energized court system.[3] The legal system became an omnipresent factor in the lives of rural people, given the almost phenomenal increase of lawyers—from thirty-four in 1780, according to one source, to a total of ninety-two in 1785—many of whom took up residence in the rural towns of the interior.[4] And other vocational pursuits opened up, such as in Springfield, where the federal arsenal continued to employ artisans after the war. Newspapers in Worcester, Springfield, and, by 1786, Northampton brought news of the world westward. Perhaps more important, the newspapers kept alive people's perceived need for cash by advertising commercial wares available at retail stores in market towns. In a tangible way, the war and postwar experiences of western farmers substantially changed their values and their expectations.[5] If only gradually and incompletely, rural people began moving away from the static and timeless patterns of traditional culture. In the search for causes, surely any objective historical interpretation of Shays's Rebellion would want to take account of this transformation.

In political terms, this change was observable in the dramatic increase in interest and participation of small rural towns in the legislature of the state. Here the elected representatives of hundreds of small farmers—often farmers themselves whose attendance at the General Court in Boston had to be fitted around the tilling, planting, and harvesting—adopted positions that reflected the concerns of their constituents. They favored paper currency and resisted when an eastern majority voted to end the legal tender provision of the state paper still in circulation after 1780. They sided with thousands of veterans in their demands that vouchers, given them during the war instead of pay, be accepted in payment of state taxes. They resisted impost and excise taxes that fell heavily on consumers, and they balked at the notion of a half-pay settlement with Continental officers when nothing had yet been done for the rank-and-file veterans. In House votes, they usually lost; but they were close enough in some votes to frighten the conservative majority, and along with the odd victory, they convinced their opponents that they represented a serious threat to the commercial and propertied interests of the state.[6]

It was these commercial and propertied interests which, of course, produced the Federalists in Massachusetts.[7] They enjoyed enormous advantages in the factional contests that took place in the legislature during the 1780s. They came from the larger towns of the state, they were better educated, they found it easier to attend the General Court and to remain through summer sessions, and they enjoyed the support of the newspapers, the courts, and the political system in general. When they occasionally lost votes in the House, they counted on the Senate to represent property, and they were not disappointed. But whatever their advantages, they rarely felt comfortably in command and anxiously observed the spreading populist tide. The extralegislative political activity of farmers fed their anxiety. During the Revolution, rural towns began organizing county conventions to state their grievances and to concert their political actions.[8] In 1782 an angry crowd of rural debtors attempted to disrupt the court in Northampton, and the old Revolutionary leader Joseph Hawley warned that law-abiding westerners were considering going over to the "mob" unless there was prompt legislative action to solve agrarian grievances.[9] By 1784 conventions in rural counties were commonplace, and conservative critics were condemning them as threats to property and a danger to the constitution of the state.[10] The divisions of Shays's Rebellion, in other words, were in evidence long before the insurrection broke out in 1786.

Thus, when Federalists came to write about the rebellion, they saw its causes in the political discord of the previous several years. They viewed the Shaysites as one and the same with the large number of inland farmers with whom they had been arguing for most of the 1780s: mad, distracted husbandmen who wanted to cheat their creditors with worthless paper money and who had no understanding of how a state must protect the property of its citizens by maintaining a stable monetary and financial system. Moreover, the Federalist analysis suggested that the insurrection had its roots in anarchic or democratic ideas—the two were interchangeable—all of which were let loose at dangerous and unconstitutional county conventions. They claimed that farmers were "ignorant" and easily manipulated by unscrupulous "gentlemen." When the Federalist George Richards Minot summed up this analysis in his *History of the Insurrections,* published in Worcester in 1788, he claimed that the society which produced the rebellion was characterized by what he called "a distinction of interests" at the root of which, as he interpreted it, lay a natural propensity for man to behave as his social and economic condition dictated. Sounding very much like the James Madison of *Federalist No. 10,* Minot suggested that the clash of interests was an inevitable feature of civil society. "These classes of people," he said of creditors or "men of property," "will ever be opposed by debtors and persons otherwise interested against them." Only the state and its constitution could stand between them and protect the few against the many.[11]

Without subscribing to the social biases of the Federalists, one can agree that it makes sense to look for the causes of Shays's Rebellion in the political turmoil of the 1780s. But if the political clashes of the decade explain the insurrection, did the insurrection cause the Federalist movement? Historians have reasonably seen a connection, arguing that the social threat posed by the Shaysites drove conservative merchants and other men of wealth to seek refuge in a stronger central government, capable of providing the security and financial stability they perceived to be lacking at the state level.[12] The public claims of Federalists at the time seem to lend weight to the theory, for mixed into their "interest-based" analysis of the causes of rebellion, they frequently added their certainty that only a strong national government could prevent such uprisings in the future.[13] Such assertions suggest that Shays's Rebellion was one cause among many leading to the calling of the federal convention and the writing of a new constitution, yet the pertinent fact about Massachusetts is that political battle lines had already been drawn before the insurrection ever broke out. Well before 1786 many conservatives, including most of Boston's merchants and traders, had already turned their back on the state and set their sights on the creation of a strong national government. For them, Shays's Rebellion tended not to shape or alter their outlook on the world so much as it simply confirmed them in their beliefs.

There was, however, yet another "cause" of Shays's Rebellion frequently mentioned by pseudonymous Federalist newspaper writers in 1786 and 1787, which showed that they feared not only an internal enemy but also an external one. This was the fairly widespread Federalist or proto-Federalist notion that the British were behind Shays, that the insurrection was an attempt to undo the American Revolution and discredit the new nation.[14] Here lies a clue to the origins of organized Federalism in Massachusetts. On the face of it, a Federalist suspicion of the British does not seem in character given what we know of the later Federalist party preference for things British. Nor does it seem to square with the past of many

Massachusetts merchants who became Federalists. Various studies have shown that Boston merchants were deeply divided by Revolutionary events, and many, perhaps even a majority of them, if not always in agreement with British measures of the 1760s and early '70s, accepted the Patriot cause most reluctantly: they had resisted commercial boycotts of British manufactures at the time of the Stamp and Townshend acts and again after the tea crisis, and by June 1774 they had openly split with the more radical Revolutionary leaders.[15] Even many who were not openly Tory resisted Independence and, once it had been declared, adopted moderate if not conservative positions on most political and constitutional issues. Moreover, both during the war and after, merchants and their conservative allies resisted all attempts to deprive known Tories of their properties and rights and were poised at war's end to welcome Tories back into their midst.[16] In fact, Timothy Pickering of Essex County went so far as to claim that the country would be better off if some of the Patriots could be shipped out in exchange for some of the Tory refugees.[17]

This seemingly pro-British attitude, moreover, appeared to fit with the commercial expectations of Massachusetts merchants at war's end. Even before hostilities were formally concluded, merchants were looking optimistically to a future in which they would revive their trade with Britain and the West Indies, reestablish credit connections, and restock their shelves with the latest in British fashions and conveniences. Some even decided to go off to England themselves to conduct their own personal diplomacy and to select new stock.[18]

It did not take long, however, for optimism to give way to frustration and anger. British houses were willing enough to ship goods to America and to do so on credit, but the prospects looked good enough also to send dozens of British factors over to collect debts, as the peace treaty permitted, and also to carry on their own direct trade with inland shopkeepers and others on the wholesale market. Boston merchants blamed the British factors for their unfair intrusion, and the first postwar feeling of hostility began to develop.[19] Merchants are competitive by nature, however, and they recognized that there were things they could do to hold on to their fair share of the import trade. First and foremost, they could expand their domestic market far beyond its limited prewar size. They could aim to do more than satiate the pent-up demand of their former customers by making consumers of people who had heretofore perhaps only nibbled at the fringe of the consumer market. This they hoped to accomplish by stimulating demand among farmers in the rural interior; the means to this end was weekly newspaper advertisements which offered every conceivable article of British manufacture on such generous terms as to convince almost any reader that such items were affordable. At hand to help were not only the several newspapers in Boston but also the more recently established weeklies in Worcester and Springfield, eager to spread the gospel of consumerism for a small advertising fee.

There was nothing new about advertisements in American newspapers; what we must recognize are the new marketing techniques of the 1780s and the powerful transformation they wrought on rural values. The British historian Neil McKendrick has written brilliantly about the commercialization of eighteenth-century England and what he correctly calls *The Birth of a Consumer Society*.[20] It is easy to see that the same techniques that were rapidly expanding consumerism into provincial England were used by American merchants in the last quarter of the eighteenth century, and with tremendous impact in the immediate postwar period. The trick was not simply to stimulate people's appetite for more or to convince people that what were once considered luxuries were now necessities or, at the least, decencies, although these, too, were essential ingredients in the sales pitch. What was strikingly new was the trader's concern to put himself in the buyer's shoes and to explain how one could actually afford to pay for these things.

The short-lived first approach was to sell "very cheap for cash." But by the spring of 1784, tantalizing lists of imported goods were being offered in exchange for "furs, bees-wax, old pewter, and all kinds of grain [which] will be received as cash." Ebenezer Storer would sell for "cash, continental Loan certificates, Massachusetts state notes, or Good Pot-Ash" at his store in Union Street, Boston. Shopkeepers White and Clap of Rutland would give both cash and goods for pot and pearl ashes, but they were also looking for "salts, furs, Massachusetts state securities, continental certificates, and New York new emission money." It was only in late summer

1784 that traders began to admit openly in their ads that the buyer did not need money or goods at all. William Moore warned that all of his fellow traders were advertising goods on credit "at the lowest terms"; he urged his "impartial Customers" to compare before they bought and "to call and judge for themselves."

Since money was no object, who could resist reading the long lists of goods that now made up the typical advertisement? The variety in some was mind-boggling. Where once merchants had simply offered English dry goods as their stock in trade, now they followed the lead of such Boston importers as S. and S. Salisbury, whose itemized lists had something for everyone, but especially for women: "broad cloths, plains, serges, rateens, frizes, flannels, shalloons, tammies, poplins, crapes, quality bindings, variety of knee straps, men's worsted and cotton caps, corduroys, milliner's needles, Sattins, modes, calicoes, Irish linens, Cambricks, Lawns, Dutch Lace, Catgut, Silk handerchiefs, Muffs and Tippets, Bonnet Paper, Italian Sprigs, Ribbons, Fans, Silk thread and Cotton ditto, Silk and Cotton jacket patterns, Jacket buttons, blankets, Diapers, Sheetings, etc." Add to this the hardwares: "window glass, nails, shot, powder, smith's anvils and vices, mill saws, steel and iron plate hand saws, holsters and pocket pistols, coffee mills, wool cards, fox and rat traps, shovels, an elegant assortment of looking glasses, frying pans, chafing dishes, bellows, best London pewter, flat irons, knives and forks, an assortment of brass handles and escutcheons, hinges, locks, English glue, white lead, red lead." And if the reader was not already hooked, there were "West India goods, groceries, crockery ware, bibles, psalters, primers, writing paper, and a large assortment of Tin Ware."[21] Life would never be the same again.

What was happening was that Massachusetts merchants were attempting to expand their home market by transforming tastes and by drawing new consumers into the retail market. We have no direct knowledge of the extent to which they succeeded with the participants in Shays's Rebellion, although it might be possible to find sufficient estate inventories in the probate records to show that Shaysites included English manufactures among their valued possessions. What we do know, of course, is that whatever they were buying, Shaysites became heavily indebted and a substantial percentage of them ended up in court because they were unable to meet their obligations.²² One way or another, these men who may have started life as subsistence farmers had, by this time, left the simple imperatives of subsistence behind them; their tastes were changing, their perceived needs were growing, they willingly risked indebtedness to expand their store of material possessions, and they now needed cash or a cash substitute to pay their debts and their taxes and perhaps also to maintain their new life-styles. Merchants would later claim that farmers bought luxuries they could not afford, but the fact is that merchants used advertising to blur the distinction between luxuries and necessities.

The newspaper advertisements, however, chart both the rise and the fall of the consumer boom. By the fall of 1784, notices of a new kind were beginning to appear. They were placed by brokers eager to buy and sell the bewildering array of paper still around at a time when hard money was fast disappearing. Joseph Ward of Boston dealt in "state notes, Continental certificates, Treasurers orders, New Emission money, and every other kind of State and Continental Securities." John Cunningham, Jr., of Boston wanted "New York and this State New Emission money, State notes payable in the next Tax, Orders from this State Treasurer, payable in Tax No. 2 and 3, and all other kinds of Publick securities." Even the postrider between Worcester and Concord, New Hampshire, carried on a paper exchange on the side and advertised for "New York Emission money and Consolidated State Notes."²³ Money men were beginning to hedge and to hoard.

By 1785, when British credit had completely dried up and cash was as scarce in the city as in the country, merchants abandoned their effort to expand the domestic market for British manufactures, turned their backs on the problems of indebted farmers, and embarked upon a single-minded course to solve their commercial difficulties. If they could do nothing further to expand the domestic market or the demand side, then they must reduce the number of suppliers to bring the two sides of the equation back into balance. Some merchants knew that they simply were best off to get out of the business. The firm of J. and J. Amory, which ideally fits the earlier description of reluctant Revolutionaries who hoped to revive the British commercial connection, announced firmly in 1785 that it was closing out its trade in British goods and would sell off its supply at cost or even below cost.²⁴ But a substantial number of other merchants believed that the best solution was to eliminate the competition of the British factors.²⁵

In mid-April 1785 Boston merchants and traders crowded into the long room of Colonel John Marston to "consider what discouragement should be given to the British Factors, who were residing here and monopolizing to themselves the benefits of commerce." Tempers were short. Even the once radical *Boston Gazette* observed of the meeting that "in every collection of men where the redress of any grievance is the object, there are some whose passions out run their reason." At an adjournment at Faneuil Hall, however, cooler heads urged the adoption of resolutions pledging not to purchase goods from British merchants, factors, or agents, nor to let or sell them warehouses, shops, houses, or ships. Moreover, in their anger they were willing to "encourage the manufacture & produce of this country," a clear offer of political alliance with the artisans of the town. But most important was their determination to get congressional action: they wanted a federal regulation of trade, blocking British exploitation of the American market and reserving it to Americans. To this end they instructed their committee to write to merchants everywhere in the nation "recommending to them an immediate application to the legislatures of their respective states, to vest such powers in Congress (if not already done) as shall be competent to the interesting purposes aforesaid, and also to petition Congress to make such regulations as shall have the desired effect."²⁶

Boston's merchants commited themselves to what they called "federal policy," which was in effect an American mercantilism. Congress must be given the power to regulate trade. And with a blind eye and a deaf ear to farmers calling for paper money or cash substitutes, they went about building a political alliance that could accomplish their purpose. Their April offer to cut off British trade and encourage American manufactures immediately attracted the support of a number of Boston's tradesmen and artisans. The latter organized a committee of their own and then exchanged letters with the merchant committee in which they celebrated their newfound unity and unanimity.²⁷ Within weeks merchants and artisans together opened a lobbying campaign to win over the new governor, Bowdoin, and the legislature to their proposition that a convention of all the states must be called to revise the Confederation by vesting it with the power to regulate trade.[28] When the legislature responded with a favorable resolution, Nathan Dane explained to Rufus King off in Congress that the "mercantile interest," as he called it, knew exactly what it wanted and had got its way.[29] What he might have added is that the organization of this mercantile interest, or coalition of merchants and manufacturers, represented a new plateau in the development of nationalist sentiment in Massachusetts. Where before there had been legislative and limited public support for granting an impost to Congress, to create a national revenue, there was now an organized Federalist movement in Massachusetts commited to political action and to popularizing its approach in the press.[30] Its rallying cry for the next two years was the need to create a national commercial policy. Writers like "Americanus," writing in Worcester's *Massachusetts Spy,* spread the gospel, urging even the farmers to believe that the shortage of cash was not the fundamental problem. Americans would one day be a wealthy people, and they must hasten that day by "encouraging manufactures, discouraging the importation of superfluities, but especially by instructing our constitutional guardians to unite our commercial interest, by committing it to the care of the grand council of these states. Under the direction of that august body," he concluded confidently, "our trade will soon be wisely regulated, and our manufactures will encrease."[31]

The frustrated attempt to restore the British import trade was an important factor in creating the Federalist movement in Massachusetts, but it was not the only factor, nor even the only commercial factor. Eighteenth-century Massachusetts merchants were a diversified lot, as much so after the Revolutionary War as before. Many eagerly sought to return to the British West Indies with fish and lumber to exchange for sugar and molasses. Besides looking to the revival of British trade links, others with equal optimism looked outside the traditional patterns of imperial trade to new opportunities afforded by Independence: Some expected to profit from the carrying trade, especially in the southern states. They looked to new markets for American staples in France, Holland, Spain, and elsewhere in Europe. Merchants of Hingham and Salem eagerly planned risky voyages to China, hoping to be the first to open that potentially lucrative trade for the United States.[32] Meanwhile, American diplomats were ordered by Congress to help facilitate the economic development of the new nation by seeking most-favored-nation commercial treaties with European powers.

Yet by 1785, almost all of these endeavors were meeting with frustration. Within a year of the peace treaty, Britain closed its West Indies to American merchants in order to favor merchants in its loyal colonies north of the United States. America's ally, France, seemed suddenly to become jealous of reviving American trade and especially resented New England's exploitation of the Atlantic fisheries and the fish trade with the Caribbean. Spain and Portugal were reluctant to grant the United States most-favored-nation status, while the American envoys sent to arrange such treaties in several European countries lamented their lack of negotiating leverage. Merchants looking to the Mediterranean soon backed off because of the risks of seizure by Barbary pirates, while congressmen expressed frustration at their total inability to do anything about it.[33] Moreover, within Congress, the sectional interests of New England and the southern states clashed over whether the treaty with Spain should allow trade with the American west through the mouth of the Mississippi.[34] The New Englanders bitterly opposed this, perhaps, as southerners said, because they did not want to see development of the interior and a trade they could not control. And finally, New Englanders discovered to their dismay that their own countrymen in the southern states were unwilling to give Yankee merchants any privileges whatever in the carrying trade. Southerners liked free trade: whoever offered them the best deal, regardless of nationality, could carry their staples to European markets.[35]

There had been times during the American Revolution when New England merchants had also sounded like free traders, or at least they longed for the removal of the many British restrictions of the 1760s.[36] But an important aspect of their change of mind in the 1780s was their growing conviction—shared by both merchants and artisans—that free trade was not in their economic interest. Southerners maintained an interest in free trade because they had a ready staple for export and were convinced that free trade would give them the best deal with respect to freight, export prices, and import prices. They accepted the most-favored-nation approach to commercial treaties with foreign countries. But northern merchants, recognizing that free trade gave privileges to their foreign competitors—especially the British—were turning to protection through trade regulations, especially the mercantilist idea of confining the nation's trade to ships of the nation.

Even as late as the fall of 1785, however, the Federalist movement in Massachusetts was still largely confined to the alliance of merchants and artisans; many of the state's leading politicians feared what might happen were there to be a convention for the complete overhaul of the Articles of Confederation. They were agreed that Congress must have an independent revenue such as would be provided by a 5 percent impost, and they saw merit in a uniform regulation of trade. But these must be accomplished piecemeal by amendment, and national trade regulation, at least, should be limited to a fifteen-year period, after which the states could resume their regulatory powers if they so chose.[37] Rufus King was firmly convinced that a tight regulatory power exercised by Congress was the only answer, but he recognized that the issue would split the states into North and South.[38] Others who were soon to make their reputations as leading Federalists, such as Theodore Sedgwick, Caleb Strong, and Nathan Dane, tended to believe that caution was essential and that the merchants demanding a constitutional convention were acting only out of self-interest. Their caution is to be explained, in part, as a persistence of the New England suspicion of Robert Morris and the other Philadelphia-centered nationalists who had dominated Congress in the early 1780s. A wholesale revision of the Articles, they feared, could produce a significant power shift to the wrong kind of men.

But a series of developments in early 1786 brought them, too, into the growing Federalist coalition. Many of these men were lawyers. During the four months or so before spring elections in 1786, Massachusetts newspapers were filled with letters denouncing lawyers as parasites on poor debt-ridden farmers, gougers whose exorbitant fees should be reduced and regulated by law, and a budding group of aristocrats growing rich on the suffering of others. Spokesmen for debtors argued that small claims should be dealt with summarily without lawyers or that honest men might represent themselves in court. Others insisted that, since so many cases went to appeal, the lower courts should be abolished as an unnecessary additional expense. The more radical even insisted that the profession of law should be abolished along with the remnants of English common law by which lawyers practiced their sophistry.[39] The opportunity was ready-made for Federalist merchants to espouse the cause of their legal brethren and draw them into their conservative analysis of events. Significantly, before the election for representatives took place in Boston, a writer calling himself "A Barber" proposed that Boston would be best served in the legislature by two merchants, two lawyers, two tradesmen, and one other. The "two good lawyers" were needed, the "Barber" argued, "to outtalk the countrymen."[40] There was a natural congruity of interests that had brought merchants and lawyers together before; by the summer of 1786, lawyers were sounding much friendlier toward the merchants' plea for a strengthened federal system.[41]

All of this shows us that the Federalist movement was growing incrementally: from a core of merchants the movement expanded outward, absorbing the interests of artisans and lawyers and—although the story cannot be developed completely here—of bankers and financiers, of holders of public securities, and of army officers. But despite its dynamic growth, the Federalist movement in Massachusetts lacked the essential backing of a clear-minded majority of the voters of the state determined to rectify the shortcomings in the Articles of Confederation by establishing a strong, regulatory national government. The reluctance of some Massachusetts Federalists to send delegates off to James Madison's Annapolis convention to discuss trade regulation must also indicate that many were not yet convinced that there was anything like a sufficient body of opinion in America sympathetic to wholesale revision of the Articles.[42] Moreover there was the growing conviction among some leading men in the state—a conviction amounting almost to paranoia—that antagonism to national commercial regulation was concentrated in the southern states and that the achievement of a truly consolidated national government could come about only after the South was eliminated from the Union.[43] Secretive talk about dismembering the nation surely indicated the depths of their desperation. What they needed, if we may interpret the state of affairs in the fall of 1786, was a dramatic demonstration of the need for a stronger national government, something that would galvanize public sentiment in favor of immediate political action, something with a broader appeal than commercial policy.[44] Enter Shays's Rebellion.

The scattered county conventions and armed actions against the courts of law in 1786 provided the Federalists with exactly what they wanted, although events needed interpretation and perhaps even "improvement." The protest was widespread, but it was also disorganized, unconcerted, mostly verbal, and largely nonrebellious. Daniel Shays and his followers gave the protest its short-lived violent edge, yet the governor's ablest informers correctly assessed the demands as modest and the threat as lacking in broad-based support.[45] But whatever the inadequacies of the protest movement, shrill hyperbole filled the eastern newspapers expressing exaggerated fears of imminent invasion by barbaric hordes of ignorant farmers.[46] Boston raised new military regiments including an expensive artillery unit. Elaborate signals were worked out as part of a defensive strategy to protect the town from the thousands of rebels who were daily expected to descend on neighboring Cambridge. And eventually thousands of dollars were voluntarily collected from Boston merchants to pay for Benjamin Lincoln's army. Nervous easterners classified all rural protest, whether armed and violent or passive and verbal, as insurrectionary; the farmers' demands for paper money and other things anathema to conservatives were rolled together with the armed action of defiant Shaysites as evidence of widespread rebellion. By any measure, Federalists overreacted. They inflated the seriousness of the threat, and at least some of their exaggeration must have had a conscious purpose. For in their public utterances, they rarely missed the chance to explain with direct simplicity their conviction that this rebellion was occurring because the United States lacked a national government capable of regulating trade and rationalizing the public debt. It was a political analysis that repeated the articles of faith in what by now was a Federalist creed.

The polemical character of the Federalist analysis, however, was best typified by the now frequent claim that the regulation was more than a farmer uprising: British agents were at work attempting to undo the Revolution and destroy the republic. Did Federalists believe this, or were they simply interpolating into their analysis of the uprising their own frustrations and changes of heart? There had, after all, been British agents, but they were commercial agents or factors who had, so it was believed, ruined the import trade for the indigenous commercial community. Even as late as the spring of 1786, Federalist newspaper writers were tracing all of Massachusetts's problems, both the "public poverty" and the "general discontent," to the inability of Congress to regulate trade on the one hand and the British menace in their midst on the other.[47] Federalists simply rolled this interpretation into their analysis of the insurrection. Perhaps for some Federalists who had been reluctant Revolutionaries, soft on independence, or forgiving of Tories, this was a chance to get right with history: they now were ready to condemn Britain and wrap themselves in the flag if that could aid their pursuit of a strong national government. Whatever their motivations, there can be no doubting their frustration over the postwar failure to renew profitable economic ties with Britain.

Shays's Rebellion, at least to certain leading men, was less a cause of Federalism than it was an opportunity to expand and popularize it. Stephen Higginson, himself a recent convert to the nationalist solution, seemed almost delighted with the turn of events in the fall of 1786. Just at a time when he had given up on the General Court as reasoned directors of public affairs, "some new event turns up to avert the evil & show us the necessity of abridging the power of the states." The Shaysite action he looked at as a godsend because of its impact on public opinion. "I never saw so great a change in the public mind on any occasion as has lately appeared in this state as to the expediency of increasing the powers of Congress, not merely to commercial objects but generally." And with amazing perspicacity, he predicted that "by the next summer I expect we shall have been prepared for anything that is wise & fitting. Congress should be making the necessary arrangements for improving this disposition, when sufficiently increased, to right & valuable purposes. They must be prepared not only to support a proper force in the field, but to consolidate the several governments into one, general & efficient."[48] When Henry Knox wrote from the capital of the Confederation, he congratulated his friends as if both the rebellion and its suppression had been a Federalist accomplishment. "The energy of Massachusetts places it in an honorable point of view," he said, adding with obvious enthusiasm, "the strongest arguments possible may be drawn from the events that have happened in that state in order to effect a strong general government."[49] In short, if Shays's Rebellion had not occurred, the Federalists would have had to invent it.

At the least, Federalist leaders who had been searching for the way to convince fellow Americans of the need to create a strong central government astutely saw the potential in exploiting the rebellion. Their task was made easier, however, by the political culture in which they operated. In Massachusetts there already was a natural audience for the Federalist message among the population of the most commercial-cosmopolitan towns.[50] Over a decade of legislative conflict with farmers over courts, paper money, taxation, and management of the public debt had sharpened the competitive attitudes of such people and accustomed them to analyzing events in terms of self-interest. For most of those who became rank-and-file Federalists, the threat of armed popular insurrection was by itself convincing proof of the need for drastic measures, and they quickly concluded where their own interest lay. It was "we" versus "they," rich against poor, or creditor against debtor, just as George Minot said. Limited by their frame of reference, moreover, Federalists—leaders and followers alike—mistakenly attributed to rural protestors a similar level of solidarity on the basis of interest. The Federalist analysis of rural discontent shows that they neither understood the problems of western farmers nor sought to do so. They did not even see through a glass darkly. For them, Shays's Rebellion symbolized their worst fears about the democratic element in their society, and beyond that it simply mirrored their anxieties: it reflected familiar images of a Massachusetts that had failed to develop economic self-reliance, was unlikely to produce an agricultural surplus for export, and the trade of which was in danger of slipping into the hands of British competitors unless a faltering state economy was absorbed at once into a national one. It was ironic that the

Federalists—the new nation's first political nationalists—included merchants who had once been tepid Patriots at best, many of whom at war's end had with great anticipation invested in renewed British ties. Yet, whatever the ironies, merchants and their associates stood converted to the national cause by a series of events of which Shays's Rebellion was only the last.

PART TWO
Political Cultures in Conflict

5

"THE FINE THEORETIC GOVERNMENT OF MASSACHUSETTS IS PROSTRATED TO THE EARTH":
The Response to Shays's Rebellion Reconsidered

William Pencak

Few rebellions in history have been suppressed as effectively or with as little bloodshed as the Massachusetts farmers' insurrection of 1786–87. Only three engagements of importance occurred, although the rebels waged a mild guerilla war against the supporters of government from late February to May 1787. Four insurgents died and a handful were wounded as a single round of cannon fire routed Daniel Shays's makeshift army before the Springfield arsenal on January 25, 1787. Aside from weather-related casualties during one of the worst winters in Massachusetts history, no one on either side apparently suffered as government troops staggered into Shays's headquarters in Petersham on February 4, chasing the surprised insurgents from their campfires and breakfasts. A final six-minute skirmish at Stockbridge, "the severest" as contemporary historian George Richards Minot noted, produced three fatalities and three wounded among the Shaysites, one death and one other casualty among the forces of law and order. Massachusetts inflicted a small number of fines, whippings, temporary disfranchisements, and brief imprisonments before pardoning all rebels sentenced to death except for two involved in late plundering. The continent could then join the Commonwealth and Minot in rejoicing over

---

From a paper presented at the Bicentennial Conference on Shays's Rebellion, 1986, sponsored by the Colonial Society of Massachusetts.

"a dangerous internal war finally suppressed, by the spirited use of constitutional powers, without the shedding of blood by the evil magistrate."[1]

During the nineteenth century the established order triumphed almost as completely in print and folklore as it had on the field of battle. Josiah Gilbert Holland's 1855 *History of Western Massachusetts* spoke for a consensus that condemned the Shaysites' "entire lack of moral power, their utter cowardice, their insolence and malice, their outrages and robberies." Popular anecdotes mocked poor "fall back Shaise," and "The Ballad of Daniel Shays" placed the blame for the revolt squarely in the jaws of Hell:

> Within the state I lived, of late,
>   By Satan's foul invention,
> In Pluto's cause, against their laws,
>   I raised an insurrection.[2]

In the twentieth century, however, supporters of the vanquished yeomen have successfully counterattacked and achieved a retrospective moral victory. Otis Hood, the Communist party's candidate for governor of Massachusetts in 1936, has not stood alone in applauding Shays as "a pioneer in fighting against the tyranny of the moneyed class." Speaking to the elite American Antiquarian Society in 1902, Charles Francis Adams compared the "intense hardship, not to say oppression," suffered by "law-abiding New England farmers and landowners" with the labor agitation and "Debs business" of the 1890s: "The historical fact is that the conditions of the people then prevailing were almost unendurable, the laws barbaric, and the people had shown themselves long-suffering." Even as scholarly conferences marked the rebellion's two-hundredth anniversary, the Commonwealth circulated a film to libraries and schools in praise of the beleaguered, liberty-loving farmers.[3]

The rebellion's most careful modern historians also echo the insurgents' own claim, shouted as they paraded through the streets of Worcester, "calling to all who wished for a redress of grievances (the only object which had led them to arms) to join and follow." In his still valuable 1905 dissertation, Joseph Warren stressed that the government's countermeasures provoked the insurrection: "In self-defense the insurgents stopped the Supreme Court, attacked the

Federal Arsenal at Springfield, and endeavored to form an organization among themselves. Then the government attacked them in force and the Rebellion was put down." The uprising's most thorough historian, Robert Feer, has argued that "conservatives accused the insurgents of wanting changes far more radical than anything which appears in their own writings." Far from constituting a planned revolt, the county conventions and court closings that "sprang up from nowhere" in the summer of 1786 were "as devoid of centralized organization as any movement involving thousands of people could be." In retrospect, "the whole affair had not been as serious as it had seemed in the excitement of the moment." And while granting that "even the most vigorous anti-Shaysites were anxious, for the most part, to end the business as peacefully as possible," Feer dismissed the Commonwealth's efforts to appease them as "too little, too late." More recently, Barbara Karsky and David Szatmary have juxtaposed the "persistent reformism" and "self-defense" of the "Regulators" with the "suppressive legislation" and "repression" of the authorities.[4]

Writings on the rebellion reconcile two usually opposed schools of historiography that converge in sympathetic solidarity with the revolting farmers. Conflict between indebted, overtaxed yeomen desiring populist reforms and a more prosperous, aristocratic, and commercial seacoast defined the issue for Progressive scholars such as Vernon Louis Parrington and Merrill Jensen, as it does for Karsky and Szatmary. Yet the insurgents' reluctant resort to force following protracted misery and their carefully limited violence also conform to the early American crowds described by Pauline Maier, which "defended the urgent interests of their communities when the lawful authorities failed to act . . . only after the normal channels of redress had proven inadequate." Gordon Wood, approvingly quoted by Szatmary, has explicitly placed the rebellion in a long tradition of crowds embodying united local sentiment. It required the uncharacteristic belligerence of a government which refused to accommodate the populace to distinguish it: "Shays's Rebellion represented something of an anomaly, largely because the farmers of western Massachusetts, unlike other groups in the 1780s, found no release for their pent-up grievances in legislative actions but instead were forcibly resisted by the authorities."[5]

Reevaluation of Shays's Rebellion is needed. First, pro-Shays interpretations offer far too simple an explanation for the behavior of the insurgency's opponents: if some of the Boston merchants may have cared only to maximize their wealth regardless of where the burden fell, the conduct of Samuel Adams, Artemas Ward, and the thousands of farmers who enlisted to suppress the revolt did not. Had the Sons of Liberty of '76 become the Tories of '86? Second, by neglecting to look carefully at the anti-Shaysites' perceptions and motives, the historiography of the rebellion has stagnated in a moralistic quagmire where virtuous, democratic country farmers struggle for the soul of the nation with callous aristocratic merchants. The work of Cecilia Kenyon, John Riche, Gordon Wood, and others has moved the study of the United States Constitution beyond such simplistic dichotomies; so should an analysis of Shays's Rebellion.[6]

This chapter argues four points. First, the Shaysites went well beyond the practices of Revolutionary crowds. An examination of the insurgents' demands, behavior, and support demonstrates that they did not attempt, reluctantly and defensively, to correct grievances within the existing constitutional framework. From the very beginning they modeled their resistance on the Revolution itself and appropriated the symbols of a cause for which they had sacrificed but little—few Shaysites had served significantly in the war. Second, the rebels sought to supplant a social order based on republicanism and a communitarian vision of civic virtue with a minimal state government guaranteeing free pursuit of private and town interests. Third, the magistrates of eastern Massachusetts and their supporters believed they were mounting a last-ditch defense of the republican vision for which they had fought and which had already been repudiated by prodebtor, antinationalist state legislatures elsewhere. Finally, by responding to the rebellion with restraint, in seeking to reconcile grievances where possible, avoiding bloodshed, repudiating the punishments imposed by James Bowdoin and his administration, and conciliating the disaffected, the official response to Shays's Rebellion offered an enduring lesson in the preservation of a republic. Through a restrained but firm defense of principle, Massachusetts in 1786–87 came up with republican remedies for popular rebellion and helped to secure the future of self-government in the new nation.

WHAT DID THE SHAYSITES want and how did they seek to accomplish their goals? They claimed their petitions of grievances, county conventions, and marches to close courts followed in Massachusetts' long-standing tradition of protests against abusive authority. Further, they insisted they had no intention to "rebel" but only sought relief from insupportable burdens, borne for the most part by a loyal Revolutionary populace. But examination of the Shaysites' specific demands, self-presentation as an armed force, and lists of identifiable rebels reveals instead that people who had done little for the Revolution forcibly sought to alter a Massachusetts constitution they had never accepted.

During the summer of 1786, inhabitants throughout the Bay State—including but by no means limited to the areas that rebelled—protested the government's policies in three ways. In ascending order, towns petitioned for redress of grievances, communities sent representatives to county conventions to reinforce these demands, and armed crowds closed or threatened to close court sessions in five of the eight counties, apart from Maine, of mainland Massachusetts. While the conventions formally repudiated the crowds' resort to force and all the conventioneers were not formally elected by their towns, the grievances voiced were fairly general. The convention of fifty Hampshire and Berkshire towns that met at Hatfield on August 22, for instance, after voting itself a constitutionally legal meeting, demanded the abolition of the state Senate, "the present mode of representation" (e.g., property qualifications for public office), and the courts of Common Pleas and General Sessions. It demanded that all government officials be elected annually by the legislature and have their salaries adjusted from year to year, which would end "unreasonable grants to some officers of the government." Many petitions especially criticized the governor's £1,100 stipend. Lawyers received vitriolic criticism, as did high taxation to liquidate the state debt. The General Court's location in Boston, which was difficult for westerners to reach, expensive to live in, and too full of money-making distractions and anti-rural lobbying, also came under attack. The convention called for "a bank of paper money subject to a depreciation" to remedy "the want of a sufficient medium" and demanded that the recessed General Court be summoned immediately to consider these matters. Aside from recommending the end of imprisonment for debt—"that abominable pagan practice" as one Shaysite wrote—and abolishing the Commonwealth's attorney general, the Hatfield convention's twenty-one demands encapsulated the general complaints on the eve of the rebellion.[7]

Further, before they marched on the government arsenal in late January, Shays and his men insisted their purpose in convening and arming was limited. "I had no intention to destroy the government but to have the courts suspended to prevent such abuses as have late taken place," Adam Wheeler, one of the four leaders not included in a general offer of indemnity, insisted. Just before the battle at Springfield, Shays himself replied to a government colonel's argument that "I am here to defend the country you are endeavoring to destroy" by stating, "If you are in defense of the country, we are both defending the same cause." Several days earlier, during an interview in which he vowed to plunder and destroy that "nest of devils" (Boston), Shays nevertheless maintained that "his ideas never extended so far as to think" of overthrowing the constitution, and he "knew no more what government to set up than he knew the dimensions of eternity." Even his opponents, on the rare occasions they distinguished the insurgents' motives from the implications of their actions, agreed: "I do not consider the present disturbances as systematically conducted to any determinate object but such is the restless spirit of the country at present that I am convinced their discontents may easily be increased to open resistance to our present government," Samuel Holden Parsons informed Benjamin Lincoln in September.[8]

But as Peter Shaw has noted regarding crowds during the American Revolution, "observers reacted not so much to the destruction of property and the physical intimidation of a few individuals . . . as to the ritual violence of the protests." Hanging and burning effigies that equated British officials with the pope and the devil—a device the Shaysites applied to Bowdoin on at least one occasion—appeared to brand the status quo as evil incarnate and proclaim a rebellion. Similarly, the 1786 rebels' actions belied their disclaimers. The insurgents had indeed traveled great lengths. They assembled in convention—which in Massachusetts indicated a belief that legitimate government had defaulted or needed reconstruction—sought to restructure the entire state administration, and presented themselves from the first not as a peaceable crowd of aggrieved citizens but a "new modelled" revolutionary army. Shays's Rebellion was a revolution against the Revolution.[9]

A Massachusetts convention denoted a state of nature which required the people to govern themselves outside established institutions or to re-create them. The Provincial Congress of 1774–75 set up a provisional government when the royal governor dissolved the legislature. The conventions of 1782 had in fact prefaced Samuel Ely's "rebellion." That of 1780 drafted a new constitution. Two conventions in 1784 had quickly and quietly adjourned after presenting their protests. But in the summer of 1786, Bristol, Worcester, Hampshire and Berkshire, and Middlesex counties all held conventions that continued to sit by adjournment throughout the autumn and winter while the rebels shut down much of the provincial government. The conventions therefore resembled an ongoing *imperio in imperium*, "a possible basis for a revolutionary government which the insurgents may well have wished to control," as historian Joseph Warren put it.[10]

Furthermore, the conventions' demands did not simply ask that debtors be relieved, taxes reduced, or paper money printed. They struck at the constitution itself. Abolishing the Senate and making the governor totally dependent on the lower house's whim for his salary would have achieved the unicameralism of Pennsylvania and Vermont. If they also succeeded in eliminating the county courts, the only level of state administration between the Supreme Judicial Court and the local sheriffs and justices of the peace, the Shaysites would have reduced government to the towns and their representatives. And while the adoption of paper money and the restructuring of debts and taxes by no means foretold the "desiring to abolish all public and private debts, and to have a general division of property" which conservatives feared, these reforms would have significantly transformed the Bay State's economic and political life.[11] Nearly every other new state had concentrated power in the hands of a democratized lower house and introduced a depreciated currency. Massachusetts, the Shaysites were suggesting, ought to get into line.[12]

Moreover, the Shaysites did not act like a prerevolutionary crowd protesting grievances. From the first they behaved like an army, as Governor Bowdoin emphasized in his proclamation, charging them with assembling "with guns, swords, and other deadly weapons and with drums beating and fifes playing." The government perceived protest as rebellion because the insurgents appeared as a military force. They also threatened violence beginning in September 1786 by pointing bayonets at Worcester County chief judge Artemas Ward, promising at Concord that "every person who did not . . . join the regulators in two hours should be driven out of town," and in one instance (Aaron Broad's) promising "to fight and spill my blood and leave my bones at the court house until the Resurrection."[13]

The rebels presented themselves as a genuine army in yet other ways. As early as September 24, they were formally enlisting men at militia musters "to break up the Supreme Court." On October 13 they summoned men "well armed and well equipped with sixty rounds" each to prepare "to turn out at a minute's notice," consciously imitating the minutemen of a decade earlier.

Perhaps the insurgents' most blatant assumption of the mantle of the Revolutionary army occurred in the placement of green boughs in their hats, which they sported as early as September 27. Such sprigs held a symbolic importance: the Continental army had donned them on special festive occasions such as the Fourth of July and victory parades. In contrast, government troops wore pieces of white paper. One could argue the boughs symbolized the "State of Nature" into which men unprotected by a cruel government were thrust, just as paper could stand for the laws and constitution the militia defended. Henry Van Schaack of Stockbridge "did not think it sage or prudent to decorate" his hat with the white paper in February, but his fellow citizens wore the twigs, pinned white paper to their backs to mock the government emblem, and "declared themselves to have no more idea of submitting to government than the wild savages." As late as April, "sundry persons" remained "very insolent" and kept "the badge of Rebellion in their hats."[14]

By adopting the green bough as their distinguishing mark, the rebels symbolically reconstituted themselves as the Continental army, claiming to continue the good fight they had begun in the Revolution. Was this boast accurate? Not only the rebels but even their opponents sometimes remarked that the insurgents did in fact include former members of Washington's regiments. Speaking to Park Holland after the skirmish at Springfield, General William Shepherd remarked "that at no time in his life was he ever called upon to perform so painful a duty, as when he ordered good aim to be taken at Shays and his men, many of whom had fought at his side and stood firm through the most trying scenes of the war."[15]

Daniel Shays and his first commanding officer, Reuben Dickinson of Amherst, illustrate Shepherd's interpretation. Born in Hopkinton of poor parents, Shays rose to local prominence as a farmer in his new home of Pelham, served as a lieutenant and then a captain in the Continental line, loaned money to the government, and received a sword for gallant service from the marquis de Lafayette. His opponents reviled him for selling it; but if he did, one can well imagine the financial distress, regret, anger, or disgust that must have driven him to such a step. Dickinson, an Amherst selectman who raised ten children besides serving as a Continental officer through much of the war, found his estate reduced from 160 acres in 1780 to 50 in 1785. Shortly after the rebellion, lawsuits forced him to sell the rest of his land, and he moved to Thetford, Vermont. The three others listed with Shays as the rebellion's "principal abettors"— Adam Wheeler of Hubbardston, Luke Day of West Springfield, and Eli Parsons of Adams—had all served as Continental officers, although Wheeler was "reported deranged" in 1778.[16]

Nevertheless, what evidence can be gleaned from comparing lists of Shaysites and those of the volunteers against them who had army records comes close to supporting Henry Lee's exaggerated claim that "the late officers and soldiers are on the side of government unanimously." A sample of 327 rebels examined by David Szatmary revealed that only about 31 percent had participated in the war at all, a mere "few" in the Continental army. My own investigation of several sets of protestors also demonstrates few insurgents with significant service. To be sure, it is difficult to trace large numbers of Massachusetts soldiers perfectly because of name duplication, omissions in the lists, and the westward movement of men away from the towns from which they enlisted. Massachusetts added no fewer than fifty-seven new towns to its number during the Revolutionary era. Setting to one side those with common names and known youths for whom no fairly probable military service could be traced, the vast majority of identifiable Shaysites only served briefly in the militia. Only five out of thirty-three leaders sufficiently obnoxious to be mentioned by name in government warrants who served in the war did so for six months or more, as did sixteen of ninety-one from a more general sampling (lists of those arrested in the Robert Treat Paine Papers, with the twenty-nine Shaysites who served as delegates to the state constitutional convention of 1787 added). As with the citizens of most Massachusetts towns, the typical Revolutionary duty of a 1786 insurgent had constituted a few days in the militia, with possible brief combat service at Lexington, Concord, Bunker Hill, or against General John Burgoyne's invasion in 1777.[17]

Contemporary accounts of the rebels' conduct under fire also refutes their self-identification with the demobilized regulars. The Massachusetts line during the war had attained such discipline that Baron von Steuben "admired" rather than "inspected" it. But at the Springfield arsenal, a single round of cannon fire caused the rebels to flee in panic, much as untrained militia frequently had throughout the war. Daniel Stebbins estimated that Shays's forces at Springfield—usually counted at about 1,100—included 400 "old soldiers" who formed the advance guard, a number consistent both with William Pynchon's estimate of 300 "continental troops who had been used to action and despised the militia" at Worcester and with Szatmary's statistics. When General Benjamin Lincoln's forces surprised the rebels at Petersham after a night march through a blizzard, "some of Shays's men retreated so hastily that the officers had all left their swords and the soldiers their firearms." At least one scholar attributes Shays's selection as general—a title and role he spurned—to his reputation as a drillmaster. This suggests that few seasoned veterans joined his cause.[18]

If the rebels were not the Revolutionaries, who were they? They included local leaders such as Job Shattuck of Groton, William Whiting, Chief Justice of the Berkshire Court of Common Pleas, and Amherst's John Billings. The average Regulator owned a substantial plot of 60 acres, less than the overall colonial average of 100 to 200 estimated by Jackson T. Main and cited by Barbara Karsky to present the Shaysites as relatively poor, but then New England farms tended to be smaller than those in the southern and middle states. Two-thirds of the rebels had been sued for debts, for which they had trouble selling their property to repay, despite their obvious eagerness to do so. They suffered shame at being unable to pay, as manifested in their replies to Worcester merchant Stephen Salisbury's dunning notices. Salisbury's papers indicate complex chains of credit stretching from farmers to local retailers to county shopkeepers to Boston merchants to British houses where people at one level had to sue to convince their creditors they were not holding out. As Caleb Strong noted, "The difficulty is that many of the rebels from this part of the country do not owe half as much as they are worth." The Shaysites, in short, represented cross sections of their respective local communities: as Ebenezer Mattoon, a pro-government defender of convicted rebel Henry McCulloh wrote, "He told me he wished he was out of it, but he could not live in Pelham unless he joined them."[19]

Still, the large number of insurgents with no traceable military experience—nearly 70 percent according to Szatmary, at least half by my estimate—in a state where perhaps two-thirds of eligible males served at least a few days in the militia, strongly suggests that reports that the Shaysites have "drawn in a large number of boys" were true. "Those in favor of the court were as fine a body of men as I ever saw," Lemuel Tyler reported from Springfield on September 26, whereas "the insurgents in general made a despicable appearance both as to dress and arms. Many of them were boys, raw, ragged, and undisciplined." The Reverend Justus Forward of Belchertown noted that the young wearers of the green bough outnumbered the old, and one witness against the Shaysites argued against them that "the elderly people ought to take the matter up and not the youth." But if the tender ages of many rebels refuted their claim to represent the Revolution, it also extenuated their folly. Bemoaning the "want of care in the education of youth" who "opened their ears to every ingenious report . . . without examination," a writer for the *Worcester Magazine* lamented that "in the late insurrections, many youths have gone forth, bearing the weapons of death, when they had no idea of the merit of the cause, and knew nothing of the nature of civil government."[20]

Who were the government troops? Their heroic exertions recall the performance of the Continentals during the last few years of the war. The rapid midwinter march to Springfield, one observer reported, "would have reflected honor on the oldest and best disciplined troops. The cheerfulness with which a militia submitted to it, and the ardor they possessed on the occasion was astonishing." One soldier described how after "being obligated to march in order" with the insurgents "running each man separately," Lincoln's men still overtook them at Petersham after tiring forced marches "through a thick crust of snow, which was sometimes up to our knees and sometimes up to our necks." Lincoln twice formally thanked his troops for their "long and distressing march of thirty miles without a halt but for a few minutes" which brought them to Petersham.[21]

Unlike the rebels, many supporters of the state had previously served for long periods in the Continental army. Brookfield, Springfield, and Newbury volunteers respectively counted nineteen of twenty-eight, thirteen of thirty, and seventeen of thirty-three men with at least six months' service. Lincoln especially singled out the Brookfield volunteers for the "fortitude and address discovered in arresting so many of the insurgents." This fifty-six-man company included seventeen justices of the peace and militia officers who enlisted as privates, as did Rufus Putnam himself. They were a far cry from the "government puppies" and "shopkeepers, lawyers, and doctors" the rebels were sure they could defeat. An association of Continental officers, although complaining of arrears in pay, taxes, and private debts, publicly offered the General Court "every possible support to such measures as shall be adopted for the restoration of order." Their overwhelming support of government proves that Shays's Rebellion marked an attempt by people who, save for a small minority, had not fought in the Revolution to appropriate its symbols and overturn the political order it had established. The General Court could therefore almost unanimously condemn the "wicked, unnatural rebellion" undertaken by those popularly mocked as "Sons of Fraud and Violence" and "Sons of Licentiousness."[22]

SHAYS'S REBELLION WAS NOT only a military contest but an ideological struggle between two regions that had experienced and imagined the Revolution in radically different ways. The east, especially Boston, plausibly considered its leading role in the decade 1765–75 and its economic and political sufferings as proof of a unique public virtue and commitment to republicanism which ought to have convinced the relatively uninvolved west of its right to govern. The western rebels, with equal plausibility, regarded the Bay State's new constitution as a minority document which enabled the commercial east to rule without regard for postwar rural sufferings. The west sought to be left alone as it had been during the colonial period. It hoped to shape a state primarily concerned with guaranteeing local autonomy and pursuit of self-interest by reducing individual burdens. The east desired to instill in the west a greater commitment to sharing the Revolution's costs and to incorporate it into a republican community.

Eastern Massachusetts's long-term suffering in the cause of liberty further explains its anger that the Shaysites would use economic hardships to justify rebellion. Virtually depopulated during the siege of 1775–76, Boston supplied over 2,300 men who served more than three months in the army, many enlisting for other towns which did not meet their quotas. And as the "poor follows . . . barefooted, bare legged, and bare-breeched" struggled on, with "nothing but virtue [to] keep the army together," according to Colonel John Brooks, who commanded the anti-Shays troops in Middlesex, the coastal towns petitioned against the "inhumanity (for it deserves no milder name)" of "wicked farmers," "insolent with their thousands," as prices rose, trade stagnated, and "many perished." The General Court legislated against hoarding and gouging, as "many persons within the state are so lost to a sense of public virtue as to withhold the necessities of life and to refuse the public bills of credit." The plight of eastern Massachusetts, cradle of the Revolution, resembled that of a Continental army "starved at pleasure," as E. Wayne Carp has felicitously entitled his account of supplying the troops.[23]

As the ports starved, they could not help but observe, as historian Ralph V. Harlow has noted, that "by far the most important feature" of the state's Revolutionary economy was "neither the high cost of living, nor the profiteering schemes of the merchants, but the unusual prosperity of the agricultural population." Harlow's observation, while only partially true, is nevertheless significant in light of Oscar and Mary Handlin's subsequent conclusion that whereas "farmers close to the market profited from ever-increasing demands," the newly settled areas from which the Shaysites drew their greatest strength were "most depressed" by the shortage of cash during the Revolution to pay the debts they had contracted to set up their holdings. Harlow's perspective, drawn from eastern Massachusetts sources, reflects the seaboard's mistaken idea that the farmers of the state all enjoyed the same boom as the commercial farmers in established communities.[24]

The east's unfortunate experience with rural suppliers during the war also casts the government's callousness in the face of agrarian misery in a different light. First, it accounts for the seaboard's persistent litany that "luxury, luxury, the great source of distress, has here taken up her dismal abode." Noah Webster pronounced it a "fact, demonstrated by correct calculation, that the common people in the country drink rum and tea sufficient every year to pay the interest of the public debt, articles of luxury which so far from doing them any good, injure their morals, impair their health, and shorten their lives." A moralizing twenty-year-old John Quincy Adams thought that "the malcontents must look to themselves, to their idleness, to their dissipation, and extravagances" to cure the "deadly poison" which threatened the body politic. The General Court suggested the farmers meet its moderate program to ease the cash shortage halfway with "a reformation of manners . . . by recurring to the principles of integrity and public spirit, and the practice of industry, sobriety, economy, and fidelity in contracts, and by acquiescing in laws necessary for the public good."[25]

Reserving for later discussion the argument that the General Court in fact adopted a sensible policy to redress the farmers' grievances, port cities such as Boston and Charlestown had suffered from overtaxation, economic distress, and population loss since at least the 1740s. Even when they admitted rural misery, they could find little merit in the west's argument that a few years of hard times warranted destruction of the state's political system. A writer in the *Massachusetts Centinel* noted the "general discomfort among the inhabitants" and "granted that taxes are heavy." "But," he insisted, "though they are a burthen we are not sure they ought to be called a grievance." The General Court, in its "Address to the People," argued that they should "bear cheerfully" the economic consequences of the war and assumed as a matter of course the incorporation of virtuous self-sacrifice into Massachusetts's collective identity: "Can we be willing, that the history of the American Revolution shall be blackened with the tale that we refused to redeem the securities we had given to effect it, and shall our posterity blush to hear of it even because the perfidy of their ancestors exceeded their glory?"[26]

Eastern Massachusetts transformed its exceptional past leadership and sufferings into both a badge of virtue and an argument that those who had guided the Revolution ought to complete it. Shays's Rebellion threatened to ruin a state which "once fixed the attention of the world," where "liberty, the fairest gift of bounteous Heaven, . . . found an asylum." "Anti-Honestus" predicted the rebels' success would initiate "a long farewell to all our greatness." The town of Boston issued a circular letter warning that "next to crucifying the Savior of the World and despising their eternal Salvation, is the sin of a people in wantonly sporting with their chartered liberties, and despising their political salvation." The government's reaction collectively echoed one "Publius" who thought the Shaysites were "throw[ing] away blessings for which other nations pine and languish in vain" by spurning a constitution founded on "the collective wisdom and experience of the ages."[27]

Although western farmers' hardships from taxation and debt cannot be denied, they shared neither the east's sense of republican destiny nor its enthusiasm for the 1780 Constitution. Western Massachusetts remained one of the few areas in the nation untouched by combat. "The laggard revolutionists," as Robert J. Taylor has dubbed them, had little to do with the resistance movement until the "Intolerable Acts" shocked them out of their complacency. After the west closed its courts in 1774, county conventions and mobs kept them shut for much of the next decade. Debts and taxes remained unpaid though uncanceled. After denying the legitimacy of a state government based on resumption of a 1692 charter granted by a British monarch and rejecting the General Court's Constitution of 1778, the west sent few delegates to Boston during a bitter winter to draft the 1780 document that was finally approved.[28]

The 1780 Constitution lacked real legitimacy in the west. Several of the provisions against which the Shaysites railed were approved only by the divided votes of a small number of mostly eastern towns. Aspects of the court system passed as narrowly as 32 to 24; the state Senate carried 57 to 39. Sixty delegates approved a clause that legislators should be paid by the towns; 20 opposed. Property qualifications for voters carried 37 to 27. Originally, 251 towns out of 300 sent delegates.[29]

Governed by county and state bodies of which it did not approve, the west could regard the new state as a mere exchange of masters. In 1776, for instance, Pittsfield contended that the new justices revealed a "disposition triumphantly to ride over" the people and "worse than renew all our former oppression." From the birth of the nation until Shays's Rebellion, hundreds of petitions complained of taxes, debts, a shortage of money, and the structure of government.[30]

The divergent behavior of the Massachusetts backcountry and the eastern region can perhaps be best explained respectively by two concepts around which Richard Bushman and Oscar and Mary Handlin have structured books. The west tended to regard the new republic, as it had the provincial royal government, in terms of what Bushman calls the "protection covenant." The inhabitants were content to be ruled by a remote and unrepresentative elite provided it protected and did not oppress them. If government became active and intrusive, and if petitioning for redress of grievances failed, the people had the right to resist as necessary. But after two decades of struggle, eastern Massachusetts regarded the state as the "Commonwealth" the Handlins describe. It represented a "moral whole" and required an active citizenry dedicated to a public interest transcending personal and local concerns.[31]

How one judges Shays's Rebellion depends on the behavior not only of the rebels but of the government as well. In fact, the legislature lived up to its claim to be "lenient and merciful."[32] During the autumn and winter of 1786, it tried to meet the grievances of the people and was slow to undertake military preparations even in the face of armed rebellion. Because many who opposed the rebels recognized the validity of their demands, the government proved reluctant to shed blood and sought reconciliation rather than retribution. Finally, the state's voters, even with the insurgents disfranchised, repudiated the Bowdoin administration that insisted on punishing them.

The special fall session of the General Court called to deal with the insurrection went a long way toward redressing the Shaysites' substantive grievances although it rejected any restructuring of the government. To ease the west's financial crunch, debtors and creditors could now try suits under £4, which constituted the majority, before justices of the peace instead of dealing with expensive courts and lawyers. Moreover, both debts and taxes could be settled with household goods as well as real estate, the value to be determined by referees. This measure was to last eight months, at which time a new court could renew it. To remedy the shortage of cash, the state prepared to mint $70,000 in coin and to sell off £163,000 of Maine lands, which would reduce the state debt by about 15 percent. The November acts clearly could have tided the protestors over until the new legislature could be chosen in May, at which time they could have made good their claim to represent the popular will. The legislature also offered to pardon anyone who would lay down his arms by January 1, 1787, and in an "Address to the People" attempted to explain the necessity of high taxes and the "ruinous effects of luxury and licentiousness," which had driven people in debt. It also explained the new laws and asserted a general disposition to accommodate grievances without undermining public credit and authority. The legislature's reforms were not without effect. Arrested insurgent Dr. Isaac Cheney commented that he was "well satisfied" with the measures and only wished they had passed "three months sooner," as then the people "would not have taken up arms against government." On January 2 the Hampshire convention urged the rebels to disarm and "join with us in our prayer to the legislature for a redress of grievances," as "the General Court, at their last session, did spend much of their time . . . and attend to the prayers of the people, and still do show a will to hear their complaints."[33]

But if the General Court's conciliatory attitude converted some recalcitrants, it was by no means the product of sheer goodwill and statesmanship. Not only was Massachusetts broke—it had to borrow £6,000 from Boston merchants to launch Lincoln's expedition and accepted articles useful for war in payment of taxes—but the insurgents' complaints, if not their mode of redressing them, were general throughout the state. The Adams family seat of Braintree expressed much the same grievances as the conventions; in Boston itself, Dr. Charles Jarvis, representing "Mr. H[ancock]'s friends," "censured the government severely" and "trumpeted it around that had *he* [Hancock] been governor this difficulty would not have taken place." John Pickering reported to his brother Timothy that "a very small part" of Essex County's people favored the insurgents, but Thomas Cabot informed Benjamin Lincoln that "even in the town of Salem, upon a small success on the side of Shays . . . a great many would have joined him, at least in sentiment." Winthrop Sargent, too, discovered "a shameful amount of exertion and a secret inclination in favor of the insurgents" in the eastern counties.[34]

Uncertainty characterized the sentiments of many from beginning to end. In early September numerous towns in both Middlesex and Bristol petitioned the governor not to use force and instead to give them a chance "to endeavor by every rational argument to dissuade those who seem refractory from measures which tend immediately to destroy the fabric of our government, and by knowing what are the real grounds of their complaints unitedly join in legal and constitutional measures to obtain redress of what may be found to be real grievances." Boston's Peter Thacher recalled how "Colonel [Oliver] Prescott of Groton and Mr. [Samuel Phillips] Savage [of Concord] came to town frightened out of their wits and begged that the orders for the militia might be recalled." Perhaps the most representative response to the rebellion came from the small town of Rowe. Addressing a letter "to all it may concern" on December 4, 1786, "the inhabitants of this town, being repeatedly requested to join in the dispute between the government and those called the Regulating party," and being "under great disadvantage as to obtaining the true cause of the dispute which renders it impossible for us to determine what is best to be done," simply decided to send as many men "as can conveniently march . . . to that place that they can obtain the best information of the true state of affairs and (if need be) join that party they shall judge to be in the right."[35]

In consequence of such ambivalence, the General Court pursued a vacillating policy. From September to November 1786, the conciliatory attitude of the House prevailed over the more militant action favored by the Senate. In November, after someone claiming to be Shays circulated a letter ordering the people to arm themselves and be ready to fight at a minute's notice, the representatives finally agreed to suspend habeas corpus; at the end of the month the General Court sent out the light horse to seize the Middlesex ringleaders even while alleviating some grievances and offering a general pardon. Only after these measures failed to halt the court closings and rumors of marches—given winter travel conditions and poor communications, it is probable many rebels had no idea what the General Court had done—did the legislature authorize Lincoln's expedition. From January to May 1787 the state was at its most repressive; the twelve prospective executions and deprivations of political rights for all identifiable rebels angered even government supporters. The bill authorizing the rebels' trials only passed the House 58 to 52 with a motion to consider failing 56 to 55. The 1787 spring elections overwhelmingly repudiated Governor Bowdoin in favor of the more lenient Hancock. Even with the Shaysites disfranchised, the voters elected a General Court sympathetic to the rebels. The legislature then proceeded to moderate the state's fiscal policy to general satisfaction and to restore to the proscribed traitors their full rights as citizens. Hancock pardoned all those under sentence except for a few looters.[36]

The confusion over what ought to be done about a rebellion whose nature, justice, and extent puzzled the government led to extreme reluctance to use force. The pains generals Shepherd and Lincoln took to avoid fighting the rebels demonstrates the hesitancy with which the government moved. After warning Shays not to pass over an imaginary line within firing distance of the Springfield arsenal which the government troops defended, Shepherd "ordered a field piece fired in a different direction from the party, in hopes to deter them from progressing further." After performing the most "painful duty . . . in his life" and firing on the insurgents, Shepherd refused some of his troops' request that he either continue to fire on or pursue the fleeing rebels. Reporting to Governor Bowdoin that "the unhappy time is come in which we have been obliged to shed blood," Shepherd stated that "had I been disposed to destroy them, I might have charged upon their rear and flanks with my infantry and the two field pieces and have killed the greater part of his whole army in twenty-five minutes." Governor Bowdoin praised Shepherd for having "answered the hopes and expectations of the country" by defeating the rebels with "the loss of so few lives." "It is not my wish to have the people of the Commonwealth destroyed, for this would weaken it, but that they may be reduced by the gentlest means possible into the path of their duty," he concluded, thereby expressing the general consensus.[37]

For his part, General Lincoln not only proceeded with his army so as to minimize confrontations but became the foremost advocate for a quick restoration to the insurgents of their full rights of citizenship. When his men marched west, Lincoln stressed that "they do not in any way insult or injure the inhabitants" and warned the soldiers "not [to] take upon themselves to determine the political character of men should violence or insult be offered." Any unauthorized "marauding or any infringing on the peace" would meet with "exemplary punishment." Lincoln's only lapse from mildness came when he found the court-martial punishment decreed for some of his own men for looting too mild: they had to stand publicly for an hour wearing signs "For Plundering." He even believed the temporary disfranchisement to be suffered by most rebels too harsh, as he explained in a private letter to Governor Bowdoin which became the basis for their quick reinstatement to full citizenship: "We have invariably said to them you are wrong in flying to arms. You should seek redress in a constitutional way. These observations were undoubtedly just, but will they not now complain, and say that we have cut them off from all hope of redress from that quarter; for we have denied them a representation in that legislature, by whose laws they must be governed. While they are in this situation, they will never be reconciled to government, nor will they submit to the terms of it from any other motive than fear enlivened by a constant military armed force entered over them." Lincoln concluded by blaming the insurgents not so much for their rebellion but for their repeated sloth in not electing representatives to the General Court: "We have much more now to fear from a certain business which has seized upon a great proportion of our citizens, who have been totally inattentive to the exercise of those rights conveyed to them by the Constitution of this Commonwealth." He had carefully considered the problem of reconciling the highly mobile insurgents, capable either of hit-and-run attacks or of depriving the Commonwealth of many useful citizens by heading north or west. He recommended "all that mercy which the good of the state shall admit . . . with a grace that she may evidence a disposition to forgive, to embrace cordially those who are forgiven."[38]

Seeking consensus in a severely divided community, the government only resorted to arms after attempts to negotiate, redress grievances, and arrest ringleaders had all failed. By delaying so long, and demonstrating the reasonableness of its final resort to force, Massachusetts ensured that a great majority would side with government even though many of the volunteers shared the Shaysites' grievances. Perhaps 7,000 men participated in the January and February expeditions, as opposed to the insurgents' maximum, short-lived strength of 3,000. In actual military operations, conducted with minimal damage after repeated warnings, the state again used force sparingly. Finally, in pardoning almost all the rebels and reintegrating them quickly into civic life, Massachusetts sought to reestablish the communal consensus that underlay early American political theory and practice. Samuel Adams's cries to hang the traitors were clearly the exception, not the rule.[39]

BY QUELLING SHAYS'S REBELLION so successfully and painlessly, however, Massachusetts reclaimed its glory as the new nation's most energetic and public-spirited state. On the eve of and during the rebellion, the Bay State was in despair: "Oh Massachusetts! Oh Massachusetts!" lamented a typical writer in the *Boston Magazine*. "Thou who wast Chief in Thy Country! The elder born and the most lovely of the daughters of Columbia! How Thou art fallen! Thy gold is truly become dust and Thy glory is departed from Thee!" But as the state began to arm, "it is more like the year 1775 than any thing I have seen since," Henry Jackson reported to Henry Knox, remarking on how citizens flocked to join quickly forming light horse regiments and volunteer companies. The *Massachusetts Centinel* noticed that "the late commotions in this state have awakened that spirit of military ambition which so nobly distinguished us in 1774 and 1775."[40]

In addition to not shaming "the ghosts of murdered heroes," Shays's Rebellion gave Massachusetts the added bonus of writing yet another glorious page in the annals of human history. As "Historicus" explained in the *Massachusetts Centinel:*

> In monarchical and aristocratical governments, when the people alone are concerned in the rebellion, as soon as it is known, the hand of power is immediately employed to crush it, if possible. From the nature of republics and democratic governments, the proceedings must and ought to be different, and time and leisure given for the operation of human passions (unless the rebellion be so daring as that self-defense requires the exertion of an immediate force), and to offer light and conviction to the deluded, a reasonable time to return to their sense of duty, and if they do not, to unite the sentiments and resolution of the body politic, by effective measures to be taken with them, and effective they must be, or government is at an end, and the peace and prosperity of the people destroyed.

The harsh repression that had hitherto characterized nations' responses to rebellions, Massachusetts realized, would poorly serve a republic dependent on the affections of the people. As Minot wrote in his history, "Upon the histories of European nations, a reliance could be placed so far only as the genius and circumstances of the people of the two hemispheres agreed. But who could say, that principles and measures which might persuade or terrify the minds of the mountaineers of Scotland or Wales, would have the same effect on the unconquerable spirit of the inhabitants of Massachusetts?" Eschewing the bloodbaths that had put down earlier civil wars, Massachusetts provided once again, as Henry Van Schaack realized, a model for the world: "I wish people cooly to view the wickedness and ill policy of those who have lived through preceding civil wars; let us in this commonwealth lay down a mode of conduct as will be worth imitating by after ages."[41]

In the *Federalist Papers,* defending the United States Constitution as a "novelty in the political world" which had "no model on the face of the globe," James Madison could nevertheless retain some hope that the United States might provide "a republican remedy for the diseases most incident to republican governments." The worst of these diseases was faction, which begat domestic insurrections of the sort that had plagued the republics of ancient Greece, Rome, and Renaissance Italy. Within four years of the Peace of Paris, Massachusetts had already pioneered in a republican remedy for the disease of rebellion. Its spokesmen were already describing America's Revolution as unique in achieving permanent political stability. None other than Shays's chief Bostonian defender, Dr. Charles Jarvis, proclaimed in 1788 that "in other countries, . . . unhappily for mankind, the history of their respective revolutions has been written in blood, and it is in this only that any great or important changes in our political situation has been effected without public commotions." Minot, too, made Massachusetts's successful resolution of the insurgency seem even more spectacular by noting that "no rebellion had heretofore marked the annals of Massachusetts, either under royal or republican rule," and that its new "Constitution was also recent in its standing, and unsettled by practice." Nevertheless, with no historical precedents to guide it, "the manner in which these difficulties were suppressed does much honor to government." "The lenity of government . . . must attach every man to a Constitution . . . which governs its subjects without oppression, and reclaims them without severity." To contemporary Massachusetts statesmen, Shays's Rebellion was quickly transformed from a manifestation of social tension into a symbol of how Massachusetts had solved the age-old problem of preventing revolution from deteriorating into a state of anarchy.[42]

The significance of Massachusetts's response to Shays's Rebellion has yet to be integrated into either the national consciousness or the historiography of the uprising, republicanism, or the "Critical Period." Its major importance lies not in the context of agrarian protest or as the catalyst of a national constitution already in the planning stage. Rather, it showed how republics could maintain the political stability that had historically eluded them. Seeking to conciliate the disaffected and dealing mildly with rebellion, Massachusetts could resume its proper role as a "City Upon a Hill."

6

REGULATORS AND WHITE INDIANS
The Agrarian Resistance in Post-Revolutionary New England

Alan Taylor

The New England "Regulators" (or "Shaysites") of 1786–87 have long posed a puzzle because their lackluster resistance fell so short of their fiery and defiant rhetoric. As farmers and rural artisans distressed by taxes and debts during the economically troubled 1780s, the Regulators had serious and pressing grievances. They spoke with dread of impending "slavery": of losing their property and so their cherished independence as freeholders. Taking up arms and mustering by the thousand, they forcibly closed the county courts and promised to repel any attempts to suppress their protests. Yet, when the Friends of Government responded with military counterforce, pressing the Regulators to surrender or fight, they quickly broke and fled. In the pivotal confrontations at Exeter, New Hampshire (September 20–21, 1786), and at Springfield (January 25, 1787) and Petersham (February 4, 1787) in western Massachusetts, the Friends of Government proved far more ready to inflict and absorb bloodshed.[1]

During the three decades following the Revolutionary War, central Maine—then a part of the Commonwealth of Massachusetts—hosted a very different agrarian resistance: diffuse, protracted, theatrical, partially successful, and little known. Determined to hold their new homesteads without buying titles from nonresident

---

From a paper presented at the Bicentennial Conference on Shays's Rebellion, 1986, sponsored by the Colonial Society of Massachusetts.

land speculators, known as "Great Proprietors," the settlers secretly organized armed companies of men disguised as Indians to frustrate enforcement of the Commonwealth's land laws. Although their rhetoric resembled the Regulators', central Maine's settlers adopted very different tactics. Eschewing the Regulators' massive, aggressive offensives against courts and state legislatures, the "White Indians" sought to nullify the local operation of offending laws by cordoning off their communities and by adopting fearsome disguises and bloodcurdling threats to scare off interloping surveyors and sheriffs. Unless deputies could serve writs on settlers targeted for prosecution and unless proprietary surveyors could run lines to prove that the accused dwelled within the proprietors' particular claim, Maine's Great Proprietors could not prosecute the ejectment and trespass suits necessary to reestablish their legal control over the contested land. Only on the rare occasions when the authorities jailed a suspected White Indian did the armed settlers muster in large numbers drawn from several settlements for a quick nighttime descent on the county seat to set their comrade free.[2]

By examining in detail two contrasting confrontations, one at Exeter, New Hampshire, in 1786 and the other in central Maine in 1808, this essay explores why the Regulation collapsed so quickly and why the White Indians persisted long enough to win a compromise settlement. I will argue that both Regulators and White Indians clung to a prerepublican political culture based upon a "protection covenant" that simultaneously inspired and limited their protests. Accepting that gentlemen would rule but insistent upon their right to suspend particular offensive laws, rural folk resorted to limited, symbolic violence. Their aim was not to seize power, or to challenge the world of ranks and orders, but to jolt and reclaim wayward rulers to a sense of their duty. However, rather than backing down, as the Regulators expected, gentlemen responded with surprising force and determination; they had renounced the protection covenant that legitimated localist, extralegal resistance. Hence, rural protest could only survive in the new republic by adopting the White Indians' techniques designed to avoid the direct battlefield confrontations with self-confident gentlemen that had so unnerved and shattered their Regulator brethren. By decentralizing their resistance and by performing frightening rituals in disguise, the settlers raised a protective barrier between their settlements and encroaching authority. The White Indians reversed the imbalanced self-assurance that ordinarily served gentlemen so well in facing down yeomen insurgents: behind masks settlers acted with a new verve against stunned officials, who often lost their nerve.

IN 1786 MANY NEW HAMPSHIRE yeomen, especially those in Rockingham County, were angry at their unresponsive state government. Ignoring urgent petitions from the countryside, the legislature had refused to alleviate debtor distress with an emission of inflationary paper money. Instead, New Hampshire's rulers passed a provocative bill removing legal impediments to British subjects collecting debts within the state. Wild but alarming rumors hinted at still worse to come: heavy taxes to compensate Loyalist refugees for their confiscated property. Driven to act by legislative indifference and inflammatory rumor, 200 men mustered on the morning of September 20 in Kingston, six miles west of Exeter, where the legislature was in session. About one-third of the insurgents bore firearms; the rest carried swords or clubs. Led by militia officers and following a beating drum, the insurgents marched that afternoon in military order into Exeter, surrounded the meetinghouse where the legislators were convened, and swore they would suffer no one to depart until they received a satisfactory response to their petitions for redress. A hostile observer, the young lawyer William Plumer, described the Regulators as "dirty, ragged fellows—many of them were young and most of them ignorant." New Hampshire's president, General John Sullivan, responded with "a cool and deliberate speech" denouncing their request as "an outrageous insult upon the Legislature." Determined to ignore the "banditti," the legislators continued to deliberate as if they were not surrounded by angry, armed men.[3]

The standoff continued until dusk when William Plumer and nineteen other "Gentlemen of the first rank and education" resident in Exeter began beating a drum, hollered "Huzza for Government!" three times, and marched unarmed directly toward the startled insurgents. "The mob were greatly frightened, and in their confusion some ran, and others leaped into the graveyard," Plumer reported. Sullivan led the legislators out onto the street while the insurgents dispersed to their camp a mile outside of town.[4]

That evening Sullivan summoned the militia from New Hampshire's eastern towns to assemble in Exeter at dawn to suppress the insurgency. In the morning Sullivan sent a body of cavalry and light infantry "accompanied by many gentlemen of the first rank and education, who appeared as volunteers" in pursuit of the insurgents. The alarmed Regulators broke and fled. Some tried to organize a stand at the bridge across King's Falls but hesitated when their officers ordered them to fire. The gentlemen and militia surged into the Regulators' ranks, disarming and capturing thirty-nine and sending the rest into headlong flight homeward. A gentleman observed that government's commander, General Joseph Cilly, a Portsmouth lawyer, "distinguished himself by rushing sword in hand among ye rioters, & pulling them as a butcher would seize sheep in a flock."[5]

To seal their triumph, the Friends of Government hauled their prisoners back to Exeter, where they ritually disgraced the captured insurgents and celebrated the militia's loyalty. While a band played "the rogue's march" and onlookers jeered, the prisoners were forced to remove their hats and parade twice through the militia drawn up on both sides of the main street, "that," in Plumer's words, "in that humiliating condition they might behold a few of the many who were ready to defend the government." He was pleased to report that the prisoners found the ritual "a mortifying situation."[6]

The next day, September 22, the ritual humiliation continued and moved indoors as the legislature separately examined and sternly admonished the captured Regulator leaders. The victors were eager to spare their prisoners' lives in return for public confessions. Plumer reported that the Regulators' two commanders, Major James Cochran of Pembroke and Captain Joseph French of Hampstead, responded as desired: "Capt. French discovered great contrition. He gave satisfactory evidence that he was an honest man, but had been seduced by designing men. He frankly confessed that he had forfeited his life and implored their mercy.... Major Cochran said but little, but was much affected. He acknowledged he had forfeited his life and fortune to the State . . . [and had] been deceived by false representations; that he had taken a false and hasty step, but as it was his first offence, he now humbly entreated that Court, whom he had so daringly insulted a few hours since, to save him from ruin." The delighted legislators pardoned and released French, Cochran, and all the other prisoners save six who were indicted by the state superior court for riot (rather than treason). Again the captives displayed humble contrition. When asked for his plea, Samuel Morse dropped to his knees and replied, "Guilty, very guilty." According to Plumer, another prisoner "fainted and fell, and it was some time before he was able to answer *guilty*." In return, the court released the indicted six on modest bail for trial at the next term, when they were convicted and punished with light fines. By so shrewdly handling power and leniency, the Friends of Government completely stifled insurgency in New Hampshire, enabling the legislature in January 1787 forthrightly to reject any program of debtor relief.[7]

The Friends of Government noted the contrast between their own assured self-confidence and their agrarian foes' insecure confusion, reassuring proof that yeoman insurgents could not withstand determined gentlemen. The Friends of Government expressed contempt for their foes as, in Plumer's words, "an ignorant lawless band of unprincipled ruffians," who were no match for troops properly commanded by genteel officers. Of New Hampshire's defeated Regulators the Congregational minister Jeremy Belknap wrote, "Had these men been engaged in a good cause, and commanded by proper officers, they would have maintained the honor of their country, and fought her battles with ardor and perseverance; but, conscious of their inconsistency in opposing a government of their own establishing, their native fortitude forsook them; and they gave an example of the most humiliating submission. Most of them professed to be ashamed of their conduct, and their shame appeared to be sincere." After the King's Falls scuffle, Plumer reported, "we returned to town in great order and regularity, without the loss of blood on either side. President Sullivan has acquired credit by his prudence, caution and firmness." Another delighted gentleman concluded, "The whole affair was conducted with much coolness and moderation." The Friends of Government saw the episode as vindicating genteel values, as proving the supremacy of moderation, coolness, order, regularity, prudence, caution, and firmness when opposed by the "banditti's" perceived excess, fervor, disorder, license, impudence, haste, and cowardice.[8]

In a few days New Hampshire's Regulators passed rapidly from mobilization through confrontation to humiliation and submission, a process that lasted months in neighboring Massachusetts. In a peculiarly telescoped form, the Exeter episode exemplifies the New England Regulators' paradoxical but characteristic volatility: their determined defiance dissolving into ashamed obeisance almost overnight. In late 1786 and early 1787 in New Hampshire and Massachusetts, rural towns once alive with angry, determined crowds quickly reverted to abashed compliance with the law once the Friends of Government displayed first their power and then their mercy.[9]

THE REGULATORS' SUDDEN COLLAPSE was a consequence of their political worldview, of the notions they carried in their minds to Exeter's meetinghouse, Springfield's armory, and Petersham's campground. Contrary to the interpretation of the Regulators as egalitarian democrats, the American Revolution had had little impact—as of 1786—on the yeomanry's adherence to the protection covenant at the heart of colonial America's political culture. This protection covenant insisted that society was fundamentally riven between "rulers" and "the ruled." The yeomanry expected political leadership from "the few," from gentlemen with the requisite social standing, wealth, education, and external contacts to successfully conduct county, state, and national governance. According to the protection covenant, "rulers" deserved grateful obedience so long as they safeguarded the liberties and property of "the ruled." But this formula could be reversed to justify crowd actions intended to discipline wayward gentlemen; rulers seen to betray liberty and prey on the people's property temporarily forfeited popular allegiance.[10]

Gathered in crowds, yeomen did not seek to supplant elite governance, but merely to "regulate" the proper balance between the rulers and the ruled, between authority and liberty, when the former encroached on the latter. By administering short, sharp rebukes, crowds meant to jolt wayward gentlemen into resuming a proper solicitude for the common good. A successful crowd action reclaimed rulers who had become threats to their people's liberty and well-being. For example, in 1766 the inhabitants of Scarborough, Maine, were angry with their leading man, the merchant Richard King, for embezzling the parish's funds and for aggressively prosecuting his many debtors. So they manhandled King, broke his house's windows, wrecked his furniture, burned his business papers, killed several of his livestock, and torched his barn. A member of the crowd explained that "it was a good thing, and would do *King good,* and *make him a better man.*" Indeed, Scarborough's residents saw no contradiction between violently recalling King to his duty while continuing to elect him to the town offices that no one else in town could perform so well.[11]

The New England Regulators did not intend to overthrow their state governments but simply to suspend execution of particular "oppressive" and "unconstitutional" laws until their rulers could rectify their mistakes. Court closings simultaneously bought time and alerted rulers that they had violated their covenant to behave as "political fathers." Once they had forced their rulers to do their duty, the Regulators believed that they could quickly and quietly return to their farms and to grateful obedience. The New Hampshire Regulators surrounded the state legislature to demand action that only the captive representatives could enact. In effect, the angry men without doors were also the hostages of the legislators within doors.[12]

Unfortunately for the Regulators, New England's gentlemen refused to play their assigned role in the protection covenant because they were ahead of the yeomanry in breaking with the colonial era's political culture. In the short run, the Friends of Government were more profoundly affected by the recent Revolution's new republican notions, albeit in a self-interested manner that sought to perpetuate their wealth and authority. In 1786 William Plumer insisted that "the Legislature ought to give, and not receive, the tone to the people. The *few,* and not the many, are *wise,* and ought to bear rule." In the wake of the Revolution, gentlemen could insist that at one annual moment—election day—the distinction between rulers and the ruled dissolved and that until the next election this moment invested rulers with the full power of popular sovereignty. In their view, the electoral moment denied the people any legitimate extralegal power to discipline their representatives between elections. Once necessary to frustrate British rule and Loyalist plots, the extralegal crowd became, in the gentlemen's opinion, a dangerous anachronism in the new republican order. If crowd actions persisted, alarmed gentlemen foresaw an anarchy that would ultimately provoke the tyranny of a military despot: a Cromwell or a Caesar. As a result, mixed fear and assurance impelled the Friends of Government to regard the Regulation as a challenge they needed forcefully to repel: fear that the infant republic would fail, assurance that only the elected few could exercise any legitimate power between elections.[13]

In sum, the Revolution wrought a dangerous divergence in the political worldviews nurtured by yeomen and gentlemen. Regulators expected that they could easily command legislative redress with direct action; instead, they provoked a violent reaction from authorities convinced that the new republican order could not survive any concession to the extralegal crowd. The Regulators failed because, to their surprise and confusion, they encountered determined gentlemen ready to kill rather than give way to extralegal crowds. The Regulators' consequent confusion and disorientation was painfully evident in their abashed submissions, their meek participation in the ritual abasements demanded by the Friends of Government. The gentlemen's unexpected prowess and subsequent leniency convinced most Regulators that they must have fundamentally miscalculated in their understanding of the prevailing balance of the protection covenant; the sequence of defeat, public humiliation, and abated punishment led most to conclude that their rulers had not transgressed. Consequently, it is small wonder that most quickly lapsed into the passive obedience that was the political norm when rulers did not seem to be encroaching on the liberty and property of the ruled. The exceptions proved the rule; in parts of Massachusetts vindictive Friends of Government did not follow victory with lenience, arousing a brief backlash that nearly defeated ratification of the Federal Constitution in that state in February 1788; but Antifederalism proved short-lived in Massachusetts, losing its majority in the former Regulator strongholds by the early 1790s to the Federalists, the renamed Friends of Government.[14]

ON JANUARY 28, 1808, a very different confrontation occurred in Fairfax (now Albion), a new hill country settlement in central

Maine. Pitt Dillingham, a merchant and a deputy sheriff, drove his sleigh northeastward away from Augusta, a commercial center on the Kennebec River, into the backcountry for a parlay with Fairfax's White Indians. He arrived at Wilder Broad's tavern to find 400 spectators waiting. Within an hour about seventy-four disguised and musket-armed White Indians (or "Liberty-Men") appeared on the crest of an adjacent hill. They marched in single file behind "an elegant standard" toward Dillingham, the tavern, and the crowd. Wheeling with military precision before the tavern, the White Indians fired a deafening volley into the air. Proceeding into an adjoining field, they formed a half circle and summoned Dillingham to enter and state his business. He described the scene:

> They were dressed with caps about three feet high, masks, blankets, moccasins on their feet. Their caps and masks were decorated with the most uncouth images imaginable. The masks were some of bearskin, some sheepskin, some stuck over with hog's bristles &c. To give a true description of them is impossible. The frantic imagination of a lunatic in the depth of desperation could not conceive of more horrid or ghastly specters. Their savage appearance would strike terror in the boldest heart ... and in that situation with about seventy-four of those horrid visages on one side under arms, about four hundred spectators on the other & encircled in this ring I was ordered to speak.

Dillingham added that their appearance "shook every fibre of my frame." Six days after his ordeal he wrote, "No earthly consideration would tempt me to go among them again provided they wore the same appearance they then did." In contrast to the Exeter confrontation, at Fairfax fear and indecision gripped the gentleman.[15]

As Dillingham attested, the White Indians took unusual pains to enact the most graphic and psychologically chilling performances they could devise. The settlers' poverty, relative isolation, hardships, and limited education led gentlemen to consider them as little better than savages, as literally "White Indians." The settlers exploited this stereotype to inculcate an inhibiting dread among their foes. Periodically the White Indians threatened to burn the buildings or poison the inhabitants of commercial communities, like Augusta, considered noxious for assisting proprietary posses and surveys. At night White Indians crept into the commercial towns to drop dreadfully imaginative anonymous letters around the homes of sheriffs, lawyers, surveyors, and land agents. These letters simultaneously threatened the recipients with destruction and demonstrated their vulnerability to secret nocturnal visits. The Great Proprietors' Augusta lawyers received sketches of themselves dangling from the gallows, sketches flanked with drawings of matching tomahawks dripping blood. Colonel Samuel Thatcher, Lincoln County's sheriff, awoke one morning to find that overnight the White Indians had left an open coffin on his doorstep. For its shock value, some White Indians killed, roasted, and ate the horses of persistent deputies before their eyes. While canvassing the backcountry for timber trespassers, Charles Vaughan, a land agent for one company of Great Proprietors, encountered a board posted to a tree addressing him by name and, in his words, "assuring me that there are Indians ready to fire at me with guns doubly charged and with a hand (*over death*) pointing to the trespassing ground, and another hand (*over life*) pointing to the road I came from." Suddenly feeling underpaid, Vaughan followed the hand of life, hastily retracing his steps homeward to devote the rest of the afternoon to a letter demanding more money from his employers.[16]

The White Indians' performances featured violent and blasphemous language, expressions of a folk culture where oaths carried a magical power to frighten and harm. Before dawn November 13, 1795, ten armed White Indians burst upon the Balltown (now Jefferson) campsite of Ephraim Ballard's proprietary survey party, awakening them with deafening shots into the air. Pressing a loaded musket to Ballard's chest, the leader profanely bellowed, "Deliver up, deliver up all, God damn you, deliver the compass, deliver up the cannister, God damn you, take nothing out, if you do you are a dead man." Ballard delivered. When Elliot G. Vaughan, a proprietary agent, visited Bristol in August 1810, a crowd gathered to warn him, "Never show your head in Bristol again." Vaughan remembered that one settler angrily "wish'd to god he could see my blood on the burying ground above there where a number of their friends and relatives were who had been wounded & killed by the Indians and in the most irritating manner added God Damn you I wish I could meet you in some convenient place." Vaughan departed to spend the night in the neighboring town, where long after midnight a crowd kept the terrified agent awake by "stoning the house & making almost every noise that can be conceived of." Vaughan did not return.[17]

Although decentralized and intermittent, the settlers' resistance could suddenly appear extensive, formidable, and elaborate. According to one chagrined deputy, the White Indians' patrols could, by sounding their tin horns, readily turn out "a number sufficient to effect any of their purposes." Deputy Sheriff Henry Johnson of Winslow testified that the White Indians "had every appearance of military discipline & subordination, and obeyed the commands of a person they called their chief. Centinels were regularly posted and relieved and . . . every avenue to their settlement was strictly guarded to prevent the approach of any officer, and [they] emphatically declared they would kill any officer who should serve any writs of ejectment or upon whom any such writs were found." The White Indians stockpiled ammunition in special magazines, sought out legal advice, levied special taxes to meet their expenses, administered local justice, and held periodic mass meetings to promulgate their "laws," burn effigies, and sustain fervor for their cause. After touring the backcountry, Pitt Dillingham described the resistance as "a very generall and serious combination [that] had been entered into by several thousands in the county."[18]

By avoiding overt confrontations with large numbers, the White Indians sustained their resistance within a legal gray area short of the legal definition of an "insurrection," rendering it impossible for the authorities legitimately to mobilize the militia. So long as the White Indians confined themselves to frightening performances conducted by small parties, the legal authorities had to rely on deputy sheriffs and posses. Charles Hayden, a proprietary surveyor, knew that posses were useless against the White Indians: "They appear in their disguise, commit an outrage & disappear. I think if the sheriff, officers & magistrates should go into that section of the country they would not find any body of armed men to read the riot act to; all would appear in peace." In February 1808 a tavern keeper sympathetic to the White Indians boasted to George Bender, an emissary to the region from Governor James Sullivan, that even if the militia invaded "tho a body of 500 Indians were assembled yet when the troops reached the spot they would find nothing to fire at but trees, nobody would know who the Indians were, or where they had gone to." Aware that considerations of expense forbade a long-lasting occupation, the settlers were confident that any militia expedition would quickly withdraw, allowing the smoldering resistance to resume.[19]

In addition to preserving a useful legal ambiguity, the settlers' tactics helped preserve the solidarity critical to the resistance's survival, for, like their Regulator brethren, few White Indians were prepared for open, sustained rebellion against their rulers. Bloodshed would invite state retribution and alienate many of the supporters of resistance. But the White Indians saw no need for their foes to know the limits on the actions which the White Indians could pursue without disrupting their tenuous coalition. Through terrifying displays, the White Indians inculcated in their foes an inhibiting dread beyond their actual danger. In this way they sought maximum leverage at minimal risk. They meant for outsiders to expect the worst and so treat them with great caution. By the shrewd manipulation of terrifying imagery the White Indians meant to enjoy the paralyzing effect of bloodshed without its corrosive consequences for their resistance.[20]

For years the strategy worked. Proprietary surveyors and deputy sheriffs repeatedly abandoned forays into the White Indians' settlements at the first sign of trouble; but, despite repeated pleas, the Great Proprietors could not persuade the governor and General Court that an actual insurrection—requiring militia—existed in central Maine. To secure permission for his deputies to serve nonproprietary writs, Kennebec County's sheriff, Arthur Lithgow, sent Pitt Dillingham to Fairfax in January 1808 to assure the White Indians he would restrain the service of proprietary writs. For a county sheriff to negotiate with and appease what, by law, was a criminal conspiracy represented a remarkable concession. But Lithgow was not alone, for Augusta's worried lawyers supported him, and his counterpart in Lincoln County, Edmund Bridge, applied to the governor for permission to suspend the service of all writs, those for creditors as well as for proprietors, in the militant backcountry. Not subject to the same pressures, Governor Sullivan in Boston felt that Maine's magistrates had taken leave of their senses; he rebuked Bridge and invited the Council to sack Lithgow. Nonetheless, Lithgow's successor and Edmund Bridge had little choice but quietly to restrain writ service in the backcountry settlements during the ensuing year.[21]

The Great Proprietors were frustrated with the settlers' ability to deter surveyors and deputies with threats and small patrols, neither of which constituted clear-cut evidence of an insurrection. In August 1801 General Henry Knox, the preeminent Great Proprietor as well as a staunch Friend of Government, fumed, "At present a shapeless rumour exists." He added, "Our great object is to oblige them to avow their designs. At present they act by dark sayings and equivocal conduct." In October 1809 a proprietary pamphleteer complained of the "unknown men, who dare not *name* or *shew* themselves . . . who are one day said to be *many and powerful* when it is designed that they shall *inspire terror,* and the next day are represented as *few and contemptible,* when it is intended to *prevent any force being kept up against them.*" In 1870 James W. North, a proprietor's grandson, wrote in his *History of Augusta:* "This mode of guerrilla warfare was worse than open and formal insurrection. In the latter, a crisis would soon be reached, and a remedy provided; but in the former, disguise and secrecy prevented the notoriety which would call for the intervention of the strong arm of government, and the guerrillas as effectually attained their object." Indeed, it is a revealing measure of their success that, in contrast to the Regulators' short, dramatic movement, the White Indians' resistance was a diffuse, protracted affair without a clear-cut climax. Their tactics worked so well that, for lack of an Exeter, Springfield, or Petersham, the White Indians have virtually escaped historians' attention.[22]

THE DIFFERENT DENOUEMENTS OF the New England Regulation and the White Indian resistance contributed to different political legacies in their respective towns. Paradoxically, the Regulation's sudden, dramatic collapse helped preserve most of its participants' allegiance to a modified protection covenant upheld on election day, but on no other day, by the Federalists. Conversely, the White Indians' protracted struggle gradually weaned them from the protection covenant in favor of active participation in the electoral crusades sponsored by the Jeffersonians. The White Indians' reluctance to attack the courts or their legislature attests that they had begun to adapt to the republican order. The stalemate that resulted from their successful resistance and the obduracy of their Federalist rulers impelled the settlers to complete that adaptation.[23]

New England's Federalist and Jeffersonian leaders were gentlemen who shared a commitment to entrepreneurial values, commercial development, and republican institutions. The two competing elites differed over how to approach the electorate for support. Entrenched in power, the Federalists hoped to sustain themselves as a governing elite with the consent of the people, by appealing to their traditional longing for a harmonious, corporate Commonwealth directed by a paternalistic meritocracy. But the upstart Jeffersonians renounced the protection covenant's distinction between the rulers and the ruled. Instead, the Jeffersonians invited the common people fully to participate in a new liberal conception of society which accepted, even celebrated, pluralism and competition in politics, economics, and religion. To retain power, the Federalists needed to preserve an apathetic or deferential electorate. To win power, the Jeffersonians needed to create a partisan constituency.[24]

Most of the defeated Regulators who persisted in their hometowns accepted their humiliation and relapsed into the "habit of subordination" that they considered normal and desirable in state politics. Indeed, once burned, twice as cautious, they became loath to invoke the logic of the protection covenant to justify extralegal violence. They modified the protection covenant by devaluing their own ability to judge whether there was oppression in the land and by elevating their respect for their rulers. Moreover, the commercial prosperity and diminishing taxes of the 1790s underlined for them the advantages of trusting in the Federalist political fathers. The swelling electoral turnout in former Regulator towns after 1800 reflected not a new popular assertiveness but an alarm, shared with the Federalist elite, at the rising Jeffersonian challenge to the traditional conception of the social order. By 1800 the Jeffersonian represented the frightening disorder that the Regulator had once perceived in the lawyer and merchant.[25]

Initially, the White Indians, like the Regulators, counted on the General Court's gentlemen legislators to take the hint from the resistance and revert to protecting the liberty and property of the ruled. Despite the Federalists' staunch support for the Great Proprietors, the inhabitants of central Maine routinely cast at least two-thirds of their votes—when they bothered to vote at all—for that party's gubernatorial candidate until 1804. The settlers' combination of extralegal resistance with electoral deference reflected their traditional conception of the polity; they accepted that only gentlemen could govern the Commonwealth but reserved the right to resist any of their actions deemed oppressive. Hence James Shurtleff, a settler leader, could champion the resistance and celebrate Federalist president John Adams in the same poem.[26]

But frustration mounted in central Maine as, year after year, the Commonwealth's rulers refused to play their part in the protection covenant. Although effective in nullifying the local operation of the land laws, the White Indians' tactics could secure only a protracted stalemate. The White Indians could suspend the Great Proprietors' litigation, but only the General Court could confiscate their land claims.

Disappointed in their quest for political fathers, the settlers became receptive to political missionaries bearing the word of Thomas Jefferson: that common men could protect and advance their interests only by engaging in organized partisan politics. Increasingly active after 1803, Maine's Jeffersonians preached that electoral politics offered a surer way to frustrate Federalist landlords than the traditional resort to extralegal violence by autonomous communities. By 1807, when they first captured the governorship of the Commonwealth, the Jeffersonians had politically transformed central Maine into a stronghold where they routinely captured three-fifths of the votes, and where most of the men voted. As their elected leaders became Jeffersonian "Friends of the People," rather than Federalist "Fathers of the People," settlers simultaneously denied special privileges to gentlemen and undermined their own justification for resisting the acts of government.[27]

To mollify the settlers without confiscating the Great Proprietors' land claims, the Jeffersonian General Court passed the Betterment Act on March 2, 1808. The act authorized juries in ejectment suits to ascertain both the value of a settler's lot in a "state of nature" and the "improved" value imparted by his "betterments"; the prosecuting proprietor then had the option of obliging the defendant to pay the wild land value to secure a title or of taking possession by purchasing the betterments. In practice, a few jury decisions under the act established $2 to $3 an acre as the regional standard for settlers to pay for proprietary title. A compromise, the act afforded neither the free land sought by the settlers nor the $4 to $7 an acre previously insisted upon by the proprietors. Initially slow, settler acquiescence to the compromise accelerated after the resistance claimed its first and only life on September 8, 1809, when a White Indian patrol shot Paul Chadwick, an assistant in a proprietary survey. Because the resistance depended so heavily on sustaining a terrifying illusion without actually shedding blood, the killing led many to rethink their commitment to the resistance, their defections eased by the existence of the Betterment Act. As a message that their political leaders could do no more, the Betterment Act, in conjunction with Chadwick's death, eroded the will to resist any longer. By the close of 1812 almost all of the White Indians' settlements had come to terms with their proprietors and permitted surveys. By then, because their resistance had been so protracted and because it had culminated in partial success through Jeffersonian auspices, most settlers had ceased to think and behave as "the ruled." They had become republican citizens.[28]

7

REINTERPRETING REBELLION:
The Influence of Shays's Rebellion on American Political Thought

Michael Lienesch

For years, scholars have cited the role of Shays's Rebellion in the creation of the American Constitution. With few exceptions, they have claimed that the rebellion was important—some say instrumental—in inspiring the Constitution. Richard Brown has recently pointed out that historians from George Bancroft, John Fiske, and John Bach McMaster in the last century to Forrest McDonald, Jackson Turner Main, and Gordon Wood in this one have agreed on this point, creating a rare historical consensus that has been relatively immune to revisionist reinterpretation. Political scientists have agreed, so much so that the consensual wisdom on Shays's Rebellion has become enshrined in virtually every introductory textbook on American government. According to Burns, Peltason, and Cronin, authors of the redoubtable *Government by the People,* now in its thirteenth edition, Shays's Rebellion "acted as a catalyst, precipitating the decision to call a convention to meet in Philadelphia in the summer of 1787."[1]

But while political scientists are certain that the rebellion was influential, they seem less sure about the nature of that influence. Thus, they write, the rebellion "heightened the movement for constitutional revision," "fuel[ed] the drive for a stronger national government," and "set the stage for the gathering in 1787 of a Constitu-

From a paper presented at the Bicentennial Conference on Shays's Rebellion, 1986, sponsored by the Colonial Society of Massachusetts.

tional Convention." In fact, the role of the rebellion in the creation of the Constitution was less causal but considerably more complex and ultimately more significant than these descriptions suggest. For while Shays and his supporters did not cause the Constitution to be created, they were active in bringing about certain changes that made it possible. Among these were conceptual changes, transformations in political thinking, what Henry Knox, writing at the time, referred to as "prodigious changes in the minds of men."[2]

To chart these conceptual changes, this essay examines the public debates taking place at this time, the rich and sometimes rancorous political discourse of the preconstitutional period, called by Isaac Kramnick the "great national discussion." Its focus is three concepts that were particularly prominent in public discussion: resistance, revolution, and reform. These three concepts, hotly disputed as they were, were conspicuous enough in the discourse of the day to constitute what have been called "keywords" or "contested concepts." Rending the Revolutionary consensus, dividing radical republicans from their conservative counterparts, the conceptual conflicts that centered on these concepts helped inspire an intensely partisan politics. Moreover, because these conflicts served not only to articulate and clarify the thinking of the time but also to transform it, they inspired a reinterpretation of the idea of rebellion that would play a part, albeit less directly, in separating supporters of the new United States Constitution from its opponents. Finally, to the extent that these transformations continue to shape our thinking, these eighteenth-century conflicts helped create a concept of rebellion that we as Americans have been living with ever since.[3]

Following a short consideration of the background of these debates, the essay charts these conceptual changes, following them from mid-1786, when popular protest began in earnest, through the framing and ratification of the Constitution. The sources are newspaper articles, essays, and reprinted speeches, along with convention debates. Many of the sources are from Massachusetts, as expected, but in order to follow the diffusion of the debate into other states, other sources are considered as well. Private letters are used at points to supplement the public statements.

EVEN BEFORE DANIEL SHAYS and his band of agrarian insurgents took up arms against the Commonwealth of Massachusetts in late 1786, a war of words was brewing. As early as midsummer, in response to county conventions that had been convened throughout New England to draw up petitions advocating paper money and more tolerant tender laws, partisans had begun to let loose with extraordinary examples of protest and counterprotest. In the popular press, especially in Massachusetts and New Hampshire, where, in addition to calling conventions, protesters had begun to close down courthouses, the debates were particularly heated, with columns that conventionally carried advice on curing sores or cultivating bigger turnips giving way to angry broadsides and impassioned denunciations. For example, writing in the *Massachusetts Gazette*, "A Citizen" blasted convention organizers as "sons of fraud and violence," "secret but active enemies to our peace and happiness," and "eminent only for their vices and depravity." At almost the same time, "A New Hampshire Freeman" was suggesting that convention opponents consisted of nothing more than "two-penny shopkeepers, usurers, speculators, or any other class of men, that delight to fatten on the distresses of mankind." "A Countryman," writing in the same edition of the *New Hampshire Mercury*, went even further, flatly branding them as "Tories and Enemies to America." By October, insinuations and insults had become commonplace, and writers on all sides and of every station did not hesitate to join in the fray. Even the laconic "Not a Mobb man," hardly a master of the pen, could contribute the choice comment that convention participants were "a Peck of Ritches which Evry Good man Ort to dispise."[4]

The intense partisanship of the discourse was not only unusual for its time, it was shocking. Throughout the Revolution, American newspapers had seen their share of hot-tempered prose. But the discourse seemed somehow more detached when rationalizing the break with England to a candid world. Even when the prose got personal, it was directed against English oppressors and almost never against republican brothers-in-arms. Postwar writers sometimes seemed to recognize that they were crossing the boundaries of civility, to say nothing of straining the bonds of republican brotherhood. "Modestus" for one commented critically on the recent proliferation of "rant or Billingsgate." At the same time, he did not hesitate to revile his opponents with terms that ran from "political Jesuits" to "Jacobites" to simply "pests." Adding insult to injury, he blamed his enemies for the decline in discourse. It was not enough for him to denounce an earlier writer for his "incoherent and laboured production"; he went on to charge that the "marks of sedition" were "evident in every sentence."[5]

Implicit in the debates was a dramatic polarization. Frequently writers spent more time attacking one another than making any original points of their own. At times their writings degenerated into a kind of verbal free-for-all, so that when "A Freeman" told the readers of the *Worcester Magazine* that "Citizen's" letter consisted of "low, dirty, and scurrilous invectives," "Monitor" attacked him in turn for his own "scurrilous, wicked, and seditious" opinions, and so forth. As local protests gave way to armed and organized resistance, the charges and countercharges became even more extreme. In midwinter, a writer calling himself "A Friend to Humanity and Good Government" was picturing the struggle in starkest terms, as a contest between "*evil*" and "*good.*" By the following spring, debate had become another version of warfare. What had once been civil discourse, counseled "Camillus," himself always ready to throw fuel on the fire, had become "infested with the harangues of the emissaries of treason."[6]

In such a situation, with enmity being felt all around, there was little room for compromise. The few calls for moderation seemed to fall flat, and most went unanswered. Worse, at least one writer who sought to steer a middle course was criticized for his closet partisanship. When "Honestus," writing in the *Independent Chronicle,* called on citizens to recognize that there were honest grievances and that those grievances could be protested peaceably, he was branded as a back-room rebel. Such pleas for reconciliation, announced an unmoved "Suffolk," were "the language calculated to make *insurgents.*"[7]

As consensus seemed to crumble, a divided discourse became the order of the day. Observers testified to the pervasiveness of the public debate, to the fact that disagreement and distrust had found their way into "almost every tavern, and conversation circle." Inflaming emotions, polarizing partisans into competing camps, closing off room for negotiation, this rancorous debate encouraged the more heated, more partisan, more uncompromising politics that would come to be called "party rage." But even more important was the effect of this divided discourse on political thinking, for the purpose of the partisans was not only to provoke passion but also to transform thought. As "Camillus" said of his opponents (and they would surely have said the same of him), their intentions were to "make that odious which was right, and that popular which was wrong." Nowhere was the transformation more dramatic than in three concepts that lay at the heart of republican political theory: resistance, revolution, and reform.[8]

IN THE POPULAR PROTESTS of the time, the concept of resistance was common. In the Whig theory of Harrington, Sidney, and Locke, insurgents found a time-honored terminology of protest, in which the rights of citizens were posed against the power of their rulers. Protesters reminded their fellow citizens that rights were fragile, never secure, and that power was grasping and never satisfied. Recalling the recent Revolution, they reminded their audience of its responsibility to resist power through constant vigilance and periodic protest. According to "A Member of the Convention," there could be no questioning the principle that "the people may, in a decent manner, seek redress of grievances; or even alter, change, or destroy, when for the good of the people."[9]

In the petitions passed by the county conventions, resistance was described as rational. Delegates went out of their way to describe themselves as responsible citizens, respectable property owners, and loyal veterans of the Revolution. In terms that today seem painfully polite, if not downright obsequious, they depicted themselves as patient and long-suffering victims. Far from sputtering like fanatics, they spoke with cool and almost philosophic rationality about their rights and privileges. After all, wrote "A Freeman," "history can produce no instance of a people's losing their freedom by Conventions of their private citizens, or even by mobs."[10]

Petitioners called on citizens to be suspicious of their rulers. Much of their wrath was focused on the magistrates, tax officials, and lawyers they held responsible for the farm foreclosures that had sparked many of the early protests, on "the court, the placemen, the pensioners." Somewhat less specifically, these debt-conscious borrowers aimed their criticism at lenders, or at least at what "Attleborough" called "that aristocratical principle too generally prevalent among the wealthy men in this State." Above all, they condemned their elected officials. Drawing on time-tested republican principles, they argued that rulers would always become corrupt and that even the best of them posed a threat to the liberties of their subjects. The fact that Americans were now governed by their own republican rulers made little difference. Indeed, some argued that independence itself posed a threat to freedom, in that citizens might be lulled into complacency by their new republican form of government. "A Freeman" was explicit in citing the danger, lest "the virtuous yeomanry of Massachusetts, who disdained to stoop to foreign tyrants, now bow their necks to internal despots."[11]

At the same time, the petitioners spoke glowingly of the people. Predisposed as they were to assume an alliance of monarchy and aristocracy against the people, these radical republicans did not hesitate to consider themselves representatives of the entire population, excluding only potential monarchists and aristocrats. As one set of resolutions put it, they spoke for "almost every individual who derives his living from the labours of his hands or an income of a farm." Among the insurgents themselves, virtually every letter from Shays and fellow protest leader Luke Day referred to their troops as "the body of the people assembled in arms" and to themselves as "officers of the people." Additionally, their supporters made it clear that the people could do no wrong, that they were, according to "A Member of the Convention," "ever humane, generous, and profligate of their favours." Throughout their thinking, the theme of self-defense ran strong, with Shays implying that it was government which was the aggressor and the people who were protecting what was rightfully their own, acting, he stated, "in defence of their lives and liberties." Above all, their thought was shaped by the principle, absolute and inviolable, that government must answer to the people. So it was that "Attleborough" seemed honestly shocked that he and his fellow protesters could be "stigmatized as traitors, incendiaries, *vile creatures,* and nearly threatened with prosecutions for daring to enquire into the present gross mismanagement of our rulers, and venturing to express their opinion that alterations favourable to the people, might be made in the present constitution."[12]

By contrast, critics of the protests questioned this conception of resistance. Although republicans, they insisted on a more conservative interpretation of republican theory, suggesting that while the idea of resistance was sound in theory, it was problematic in practice, at least in a republic such as their own. Writing in the *Independent Chronicle,* "Jonathan of the Valley" suggested that resistance was only legitimate when grievances were real, and the so-called grievances of the convention petitioners were in fact nothing more than "inconveniences." Adopting medical metaphors, critics described the protests as social ills, in terms that ranged from the mild ("a few peccant Humours") to the drastic ("The whole State is diseased."). Alexander Hamilton proved particularly adept at this symbolism, and his *Federalist No. 28* was heavily laced with medical imagery, including references to "maladies as inseparable from the body politic as tumors and eruptions from the natural body." Even more ominous was Hamilton's suggestion that for such diseases, there could be "no remedy but force." In general, these critics seemed to be searching for an alternative terminology, referring to protests not as examples of rightful resistance, what protesters called "regulation," but rather as "commotions," "disorders," "emergencies," "seditions," or simply "insurrections."[13]

In defining insurrection, and distinguishing it from resistance, these conservative thinkers made a point of depicting the protests as hopelessly irrational. Their descriptions teem with references to fury, madness, and "phrenzy." Protesters were described as madmen and fanatics, their actions as "extreme folly." Henry Knox captured the sentiment best in referring to the events in western Massachusetts as a "rebellion against reason." Unlike their radical republican counterparts, who depicted reason as inherent in human nature, such conservative republicans saw passion as the hallmark of the human character. Reason, they argued, was the product not of nature but of civil society, having to be imposed from without, through institutions and laws. Because reason and passion were opposites (radicals preferred to think of reason as the opposite of ignorance), the two forces were in constant conflict. Hence conservatives could describe a protracted struggle between reason and passion, identifying themselves as soldiers of rationality while branding protesters as the armies of madness. "Cassius" made the case in a January 1787 letter to the *Worcester Magazine:* "Now is the time when men act before they reflect; every measure is taken to prejudice the unthinking part of the community; the passions are inflamed, the solid principles of reason and truth scarcely examined, and the understanding inveloped in a mist of errours."[14]

More important was the treatment of vigilance. Supporters of the state made much ado about the differences between colonial and republican rulers. Unlike kings and aristocrats, who would never be worthy of trust, popular representatives could be trusted implicitly. Beyond this practical consideration, however, these Friends of Government turned to the larger matter of the relationship between liberty and power. They began with liberty, arguing that their radical counterparts had misconstrued the concept and would "not know her when you meet her," as "A Member of Society" bluntly told insurgent Adam Wheeler in an open letter. Recalling a line of thought at least as old as John Winthrop, "Nestor" distinguished between "natural" and "political" liberty. Natural liberty, "Nestor" argued, was synonymous with license and was found "in common with the wild beasts." By contrast, political liberty came through obedience to the laws of society, by *"being subject only to laws made in an equitable constitutional manner, and binding alike on all the citizens of the state."* In short, real liberty consisted in being "good subjects." With this assumption in hand, republicans ought to reconsider their traditional suspicion of their rulers. There was, "Bostonian" informed his readers, "a wide difference between manly jealousy and mean suspicion."[15]

For at least some of these thinkers, the notion of suspicion itself was open to question. In the absence of a clear conception of fundamental law, suspicion could seem uncomfortably close to sedition. In other words, to question rulers was to question rules and, by extension, to question government itself. "An Other Citizen" took the argument to its logical extreme, arguing that power could be compatible with republican freedom after all: "For though all power originates *from* the people, it does not remain *with* them . . . [and] may not be reassumed, nor the constitutional exercise of it disturbed with impunity; and in some cases not without incurring the guilt of treason."[16]

Perhaps most important, these more conservative republicans let out all the stops in descriptions of "the people" that were distinctly unflattering. They began by making it clear that far from the population as a whole, or even a majority of it, the protesters represented a mere "minor part." Here they could draw on the traditional republican fear of factions. More often, they made clear the distinctions between the insurgents and themselves, pointing out that the disaffected few were not only poor but "vulgar." (One minister thought it important to note that the malcontents did not live in "the most conspicuous and best educated towns.") Especially in their letters, commerce-conscious conservatives were adamant about the economic implications of the protests. For example, both Henry Knox and Henry Lee sent almost frantic accounts of the rebellion, warning their fellow conservatives that the true intentions of the rebels included not only the abolition of debts but also the redistribution of property. Even in their public writings some made the same case, presenting the protesters as levellers and members of what "Camillus" called "the Robinhood society." Absent in the criticism was any concept of a common people, united in some commitment to a common good. Instead, some conservatives went so far as to equate "the people" with "the mob." As Fisher Ames would tell the Massachusetts ratifying convention, democracy was "a volcano, which conceals the fiery materials of its own destruction."[17]

Apparently the arguments were persuasive, for among those who in theory ought to have been sympathetic to the cause of resistance, there was in practice a good deal of equivocation. Indeed, to Samuel Adams himself, whose radical republican credentials could hardly be questioned, the county conventions were at best mild embarrassments, and the armed protests were nothing less than criminal acts. In Adams's case there were many considerations involved, but the fact is that among leading radical republicans, the protests in Massachusetts found surprisingly little support. New York's scholarly "Brutus" would dismiss them as "violent commotions." For Richard Henry Lee, lumping them together with similar activities in his native Virginia, they were "riots and mobbish proceedings." Closer to home, Boston's "A Columbian Patriot" saw them as a "dangerous insurrection." For these old Patriots, Shays's actions had been troubling enough to provoke a serious rethinking of the principle of resistance. Even the eminent Revolutionary James Warren found himself revising his views: "The Truth of the Matter is," he wrote to John Adams in a bitter denunciation of the protests in Massachusetts, "the People resemble a Child."[18]

NOT SURPRISINGLY, SHAYS AND his fellow insurgents described themselves as revolutionaries. Many were in fact veterans of the Revolution, who stressed not only their service but also the sacrifices they had made. At times, they seemed to be reliving the Revolution, calling on their compatriots to assert their "rights," defend their "lives and liberties," and stand fast against "tyrannical government in Massachusetts."[19]

In reassuming the role of revolutionaries, they relied on the classical republican conception of revolution. From Machiavelli to Burgh, classical republicans had described revolution as a cyclical reversion, a return from corruption to original purity, or a recapturing of what were called "first best principles." Adopted in the eighteenth century by radical Whigs like Trenchard and Gordon, this conception had become widely accepted in America by 1776, so that Samuel Adams and his compatriots could consistently describe the American Revolution not as a radical thrust toward economic (or even political) equality but as a recovery of lost liberties. Thus it was not surprising that agrarian protesters portrayed themselves as part of this tradition, attempting not to install a new government but to restore the virtue of the old one. Explained "A Member of the Convention": "To revert to the principles of the [state] Constitution, on certain occasions, is not only lawful, but a duty."[20]

Theirs was a remarkably benign conception of revolution. Radical republicans had long maintained that in returning to original principles, revolutionaries would be returning to the original state of society, which they described as harmonious in all its aspects. Revolution would be a reversion not to anarchy but to freedom. Anarchy itself was an illusion, what "Candidus" called a "bugbear." But even assuming some chaos, such a state could not last for long. Indeed, as Pennsylvania's "Centinel" put it, "the greater its violence, the shorter the duration." Besides, as Shays and Wheeler had said, "one moment of liberty" was "worth an eternity of bondage." Working from these assumptions, radical republicans could be almost blithe in their defense of periodic revolutions, what Thomas Jefferson liked to call "instances of irregularity." As Jefferson himself explained in a letter dealing with the events in Massachusetts, "If the happiness of the mass of the people can be secured at the expence of a little tempest now and then, or even of a little blood, it will be a precious purchase."[21]

By contrast, conservative writers alarmed by Shays worked overtime reinterpreting the concept of revolution. Prominent among their problems was finding an appropriately pejorative label for the protests. Throughout late 1786 they continued to refer to them in a variety of ways, fishing, as it were, for the proper description. By early 1787, as Madison reported to Washington, the term of choice had become "rebellion." In fact, in February 1787 the Massachusetts General Court would officially declare the existence of a state of "open, unnatural, unprovoked, and wicked rebellion." Here pro-government conservatives were adopting a term that had always seemed suspect to republicans. By referring to the protests as a rebellion, they could distinguish them not only from earlier republican revolutions but, far more important, from the American Revolution itself. Indeed, by assigning "rebellion" to their opponents, while expropriating "revolution" to themselves, conservatives could depict the protesters as counterrevolutionaries, the insurgents having "turned against their teachers," according to "Camillus," "the doctrines, which were inculcated in order to effect the late revolution."[22]

Beyond the labels, conservative thinkers critically confronted the principles of Whig theory, beginning with the state of nature. In general, they described human nature in terms more reminiscent of Hobbes than Locke or Rousseau. Their descriptions were rife with references to barbarism, cannibalism, and savagery of all kinds. "Do they [Americans] wish to become as HOTTENTOTS," asked an incredulous "Brutus," "or set up a government upon the lawless sentiments of the ALGERINES?" For these thinkers, the state of nature was the state of war; rebellion assumed a return not to innocence but to violence. In their writings, anarchy became synonymous with confusion, chaos, and internal conflict, that "rude violence, in which every man's hand is against his neighbor." Moreover, with Shays, anarchy had come close to home and seemed far more real as a result. Even allowing for bombast, "Cassius" seemed terrified at its specter: "Anarchy, with her haggard cheeks and extended jaws, stands ready, and all allow that unless some efficient form of government is adopted she will soon swallow us."[23]

Implicit in this conception of revolution was a noncyclical view of popular protest. Unlike radicals, who saw anarchy as allowing for a return to first principles, conservative republicans described it as part of a pendulumlike process in which anarchy led not to freedom but to tyranny. In turn, tyranny would revert to anarchy. The result would be an unrestrained reaction, the pendulum gathering momentum with every swing, leading inevitably to violence. Hamilton described the theory in his *Federalist No. 9*, where he pictured the classical republics as in "a state of perpetual vibration between the extremes of tyranny and anarchy." But it was John Adams, writing in his multivolumed *Defence of the Constitutions of Government of the United States*, who made the clearest case, relying on Thucydides to show how the conflicts between democratic and aristocratic parties had been exacerbated by the Peloponnesian War, culminating, in his words, in "perpetual alterations of rebellion and tyranny, and the butchery of thousands upon every revolution from one to the other." Writing after Shays, Adams's point was unmistakable: "Human nature," he concluded, "is as incapable now of going through revolutions with temper and sobriety, with patience and prudence, or without fury and madness, as it was among the Greeks so long ago."[24]

The idea of imbalance came heavily laden with baleful implications. First among these was anarchy itself, replete with conflict, what New York's "Caesar" preferred to call "anarchy and wild uproar." More important, however, was anarchy's counterweight, tyranny. In his *Defence,* Adams reminded his readers that this state posed a particular threat, for while anarchy would never last long, "tyranny may be perpetual." Conservatives minced no words in describing Shays as such a tyrant. Connecticut's "Landholder" made the connection with characteristic bluntness: "Had Shays, the malecontent of Massachusetts, been a man of genius, fortune, and address, he might have conquered that state, and by the aid of a little sedition in the other states, and an army proud by victory, become the monarch and tyrant of America."[25]

To these conservative thinkers, however, there was a more threatening prospect than democratic despotism. Shays notwithstanding, they hinted at the possibility of a return to monarchy. Many, including Adams, Franklin, and Madison, thought monarchy was inevitable, if not now, then at some point in the future. More important, at least a few thinkers of the time thought it was desirable and were prepared to express their preference for monarchy publicly. As a practical matter, the reintroduction of a king seemed "out of the question." But the possibility alone was enough to pose a threat, and conservatives used it to ward off popular protest: "If we incline too much to democracy," Hamilton would tell the Philadelphia convention, "we shall soon shoot into a monarchy."[26]

Beyond monarchy, however, there lay an even more ominous outcome. Throughout the 1780s there had been talk in certain circles of a dictator, presumably a military man such as Washington. By late 1786 the talk had become serious enough that responsible conservatives had become alarmed: the "best" citizens, Jay told Adams, seemed disillusioned at the prospects for self-government and had begun to "look to other systems." With Shays, however, the potential seemed even greater than before. For in responding to the rebellion, Massachusetts officials had acted swiftly and with alarming severity, not only in the field, where protesters were met with massive force, but also in the courts, where they faced prosecution, along with disfranchisement and disqualification from office. By mid-1787 many conservatives had become critical of the repression. "Cassius," for example, warned that repression would incite further resistance and denounced "Numa" and his "aristocratick clan" for advocating extreme measures that could only "stir up sedition and rebellion."[27]

Thus more cautious conservatives could be found simultaneously warning counterrevolutionaries and radicals alike of the dangers of both extremes and positioning themselves as the responsible middle way. Their efforts were by no means merely strategic. If anything, the bulk of these thinkers seemed more deeply disturbed at the potential for counterrevolution than radical revolt. Having witnessed the ferocity of Shays's opponents, as well as the force used to put down the Massachusetts protests, they seemed chastened. Even Hamilton himself, who had flirted with the idea of a coup d'état at the close of the war, seemed to shrink from the possibility of a reactionary counterthrust. "That the human passions should flow from one extreme to another, I allow, is natural," he would tell the New York ratifying convention. "Hence the mad project of creating a *dictator*."[28]

For a variety of reasons, radical republicans were not immune to the threat of anarchy followed by tyranny. In some cases, such as that of New York's Governor Clinton, who feared lest the protests spread into his bailiwick of New York, the concern was pragmatic. In others, like that of the moderate "Cato Uticensis," it seemed more philosophical, with "Uticensis" adopting the pendulum theory hook, line, and sinker ("How natural the transition is from one extreme to the other; from anarchy to tyranny."). But after Shays, and especially after the repression of the rebellion, radicals had to take seriously the threat of anarchy and tyranny, and as a result found themselves embracing this more conservative concept of revolution. Like it or not, New York's "Cato" had to admit that Americans were "like other men in similar situations, [and] will as readily produce a Caesar, Caligula, Nero and Domitian in America, as the same causes did in the Roman Empire."[29]

WITH THE DEFEAT OF SHAYS and his forces in January and February 1787, when they were routed in battles in Hampshire and Berkshire counties, radical republicans became surprisingly quiet. Although scattered protests would continue for several months, by June 1787 the rebellion had come effectively to an end. Regulator-type activities continued to be carried on in several other states, some inspired at least in part by Shays, but these, too, were fewer and less formidable than before. There were many reasons for the decline in dissent, but Shays's failure was prominent among them, providing an object lesson for protesters and public officials alike. From this time on, protesters seemed more cautious, while public officials seemed less reluctant to use coercive means to put them down. At the same time, officials had learned the lesson that repression had its limits. For their part, having raised the important issues, the rebels themselves seemed willing to wait, more or less confidently, for their resolution. As Shays wrote to General Benjamin Lincoln, requesting clemency for himself and his followers, "The people now in arms, in defence of their lives and liberties, will quietly return to their respective habitations, patiently waiting and hoping for constitutional relief, from the insupportable burdens they now labour under."[30]

Yet the calling of the Philadelphia convention, coming close on the heels of the protests, left radicals perplexed. Having asked for changes, they now got them, and with a vengeance. To most, the plans for a radically revised constitution seemed all wrong. Predisposed as they were to think in cyclical terms, considering reform to be part of a process of reverting to first principles, they saw the proposed changes as departures from established ways. Thus radicals found themselves suddenly cast in the role of conservatives, denouncing the new plans for being in effect too radical, for "taking us from the good old way," in the words of "Countryman," "and leading us into new schemes and devices."[31]

At best, their position was problematic, for having demanded reforms, they could hardly now revert to a blind defense of the existing system. Like their conservative counterparts, radicals believed that the Confederation was badly in need of revision. According to Patrick Henry, who would become a leader of the Antifederalist opposition, all agreed on the need for reform: "Every man says that something must be done." Moreover, they had relatively little commitment to the existing government. Whether the Articles of Confederation remained or not, announced "Federal Farmer," was "but of little importance." Indeed, many were willing to admit that the time did seem ripe for constitutional change. As "Federal Farmer" put it, "I know our situation is critical, and it behoves us to make the best of it."[32]

Compounding the dilemma were practical political problems. Although most radical republicans moved easily into the Antifederalist ranks, once there they found themselves disagreeing with more moderate Antifederalists, not only about the character of the proposed changes but also on their timing. Here perceptions of the recent rebellion came heavily into play. Typical among the moderates were those like Melancton Smith, who dismissed the insurgency as insignificant, an unfortunate aberration in an otherwise happy transition to independence. Writing as "A Plebeian," Smith could conveniently overlook almost all the troubles of his times, assuring his New York readers that "neither the hand of private violence, nor . . . legal oppression, are reached out to distress us." Others found it harder to forget the Massachusetts uprising. Boston's "Agrippa," for example, thought to be Harvard's James Winthrop, had been deeply disturbed by events in the countryside and had personally volunteered to lead troops against Shays. Even so, "Agrippa" found solace in the suppression of the rebellion and saw Shays's failure as further proof that reform was not needed, the "damage," he wrote, having "been repaired." Still others took an even more paradoxical position, arguing that the protests had been terrifying in and of themselves, but that the proposed constitutional reforms were even worse. Writing in the *Massachusetts Gazette,* "Vox Populi" would take this stance, denouncing the Constitution's framers as—of all things—reincarnations of Shays: "I say let them consider in what respect such a revolution would differ from the *bold* and *unprovoked* one which was attempted to be made last winter!"[33]

Antifederalists argued that the proposed Constitution was too much too soon. Even while admitting that changes were in order and that the time for them was right, they continued to counsel caution. What was needed, advised "Federal Farmer," was not simply reform but "cool and deliberate reforms." Periods like the present were fraught with uncertainty, offering equal possibility for failure and success. Under the circumstances, they thought it best to be deliberate and in carrying out changes, in the words of "An Old Whig," to "consider carefully." Thus they bridled at the haste shown by the Constitution's supporters. "Brutus, Jr." warned his compatriots to be careful, because "those who are anxious to precipitate a measure, will always tell us that the present is the critical moment; now is the time, the crisis is arrived, and the present minute must be seized. Tyrants have always made use of this plea;" he advised, "but nothing in our circumstances can justify it." One incredulous Antifederalist put it succinctly to the Massachusetts convention: "Why all this racket?"[34]

For their part, conservatives reacted to the decline in popular protest with an escalation of their own antiradical activities. Surprisingly, the increase coincided not with Shays's successes but with his failure. Concerned conservatives feared the aftereffects of Shays, as the protests continued to reverberate. Writing to his father in late February, James Madison warned that the protests were far from over; there remained, he observed, "a great deal of leaven in the mass of the people." Repression only compounded the problem, and the election of John Hancock as governor of Massachusetts, coming at least in part as a reaction to the harsh treatment of the rebels, gave conservatives further cause for concern. "The Insurrection in Massachusetts is suppressed," Jay wrote to Jefferson in April, "but the Spirit of it exists and has operated powerfully in the late Election." Mostly, conservatives worried about the possibility that protests would spread to the other states. As Washington wrote to the near-frantic Henry Lee, "Precedents are dangerous things."[35]

Adding to this concern was a desire on the part of some for further punishment and retribution. In the popular press, a few unrepentant reactionaries gave strong support to repressive legislation, including sedition and riot acts, along with the suspension of habeas corpus. Throughout the spring of 1787 they criticized acts of toleration on the part of the state and called for punishment in terms that ranged from the stern to the positively sadistic. "Phineas" thought it was time that the "sons of sedition and tumult" be given "a little wholesome severity." "The Republican" observed that such "atrocious criminals" deserved "the severest punishments," and that the ringleaders should be made to "atone with their blood." One writer in the *Massachusetts Centinel* went even further still in condemning the rebels, suggesting that law-loving citizens should "cut them off, and wipe from the world the blot their existence now makes in it." Taking on a momentum of their own, the calls for retribution soon became so extreme that Washington himself felt called upon to counsel restraint, observing to Madison that harsh treatment of the rebels "probably may give birth to new, instead of destroying the old leaven."[36]

By mid-1787, however, conservatives of almost all stripes had seized on Shays as a kind of archetype for anarchy, so that the further they removed from the actual rebellion, the more determined they seemed to become in their denunciations. Crucial in this regard was the publication of the mock-epic poem *The Anarchiad*, the product of the self-styled "Connecticut Wits," which appeared in the *New-Haven Gazette* in twelve installments from October of 1786 through September of 1787. Reprinted widely, the poem had the effect of elevating Shays from local leader to a kind of national nemesis. Part of the epic's power was its contemporaneousness, in that the installments coincided with the protests themselves. Thus in the first installment of October 26, 1786, Shays was only one of several leaders involved in the popular protests:

> In visions fair the scenes of fate unroll,
> And Massachusetts opens on my soul;
> There Chaos, Anarch old, asserts his sway,
> And mobs in myriads blacken all the way:
> See Day's stern port—behold the martial frame
> Of Shays' and Shattuck's mob-compelling name.

By January 11, in the fourth installment, he not only had emerged as the leader of the resistance but had taken on considerable symbolic significance, standing in league with the devil himself:

> Behold the reign of anarchy, begun,
> And half the business of confusion done.
> From hell's dark caverns discord sounds alarms,
> Blows her loud trump, and calls my *Shays* to arms.

Yet Shays's full symbolic significance is seen only after the rebellion's suppression, when in the seventh installment of March 15, 1787, he is pictured presiding over an anarchic America:

> O'er WASHINGTON exalt thy darling Shays;
> With thy contagion, embryo mobs inspire,
> And blow to tenfold rage the kindling fire;
> Till the wide realm of *discord* bow the knee,
> And hold true faith in *Anarch* and in thee.[37]

Nevertheless, the most important factor in the creation of the anti-Shays campaign was the calling of the federal convention. In this respect, some of the escalation was almost certainly calculated. Early in the protests, conservatives such as Abigail Adams felt that the troubles would in fact prove functional, showing once and for all the absolute necessity of constitutional revision. As the protests continued, however, and the ill-starred Annapolis convention came to naught, conservative writers showed growing pessimism about the chances for constitutional reform. By the time the Philadelphia convention was called, they were warning of coming catastrophe: "Sedition, though intimidated, is not disarmed," warned "Camillus." Predicting anarchy and tyranny, along with civil war, they reminded their readers repeatedly of the recent protests. "We cannot look back, without terror," wrote "Camillus," "upon the dangers we have escaped—Our country has stood upon the verge of ruin." Above all, they called for action, arguing that audacity was the only thing that could save them from what would otherwise be certain doom. "Anarchy and government are both before us," "Camillus" told his Massachusetts audience, "and in our choice. If we fall, we fall by our folly, not our fate."[38]

Following the framing of the Constitution, its supporters continued to recall the rebellion, wielding it like a weapon in the state ratification debates. Interestingly, Federalists seemed to avoid references to Shays himself. By and large, they found direct assaults unnecessary, contenting themselves with more oblique references to the dangers of anarchy. A few delegates, including several in the Massachusetts ratifying convention, were slightly more specific, referring back in shadowy terms to the events of the previous year, when the state was "on the point of civil war." In the Massachusetts convention, the topic was addressed head-on only once, when a renegade delegate, a supporter of the Constitution and a westerner, describing himself as a "plain man" and addressing his "brother ploughjoggers," pointed to the "effects of anarchy" brought about by Shays in his region and stated his willingness to accept any system that provided "a cure for these disorders." The records show that the convention was immediately thrown into tumult, with Antifederalist motions from the floor to declare the delegate out of order. Federalists themselves seemed embarrased by the references to Shays and beat a rapid retreat. The fact is that Federalists found it more effective to refer to Shays, if at all, in only a secondhand manner, allowing the Constitution to stand on its merits, while avoiding excessive antagonism. Innuendo was more than enough to make the message clear: "Have we not reason," the Reverend Thomas Thacher asked ominously, "to fear new commotions in this commonwealth?"[39]

Outside the ratifying conventions, by contrast, supporters felt no such compulsion. In the newspaper essays and pamphlets of late 1787 and 1788, the link between Shays and the Antifederalists was direct and unrelenting. Opponents of the Constitution were not simply "harpies, knaves, and blockheads," "Cassius" told his readers; they were also "insurgents." Similarly, in his reply to "Cato," New York's "Caesar" reminded his readers that they had heard Antifederalist arguments before, having been "already disseminated in a neighboring State by the glorious defenders of *Shaysism*." Shays himself was no longer a threat; with a group of supporters he had moved into quiet exile in Vermont. But his specter loomed large in the campaign for the Constitution. The choice was clear, explained Virginia's "A Plain Dealer": either "the dominion of Shays" or "that of the new Constitution."[40]

Under the circumstances, Antifederalists could do little. Throughout the state conventions, many continued to complain that Shays had provided a pretext, an excuse that supporters had used to fend off criticism of the Constitution. "The most trifling events have been Magnified," an angry Uriah Forrest wrote to Jefferson of this tactic, "into Monstrous outrages." Realistically, however, Antifederalists looked on the insurrection with resignation, describing it as a hurdle they never had managed to surmount. As Pennsylvania's "Centinel" wrote in the last of his letters, the Constitution had been viewed "through the medium of a SHAYS," and as a result, supporters of the existing system had "lost her ablest advocates." In terms of strategy, Shays had placed the Antifederalists in an untenable position: trapped, as it were, between rebellion and counterrevolution, supporting neither Shays nor his aristocratic enemies, they tried to hold a tenuous middle ground "between these two parties." But because supporters of the Constitution had already claimed the middle, its opponents were reduced to calling for caution, their radical concept of reform watered down almost beyond recognition into a desire for incremental changes within the existing Confederation. A measure of their transformation was the fact that the strongest Antifederalist arguments were often framed as antidotes to rebellion. So it was that in criticizing the Constitution for its lack of a bill of rights, "Agrippa" could contend that personal liberties would provide the best protection against popular uprisings: "But for want of a bill of rights the resistance is always, by the principles of their government, a rebellion which nothing but success can justify."[41]

WITH RATIFICATION, FEDERALISTS could consign the insurrections in Massachusetts to the past. The Confederation was history, but it was a history that Federalists were determined to remember, and in their own terms. Thus Ames told his friend George Richards Minot that he for one would take every opportunity to recall the Confederation as a time when "the corn would not grow, nor the pot boil." Minot did even better, taking it upon himself to write the history of the rebellion itself. In his *History of the Insurrections in Massachusetts,* he could place these relatively recent events well in the past, looking back philosophically on the rebellion as a "period of misfortune" that had provided "the most fruitful source of instruction." Nevertheless, even for Minot, the moral of the rebellion was a timely one, that freedom could only flourish when every citizen embraced the new Constitution, "which, from a happy principle of mediocrity, governs its subjects without oppression, and reclaims them without severity."[42]

Yet even in Antifederalist history, the depiction was more or less the same. Shays himself, reportedly reduced to penury, found few if any defenders. Indeed, in her *History of the Rise, Progress, and Termination of the American Revolution,* the ardent Antifederalist Mercy Warren would describe the events in western Massachusetts in terms that sounded more like Minot than Minot did. Thus she turned her spleen full force on the insurgents, that "incendiary and turbulent set of people" who, armed with resolves that were "most of them absurd in the extreme," had "seemed to bid defiance to all law, order, and government." While willing to lay some blame on conservatives, she was as warm in her adulation of the authorities as she was scathing in her denunciation of the protesters and went out of her way to praise the stolid General Lincoln for his "mildness and humanity." Writing not only after ratification but following several years of successful national government, even this old Antifederalist seemed unable to divorce rebellion from ratification, so that for Warren, too, Shays had become only a catalyst to constitutional order, having "awakened all to a full view of the necessity of concert and union in measures that might preserve their internal peace."[43]

Having consigned Shays's rebellion to history, revisionists did not stop there but turned to relegating rebellion itself to the past. Thus the concepts of resistance, revolution, and reform continued to be reinterpreted. As the new federal union gained support, resistance to it seemed less and less acceptable. With the horrors of the French Revolution, revolution at home became unthinkable. And by the early nineteenth century, as the Constitution became more and more a kind of national monument, reform became synonymous with constitutional revision, with changes taking place only incrementally within its benevolent boundaries. In each case, radical concepts continued to be transformed into constitutional ones. As to Shays's Rebellion, by 1813 John Adams was describing it in one of his letters to Jefferson as an act of "terrorism." The Constitution was secure, but rebellion had lost its legitimacy and had been relegated to the preconstitutional past.[44]

PART THREE
A Splintered Society

8

SHAYS'S NEIGHBORS:
The Context of Rebellion in Pelham, Massachusetts

Gregory H. Nobles

> *My name is Shays; in former days*
> *In Pelham I did dwell, sir;*
> *But now I'm forced to leave that place*
> *Because I did rebel, sir.*

The old tavern ballad goes on for many more stanzas, denouncing and deriding Daniel Shays and ultimately dispatching him to Hell.[1] This first stanza, however, makes a simple point worth our attention. It introduces Daniel Shays, the alleged leader of the rebellion that bore his name, as an inhabitant of a particular town—Pelham, Massachusetts. The identification of Shays with Pelham helps humanize him, bringing him back down from his mythical proportions in legend and literature to his real stature as a farmer in a small New England village. It also helps bring the insurrection as a whole down to human scale. By seeing Daniel Shays as a common man within the context of a community, we can begin to see more of his neighbors, the small farmers who likewise "did rebel." Shays's Rebellion was as much their rebellion as his, perhaps even more.

Historians have not always done enough to emphasize that point. Many have tended to discuss Shays's Rebellion primarily as a foot-

---

From a paper presented at the Bicentennial Conferences on Shays's Rebellion, 1986, sponsored by the Colonial Society of Massachusetts and Historic Deerfield, Inc.

note to the Constitution, turning our attention away from the farmers in Massachusetts to the framers in Philadelphia. Admittedly, there is good reason for that focus. Shays's Rebellion did indeed add to the sense of urgency at the constitutional convention. Yet focusing only on the immediate political implications of Shays's Rebellion can obscure other important aspects of its historical significance. The insurrection was a short-term crisis that crystallized and clarified long-term trends in rural society. The Shaysites had serious grievances that grew out of their own historical experience. Their complaints about the inequities of their society—especially the small farmer's vulnerability in an increasingly complex and impersonal political and economic system—did not stem simply from the chaos of the Revolutionary era but were rooted much deeper in the past. In a sense, the Revolution did not so much create new problems as exacerbate old ones. Accordingly, some historians of Shays's Rebellion—among them David Szatmary and Barbara Karsky—have attempted to analyze the rural uprising within a social context that extends beyond the Revolutionary era and, indeed, suggests connections that transcend regional and national boundaries.[2]

That task is far from complete. After more than twenty years and more than twenty book-length community studies, our view of rural New England society in the eighteenth century is still surprisingly limited and even somewhat skewed. Much of what we know comes from analyses of older, well-established towns in eastern Massachusetts. We know comparatively little about the dozens of smaller and newer towns in the west that were the main sources of Shaysite activity. Moreover, the primary emphasis in most community studies has been on economic and demographic development. Political analysis, if it enters the story at all, is generally confined to parochial problems, the occasional (and exceptional) disruptions of internal harmony in the "peaceable kingdoms." Only a very few community studies have attempted to make an explicit link between local conditions and larger political movements.[3]

Shays's Rebellion presents an especially useful opportunity for exploring further the connection between society and politics in rural New England. As was the case in the early stages of the Revolution, collective action was essentially a form of communal action; thus the town still constitutes a useful unit of study. Yet unlike the Revolution, Shays's Rebellion was not an occasion when all New England towns, presumably with common problems, united in common cause against an external enemy. Rather, it revealed divisions in New England society that reflected distinctions among rural towns.[4] For that reason, studies of supposedly representative communities in the Revolutionary crisis do not provide adequate models for our understanding of the nature of the post-Revolutionary insurrection.

This essay examines the social and political context of Shays's Rebellion from the perspective of the people in one of the leading rebel communities—Pelham, Massachusetts. Located in the hills rising to the east of the Connecticut River valley, Pelham lay near the center of Shaysite activity in Hampshire and Worcester counties. Not only did Daniel Shays live there at the time of the rebellion, but as many as ninety Pelham men—around 40 percent of the town's adult male population—took up arms in the insurrection.[5] In many respects, Pelham was reasonably typical of many other towns that rose up against the government. It ranked twentieth among fifty-eight Hampshire County towns on the 1786 tax list. Likewise, its population of around a thousand inhabitants placed it just slightly above the county median.[6] In general, Pelham's centrality—geographic, military, and developmental—makes it a valuable focus for a case study of a rebellious community. Moreover, its history reveals a tradition of resistance and rebellion that permeated parts of rural society long before Shays's Rebellion (or even Daniel Shays) appeared on the historical landscape.

Pelham was first settled in 1740 by a group of Scots-Irish Presbyterians who had lived briefly (and unhappily) in Worcester. Like thousands of other refugees from Ulster who flooded the American colonies in the 1720s and 1730s, these migrants to Massachusetts escaped discrimination in the Old World only to find it in the New. When the Presbyterian newcomers began to build their own church in Worcester, the townspeople "gathered tumultuously by night, and demolished the structure." According to an early Worcester historian, "Persons of consideration and respectability aided in the riotous work of violence."[7] Clearly the Anglo-American Congregationalists of this prosperous market town had little tolerance for members of an ethnic and religious minority in their midst.

The Scots-Irish migrants soon sought refuge on the frontier. In

1739 they purchased a 17,000-acre tract of hilly land in the wilderness of western Massachusetts, and the next year forty families moved west to establish a new town. Set apart in their own community, the Pelham Presbyterians perhaps seemed less a threat to the religious and social order of the established towns. There is no evidence, at least, of further persecution or open antagonism on the part of neighboring Congregationalists. In the early years of settlement, Pelham existed on the cultural fringe of the region, neither fully integrated nor isolated.[8]

The town was by no means unique in that respect. Between 1740, the year Pelham was settled, and the time of the American Revolution, dozens of other new towns were carved out of the Massachusetts interior. In Hampshire County alone, the number of incorporated towns rose from nine to forty-four; by 1775, almost three-fourths of the county's inhabitants lived in communities established after 1740.[9] In the space of a generation, backcountry communities filled in the frontier; to a large degree they changed not only the physical environment of western Massachusetts but the political and social environment as well.

The settlement of the backcountry had important implications throughout the American colonies. Backcountry farmers increasingly defined a distinct social group; indeed, to some extent they developed a regional counterculture that stood in sharp contrast to—and often in conflict with—the established culture of the colonial elite. In Pennsylvania, Scots-Irish settlers on the western frontier resented the political dominance of the Quaker elite in the east, and in 1763 the "Paxton Boys" marched on Philadelphia, only to be dissuaded by the intervention of Benjamin Franklin. In Virginia backcountry Baptists gained converts by denouncing the worldly excesses of the Anglican gentry. In North Carolina yeomen in the western counties took even more forceful action and rose up in armed revolt against the eastern elites who controlled the provincial government. (It was not coincidental, in fact, that in 1786 the rebellious farmers of Massachusetts adopted the same name that their North Carolina counterparts had used twenty years earlier—Regulators.)[10]

In rural New England social and religious distinctions were not as extreme as they were in the other regions, nor was social conflict as violent—at least not until the outbreak of Shays's Rebellion. Still, in the pre-Revolutionary era there was increasing evidence of important social, economic, and political differences between the inhabitants of the older, established towns and the people of the new backcountry communities. Those contrasts not only underlay the insurrection that erupted in the 1780s, they also provided the source of regional discontent many years before.

The basic elements of this contrast are perhaps best captured in an old anecdote that dates from the 1740s or 1750s. It is a joke told on a prominent Northampton merchant, Deacon Ebenezer Hunt, but it also tells us something about social relations in the region long before Shays's Rebellion. An early nineteenth-century historian recorded the story:

> One season there was a great scarcity of corn in this vicinity. A man from Pelham came to the Deacon for a bushel of corn and was very urgent. The Deacon refused—said he had no more than he wanted for his family. "I curse you," said the man. "What! What!" said the Deacon. "I curse you. God commands me to curse you." "What do you mean by such language?" said Hunt. The man called for a Bible and read the verse in Proverbs about the peoples cursing him that withholdeth his corn from the poor. The Deacon ordered a bushel put up. "Now," says he to the man, "go and curse a bushel out of the Clarks."[11]

Whether literally true or not, the anecdote is a revealing bit of local folklore. In order to "get" the joke as fully as Deacon Hunt's contemporaries would, we have to understand the characters within the cultural context of the region. Certainly the identification of the poor man with Pelham adds to the texture of the tale. He is the backcountry beggar who badgers the valley merchant for a bushel of corn. He is the Scots-Irish Presbyterian who curses the Congregational deacon and then gives him a theological beating with his own Bible. Above all, he is the outsider whose independent status allows him to confront a member of the local elite with defiance rather than deference—and get away with it. In hearing the anecdote, local residents no doubt understood implicitly the nature of the Pelham man's stance because they understood the nature of his community within the broader context of the region.

Like the brash beggar in the story, inhabitants of Pelham and other hill towns had only to go down into the established valley towns to encounter a very different world. There they would see signs of much greater wealth and economic development. The major towns in western Massachusetts—Worcester, Springfield, Hadley, and Northampton—were productive and prosperous farm communities. In his travels through the region, Timothy Dwight noted their natural advantages, especially the abundance of "fertile and delightful" land. There were "no more productive grounds in New England" than in the Connecticut River valley, Dwight asserted, and he observed that for most farmers in the established valley communities, work appeared to be "rather easy than toilsome, and much less strenuous than that of the people in the hills." Moreover, by the second half of the eighteenth century, the economy of these older towns had become increasingly diversified. The growing numbers of merchants and artisans testified to the expansion of trade, both within the towns themselves and with communities in the surrounding area. These rural market towns defined and dominated the economic and political life of a rapidly expanding region.[12]

The comparability of these communities like Pelham to the older towns is still not entirely clear. Until recently, the only sustained analysis of a new town in New England was Charles Grant's study of Kent, Connecticut, a town settled in 1739, about the same time as Pelham. This Connecticut frontier town apparently offered great opportunities for economic gain, and according to Grant the first inhabitants scrambled to make the most of the situation. Motivated by a "drive for profits," the "aggressive opportunists" of Kent engaged in land speculation, commercial farming, and an "almost frenzied determination" to develop nonagricultural enterprises.[13]

Between 1740 and 1790, however, economic prospects gradually declined in Kent. The town became "overcrowded," and an increasing number of Kent residents were landless and poor. Like the inhabitants of older New England communities, the people of Kent found themselves confronting what Robert Gross has called a "world of scarcity" by the Revolutionary era. Yet Grant is careful to note that Kent was not seriously affected by the "Shaysite contagion." In that regard he suggests that "this history of an 'exceptional town' on the New England frontier may provide some counterbalance to those radical communities which historians have found plagued with internal and external class rivalries."[14]

Grant raises an important question about the nature of new towns. In light of the many community studies that have followed his 1961 work, the frontier town of Kent seems very much within the economic and political mainstream of eighteenth-century New England. The task remains, then, to examine one of those "radical communities" like Pelham to see where the "Shaysite contagion" bred and how it spread.

One difference is clear. The inhabitants of Pelham did not experience a decline from abundance to privation: they lived in a "world of scarcity" from the beginning. In 1745, five years after the original settlement of the community, over half the families in Pelham had fewer than ten acres of land cleared for production; indeed, over 90 percent of the households had fewer than twenty acres of improved land.[15] According to standards of land use suggested by some studies of other New England communities, the people of Pelham barely met the requirements for subsistence. Grant's figures for Kent, for instance, suggest that with about five acres of tillage land and another thirty-five acres of other improved land, a farm family could probably get by, "if not burdened with too many mouths to feed."[16]

The early inhabitants of Pelham were perhaps fortunate in that regard, because they had comparatively small and young families: in 1746 only nine of the seventy-three heads of households had sons over the age of sixteen. Throughout the next three decades, while the young people of Pelham were growing, so was the town itself. In the early 1760s a group of Pelham families migrated to New York; but in the wake of the French and Indian War, an influx of new settlers in Pelham quickly took their places. Between 1765 and 1776 the population of the town almost doubled, rising from 371 to 729.[17]

This rapid population growth did not bring on a serious crisis of overcrowding, nor did it result in a significant shrinking of the average farm size. Indeed, what is most striking in the case of Pelham is the relative degree of continuity in the process of agricultural development. Some families did expand their holdings; by 1771 sixteen Pelham households had over thirty acres of improved land, close to (but still below) Grant's estimate of the level needed for a comfortable and secure existence. At the same time, however, almost two-thirds of Pelham's 131 households worked farms of less than twenty improved acres. By 1780 the average farm size rose only slightly, to just over twenty-five acres of improved land. After four decades of settlement, the pace of expansion had been slow, and most people still farmed on essentially the same scale as the first inhabitants.[18]

Small-scale farming does not necessarily denote scarcity, of course. As Bettye Hobbs Pruitt has recently shown, the standards of land use suggested by Grant and others probably overestimate the amount of land needed for a "middle-class" standard of living. Her analysis of the 1771 Massachusetts tax valuation reveals that the median farm size was twenty improved acres—that is, about the size of most Pelham farms. Moreover, she argues that the exact measure of agricultural subsistence, or "self-sufficiency," is difficult to determine for New England farms. Individual households may not have been able to supply all their own food, but they could fulfill their basic needs by engaging in exchanges with other households; thus "communities could be self-sufficient though individuals were not."[19]

Still, no matter what amount of land Pelham farmers used for growing crops, they could not expect much of a return. The soil in Pelham, like that in most of the new hill-town communities in central and western Massachusetts, was thin, rocky, and unproductive. In nearby Ware, for instance, the land was jokingly compared to self-righteousness: the more a man had of it, people said, the poorer he must be. Pruitt's figures for grain growing confirm the anecdotal evidence: Pelham, Ware, and other surrounding hill towns had relatively low levels of production (20–29 bushels per poll) compared to the towns in the rich lowlands of the Connecticut River valley (40+ bushels per poll). She notes, however, that there are other measures of agricultural production, like cattle raising, that suggest a rough comparability between hill towns and valley towns and thus "belie the familiar distinction between the 'commercialized' towns along the Connecticut River and the upland towns that were supposedly cut off from the market and isolated in their self-sufficiency." To be sure, cattle driven to the Boston market were a "cash crop" of sorts in western Massachusetts. Yet Pruitt's figures for cattle raising (an average of 2.3 per poll in the valley towns and 2.2 per poll in the hill towns) do not indicate a sizable enough livestock surplus to suggest that cattle production alone represented significant market involvement, much less income. In general, given the limitations of their land, hill-town farmers had a limited opportunity to produce a substantial agricultural surplus for the market.[20]

Not only did Pelham farmers fail to engage in large-scale agricultural production for the market, they also failed to develop nonagricultural commercial ventures. By 1771, for instance, Pelham had no shops, one tannery, and two mills. Ten men had money lent at interest, all for a total of only £24.9.7. The town remained essentially unchanged by the time of Shays's Rebellion.[21] The absence of economic development in a town like Pelham does not necessarily indicate an absence of economic desire among the town's inhabitants. Few people in Pelham had sufficient surplus capital to invest heavily in commercial ventures or to buy large tracts of land. Still, the early history of Pelham yields little evidence of either the intense "drive for profits" Charles Grant claimed for the people of Kent or the degree of market involvement Pruitt and others have suggested for Massachusetts towns in general.

The more compelling feature of the town's eighteenth-century economic profile is the occupational similarity and economic equality of its inhabitants. According to recent typologies of New England communities, Pelham was an "egalitarian farm village" that showed little evidence of social stratification; in 1771 the top 10 percent of taxpayers controlled less than 30 percent of the town's wealth.[22] The people of Pelham remained small-scale farmers, neither hopelessly poor nor especially prosperous—in short, more or less typical of the thousands of settlers that populated the backcountry hill towns of Massachusetts in the third quarter of the eighteenth century.

The limits of economic development eventually bred economic disadvantages for inhabitants of these small agrarian villages. David Szatmary has offered a very perceptive analysis of the yeomen's position at the end of the global "chain of debt." They felt increasing pressure from merchants in the region's market towns for repayment of debts that had often been carried for years. Especially in western Massachusetts, debt proceedings increased dramatically in the 1780s. Moreover, the fear of confiscation of one's property or imprisonment for debt heightened the anxieties of farmers who never actually had to go to court. As the inhabitants of Conway wrote, the "*mortgage of our farms,*—we cannot think of, with any degree of complacency. To be *tenants* to *landlords* . . . and pay rent for lands, *purchased with our money,* and converted from howling *wilderness,* into fruitful fields, by *the sweat of our brow,* seems . . . truly shocking."[23]

Similar anxiety over anticipated losses may well have motivated many of the rebels in Pelham. In some respects, the ninety men who actually took up arms in the insurrection do not fit the classic characterization of the Shaysite—that is, the debt-ridden Revolutionary War veteran dragged into court by his creditors. Biographical information is incomplete for all of Pelham's insurgents, but the town's vital records suggest that most of them were young men in their late twenties or early thirties, many of whom were just at the point of marrying and establishing themselves as independent householders. About half of them had served as soldiers in the Revolution, but usually only for a very short period of time near the end of the war. Only three Pelham Regulators (one of whom was Daniel Shays himself) were defendants in debt cases in the years just preceding the insurrection, and none suffered confiscation of property or imprisonment for debt.[24] But one did not have to suffer personally at the hands of the legal system to feel vulnerable and threatened. One had only to be aware of the laws as they stood, aware of the experience of other men, and aware of the marginal nature of one's own situation. For young men starting out in economic circumstances that were already generally strained, prospects for the future were as important as the reality of the present.

Yet economic conditions, or even economic concerns, cannot alone provide an adequate explanation for Shays's Rebellion. If that was the case, we could reduce the rebellion to a formula that derives political behavior from economic background. And if we did so, we would no doubt be disappointed and perplexed by the results. We would find, for instance, that the inhabitants of Daniel Shays's old hometown of Brookfield, which was much like Pelham in economic terms, remained largely loyal to the government during the insurrection.[25] So, too, did people in many other poor farm towns.

In order to understand the uprising of rural rebels in 1786, it is also important to consider carefully the communal patterns of political behavior—and not just in the insurrection itself but over time. On one level, people in New England shared a common political culture that provided clear standards of order, especially about the importance of peace and compromise. Yet just as there were differences in the economic development of New England towns, so were there differences in political development; to a large degree, of course, the two are related. Still, each town had its own history of political behavior that created a distinct, and sometimes distinctive, political culture for the community.

Certainly in the case of Pelham, the inhabitants developed a local political culture that set them apart from the dominant political powers of the region. Long before Daniel Shays came to Pelham, the town had a history of active opposition to external authority. In 1762, for instance, a Hampshire County deputy sheriff received a harsh welcome when he came up the hill to serve a warrant in Pelham. A group of men and women confronted him "with Axes, Clubs, sticks, hot water and hot soap in a riotous and tumultuous manner . . . [and] uttered menace and threatenings of bodily hurt and death . . . and with force of arms obstructed, opposed, hindered and wholly prevented" him from doing his lawful duty.[26]

During the early stages of Revolutionary protest, the Pelham people became even more aggressive. Not content to wait for officials to come to them, they were active in taking collective action against suspected Tories in neighboring towns. In February 1775 a mob from Pelham descended on Israel Williams of nearby Hatfield, one of the most prominent and powerful of the Connecticut Valley's "River Gods" and a leading Loyalist in the region. They locked Williams and his son in a house with a clogged chimney and smoked them overnight. After being kept "under Keepers who insult him very highly," Williams agreed to sign a confession of his political sins. Then the Pelham crowd moved on to Northampton, where their victim was Solomon Stoddard, likewise one of the wealthiest and most notable men in the county. Not only did the Pelham people suspect Stoddard of being a Tory, but some of them apparently also owed him money; he was therefore a doubly attractive target. The mob spared him the smoking they gave Williams, but they did extract a signed confession.[27]

Some people, especially most of the Whig leaders in Northampton, condemned the actions of the Pelham crowd, but they were powerless to do anything. As a local minister, the Reverend Jonathan Judd of Southampton, observed, "The Committee of Correspondence meet and know not what to Do, are irresolute, nonplussed, & Divided." Undeterred by local opposition, the mob from Pelham completed its "tour of education" according to its own sense of political direction. As the Reverend Mr. Judd noted with disgust, "They act like mad people, tho' well for a Mob."[28]

Another sometime minister, the notorious Stephen Burroughs, had an even dimmer view of the Pelham people. An itinerant imposter who filled the Pelham pulpit for a brief time in 1784, Burroughs was discovered to be a fraud and run out of town. After barely escaping with his life, he wrote disdainfully that the inhabitants of Pelham were "a people generally possessing violent passions, which once disturbed, raged, uncontrolled by the dictates of reason." These "unpolished" people, he continued, had "a jealous disposition; and [were] either very friendly or very inimical, not knowing a medium between those two extremes."[29] As Burroughs learned firsthand, they could be very inimical indeed to anyone who threatened the integrity of the community.

This was the background of Shays's neighbors when he moved to Pelham in 1780. Although some local observers accused them of emotional extremism and irrationality, they were not "mad people," nor were their passions "uncontrolled by the dictates of reason." Their actions reflected patterns of collective political behavior that were common throughout Europe and the American colonies. Urban and rural crowds often acted autonomously and aggressively for their own political purposes. Especially in a town like Pelham, whose original settlers had once suffered the scorn heaped on the Scots-Irish in New England, people felt they had good reason to be especially wary of external enemies. Throughout the short history of the town, the inhabitants of Pelham had repeatedly risen in forceful and sometimes violent defense of what they defined as their local rights and interests.

That tradition of local mobilization provides an intriguing approach to understanding the role of Daniel Shays in Pelham—and more generally, to understanding the nature of political behavior in Shays's Rebellion. At the time of the insurrection, Massachusetts officials identified Shays as the primary leader of the uprising, the "generalissimo" of the rebel forces.[30] Similarly, most early historians of the insurrection attacked Shays as a dangerous demagogue who pushed the populace to political extremes. According to one account, Shays was

> a brave man, ambitious, of good appearance and pleasing address, but seemingly utterly devoid of principle. He found it easy to enlist men for carrying out his projects however visionary, and was thoroughly unscrupulous as to the means employed in attaining his purposes. Such a man was the natural leader of the discontented, rebellious victims of a state of public and private affairs for which they held others to be blamed.[31]

His fellow farmers were, as George Richards Minot so often put it in his *History of the Insurrections in Massachusetts*, "deluded"—usually by a combination of demagoguery and drink.[32] Other critics wrote of Shays's "tavern harangues" in which he "encouraged the talk of rebellion and used the open space in front of the tavern as a training-field." "A natural if not a necessary feature of this training," noted one writer, "consisted of frequent visits to the bar-room."[33] Even the mother of one of Shays's alleged lieutenants complained that her son had been "in several insurrections, [because] his passions have been in many instances raised unduly, by going in company with others, and freely using strong liquors [so that he] has been guilty of rash expressions, which upon cool reflection he heartily lamented." Her son, Henry McCulloch, also argued that he had been deceived and "was persuaded, merely for Show, to take an Old Cutlass just before the attack at the Arsenal." He claimed he was taken to be a leader of the rebels only "because he rode a good horse and had a foolish fondness to be thought active and alert."[34]

Such explanations may be amusing, but they provide a misleading and, at best, patronizing view of the origin of the insurrection in Pelham. They portray Shays as far more important, and his followers as far more impressionable, than was the case. Daniel Shays was by no means the most prominent or powerful political leader in Pelham in the 1780s. A relative newcomer, he held a few minor town offices but never the post of selectman or moderator. He served as one of Pelham's delegates to a county convention in 1782, but on the eve of the insurrection, other Pelham men represented the town in the conventions that drafted the lists of grievances. In arguing for her son's innocence, Sarah McCulloch identified Shays as only one of "a number of Men in town . . . [including] Capt. Daniel Gray, Thompson, Capt. Cowden, Capt. Conkey who all belong to Pelham" and who were the local instigators of the insurrection. Shays was a clearly leading figure among the Pelham Regulators, but hardly a lone figure. Indeed, Shays always denied responsibility for the rebellion that bore his name. Somewhat like Henry McCulloch, he argued that he had been a reluctant rebel pushed to the forefront by his fellow townspeople because of his military bearing and experience.[35]

We cannot take such disclaimers completely at face value, of course: Shays made these self-serving statements in an attempt to save his own neck. But we cannot completely dismiss them, either. In his classic study of *Western Massachusetts in the Revolution*, Robert J. Taylor noted that the Regulator uprising was hardly a single, unified movement. Rather, it was initially a series of local protests led by local leaders—only one of whom was Daniel Shays.[36] Moreover, when we look at Shays within the context of his own community, we can hardly see him as a designing manipulator, or even the main instigator, of his neighbors. Shays rose to local prominence in a political environment that had been long established by the people of Pelham. There may have been some people in the community who, like Henry McCulloch, claimed to have felt uncomfortable with—or even coerced by—the political culture of Pelham. Still, the remarkable record of mobilization, both before and during Shays's Rebellion, indicates that the people did not simply respond to the direction (or deception) of a demagogue. Given Pelham's communal history of collective action, Shays perhaps understood that popular movements often create their own leaders. Certainly he knew better than some of his detractors that one man does not make a movement.

Neither does one town. Pelham was only one of several communities in western Massachusetts with a sizable insurgent population and a reputation of rebellious action. In the immediate vicinity of Pelham, for instance, several other towns—Amherst, Leverett, Shutesbury, and Greenwich—formed a core of Regulator strength in Hampshire County. There were also important rebel strongholds elsewhere in Hampshire County, as well as in Worcester and Berkshire counties. It is far beyond the scope of this essay to provide a town-by-town survey of the political histories of each of these towns. It is possible, however, to look briefly at instances when people from several towns acted in concert, both in Shays's Rebellion and before. By doing so, we can gain useful insights into the patterns of political behavior that had become common in the countryside.

The history of western Massachusetts in the second half of the eighteenth century is peppered with political unrest. We know, for instance, that Pelham was by no means the only town with a record of mob activity or resistance to external authority. Especially in the early stages of the Revolutionary era, people from many of the newer communities in the region asserted themselves aggressively. They took collective action, both as mobs from single towns and as part of huge crowds drawing on dozens of communities, to close the county courts and unseat the Tory elite.[37]

Moreover, once they had deposed the Tories, they repeatedly challenged the authority of the emerging Whig elite, both in western Massachusetts and in Massachusetts as a whole. Beginning in 1775, several towns in Berkshire County led the agitation for a new written state constitution. These Berkshire Constitutionalists did not seek to create a strong centralized state government; rather, they wanted to establish clear limits on the power of the state and thus maintain a large degree of control at the local level. In 1778, however, the initial draft of the Massachusetts constitution created another opportunity for opposition. Despite the widespread western support for the Berkshire Constitutionalists' call for a written constitution, only a handful of towns in the region—the older, more commercially and politically integrated market centers—gave their approval to the document proposed by the General Court.[38] People in the newer towns remained much more resistant. As the people of Pelham argued, the new constitution "labours under several material Defects [and] seems in some particulars too favourable to some Classes of Men while it excludes others." Their neighbors in nearby Greenwich echoed that sentiment, complaining that the constitution "Intirely Divests the good People of the State of Many of the Priviledges which God and Nature had given them ... Giving away that Power to a few Individuals, which ought forever to Remain with the people inviolate, who stile Themselves free and Independent."[39]

Throughout the Revolutionary era, even after the ratification of the revised draft of Massachusetts's constitution in 1780, people in many western communities still continued to "stile Themselves free and Independent." They repeatedly resorted to extralegal activity to deal with their grievances. Not only did they assemble at county conventions, they also took direct action as mobs. Samuel Ely, the migrant minister who came to western Massachusetts in 1782 with his own version of a state constitution that he claimed "the Angel Gabriel could not find fault with," became the focus of a rural uprising that gave a foretaste of the Regulation of 1786. Ely urged people to attack the justices of the county court and "knock their grey wigs off, and send them out of the world in an instant." Not surprisingly, the justices put Ely in jail. Several hundred supporters from the Hampshire County backcountry then rallied to his support, and on two occasions they forced local authorities to set Ely free. Even after the so-called Ely riots had subsided, western Massachusetts witnessed several other smaller mob actions and jailbreaks in the years before Shays's Rebellion.[40]

Shays's Rebellion represented the culmination (and the combination) of these various forms of rural unrest. In 1786, when people in the Massachusetts backcountry assembled in conventions and then in mobs, they drew upon patterns of political behavior that they knew well from their previous political experience.

The closing of the county courts provides the most compelling example of this behavior. The courts were obvious targets for very practical reasons. They were the main governmental institutions controlling the countryside; they were also the institutions that gave legal sanction to the power of creditors, lawyers, and sheriffs over indebted farmers. Yet the closing of the courts often involved a political display that embodied more than immediate political purposes. When rural people acted in concert to close the courts, they gave a dramatic demonstration of their self-conscious role on the political stage.

Consider, for instance, two court closings in Springfield—one at the beginning of the Revolution, the other in the early days of the Regulation. On September 30, 1774, several thousand people from all over western Massachusetts descended on the county court and forced the justices to renounce their royal commissions. Once they had extracted contrite confessions from the justices, the "people of each town being drawn into separate companies marched with staves & musick . . . trumpets sounding, drums beating, fifes playing, and Colours flying."[41] The parade of the crowd in individual town units underlined the political emergence of many of the new communities in western Massachusetts.

Twelve years later, almost to the day, a crowd of some fifteen hundred Regulators led by Daniel Shays occupied Springfield again, this time seeking to stop the Superior Court from sitting. For three days, while the Regulators faced progovernment militia units from Springfield and other towns in the region, the court did no business. Finally, on September 28, 1786, the court adjourned. Then, according to one observer, "the Committees agreed that the Militia [should] march to the Labratory Hill & there disband, that Capt. Shays might march thro' the Town & counter march his men to the ground [which] they occupied before & then dismiss them . . . that they [would] each Throw off the Badges a white paper in ye Militia Hats, Green Bush in ye Mobb, & go Home friendly."[42] This peaceful, almost polite, exchange of space is remarkably revealing. It demonstrated very visibly the difference between the political power of the justices inside the courthouse and the power of the people "out of doors." In the context of the region's political culture, everyone understood the significance of the symbolism. By agreeing to withdraw temporarily and let the Regulators occupy the grounds surrounding the courthouse, the authorities implicitly recognized the legitimacy, if not the legality, of the insurgents' actions. Then, once both sides had played their respective parts in this political pageant, everyone could indeed "go Home friendly."

In the course of Shays's Rebellion, however, the terms of political conflict changed dramatically—and disastrously. Despite several Regulator appeals for peace and pardon in late 1786, both sides took steps to increase their military strength. By January 1787 the government put in the field a massive militia force recruited largely from eastern towns and financed by eastern merchants. In the face of growing government manpower, Shays staged a daring attack on the Springfield arsenal to seize arms and supplies. However, three artillery blasts from the militia forces defending the arsenal quickly scattered Shays and his men. This final confrontation at Springfield clearly signaled that government officials would no longer make concessions to crowd behavior; the state would now assert its authority through force of arms. Only after the militia had broken the Regulator forces into small bands of die-hard resisters did the government offer pardon to those insurgents who would agree to surrender their arms—and some of their political rights.[43]

Yet even then, some astute observers realized that the military power of the state could guarantee submission but not acceptance. Ebenezer Mattoon, a Friend of Government from Amherst, urged conciliation when seeking clemency for a Shaysite who had been captured and condemned to die—Henry McCulloch of Pelham. A display of official mercy in McCulloch's case would "be attended with very happy consequences." Mattoon argued that "if he is spared the town of Pelham is attached to government, [but] if he is executed . . . the affections of the town is lost."[44] Mattoon understood—and helped the government understand—that armed force alone would not destroy the roots of resistance that ran deep in western Massachusetts. By agreeing to pardon McCulloch, Massachusetts officials made a conscious concession to Pelham and to many of the other rebel communities that had never been strongly "attached to government." Even in defeat, those towns had a tradition of political autonomy that the leaders of the new state government could hardly ignore.

In the final analysis, however, Shays's Rebellion was the political cataclysm, or perhaps catharsis, that brought an end to the traditional forms of rural protest—at least in Massachusetts. In the wake of the insurrection, former Regulators turned from violence to the vote, usually giving their support to the Republicans. In that regard, they still remained somewhat outside the political mainstream of Massachusetts Federalism.[45] More important in the long run, though, was the integration of these rebels—and their rural communities—into the established system of the state. Their political future lay with the new republican order. In that light, part of our future research as historians must be to analyze how these former Regulators understood and accepted the promise of republicanism.

And yet, in order for us to understand their political future, we must still ask questions about their political past. How did settlers of the Massachusetts backcountry communities define their collective political identity? How did they understand their relationship to the established political order? And finally, how and why did they take extralegal collective action, both before and during the Revolutionary era? Shays's Rebellion gives us a brief historical moment that helps us answer some of these questions on a broad regional scale. Still, to appreciate fully the varieties of political behavior in rural society, we also need to examine these questions more carefully in the context of particular communities and over a longer period of time.

This essay does not issue a call for even more studies of New England towns. It does argue, however, that the community studies published so far, excellent though they are, do not tell us all we want to know about the political culture of rural society. Two hundred years ago, the inhabitants of dozens of small farming villages in western Massachusetts tried to get the attention of their state government, which had traditionally shown a greater concern—even bias—for towns in the east. When the government failed to respond, the western farmers rose up in arms. The people of those rebellious communities still deserve attention. Perhaps now, in commemorating the bicentennial of their uprising, historians have finally given them their due.

9

A DEACON'S ORTHODOXY:
Religion, Class, and the Moral Economy of Shays's Rebellion

John L. Brooke

One day during the tension-filled autumn of 1786, Robert Forbush of Holden, Massachusetts, stopped at the house of a fellow townsman to discuss public affairs. "Conversation turned upon the Riot Act," Forbush told a court of inquiry the following April. Taking out a copy of the act and reading it aloud, his neighbor Aaron Broad had declared his loyalty to the insurgents' cause: "I am determined to fight and spill my blood and leave my bones at the Court House till the Resurrection." In similar fashion, his neighbor Isaac Chenery exclaimed at the Worcester court closing in December that "I had rather be under the Devil than such a Government as this."[1]

These religious allusions remind us that the Regulator insurgents of Shays's Rebellion were immersed in a public culture profoundly shaped by a powerful Protestant tradition. If these exclamations suggest a habitual, rough language, redolent as much of tavern profanity as meetinghouse piety, the words attributed to the Reverend Caleb Curtis of Charlton ring of the revolutionary evangelical Protestantism we have come to expect in the last two decades of historical study. Curtis was an archetype of the "black regiment" of orthodox ministers who had exhorted the people to resistance and rebellion in 1775; he had resigned his ministry to serve in the General Court in 1776. Addressing a militia company mustering to support the government in December 1786, Curtis turned them

From a paper presented at the Bicentennial Conference on Shays's Rebellion, 1986, sponsored by the Colonial Society of Massachusetts.

against their officers with an impassioned speech: "Don't mind your Governor, nor your General Warner, nor your Colonel Towne, nor your Ammidowns, but in the name of God turn out and stop the sitting of the court, and I will support you with my life and Fortune." In the manner of the ministerial exhortations at the Lexington alarm eleven years before, Curtis then prayed with the Regulators who marched to Worcester.[2]

Curtis's role in the insurgency highlights several important perspectives on the dynamics of Shays's Rebellion—or the Regulation, as it more properly should be known. His speech illustrates the insurrection's challenge to specific local gentry elites, and it points to the role of patronage of the Regulators by other men of gentry status. It also poses the problem of the religious context of the rebellion: Curtis was invoking the Protestant God in calling out the Charlton Regulators. The religious context of the Regulation was not of central importance for an earlier generation of scholars; written in the great Progressive tradition, the seminal studies by Robert Taylor, Robert Feer, and Van Beck Hall focused on the interwoven problems of economy and politics which were of first importance to a state-level analysis. But ever since the publication of Alan Heimert's *Religion and the American Mind from the Great Awakening to the Revolution,* historians have been attuned to the religious dimensions of political action in the Revolutionary era. Inspired by Heimert's work, there emerged a school of historians who saw in the evangelical fervor of the Great Awakening the seedbed of eighteenth-century American political radicalism.[3] The evangelical interpretation of political dissent has been applied to Shays's Rebellion as well. In 1971 William McLoughlin argued that Baptists in the western counties "provided more than their share of men to Shays's rebels." In 1982 Stephen Marini introduced his *Radical Sects of Revolutionary New England* with an evocative description of the backcountry, suggesting that Shays's Rebellion and the emergence of Arminian Free-Will Baptists, Universalists, and Shakers were part and parcel of a single "deeply radical . . . Antifederalist culture."[4]

At first glance it would seem reasonable to assume a relationship between simultaneous and contiguous movements that challenged the structures of civil and religious order. But such an interpretive thrust also has attracted its critics. In his 1980 study David Szatmary gave only passing notice to the religious context of the Regulation, but he argued that the Baptists were only weakly represented among the Regulators, and that the majority were Congregationalists. Most recently, Ruth Bloch found millennial language decidedly absent in the rhetoric of the insurrection in her review of political millennialism in the late eighteenth century and has concluded that Shays's Rebellion "did not give rise either to revolutionary aspirations or to desires to remake the world anew."[5]

This essay argues, with David Szatmary and Ruth Bloch, that popular participation in the Regulation did not emerge from the evangelical, sectarian impulse. Instead, Shays's Rebellion was rooted in the old organic culture of the orthodox communities. In these places, including a majority of the interior farm towns, people held to the Congregational faith of New England tradition, worshiping together in a single church, taxing themselves to sustain minister and parish, and sustaining bonds of community born of a common Puritan ancestry and a shared agrarian way of life. Rather than a harbinger of the democratic politics of interest of the century to come, the Regulation was a final expression of a corporate political culture, wherein "the body of the people" rose to "regulate" the relationship between rulers and the ruled and to defend an ancient and eroding conception of a moral economy.

If the Regulators were situated in established orthodox communities that could claim a heritage running back to seventeenth-century Puritanism, this was by the 1780s an incomplete, truncated orthodoxy. The orthodox roots of the Regulation owed nothing to the established ministry, Caleb Curtis notwithstanding. As a body, the ministry opposed the insurgents, siding with a broader gentry class rather than the local community.[6] Support for the Regulation was strongest in those orthodox communities where the gentry class was absent and the minister isolated from his social class or missing altogether.

Important as they were, the ministers did not in themselves define the orthodox world. Their authority over the religious lives of the community was shared with officers drawn from the laity. In particular, one can distinguish between a ministerial orthodoxy and a deacon's orthodoxy. Through their preaching and pastoral duties, ministers carried out the larger, sacred purposes of bringing people to God. The deacons, by contrast, were responsible for the mundane problems of institutional continuity, of managing the secular affairs of church and parish. While they served at the communion table and lined out the Psalms for the congregation, the deacons' most important responsibilities involved keeping the church accounts. They gathered the money required to supply the communion table, to pay the minister, and—most importantly—to take care of the poor, "such as were in necessity." The key to the deacon's orthodoxy lay not in questions of fundamental doctrine but in a distinctive social role: in the words of the Cambridge Platform, their office was "limited unto the care of the temporall good things of the church." The deacon's place was to insure institutional continuity and collective well-being.[7]

Such concerns also were paramount for the men who led the people into the Regulation. For better or worse, the responsibility for raising the rebellion lay with men of local standing in orthodox communities: innholders, militia captains, deacons, and selectmen. Their concerns reflected the priorities of local officials of town and church: the survival of independent households in an interdependent community. Rather than a disorderly assault on established institutions, as its critics charged, the Regulation was an effort to stabilize a society disordered by economic upheaval in the larger world. It was deeply rooted in a moral economy that cherished a social ideal of republican independence, and that shaped a critique of individualistic economic relationships which were taking on a new legitimacy in the post-Revolutionary years. But only in towns where a deacon's orthodoxy prevailed, structuring social relations in the absence of both organized dissent and gentry authority, would this sense of order be expressed in an ardent and united support for the Regulation.[8]

MINISTERIAL JEREMIADS COMPLAINING of an erosion of orthodoxy during the Revolutionary years had a solid grounding in reality. The Revolutionary crisis of 1774 had worked briefly to reinforce the position of the Congregational covenant, but this initial momentum was difficult to maintain in the years to follow. After a burst of church admissions in the crisis years of 1774 and 1775, church records reveal a dramatic decline in the rate of new membership, which would generally not be reversed until the 1790s or later.[9] Similarly, all was not well in the relationship between ministers and congregations. The rate of ministerial vacancies in the orthodox churches in the three western counties of Worcester, Hampshire, and Berkshire doubled from 16 percent on the eve of the Revolution to 33 percent in the mid-1780s. The tendency was noticeable particularly in Hampshire County, where the intransigence of Tory ministers at Amherst, Northfield, Shutesbury, Warwick, Deerfield, and Greenfield led either to abrupt and sometimes violent dismissals or to a continuing undercurrent of ill will. Other orthodox ministers, like Caleb Curtis of Charlton, withdrew from the ministry to commit themselves to secular politics of the Revolution. Simultaneously, life in the army camps provided a fertile ground for the development of a secular worldview among the young men drawn from the towns by either the prospects of glory or the demands of the draft. Daniel Shays became a Freemason during the war years, and he and Luke and Elijah Day, other leading Hampshire County Regulators, joined a new Masonic lodge in Northampton early in 1786, only to be "recorded in infamy" on the Grand Lodge minutes following the Regulation. Their Masonic membership points to the gentry aspirations of some of the leading Regulators; it also poses a particular problem for any evangelical interpretation of Shays's Rebellion.[10]

The decadence of the orthodox establishment was only one side of the religious experience in Revolutionary New England. The other side was the rise of dissenting, sectarian denominations in a long explosive revival sequence between 1776 and 1782 which Stephen Marini has neatly defined as the "New Light Stir." The greatest beneficiaries of this Revolutionary revival were the Separate Baptists. From Middleborough in Plymouth County to New Providence in Berkshire, Baptist churches reported startling increases in church membership, and between 1777 and 1782 the membership of the Warren Baptist Association tripled, with fifteen churches added to the rolls. This revival coincided with efforts by Baptists throughout the state to have the old charter set aside and a new constitution written and ratified under the Lockean principle of the state of nature.[11] Marini has described the second great result of the

"New Light Stir": the proliferation of new dissenting denominations and sects. Building on experiences in the young American army in the siege of Boston, Universalist exhorters began to draw converts from upcountry Baptists in the winter of 1775–76. The next year a series of revivals spread through southeast New Hampshire which would lead to the Free-Will Baptist movement. And most dramatically, 1780 would bring the first of Mother Ann Lee's missions across Massachusetts in search of converts for the fledgling Shaker order that had settled in Niskeyuna, New York, in 1774. The Shakers would be the most successful of a host of enthusiastic sects emerging in the New England hinterland in the unsettled years following the Revolution. Where Mother Ann Lee managed by the adoption of strict hierarchical rule to perpetuate her claim to a prophetic mantle, Shadrack Ireland, Jemima Wilkinson, and William Dorrell failed. The ephemeral small sects gathering around these prophets of new faiths were less significant for their numerical following than as a symptom of religious unease and anxiety in the raw settlements of the post-Revolutionary New England frontier.[12]

An aggregate analysis of religion and politics in the towns of the three western Massachusetts counties, though not particularly conclusive, indicates that the absence of orthodox ministers may have been one social precondition to the Regulation. This analysis does not, however, suggest any strong correlation between the explosion of dissenting religion and the Regulation. Using court records and militia muster rolls to identify the residences of both leading Regulators and militia captains who raised companies for government service, I have divided the western towns into Regulator towns, militia towns, conflicted towns, and all others (see table 9.1 and Appendix A). Broadly, the differences among these towns were not drastic, but there were certain distinctions in the religious context of local political action. The militia towns stand out as being the least likely to have had either dissenting societies or vacant Congregational pulpits. In these places it appears that a traditional orthodoxy remained intact; town and church were one, ministers filled the pulpits, and dissenters were few and far between. The core Regulator towns, by contrast, were most notable for having the highest proportion of vacant Congregational pulpits. They were not, however, havens for religious dissent.

TABLE 9.1. Dissenting societies and Congregational ministerial vacancies in western Massachusetts, by political stance, 1786–87

Towns	Militia towns	Conflicted towns	Regulator towns	All other towns	Total
All three counties					
Total towns	31	44	33	26	134
With dissenting societies	8	20	13	9	50
% of total	25.8	45.5	39.3	34.6	37.3
Without Congregational minister	8	13	16	10	47
% of total	25.8	29.5	48.5	38.5	35.1
Berkshire County					
Total towns	2	10	9	4	25
With dissenting societies	1	4	4	2	11
% of total	50.0	40.0	44.4	50.0	44.0
Without Congregational minister	0	3	6	2	11
% of total		30.0	66.7	50.0	44.0
Hampshire County					
Total towns	16	19	15	10	60
With dissenting societies	2	7	7	2	18
% of total	12.5	36.8	46.6	20.0	30.0
Without Congregational minister	4	7	7	5	23
% of total	25.0	36.8	46.7	50.0	38.3
Worcester County					
Total towns	13	15	9	12	49
With dissenting societies	5	9	2	5	21
% of total	38.5	60.0	22.2	41.7	42.9
Without Congregational minister	4	3	3	3	13
% of total	30.8	20.0	33.3	25.0	26.5

Categories and sources: See Appendix A.

Among those places having difficulty maintaining an established minister in the years before the Regulation was the town-supported Presbyterian church in Pelham—the archetype of the Regulator towns. Here problems of class were as important as those of religion. One who unsuccessfully filled the Pelham pulpit, the great imposter Stephen Burroughs, described the Pelham people as "strict Presbyterians" with a high regard for "the nice distinctions between orthodox and heterodox principles and practice." But they also objected to the gentry style of the ministers of the day; Burroughs's predecessor had been criticized less for heterodox principles than for "practicing upon a system of manners more refined than that what was prevalent in the place." The Pelham people wanted a minister who would be of one mind with them, and they objected to those who aspired to the grand style of the River God gentry.[13] In failing to settle a minister, the people of Pelham and many of the other Regulator towns were insulating themselves from the conservative counsel of the clergy. They would turn to Daniel Shays, whose claim to gentry status came not from traditional sources but from his Revolutionary career.

The religious circumstances of the conflicted towns—where local notables raised men for both the Regulators and the government—were far more diverse than the militia or Regulator towns. In these places, ministers were settled in a preponderance of the Congregational churches, but they faced stiff competition in the community at large. These politically conflicted towns were the most likely of the four groups of towns to have had organized dissenting societies. It is tempting to suggest that this religious diversity directly underlay the political conflicts of 1786. But such an argument would proceed from a simple analysis of data which masks a far more complex situation. To understand the context of mobilization in 1786 we need to arrive at a much closer view than this sweeping aggregate. This fine-grained resolution can be achieved through what Charles Tilly calls a "census of the rebellion": an analysis of the collective biographies of hundreds of individuals participating in the confrontations of 1786–87. Such an endeavor necessarily must be limited in scope—the following analysis focuses on six towns—but it allows us to begin to develop some very specific arguments about the dynamics of class and community during this short insurgency.[14]

THE WORCESTER COUNTY TOWNS of Leicester, Spencer, Oakham, Brookfield, Charlton, and Sturbridge lie just west of the county seat of Worcester, within a broad band of towns which sent both companies of Regulators to close the courts and companies of militia to support the government in the critical months of 1786–87. Approximately 600 men, or 20 percent of the ratable polls in these six towns, marched with the Regulators or the government militia. Oakham and Spencer were among the core Regulator towns; the other four were conflicted, divided between notables supporting both the Regulation and the government. The focus of the Regulators' action, the county Court of Common Pleas had adjudicated cases of debt involving 134 debtors and 82 creditors from these same towns between December 1785 and July 1786 (see tables 9.2–9.4). The collective biography of these individuals, debtors and creditors, Regulators and Friends of Government, allows us precisely to define the context of religion and class in this insurgency, and to suggest its broader significance.[15]

An interior hinterland between coast and river valley, Worcester County was settled only after the Peace of Utrecht had brought an end to New England's first long sequence of war with the French and Indians. To the west, in Hampshire County, and to a degree in Berkshire, the social landscape was marked by the stark contrast between ancient and orderly valley towns and raw, newly settled towns in the surrounding hills. But in Worcester County a rolling topography punctuated by scattered stream valleys helped to shape a mosaic of class and community. Gentry-dominated towns were strung out at intervals on the province roads, linked to the cosmopolitan world of the capital in Boston. Interspersed among them were small towns, often off the main roads, where few gentlemen were seen apart from an orthodox minister and a resident justice of the peace. Dissenting religious societies, mostly Separate Baptists affiliated with the Warren Baptist Association, had emerged in the decades following the Great Awakening, particularly in the southeastern tier of towns closer to Rhode Island, rather than the northwestern towns closer to Hampshire County. Settled in open neighborhoods spanning some of the region's stream valleys, and comprising almost a quarter of the population in these six towns, the dissenters had achieved a solid position by the 1780s. How-

TABLE 9.2. Regulators, Friends of Government, debt, and credit in six Worcester County towns, December 1785–February 1787

	Nondissenters				
	In an orthodox gentry town	In plural towns	In two small orthodox towns	All dissenters	Total
Population, 1790	2,852	2,880	1,879	2,339	9,950
% of total	28.7	28.9	18.9	23.5	100.0
All Regulators	47	56	108	53	264
% of total	17.8	21.2	40.9	20.1	100.0
All Friends of Government	189	89	8	45	331
% of total	57.1	26.9	2.4	13.6	100.0
All debtors	35	32	37	30	134
% of total	26.1	23.9	27.6	22.4	100.0
All creditors	36	21	10	15	82
% of total	49.6	25.6	12.2	18.3	100.0
Regulators from first quintile households	12	12	34	8	66
% of all Regulators	25.5	21.4	31.5	15.1	25.0
Friends of Government from first quintile households	65	42	3	24	134
% of all Friends of Govt.	34.4	47.2	37.5	53.3	40.5
Regulators among debtors	6	7	23	7	43
% of all debtors	17.1	21.9	62.2	23.3	32.1
Friends of Government among debtors	18	14	0	6	38
% of all debtors	51.4	43.8	0	20.0	28.4
Regulators among creditors	1	3	5	6	15
% of all creditors	2.8	14.3	50.0	40.0	18.3
Friends of Government among creditors	23	5	0	2	30
% of all creditors	63.9	23.8	0	13.3	36.6

Categories: Orthodox gentry town: Brookfield; plural towns: Charlton, Leicester, and Sturbridge; all dissenters: all individuals who can be linked with dissenting societies or by kinship to the broader dissenting orbit; small orthodox towns: Spencer and Oakham.

Note: Individuals from first quintile households include heads of households, nontaxpaying sons, and sons in ninth and tenth deciles.

Sources: 1783 tax valuation, Massachusetts State Library, and sources listed in Appendix B.

TABLE 9.3. Political action of debtors from six Worcester County towns, 1786–87, by location of debt

	Orthodox gentry town		Nondissenters in plural towns		All dissenters		Small orthodox towns		Total	
	N	%	N	%	N	%	N	%	N	%
All debtors	35	100.0	32	100.0	30	100.0	37	100.0	134	100.0
Regulators	6	17.1	7	21.9	7	23.3	23	62.2	43	32.1
Unknown	11	31.4	11	34.3	17	56.7	14	37.8	53	39.5
Frds. of Govt.	18	51.4	14	43.8	6	20.0	0	0	38	28.4
Metropolitan debts	9	100.0	11	100.0	3	100.0	6	100.0	29	100.0
Regulators	1		2		1		4	66.6	8	27.6
Unknown	2		2		0		2		6	20.7
Frds. of Govt.	6	66.6	7	63.6	2	66.6	0		15	51.7
Regional debts	6	100.0	5	100.0	5	100.0	6	100.0	22	100.0
Regulators	1		0		0		5	83.3	6	27.3
Unknown	1		3	60.0	4	80.0	1		9	40.9
Frds. of Govt.	4	66.6	2		1		0		7	31.8
Debts in adjacent towns	5	100.0	8	100.0	16	100.0	23	100.0	52	100.0
Regulators	1		1		6	37.5	12	52.2	20	38.5
Unknown	3	60.0	4	50.0	7	43.7	11	47.8	25	48.1
Frds. of Govt.	1		3	37.5	3		0		7	13.5
Debts within same town	15	100.0	8	100.0	6	100.0	2	100.0	31	100.0
Regulators	3		4	50.0	0		2	100.0	9	29.0
Unknown	5	33.3	2		6	100.0	0		13	42.0
Frds. of Govt.	7	46.7	2		0		0		9	29.0

Political categories: See table 9.2.
Metropolitan debts: Owed to creditors in Boston, Cambridge, Plymouth, and Newport.
Regional debts: Owed to creditors in various inland towns that were not immediately adjacent to the debtor's hometown.
Note: In the cases where a debtor owed several debts, the location of the debt or debts with the highest value was used.
Sources: See Appendix B.

TABLE 9.4. Political action of creditors from six Worcester County towns, 1786–87, by location of debt

	Orthodox gentry town		Nondissenters in plural towns		All dissenters		Small orthodox towns		Total	
	N	%	N	%	N	%	N	%	N	%
All creditors	36	100.0	21	100.0	15	100.0	10	100.0	82	100.0
Regulators	1		3		6	40.0	5	50.0	15	18.3
Unknown	12	33.3	13	61.9	6	40.0	5	50.0	36	43.9
Frds. of Govt.	23	63.9	5		3		0		31	37.8
Metropolitan debts	0		0		0		0		0	
Regulators	0		0		0		0		0	
Unknown	0		0		0		0		0	
Frds. of Govt.	0		0		0		0		0	
Regional debts	12	100.0	3		2		2		19	100.0
Regulators	0		0		0		1		1	11.1
Unknown	4		2		1		1		8	42.1
Frds. of Govt.	8	66.6	1		1		0		10	52.6
Debts in adjacent town	12	100.0	11	100.0	9	100.0	6	100.0	38	100.0
Regulators	0		1		3	33.3	3	50.0	7	18.4
Unknown	4		7	63.6	4	44.4	3	50.0	18	47.4
Frds. of Govt.	8	66.6	3		2		0		13	34.2
Debts within same town	12	100.0	7	100.0	4	100.0	2	100.0	25	100.0
Regulators	1		2		3	75.0	1		7	28.0
Unknown	4		4	57.1	1		1		10	40.0
Frds. of Govt.	7	58.3	1		0		0		8	32.0

Categories: See tables 9.2 and 9.3.
Sources: See Appendix B.

ever, though they owned wealth in amounts roughly comparable to their orthodox fellow townsmen, the leading families among the dissenters had not yet begun to acquire the trappings of judicial placeholdings, college education, and extralocal affiliation which distinguished the gentry class among the orthodox. Importantly, something of a pluralistic accommodation was taking hold in the 1780s in the towns where dissenting societies had long been situated.

Though dissenters were in a minority in these towns, the pluralist towns had disproportionately voted in 1780 against the provisions in the new state constitution for state support for religion. Over the following decade these pluralist towns began to formalize the outlines of the nineteenth-century denominational order, releasing dissenters from ministerial rates and from the costs of rebuilding the old town meetinghouses. No such accommodations were evident in the purely orthodox towns.[16]

A host of economic problems beset Massachusetts in the mid-1780s. On the one hand, holders of public securities had engineered legislation early in 1781 which simultaneously devalued and retired paper currency and guaranteed the payment of their loans at full value, in gold and silver raised by high levels of taxation. And following a postwar commercial boom, a crisis among British merchants led to a chain of debt prosecutions running from Britain to American merchants in the coastal towns to merchants in the interior, and from these men to a host of local debtors. Worcester County was particularly hard hit, with per capita prosecutions for debt double the state average.[17]

But, at least as measured by the actions of debtors and creditors in these six towns, support for the Regulators or the government did not simply reflect levels of debt and credit. The economic crisis was certainly the cause of the confrontation in 1786, but mobilization was conditioned by the varying configurations of class and religious tradition within these towns. Orthodox towns stood out at the two extremes of political action in 1786, extremes which simultaneously articulated and denied class interests. Support for both the Regulators and the government flowed along channels of corporate obligation and hierarchy that were still powerful among the orthodox and decidedly absent among the dissenters. Within particular orthodox communities, political action transcended lines of class and interest to unite the people behind local leaders either for or against the court closings. By contrast, the radically simplified dissenting communions were splintered by this political action, with minorities of notables acting to support the government, minorities of hard-pressed debtors joining the Regulation, and the majority withholding support from either side.

Brookfield, the second largest town in the county, long had

been a center of gentry influence, with long-standing connections among the Hampshire River Gods. No fewer than five companies of government militia and gentleman volunteers were raised in this town, and when Regulator sympathizers managed to pass a petition for clemency in a December town meeting, Justice Dwight Foster organized a counterpetition signed by ninety-six inhabitants. This orthodox gentry town, encompassing 29 percent of the region's population, accounted for only 18 percent of the Regulators and 57 percent of the Friends of Government (see table 9.2). Here debt relations and religious affiliation worked together to reinforce support for the government. The Brookfield gentry, along with a group of Worcester merchants and to a lesser extent the gentry in the pluralist towns, were commercial intermediaries. Owing large debts to coastal merchants, they in turn were owed money in a host of small local debts (see table 9.4). Such men were pillars of the government cause in 1786. Brookfield men with debts to merchants in Cambridge and Boston sided overwhelmingly with the government, as did the creditors living in the town (see table 9.3). But Brookfield also stood out as the only location where debtors owing money to creditors within a given town also served with the government militia in significant numbers; in other contexts such debtors remained neutral or supported the Regulation. A local creditor gentry, with their own obligations to metropolitan creditors, thus played a key role in turning their townspeople toward the government. Religious unity also played a role in this allegiance to the government. Roughly two-thirds of the progovernment militia in Brookfield were church members or the close relatives of church members. As would be the case under the Federalists in the following decades, the structures of the orthodox church, supported by an active ministry and a few progovernment deacons, apparently worked to reinforce class relations of deference in this gentry-dominated town.[18]

The smaller orthodox yeoman towns of Spencer and Oakham present a very different picture. Small towns incorporated from subordinate districts in 1775, they had neither dissenting societies nor a substantial gentry class; the town selectmen were men of local reputation, at best Congregational deacons or innholders. Well-organized companies of Regulators marched from these towns to close the courts in Worcester, and none of the local militia captains even attempted to raise companies for the government. Comprising roughly 19 percent of the population in the six town area, the orthodox population of these towns accounted for 45 percent of the Regulators and only 3 percent of the Friends of Government. The configurations of debt and the mobilization of debtors drastically different from the neighboring gentry-dominated Brookfield (see tables 9.2–9.4). Roughly two-thirds of all relations of debt and credit were with men in adjacent towns, rather than with local and metropolitan partners, and 62 percent of the debtors were represented among the Regulators, as against 20–25 percent of the debtors in all other circumstances. In sharp opposition to the gentry town of Brookfield, none of the debtors served with the government militia and, most importantly, five of the ten creditors supported the Regulation.

Among these creditor-Regulators were several who might be called Regulator notables, men who seem to have been acting on altruistic motives, on a sense of obligation to the corporate locality that transcended individual private interest, men whose leadership facilitated the dramatic mobilization of debtors in these towns for the Regulation. Deacon Oliver Watson of Spencer had served as the town's delegate to a county convention in 1784. On several occasions in 1785 and 1786 Watson appeared in the Supreme Judicial Court as a lay attorney for his neighbors when they appealed cases of debt, so that they might avoid an obligation to the court's phalanx of attending lawyers. In June 1786 he allowed his case against neighbor Benjamin Bemiss to be continued and served on the committee which called the county convention at which Bemiss served as a delegate from Spencer. Two of Watson's householding sons, one a selectman in 1786, would serve in the ranks of the Regulators, as would a dependent son of Benjamin Bemiss. In Oakham there were three selectmen in this group of creditor-Regulators. One, innholder Richard Kelly, was in court as a plaintiff in five different cases in 1786, but he, too, supported the Regulation and, after its defeat, took the oath of allegiance to the government. A second Oakham creditor, selectman Ebenezer Nye, "acted in the capacity" of a captain for the Regulator company that marched from Oakham, and his son Timothy signed an oath as well. A third creditor in Oakham, innholder Joseph Chaddock, the town's delegate to the

1786 convention, was accused of being "very busy in Encouraging" the Regulators and of giving them the town's store of ammunition. In total, these creditors were owed £176 in ten different debts, and only one of them was a defendant in one case amounting to £14. It would have been in their immediate interest to keep the courts open in September 1786, yet the focus of collective obligation within these communities impelled them into the dangers of the Regulator movement.[19]

These creditors were part of a larger group of leading men in the small orthodox towns for whom aid for debtors was the prelude to support or sympathy for the Regulation. Deacon Jonathan Bullard, a Regulator leader in Oakham, acted as local debt arbitrator. Oakham and Paxton Regulators John Gould, Seth Snow, and Jonathan Clemons all stood as sureties for debtors at the Supreme Judicial Court in the place of the cadre of Worcester lawyers. Justices Edward Rawson of Leicester and John Bisco of Spencer stood as sureties and agents for at least seven debtors in 1786. Justice Bisco also served on a committee to consider the conditions of the county jail in December 1785, with Regulator sympathizers Amos Singletary and John Fessenden.[20] In the spring of 1787 dozens of Regulators would bypass progovernment justices to sign oaths of allegiance with Bisco and Rawson, and their colleague Percival Hall of New Braintree,[21] apparently because of their known sympathy for the debtors' cause.[22] While the Congregational ministers in both Oakham and Spencer probably opposed the Regulators, five of the seven deacons serving in the 1770s and 1780s were Regulator supporters, and a sixth was moderator of the Oakham town meeting throughout the period, a sign of some popularity in an overwhelmingly Shaysite town. In gentry-dominated Brookfield, moral unity reinforced deference to the interests of the creditor-gentry; in smaller orthodox towns such moral unity worked to equate the elders' traditional obligation to the community with the interests of the debtors. In the former, a ministerial orthodoxy prevailed; in the latter a deacon's orthodoxy shaped the community's endorsement of the Regulation.

The dissenters and Congregationalists in the pluralist towns present a quite different pattern. Again, we have something of a paradox. The economic interests of debt and credit so evident in the orthodox towns seem to have been of relatively little importance in determining the loyalties of dissenters and their orthodox neighbors in the pluralistic towns, yet support for the government or the Regulation was more sharply divided along class lines (see table 9.2). Among both of these groups only a fifth of the debtors appearing in the Court of Common Pleas in the previous year were drawn into the Regulation, as against almost two-thirds of the debtors in the orthodox yeoman towns. Conversely, only a fifth of the creditors supported the government, as against almost two-thirds of the creditors in the orthodox gentry town of Brookfield. The Regulators' threat to contract apparently was not particularly important to these dissenting creditors, and conversely, something was working to impede the mobilization of dissenting debtors behind the Regulation. At the same time there was far less support for Regulation among the wealthiest fifth of the population, the traditional stratum of town leadership, than in the small orthodox towns, and also far less support for the government among the poorer four-fifths of the population than in the gentry town of Brookfield. Where the virtual civil war of 1786 united the orthodox towns on one side or the other, the dissenting communities and the orthodox in the pluralistic towns were splintered and divided along class lines.

Such divisions also characterized the dissenting churches themselves. Where orthodox Regulators were drawn from the core families of the Congregational churches, Baptist Regulators came from the fringes of their religious communities. Where Congregational deacons openly supported the Regulators, their Baptist counterparts opted for the government or took no position at all. Among the six deacons of the Baptist churches in Leicester, Sturbridge, and Charlton, two were closely related to government militia men, and the other four had no connections with either side. Similarly, if the orthodox Regulators were not often full church members, they were from families in good standing with their church, while the vast majority of the Baptist Regulators were probably only attenders, contributing to subscriptions on occasion, and often can only be connected to Baptist meetings by broader family connections (see table 9.5).

The ambiguous relationship of mobilization in the pluralist towns to patterns of debt derived from the voluntarizing dynamic of reli-

TABLE 9.5. Congregational and Baptist church affiliations of Regulators in Spencer, Leicester, Charlton, and Sturbridge

	Spencer Congregational Church			Three Baptist churches in Leicester, Sturbridge, and Charlton	
	N	%	%	N	%
Church members in good standing	5	13.5	8.5	4	8.2
Church members in bad standing	1	2.7	1.7	3	6.1
Sons of male church members	14	37.8	23.7	2	4.1
Other affiliations to church*	17	45.9	28.8	40	81.6
Subtotal	37	100.0	62.7	49	100.0
Town residents with no known affiliation to church	22		37.3		
Total	59		100.0	49	100.0

*Pew-lists, subscription lists, kinship ties.
Note: The Spencer Congregationalists practiced the Half-Way Covenant; the status of church members was not available for the Charlton Baptist church.
Sources: See Appendix B.

gion and politics that had been at work among the dissenters and in the pluralist towns over the previous decade. The constitution-making process of 1776 to 1780 made an especially important impact in dissenting societies and pluralist towns. Where the orthodox in Worcester County had seen little reason to abandon the charter in 1776, the Baptists had insisted that the province lay in a state of nature, that the old charter be set aside and a new constitution drawn up. The Congregationalists in the pluralist towns had seen the verities of the orthodox social order challenged by religious dissenters and in the early 1780s had begun to come to terms with the new order that the constitution seemed to have established. A series of local compromises mitigated the constitution's coercive requirement that "religious teachers" be publicly supported. Congregationalists began to define themselves as distinct "societies," rather than parishes with territorial prerogatives; the leading gentry in these towns had joined together in 1784 to incorporate the Leicester Academy, the region's first secular voluntary association. Thus the religious voluntarism of the dissenters had worked with the constitutional politics of the Revolutionary era to shape the outlines of the nineteenth-century social order: voluntary association among a plurality of institutions.[23]

Rather than acting simply in defense of the interests of creditors, the Friends of Government in the pluralist towns acted to defend this new constitutional order in 1786. Particularly among the dissenting Baptists and Universalists, recruits for the government militia and light horse were drawn from the elite, over half from the top fifth of the valuation, several from the households of deacons and selectmen. Some of these were men who had been active in the constitution-making process and in the forming of the Leicester Academy. Others were ambitious for place and position in the new governmental structure; all were willing to take the government's pay to serve against their neighbors among the ranks of the Regulators.[24] But, unlike the orthodox creditor gentry in Brookfield, these ambitious voluntarist gentry were unable to command the deference of the poorer households in their communities. Unlike the innholders, deacons, and selectmen in the small, orthodox towns, they felt no particular moral obligation to lead those lesser men against the government. The few Baptist-affiliated debtors who did join the Regulation were particularly exposed and isolated. They were distinctly poorer than other dissenting debtors who remained neutral, and though their total indebtedness was equivalent, they were burdened with roughly twice as many individual debts. Though a number of Baptist and Universalist notables had stood as sureties for debtors in the Supreme Judicial Court, they rarely supported the Regulation, as did their counterparts in the smaller orthodox towns.[25] Vertical reciprocal ties of deference and obligation had been dramatically eroded in those places and in communities where the new voluntary and pluralistic order had begun to take shape. The result was sharp divisions along class lines within these communities and lower rates of participation on either side of the confrontation, as progovernment notables had few followers and potential Regulators had few leaders.

Caleb Curtis was acting on just this absence of a regulating leadership in the pluralist towns when he appeared on the Charlton militia field in December 1786 and exhorted the men to march to close the courts, offering to support them with his "life and fortune." And in urging them to disregard the governor and their officers, Curtis was articulating the collapse of deference and obligation in the voluntary towns. A former orthodox minister in a town divided among Congregationalists, Baptists, and Universalists, Caleb Curtis occupied a unique rather than a typical position. Many men in Charlton were disposed to desert their gentry officers, but they found few leaders among the traditional stratum of local notables. It is important that the Regulator emergence in the dissenting towns of Leicester and Charlton came in December, not at the initial court closings in September. Curtis's appeal may have been as much political as it was debt-related; David Dresser of Charlton later testified that he had only taken up arms against the government "when [he] heard the Light Horse was coming." The mobilization of Regulators in these dissenting towns did not flow from a structured response of leading men to the pressure of debt in their communities, as it did in the small orthodox towns, but in a secondary, ad hoc fashion in response to the government's threats of violent action.[26]

Without the leadership and organization flowing along the corporate channels of a deacon's orthodoxy, dissenting Regulators in one suggestive but isolated instance drew upon the framework of voluntary association. On February 2, 1787, in the only truly violent incident of the insurgency in Worcester County, a band of Regulators encamped at New Braintree fired on a party of government men, wounding two of them. The government party had been sent to free two sheriff's deputies, Samuel Flagg and John Stanton of Worcester, from the hands of the insurgents. Flagg and Stanton had been captured when they had attempted to serve a writ of execution against Isaac Southgate, the son of a Baptist elder in Leicester. They encountered a determined group of Southgate's neighbors, who had apparently signed a formal pledge to defend "each individual among the Subscribers who may be injured" by writs of execution. But the group shared more than economic worries. According to later court testimony, at least thirteen men participated in the affair; all were drawn broadly from the dissenting orbit in the pluralist towns of the southern half of the county. Three were Universalists from Oxford and Ward, at least five were from Baptist families, and two were from the town of Uxbridge in the Blackstone valley, a region rife with religious dissent. In effect, the subscribers had established a private debtors' society, based on the voluntary principles which shaped the dissenting societies. Their purposes were quite different from the Regulator mainstream. Where the majority of the Regulators acted as a corporate force to close the courts until public grievances were met, these voluntarist Regulators banded together simply to protect private property from attachment by the sheriff.[27]

This group was only a minor element among the Worcester County Regulators in 1786, but its organization, purposes, and profile of participation was quite similar to that which had characterized a series of small riots in 1782 and 1783. Usually aimed at stopping "vendue sales" of cattle, these riots had been the first sign that the economic pressures of taxation and private debt were straining the social fabric to the breaking point. But these episodes were firmly rooted in Baptist and Universalist families and neighborhoods and bore no obvious relationship to the broader patterns of Regulator mobilization of 1786. A few future Regulators even testified against these rioters, and more of the rioters ended up in the ranks of the government militia than among the Regulators. Among the latter was Reubin Lamb of Oxford, who would be among those holding Flagg and Stanton in New Braintree in February 1787. And like this group of voluntarist Regulators, the rioters were bound together by agreements of mutual protection, involving cooperation among "reformation men" from the southern Worcester towns as well as Rhode Island and Connecticut, who chose officers and stood "ready to assist at a minutes Warning."[28]

Thus, while orthodox institutions shaped a sense of inclusive moral economy which legitimized public action against the county courts, New Light dissent informed more circumscribed efforts to protect private property. In short, the orthodox were inclined toward "public mobs," and dissenters toward "private mobs."[29] Disputes erupting within dissenting and orthodox churches in the wake of the rebellion underscore the very different linkages between moral and economic categories among the orthodox and the dissenters. The Baptist church at South Leicester was wracked with turmoil in 1787, but the lines were not drawn between Regulators and Friends of Government. Two factions fell into dispute over a plan to grant the minister a regular salary. A band of "Disaffected Brethren" led by Samuel Denny and Deacon Isaac Choate charged that the Reverend Isaac Beals was a "lazy . . . discontented person" who "wearied out the church with [his] unreasonable complaints" for support. The minister countered that Deacon Choate had asked him "the market price for Pork, that was not well fatted." Despite their financial grievances, none of the "Disaffected Brethren" joined the Regulation, and Denny's son served with the government light horse in the winter of 1787. There were some Regulators among the Leicester Baptists, but rather than quarreling over the minister's salary, most of them simply stopped attending. Of eight Regulators once affiliated with the church, only three were still active in 1786. Of four actual church members, three were excluded or admonished in 1787 for long neglecting their "travel with the church." Their censure had nothing to do with their role in the rebellion. The fourth Regulator among the membership remained in good standing, paid his 1786 dues, and was elected to a standing committee in 1787. In the spring of 1788 the Leicester Baptists articulated explicitly their disassociation of moral and economic categories in revising the language of a 1784 vote governing civil suits among brethren. This vote had directed that the creditor negotiate with a debtor as prescribed in Matthew 18:15–17, meeting with him in the presence of witnesses and before the congregation; that failing, the creditor was to treat the debtor "as he would a pagan or tax-collector." The vote originally had stipulated that the church would judge whether either party had violated "moral order." In April 1788 the church changed the language to read "gospel order." "Moral order" was too imprecise for these Baptists, suggesting a broader scope of action than the limited absolutes of the gospel church.[30]

Where the Baptists were silent about the role of their members in the Regulation, apparently maintaining a strict separation of church and state, the ministers of the Congregationalist churches were less circumspect. In the aftermath of the Regulation a series of confrontations broke out between ministers and laity in the small orthodox towns over their respective behavior during the rebellion. In

Spencer, the church finally had to vote to overrule the minister, Joseph Pope, in his efforts to censure one church member among the Regulators, Samuel Rice. And after another protracted series of meetings the church voted in April 1788 "that the conduct of Brother Samuel Tucker in their opinion, was not criminal, and ought not fall under ye reprehension and censure of the ch[urc]h for the part he acted in ye late insurrection." Nearby to the west, a bitter fight erupted between orthodox minister and people in the Hampshire County town of Ware. When the Regulator leaders called on the Reverend Benjamin Judd to pray for their cause, he called one of them a "Hell-Hound" and declared that "he would as soon pray for the Devils in Hell as for ye Insurgents." Inverting Isaac Chenery's exclamation that he would rather live "under the Devil than such a Government as this," the Reverend Mr. Judd scolded the congregation in Ware that "if the Devil was Governor or Ruler the People ought to Obey him." The ecclesiastical council that met to resolve the quarrel absolved Judd for his "harsh expressions" and censured two deacons and five other prominent men for various charges of nonattendance and for supporting the "most wicked and unprovokable" rebellion, "a crime of ye most aggravated nature." In both cases, clergy and laity had dramatically different interpretations of the covenant order. But both drew upon the blending of sacred and secular, of civil and religious, which stood at the heart of the orthodox way, impelling both Regulator requests for prayers and ministerial efforts to discipline them for their assault on civil institutions.[31]

IN NOVEMBER 1786 Captain Adam Wheeler, recently a Revolutionary officer, a former selectman, assessor, and town treasurer, and a founding member of the orthodox church in Hubbardston, wrote a brief statement explaining to the public his leading role in the closing of the Worcester courts. "He had no Intentions to Destroy the Publick Government but to have the . . . Courts of Common Pleas and gen[era]l sessions of the peace . . . suspended, to prevent Such abuses as have of late taken place by the sitting of those Courts." Wheeler was particularly "Distressed to See Valuable and Industrious members of Society dragged from their families to prison, to the great damage not only of their families but the

Community at large."[32] Wheeler's language contained no dramatic religious metaphors, yet it spoke of a basic moral concern. Adam Wheeler made a choice between the legal enforcement of contract and the preservation of household independence. His decision to lead men against the courts, in an almost ritual tradition of collective action that sought only a redress of public grievances, flowed from his particular circumstances as a leading man in a small, orthodox town.

The Regulation has long been seen simply as a confrontation of debtors and creditors. Obviously, debt relations were powerful determinants of political action in the 1780s. But this political action was also decisively shaped by expectations and relationships forged in very different religious communities. The corporate assumptions of the orthodox laity shaped a unified Regulator militance in the yeoman towns; men of local standing acted on an understanding of mutual obligation to lead debtor-neighbors against the courts. But corporatism could also contribute to debtor deference to a powerful creditor-gentry and to ministerial assumptions of such deference. Conversely, Lockean voluntarism undermined expectations of both mutual obligation and hierarchical deference. Its privatistic impulses shaped the most striking patterns among the dissenters: small-scale rioting in 1782 and 1783 and the general failure of debtors to mobilize—other than in minor private efforts—in 1786 sharply contrasted with the staunch progovernment action by leading dissenting households. What differentiated the Regulators most particularly was an expectation of governmental adjustment, a willingness to interfere with the adjudication of individual contract, and a social structure conducive to collective action.

In summary, then, Shays's Rebellion was centered in the orthodox world, in the expectations of social reciprocity of a people united in the territorial structures of corporate church and town. Rather than being driven by any millennial, otherworldly fantasies, the Regulators were very much of this world, and they expected religion to serve worldly purposes. Their worldview was not shaped by the intense fervor and separatist impulses of the evangelical revival but by a profound sense of the moral context of human behavior. Rather than being devout church members, they were more typically affiliated by the inclusive forms of infant baptism and the

Half-Way Covenant, the sacred safety net of a conditional birthright contract inherited from the late seventeenth-century compromise of Puritan divinity. This orthodox Regulator mentality was perhaps tribal in its focus in the household and corporate community. It certainly was grounded in assumptions about church and state that we reject and contributed to a fundamental misunderstanding of constitutional government. But these religious sensibilities never provided the intellectual roots of a millennial imperialism, and they informed a moral critique of individualistic economic relationships which is the lasting legacy of this brief insurgency.

APPENDIX A: Religion and the Regulation

The following lists summarize the religious circumstances and political loyalties of the 134 taxpaying towns and districts in the three western counties (see table 9.1). The following data were also used in the analysis for a parallel essay, "To the Quiet of the People: Revolutionary Settlements and Civil Unrest in Western Massachusetts, 1774–1789," *WMQ*, 3d ser., 46 (1989): 453–57.

Key: B = Baptists; Q = Quakers; E = Episcopalians; UN = Universalists; S = Shakers; SEP = Separates; v = Congregational ministerial vacancy.

Sources:

Dissenting societies: *Pocket Almanack for 1787 . . . Massachusetts Register* (Boston: Fleets, 1786), 57–60; *Minutes of the Warren [Baptist] Association, at Their Annual Convention, Held at Mr. Blood's Meetinghouse in Newton, 1786* (Charlestown, Mass.: John W. Allen, 1786), 2–3; David D. Field and Chester Dewey, eds., *A History of the County of Berkshire, Massachusetts* (Pittsfield: S. W. Bush, 1829); John R. Lockwood, ed., *Western Massachusetts: A History, 1635–1925*, 4 vols. (New York: Lewis, 1926); Nathaniel B. Sylvester, ed., *The History of the Connecticut Valley in Massachusetts*, 2 vols. (Philadelphia: L. H. Everts, 1879); *History of Worcester County, Massachusetts*, 2 vols. (Boston: C. F. Jewett, 1879). Shaker locations provided by Stephen Marini.

Congregational ministerial vacancies: *Pocket Almanack for 1787 . . . Massachusetts Register* 57–60.

Government militia captains: The distribution of captains who raised companies for government service was used to establish the geography of support for the government in the fall and winter of 1786–87. The names of these militia captains were found in the militia muster rolls filed in volumes 191 and 192 of the Massachusetts Archives Collection, part of the Archives of the Commonwealth, located at the Massachusetts State Archives building, Columbia Point, Boston. These names were linked with towns using the 1790 census, *Heads of Families at the First Census of the United States Taken in the Year 1790: Massachusetts* (Washington, D.C.: U.S. Bureau of the Census, 1908).

Regulator leaders: I have used lists of those individuals singled out for arrest and prosecution to establish the distribution of the leadership for the Regulation in the fall and winter of 1786–87. Because the oaths of allegiance signed in the spring of 1787 were somewhat erratically administered and were aimed at the rank and file, not the Regulator leadership, I did not use them to establish this geographic profile. Sources include warrants, indictments, and imprisonments listed in the following sources: Massachusetts Archives, 189:75–76, 81–84, 100–102, 135, 210; Suffolk Files Collection, file no. 155325 (initial list of 21 indictments) and no. 155296–7; Supreme Judicial Court Docket Book, 1787, 58–60, 63, 77–80, 101–2 (and September Session, Worcester County, n.p.); Jail Register, Worcester County, Mass., Papers, folder 1, box 2, American Antiquarian Society; Prison Lists in Original Papers of Shays's Rebellion, Berkshire Athenaeum; and court notes in Robert Treat Paine Papers, box 23, Massachusetts Historical Society. The Suffolk Files Collection and the Supreme Judicial Court Docket Books, formerly located in the Suffolk County Court Building, are now part of the Judicial Archives located at the Massachusetts State Archives building, Columbia Point, Boston.

"Plus Black List": The "Hampshire County Black List," Robert Treat Paine Papers, box 23, identifies 139 leading Regulators in Hampshire County. This list allows for more of Hampshire's sixty towns and districts to be classified, adding four towns to the "Regulator" category and shifting three towns from the "Militia" to the "Conflicted" category.

For suggestive discussions of the importance of local militia captains as "notables" and of politics as a form of militia muster, see Fred Anderson, *A People's Army: Massachusetts Soldiers and Society in the Seven Years War* (Chapel Hill: Univ. of North Carolina Press, 1984); Van Beck Hall, *Politics without Parties: Massachusetts, 1780–1791* (Pittsburgh: Univ. of Pittsburgh Press, 1972), 207–8, and Robert H. Wiebe, *The Opening of American Society: From the Adoption of the Constitution to the Eve of Disunion* (New York: Random House, 1984), 37–38.

Berkshire County Towns

Towns	Relig. dissent	Congreg. vacancy	Govt. militia captains	Regulator leaders
Adams	BQ	v		3
Alford				2
Dalton		v		10
Becket	B			
Egremont				10
Great Barrington	E	v	3	4
Hancock	BS	v		
Lanesborough	BE		2	3
Lee		v		10
Lenox	B		3	3
Louden		v		
Mount Washington				
New Ashford		v		4
New Marlborough		v	3	1
New Providence*	B			
Partridgefield			2	4
Pittsfield	BS			15
Richmond	S		3	
Sandisfield	B		3	1
Sheffield		v	2	8
Stockbridge			2	
Tyringham	S	v		3
Washington	BS		1	5
West Stockbridge	BS	v		16
Williamstown			1	7
Windsor			1	4
Total			26	113

*Not a taxpaying district in 1786; not used in final analysis.

Hampshire County Towns

Towns	Relig. dissent	Congreg. vacancy	Govt. militia captains	Regulator leaders	Regulator leaders plus Black List
Amherst			1	2	7
Ashfield	BS				2
Belchertown	S		3	3	4
Bernardston			1	5	3
Blandford		v	2	1	5
Brimfield			3		
Buckland		v	1		
Charlmont			1	1	2
Chesterfield		v	4	2	2
Colrain	B			3	4
Conway				1	4
Cummington					
Deerfield		v	1		
Easthampton		v	4		
Granby	BS	v			
Granville		v	4		1
Goshen		v	1		
Greenfield			1	1	2
Greenwich				3	9
Hadley			2		
Hatfield			2		
Hawley		v			
Heath			1		
Holland					
Leverett	B	v			7
Leyden		v		2	2
Longmeadow		v		1	1
Ludlow		v		1	3
Rowe		v			
Middlefield		v			
Monson	B		1		1
Montague	BS		1	2	5
Montgomery		v	1		3
Chester			1		
New Salem	B			1	5
Northampton			2		
Northfield			1	3	4
Norwich		v	3	2	2
Orange			1		

Hampshire County Towns *Continued*

Towns	Relig. dissent	Congreg. vacancy	Govt. militia captains	Regulator leaders	Regulator leaders plus Black List
Palmer					
Pelham	B	v		2	8
Plainfield		v			
Shelburne	S		1		
Shutesbury	B	v		1	10
South Brimfield	B			1	2
South Hadley			3		
Southampton			3	1	1
Southwick	B		1	1	3
Springfield			1		
Sunderland	B				
Ware		v			2
Warwick			1		1
West Springfield	BS		2	2	10
Westfield	B		1	4	6
Westhampton			1		
Wendell	B		1		
Whately				1	7
Wilbraham	B	v	1	1	4
Williamsburg					
Worthington		v	3	2	7
Total			61	50	139

Worcester County Towns

Towns	Relig. dissent	Congreg. vacancy	Govt. militia captains	Regulator leaders
Ashburnham	B			
Atholl	SEP	v		
Barre				1
Berlin				
Bolton	BQS	v	1	
Boylston			1	
Brookfield			6	2
Charlton	B		2	2
Douglass	BQ		2	
Dudley	B		1	1

Worcester County Towns *Continued*

Towns	Relig. dissent	Congreg. vacancy	Govt. militia captains	Regulator leaders
Fitchburg				
Gardner		v		
Grafton	BS		2	2
Harvard	BS			1
Hardwick	B	v	1	14
Holden			1	5
Hubbardston				2
Lancaster				
Leicester	BQ		1	1
Leominster			1	
Lunenburg			1	
Mendon	QQ	v	2	
Milford	UN		1	
Northbridge	BQ			
Northborough			1	
New Braintree			1	3
Oakham		v		1
Oxford	UN	v	1	2
Paxton		v		4
Phillipston				
Princeton		v		5
Petersham	BS		1	
Royalston	B			
Rutland			1	1
Southborough		v		
Shrewsbury			1	1
Spencer				6
Sturbridge	B		2	5
Sterling				
Sutton	B		2	1
Templeton	B			1
Upton	B			
Uxbridge	Q		1	3
Ward				1
Westborough		v	1	
Winchendon			1	
Westminster			1	
Worcester		v	4	2
Western		v	1	
Total			42	67

APPENDIX B: Sources on the Regulation in Worcester County

The material identifying the insurgents in southwest Worcester County was produced in two judicial contexts and is presently held in four different archives. First, oaths of allegiance were administered to the rank and file of the movement by the justices of the peace in the towns, a few as early as December 1786 but the majority in February and March 1787. Oaths were located for all the towns considered here except Charlton and Sturbridge. The original lists returned by the local JPs are to be found in Massachusetts Archives (MA), 190:80, 107, 131, 151, 165–66 & ¾, 169, 205, 216, 225B. Second, a body of material produced by the Supreme Judicial Court sitting in Worcester is located in three archives. Extensive testimony heard against a small number of insurgents in January, February, and March 1787 by justices in Worcester is located in folder 5, "Arrests and Trials of Several Insurgents, 1787," Shays's Rebellion Collection, American Antiquarian Society (AAS). This material was apparently part of a larger body of evidence brought before the Supreme Judicial Court at its special April 1787 session in Worcester. A set of notes and lists taken down by Robert Treat Paine and others at this April session is located in the "Box on Shays' Rebellion," Robert Treat Paine Papers, Massachusetts Historical Society. Finally, the indictments handed down at this session are located in the Suffolk Files Collection, file no. 155325 (throughout), Judicial Archives. MA vol. 189 contains a considerable amount of useful material from the months following the April session, including a letter about Josiah Walker of Sturbridge (163–66) and petitions from Caleb Curtis of Charlton (200, 237).

The evidence on the Friends of Government is drawn predominantly from the Massachusetts Archives. Muster rolls of the militia and volunteers raised to put down the rebellion are located in MA, 191:113, 113a, 157, 158, 175, 176, 180, 188, 211, 212, 220, 221, 275, 285 and 192:1–3, 17, 35, 37, 69, 75–79, 128, 157, 161, 176, 191. Unlike the insurgents, the militiamen are not identified by town, but generally each unit was drawn from a relatively small area of between one and four towns. These muster rolls were compared with the 1790 U.S. Census to link men with towns; names that did not appear in the census were located in the Vital Records. (In general, the relative short period of settlement [forty to fifty years] meant that clusters of family names did not predominate, as they did in the eastern towns, and thus the linking of various types of records is quite accurate.)

Another important source for identifying Friends of Government is the list of ninety-six inhabitants who signed the Brookfield Protest against a pro-Regulator petition in January 1787, located in MA, 190:313. Other sources for the Friends of Government in southwest Worcester County are: Dwight Foster Journal, 1772–87, entries for Jan. 31–Feb. 3, 1787, Foster Family Papers, vol. 1, AAS; Ephraim Ward Diary, 1787, Jan. entries, misc. MSS, box W, AAS; Emory Washburn, *Historical Sketches of the Town of Leicester, during the First Century from Its Settlement* (Boston: John Wilson and Son, 1860), 239–329; Emory Washburn, "Topographical and Historical Sketch of the Town of Leicester," *Worcester Magazine and Historical Journal* 2 (1826): 116–19; Josiah H. Temple, *History of North Brookfield, Massachusetts* (North Brookfield: Published by the town, 1887), 245–46.

The evidence on debtors and creditors is drawn from the Worcester County Court of Common Pleas Record Book, 13 (1785–86): 1–280, and from the appeals to the Supreme Judicial Court recorded in the Suffolk Files Collection, files no. 154708–155293. See also Supreme Judicial Court Docket Books, April and September 1786 sessions. The Worcester County Court of Common Pleas Record Books, formerly located at the Worcester County Court House, are now part of the Judicial Archives located at the Massachusetts State Archives building, Columbia Point, Boston.

Evidence on religious affiliation is drawn from a wide range of manuscript and printed sources. The manuscript sources include the membership Book, First Congregational Church of Spencer, Mass. (MSS, church vault); Greenville (Leicester, Mass.) Baptist Church Records, vol. 1, Andover-Newton Theological School, Newton, Mass.; the Records of the Baptist Church of Christ in Sturbridge, Mass., microfilm, Research Library, Old Sturbridge Village; and the Second Religious Society in Oxford and Adjacent Towns (Called Universalist), Record Book, 1785–1845, Andover Harvard Theological Library. Other dissenting affiliations in Leicester have been drawn from Washburn, *Leicester*. The records for Congregational churches in the three precincts of Brookfield are listed in *The Confession of Faith and Covenant of the First Congregational Church in North Brookfield, Mass., with a Catalogue of Members (1752–1878)* (West Brookfield, Mass.: Thomas Morey, 1878); *Catalogue of the Members of the Congregational Church in West Brookfield, from 1758–1861* (West Brookfield, Mass.: Thomas Morey, 1861); *Rules of Order and Discipline, Articles of Faith, and Covenant of the Evangelical Congregational Church in Brookfield, Mass., with Historical Notes* (West Brookfield, Mass.: Thomas Morey, 1878). The membership of the Charlton Baptist church is listed in Holmes Ammidown, *Historical Collections*, 2d ed., 2 vols. (New York: n.p., 1877), 2:176–78. The Congregational attenders in Sturbridge and Leicester are identified on a 1783 pew list in the Sturbridge Town Records, vol. 3, Sturbridge Town Hall; and a 1783 pew list in Leicester General Records (1745–85), 338–40, Leicester Town Hall. Spencer attenders are identified in a 1771 pew list in James Draper, *History of Spencer, Massachusetts* . . . (Worcester, Mass.: H. J. Howland, 1860), 138–39. The Charlton and Oakham Congregational records are very fragmentary. For Charlton, see 1773 pew list in D. Hamilton Hurd., comp., *History of Worcester County, Massachusetts* . . ., 2 vols. (Philadelphia: J. W. Lewis, 1889), 1:750; 1782 church records recorded in the Stone Family Account Books, 1772–1830, folio vol. 2, AAS, and the 1798 Congregational proprietors' list in Ammidown, *Historical Collections* 2:172. For Oakham, see the account of the church and a list of men working on the minister's dwelling, Jan. 1786, in Henry B. Wright and Edwin D. Harvey, *The Settlement and History of Oakham, Massachusetts* (New Haven: n.p., 1947), 115–29. Using the Vital Records and numerous town and family genealogies, all of this evidence had been recorded on family reconstitution cards.

10

THE RELIGIOUS WORLD OF DANIEL SHAYS

Stephen A. Marini

What was the religious world of Daniel Shays and what role if any did it play in the insurrection of 1786–87? Clear answers to these questions are not easy to obtain. Writers on the rebellion from George Richards Minot to Marion Starkey neglected religion altogether. In 1969 William G. McLoughlin opened a new line of inquiry with the claim that "the Separate-Baptists in western Massachusetts were prominent among the supporters of Daniel Shays."[1] A decade later David P. Szatmary replied that McLoughlin's opinion "may be overstated" and interpreted religion as a variable that identified the Regulators but did not distinguish them from other citizens. "The militants were homogeneous in religious affiliation," he wrote. "While some Baptists undeniably fought against government, most militants probably were Congregationalists."[2]

The careful subsequent research of John Brooke sustains Szatmary's opinion; in fact, his evidence suggests that Separate Baptists may even have been proportionately underrepresented and that the sectarians' motivations were primarily economic. Poor Baptist farmers rebelled, middling ones did not. Brooke's most recent research on the Regulation makes a compelling case that the Regulators were not dissenters but rather Congregationalists and "men of local standing: selectmen, low-ranking militia officers, and deacons" from "those orthodox communities where the gentry class was absent and the minister isolated from his social class or missing altogether."[3] Brooke argues that a popular religious culture of

From a paper presented at the Bicentennial Conference on Shays's Rebellion and the Constitution, 1986, sponsored by Historic Deerfield, Inc.

orthodoxy disposed such men to act in restoration and defense of a collapsing socioeconomic order. In towns that enjoyed greater economic diversity and a more stable ministry, this same "deacon's orthodoxy" aligned itself with the government against the Regulation.

All of these interpretive claims suffer from a common liability. There simply is no thorough description of religious development in Shaysite Massachusetts available upon which to ground interpretive generalization and theoretical insight. The most complete work on any one religious body is William McLoughlin's many capable studies of the Separate Baptists, but surprisingly, the researcher today must still rely on unstudied manuscript sources and nineteenth-century town and church histories for information on Congregationalism and on fragmentary evidence and scholarship on other dissenting groups.[4]

Historians have long accepted the judgment of late eighteenth-century Congregationalist ministers that New England's religious institutions and popular piety languished during and after the Revolution. No less an authority than Sydney Ahlstrom called the 1770s, 1780s, and 1790s an era of "religious depression," during which the people of New England turned their attention away from questions of faith and toward issues of politics.[5] Several scholars, most notably Nathan Hatch, have since drawn attention to the vibrant note of millennial expectation that suffused post-Revolutionary Congregationalist and Federalist utterance in New England, and William McLoughlin has argued that the religious dissent of Separate Baptists motivated their political transition to Antifederalism and Jeffersonianism.[6] Neither interpretation, however, has challenged Ahlstrom's basic notion that the Revolution left all religious groups in essentially the same situation, weakened and culturally subordinate to politics.

Therefore in this essay my first goal has been to establish a general description of religion in Shaysite Massachusetts. The results of that inquiry have not produced the sort of clear and distinct patterns that historians hope to uncover and use for new interpretations. To the contrary, the evidence suggests quite a different kind of religious situation from that described by Ahlstrom and Szatmary, one of disorder and breakdown, instability and change. The "depression" of which Ahlstrom wrote was actually a deep institutional and intellectual crisis in Congregationalism that crippled its cultural hegemony even as its political allies sought to preserve it in the state constitution of 1780. Yet Shays's Rebellion also occurred in the midst of Massachusetts's most powerful revival since the Great Awakening, led by dissenters who mounted fundamental challenges to Congregationalist polity, theology, and cultural influence, but who themselves were riven by theological and ecclesiological divisions.

All this created a moment of dramatic religious change that mirrored and, indeed, reinforced the Revolution's own political and economic dislocations, of which Shays's Rebellion was a principal manifestation. This time of religious change generated multiple sociocultural consequences relative to Shays's Rebellion. The institutional weakness and intellectual division of Congregationalism seriously hindered its ability to perform its major cultural function, the sacred legitimation of the sociopolitical regime. Though it continued to provide legitimation through such traditional media as the annual election sermon at Boston, the Standing Order's inclusive genius was severely tested, issuing in the paradoxical pattern Brooke describes and the grim reality of coreligionists making civil war against each other. In strictly religious terms Congregationalist hegemony also broke down under the pressures of heightened internal theological dispute and unprecedented external challenge by dissenters. Shays's Rebellion, the first major episode of political dissent in post-Revolutionary New England, occurred at precisely the same moment that Congregationalism lost its religious hegemony in rural Massachusetts and a new world of religious pluralism commenced in the New England hinterland.

ON JUNE 28, 1786, the Great and General Court of Massachusetts assembled at Boston passed an act "incorporating the easterly part of Pelham and the southwest part of New Salem in the county of Hampshire, and the inhabitants thereon into a separate Parish by the name of the second parish in Pelham."[7] This apparently unexceptional event vested in the new East Pelham organization all the powers of religious taxation and responsibilities for church management permitted under the state constitution. "To promote their happiness and to secure the good order and preservation of their government," Article 3 of that document's Declaration of Rights declared that the legislature shall "authorize and require, the several towns, parishes, precincts, and other bodies politic, or religious societies, to make suitable provision, at their own expense, for the institution of the public worship of God and for the support and maintenance of public Protestant teachers of piety, religion, and morality, in all cases where such provision shall not be made voluntarily."[8]

Parish incorporation allowed the citizens of the East Pelham district to organize "a body politic" possessing a glebe lot of land for the minister and a second lot for the parish meetinghouse, along with powers of municipal taxation to create revenues for "settlement" of a minister in the community. Settlement usually entailed an elaborate contract between the parish and the candidate. In Shaysite country settlement typically included the parish's provision of a lifetime salary—usually stipulated between £50 and £70 and then increased by increments of £5 for ten years to a permanent maximum. The terms also included a stipend to the candidate, typically two years' salary payable after the second year of service, besides a parsonage or at least an arrangement for the construction of one on the parish glebe and a meetinghouse for worship or again a legal promise to construct one on the parish lot.

East Pelham's decision to petition for incorporation, however, was not the immemorial Puritan act it had been before the Revolution, whereby Congregationalists routinely subdivided earlier towns or set up public worship in newly settled communities. The East Pelham petitioners were Presbyterians, dissenters from the Standing Order, non-Congregationalists who were nonetheless permitted under the state constitution to claim the entitlements and responsibilities of parish organization. Their Presbyterian religious identity was a product of their Scots and Scots-Irish ethnic heritage. The original settlers of Pelham were part of a modest but significant stream of Scottish immigrants that flowed into New England between 1710 and 1740.[9]

The incorporation of Pelham East Parish was the outcome of not only the steady growth of the town but also the more than forty years of unrest in the community's First Parish. Pelham's first minister was Robert Abercrombie (1711–1786), a member of the Secession church educated at the University of Edinburgh and ordained in 1744 in the Pelham church by the Presbytery of Londonderry, New Hampshire. Jonathan Edwards preached his ordination sermon. The Great Awakening was at its zenith, and Abercrombie, a strong supporter of the revival and its Evangelical Calvinist theology, attracted the support of a majority of Pelham Presbyterians.[10] But as happened in so many towns, the Awakening had divided the Pelham parish into rival parties, and twenty-one church members, including one of the town's original settlers and the two men who had built the town meetinghouse in 1743, protested Abercrombie's call.[11]

Within a few years Abercrombie's severe New Light ministry sparked open controversy similar to that which engulfed Edwards at Northampton at the same time. Abercrombie, like Edwards, demanded that the church be made up only of the regenerate, and sometime in 1747 he began to refuse communion and baptism to the unregenerate and their children. Outcry in the parish led to a protracted controversy between Abercrombie, the church, and the Presbytery of Boston. The presbytery dismissed Abercrombie in 1755; the minister denied its authority to do so, and a four-year pamphlet war ensued.[12] Meanwhile Abercrombie sued the parish to recover his salary and won the case in 1759. Four years later when the town voted to settle his replacement Richard Crouch Graham, the pro-Abercrombie party refused to pay tax support for Graham and in 1764 sued for exemption on the ground that Abercrombie remained the legal minister of Pelham.[13]

Graham's pastorate was short, lasting only until 1771. For four years Pelham's pulpit was vacant, and Abercrombie occasionally supplied it. In 1775 the town called Nathaniel Merrill but proved unable to meet its contract with him. Wartime inflation wrought havoc with Merrill's salary, which grew from £80 in 1775 to £2,500 by 1780.[14] Pelham apparently defaulted in 1780, and the pulpit fell vacant until 1793. It was during this third vacancy, in 1784, that the famous episode of Stephen Burroughs, the impostor, occurred. Burroughs was the son of Eden Burroughs, prominent Presbyterian minister at Hanover, New Hampshire; young Burroughs under the assumed name of Davis succeeded in convincing the Pelhamites that he was a legitimate candidate by presenting to Pelham's Deacon

Daniel Gray a letter of recommendation from the Reverend Moses Baldwin of Palmer, reading some of his father's old sermons, and doing some effective extempore preaching of his own. News of his true identity reached town, and Burroughs fled. He was pursued to a haymow in Rutland where, "after laying Dr. Nehemiah Hinds senseless with a stone," he engaged his pursuers in a long parley and was eventually taken. Soon after he escaped Pelham altogether.[15]

This, then, was the immediate religious context out of which the East Pelham parish emerged, a context fraught with doctrinal controversy, fiscal difficulty, chronic pulpit vacancy, impostors, and even violence. It is not surprising that the settlers of East Pelham thought they could do a better job of "preserving the happiness and good order" of their neighborhood by forming a parish of their own. The East Parish covenant of 1786 enumerated five promises: to take the Scriptures as "the only rule of faith and manners," to adhere to the Westminster Confession of Faith, to observe "the Presbyterian government and discipline of the Church of Christ," to maintain "the peace and unity of the church," and to "engage as fellow citizens with the saints and household of God . . . for our mutual good."[16]

Eleven men signed the covenant, but the earliest church membership record listed twelve married couples, two men whose wives did not join the church, seven women whose husbands did not join, and three widows—thirty-six adults in all. Students of Shays's Rebellion will recognize a number of these East Pelham Presbyterians as leaders of the insurrection in Hampshire County, including Dr. Nehemiah Hinds, proprietor of the Horse and Groom Tavern where the Shaysites bivouacked before their retreat to Petersham on February 2, 1787; Deacon Daniel Gray, author of the people's address at the Hatfield convention of August 22, 1786; and Abigail Shays, wife of the Rebellion's eponym. Captain Daniel Shays himself is listed in the membership record as one of the "men whose wives have joined the church and they have not."[17]

The parish records indicate that Nehemiah Hinds also served as first moderator and William Conkey, Jr.—kinsman of the proprietors of Conkey's Tavern—acted as first assessor of the new parish. Even as the Rebellion swirled through their community, the parish continued to meet through 1786 and 1787, seeking to raise funds and find a suitable ministerial candidate for settlement. East Pelham made several offers, but the parish found it quite difficult to secure its pulpit. In the first five years of the parish, five different candidates served as supply; the first settled minister, Matthias Cozier, became embroiled in controversy with Hinds, Gray, and the Conkeys almost immediately, and he resigned in 1798 after four stormy years at East Pelham. It would not be until 1833 that an East Pelham minister served longer than Cozier.[18] This account summarizes what little is known about the religious world of Daniel Shays in its most narrow definition. Yet even from these fragments a number of perhaps surprising facts can be established. The Shaysites, or at least these Shaysites, were religious people, actively seeking to improve the condition of the church in their community even while in the act of rebellion against civil government. East Pelham was responding to endemic doctrinal conflict and weak ecclesial institutions that produced outright religious disorder in the early 1780s. The East Pelham parish was not Congregational; rather it was made up of ethnic dissenters—Scots-Irish Presbyterians—who were able to take advantage of the religious settlement of 1780, which had largely been designed to maintain the Standing Order. Ironically, the Pelhamites sought religious order under the provisions—including religious taxation—of the very constitutional system whose courts and civil taxes they so vigorously opposed. What all this most clearly indicates is that the religious world of Daniel Shays was not one of good order and sacral stability. Rather it was a religious culture caught in the throes of change at many different levels, intellectual, institutional, and constitutional.

PELHAM'S RELIGIOUS TROUBLES might seem exceptional, especially since the town itself was a Scots-Irish immigrant island in an indigenous English cultural stream. But the same level of religious discord prevailed in different forms in other central Massachusetts towns. Petersham, the largest town in the area, deeply divided between local leaders who were Friends of Government and many Shaysite farmers, and the site of the Shaysites' last major military action, experienced even more traumatic religious conflicts, some of them politically based. In 1738 the town called Aaron Whitney, Harvard class of 1736, to its Congregational pastorate. Whitney ministered to the parish nearly forty years before the Revolutionary crisis. In 1768 revival and itinerancy helped the Separate Baptists form a congregation in Petersham under the leadership of Elder Samuel Dennis. During the early 1770s political as well as religious differences emerged between the two spiritual leaders, with Whitney proclaiming his Toryism while Dennis emerged as a local Patriot leader.

When Whitney denounced Patriot resistance in the spring of 1775, the town almost immediately resolved that it "will not bargain with, hire, nor employ the Rev. Mr. Whitney to preach for them any longer."[19] Further resolutions labeled Whitney "an enemy to his country" and summarily banned him from the pulpit, ordering "that publick worship be not disturbed by any person or persons going into the desk but such persons as shall be put in by the Town's Committee." Meanwhile Baptist Samuel Dennis moved to the forefront of the Revolutionary movement in Petersham, writing the town's replies to the Boston Committee of Correspondence and serving as its representative to the 1777 General Court. Aaron Whitney died in 1777 and three more years passed before the parish was able to settle Solomon Reed in 1780. Reed's twenty-year ministry, however, was plagued by his recurrent intemperance.

Meanwhile revivals had again begun in Petersham, and in December 1781 Mother Ann Lee and the Shakers first visited the town, bringing their charismatic style of worship, apocalyptic spirituality, and controversial teachings of confession, communalism, and celibacy. *The Testimonies of Mother Ann Lee,* the classic Shaker account of Mother Ann's ministry, reported that "the inhabitants generally manifested a desire to see and hear [the Shakers] for themselves." According to the Shaker account, however, "a company of lewd fellows from the middle of town" broke up a public evening meeting, then later abducted Mother Ann and "dragged her, feet foremost, out of the house, and threw her into a sleigh." They drove to Samuel Peckham's tavern "to find out whether she was a woman or not," but the Shakers secured her release after threatening to report them to the town authorities. After this incident "the most vile and vicious accusations . . . were uttered" against the Shakers. "Witchcraft and delusion was the general cry; even in their solemn assemblies of worship, the preachers would vent their malicious spleen, and mock and mimic the operations of the power of God, which they had seen or heard of among the people."[20]

This ministerial opposition apparently was not entirely effective, for the Baptist congregation in Petersham suddenly collapsed. Elder Samuel Dennis died in 1783; the church relocated to Hardwick and reorganized under a new elder, John Sellon. Only eleven men, however, signed the new church covenant.[21] Samuel Dennis's flourishing Separate Baptist congregation had become a small refugee community under the unsettled circumstances of the early 1780s. Many of Petersham's Separate Baptists likely were attracted by the new gospel of the Shakers, who returned to Petersham in July 1783 from Shirley "accompanied by a considerable number of Believers."

On the third day of the visit, a crowd "returning from a funeral" gathered around the house where the Shakers were staying, exhibiting "riotous and persecuting spirit and conduct." Shaker elder James Whittaker confronted the crowd by reading Article 3 of the Massachusetts Declaration of Rights, claiming under it "equal rights and privileges in the exercise and enjoyment of their religious profession and worship." Mother Ann "spake boldly of their brutal and ungodly behavior, and related what she and the Elders had suffered before in this place, by their wicked hands." The Shakers moved through the crowd exhorting, reproving, and singing. At length one of the Believers, Aaron Wood, was knocked unconscious, and the mob quickly dispersed. The next evening the crowd returned, "mocking, hooting, and yelling like savages"; at one point a shot was fired in an attempt to disturb the singing and dancing of the Shakers at worship. The mobbings continued for ten more nights until Mother Ann left town for the last time.[22]

Not enough Shaker converts had been made to organize the movement at Petersham, and soon the continuing revivalism of the New Light Stir revitalized the Hardwick Separate Baptists. The congregation's subscription list of November 3, 1786, named thirty-six members, a more than threefold increase over the church covenant of 1783.[23] Hardwick's Congregational church, meanwhile, suffered its first vacancy in nearly fifty years. David White, Yale class of 1730 and pastor at Hardwick since 1736, died in 1784, and the parish could not find a successor until 1789. Under White's pastorate Hardwick had suffered and then survived a Separate schism from 1740 through

1765; two decades later the Separate Baptists organized in the town during the last year of his life and were able to exploit the resulting hiatus in the ministry to grow and prosper.

The religious situation in Petersham bore significant resemblance to Pelham's. Both of these Quabbin towns were experiencing powerful episodes of religious disorder and change during the mid-1780s. But Petersham also differed from the Pelham Presbyterians in that they had been unable to contain the disruptive forces within the normative parish system. Local traditional institutions in Petersham were themselves divided or ineffective while new sectarian religious alternatives entered the scene and flourished at least for a season.

THE PROBLEMS THAT BESET Pelham and Petersham prevailed widely throughout Shaysite Massachusetts. To better understand the magnitude and complexity of religious change in the region, however, it is necessary to expand these more detailed narratives into broader institutional and intellectual patterns. Any aggregate description of the Shaysites' religious environment must begin with Congregationalism, the traditional and legally established religion in colonial Massachusetts. Upon first inspection, rural Massachusetts in the 1780s seems to have been, as Szatmary claimed, a "homogeneous" Congregational domain, and hardly a "depressed" one at that. "In 1789," according to Szatmary, "over 77 percent of all Massachusetts churches and 80 percent of the population adhered to the Congregational faith."[24]

Yet to leave the matter at this level of generalization represents a failure to inquire whether Congregationalism in specifically Shaysite areas was more heterogeneous and unstable than elsewhere in the Commonwealth and hence might have contributed to the insurrectionary environment. John Brooke has quite recently taken up this question for the three western counties of Worcester, Hampshire, and Berkshire. His investigation concludes that an exceptionally high rate of "vacancy," the absence of a settled minister, and "destitution," the absence of an organized parish, did play a significant role in the Regulation. In Brooke's formulation, the lack of effective ministerial presence in Shaysite towns crystallized "a deacon's orthodoxy," a parochial, laicized religious persuasion dedicated to preserving traditional values and norms against what it perceived as a changing and unreliable public culture. When the policies of state government precipitated economic and political unrest in Shaysite towns, this "deacon's orthodoxy" served to legitimate the Regulation.[25]

Brooke's is a far more substantive interpretation of religion's role in the events of 1786–87 than Szatmary's, but if the latter proves too little, the former proves too much. If Szatmary wrongly dismisses religion altogether from the Shaysite movement, Brooke is tempted to find the key to the Regulation in a single religious variable of vacancy and destitution. Congregationalism in Shaysite country was anything but homogeneous and stable, but the causes and consequences of its difficulties were not as simple or as clear-cut as Brooke's hypothesis implies. Congregationalism in rural Massachusetts suffered from a number of problems, some of them internal to it, some of them brought on by the challenge of religious dissent. Nor was the pattern of malaise the same from county to county, even in western Massachusetts. All this makes generalization about religion in the Regulation more difficult, but it is essential to reconstruct the situation in all its complexity before proceeding to historiographical judgments.

The effectiveness of Congregationalism depended fundamentally upon the geographical parish system and the ordained clergy it supported. In rural Massachusetts ministers comprised a critically important local elite, possessing a rare combination of university education, a parsonage, public land, and a lifetime contract, while they conducted their public ministrations in the meetinghouse, the most costly and elaborate building in town. As "fathers" of their communities—many of them only the first or second settled ministers in the history of their towns—they baptized, catechized, married, and buried not only Shaysites and Friends of Government but also their parents and children as well.

During the 1780s the recruitment of ministers became acutely difficult for rural Massachusetts towns. The Revolution had disrupted the sensitive balance between ministerial supply and demand. Through the war years theological education came to a virtual standstill. New England's colleges barely functioned, and many pastors gave up their theological tutorials in order better to serve the war effort at home or in the field as chaplains and officers. In 1780 President Ezra Stiles of Yale counted 245 pulpits in New England either vacant or destitute. His finding meant that more than one-third of all New England towns, most of them in rural locations, lacked a settled minister. Even more distressing, Stiles knew of only 80 qualified candidates available to supply them. He listed 80 vacancies in Massachusetts alone; proration of the supply side of his finding shows 30 qualified candidates for these pulpits.[26]

Vacancy afflicted rural and frontier towns the most severely. In Shaysite country it was particularly acute. Twenty-one of forty-two parishes in Regulator towns, exactly half, experienced more than two years of vacancy between 1776 and 1786 (see Appendix). By contrast, John Brooke reports only a 16 percent vacancy rate in the Militia towns of western Massachusetts. But vacancy in Regulator towns varied significantly from county to county. In the older and more prosperous counties of Middlesex, Bristol, and Hampshire, vacancy in Shaysite parishes ran below 50 percent, while six of ten Shaysite towns in Worcester County and six of nine in Berkshire County had vacant pulpits during the Revolutionary years. This very high rate of vacancy supports Brooke's "deacon's orthodoxy" hypothesis; many Shaysite towns did indeed endure the trying times of war without the conservative cultural leadership of a minister. In these locations, vacancy could readily precipitate "a deacon's orthodoxy" and its concomitant political effects. But there is some confusion about the precise significance of vacancy. If there was a "deacon's orthodoxy" reaction in Shaysite towns, how long did it take to develop? Is the best measure an extended vacant period, such as the two years reckoned above, or vacancy at the moment of the Rebellion? By the latter standard only sixteen of the same forty-two parishes (38 percent) were without a stated minister.

Vacancy, moreover, was only part of the Shaysite religious context. In many Shaysite parishes, well-established ministers were not able to prevent their charges from resisting the state government. Another sixteen of the same forty-two parishes in 1786 (38 percent) were served by incumbents who had been settled ten years or more. The average term of incumbency for all twenty-seven parishes with a settled minister was 13.2 years. Sheer longevity, of course, was not necessarily a sign of powerful ministerial authority. Ten years of service during a revolution was plenty of time for a minister to make enemies or to fall into ineffective patterns of ministry. Indeed, such was the case in many of these towns. But the first point to be observed is that Brooke's hypothesis is inadequate on its face because in 1786 just as many Shaysite towns had long-term incumbents, and presumably no "deacon's orthodoxy," as had vacancies.

Though vacancy was indisputably important in the religious world of Daniel Shays, Congregationalism was suffering from other deep-seated problems that also significantly impaired its cultural influence. Ironically, the very institutional arrangements that had made Congregationalism such an effective state religion before the Revolution suddenly became severe liabilities after it. Intellectually, long-smoldering theological conflict that had lain relatively quiet during the Revolution broke forth in renewed and acrimonious dispute.

In simplest terms, during the mid-1780s the parish system was too expensive for many rural Massachusetts towns to maintain. The parish system, like the rest of the rural economy, suffered from ruinous inflation. The Congregationalist parish carried many financial obligations for its community, of which ministerial salary was only one, and not necessarily the most costly. Parish costs comprised a major public expense and hence a potential tax grievance in Shaysite country. Town and parish records of rural Massachusetts during the 1780s are strewn with financial controversies regarding ministerial salaries and meetinghouse construction. Parish finances were perhaps the most debated local political or economic issue during the 1780s. In Amherst, for example, when David Parsons II accepted the call of First Church to succeed his father as pastor, he stipulated in his acceptance letter of August 12, 1782, that "the several sums which you offer me in settlement and salary I understand to be in silver money, Spanish milled Dollars at six shillings, or other silver or gold equivalent . . . and I understand it to be your intent that no advantage shall ever be taken of any paper currency Depreciated or of any act of government that may be passed, to avoid the fair, honest, and equitable intent of the contract."[27]

Parsons's hard bargaining certainly could be justified by the prevailing economic conditions, but a significant number of the parishioners found it offensive and the amounts promised exorbitant. Led by Captain Ebenezer Mattoon, this group withdrew from First Church and demanded an ecclesiastical council. The council found that Parsons's demands were "unequal and unjust" and instructed the seceders "to organize and settle a minister" of their own.

One historian of the Parsons affair observed that "warm contentions and unfriendly dispositions, which were lasting, grew out of this division."[28] The implications of this remark are large when extended to the many Shaysite towns that faced growing mandatory religious expenses with diminishing resources. The colonial assumption that the civil and ecclesial arms of government would combine under the benign oversight of a homogeneous citizenry became at the first post-Revolutionary stroke an alliance between church and state against an economically distressed and politically divided people.

Financial instability was not the only problem facing Congregationalism in Shaysite Massachusetts during the 1770s and 1780s. Political, liturgical, and theological controversies plagued the Standing Order as well. In at least a few Shaysite towns incumbent ministers in 1775 were Loyalists. Four of them, Samuel Dana of Groton, Aaron Whitney of Petersham, Abraham Hill of Shutesbury, and Timothy Fuller of Princeton were dismissed immediately by their irate parishioners.[29]

Fuller's case illustrates the volatility and occasional paradox of religiopolitical opinion in Shaysite country. When this successful pastor, settled more than nine years at Princeton, delivered a cautionary sermon to the town's minutemen and refused to observe the General Court's fast day after the Battles of Lexington and Concord, he was charged with Toryism and dismissed. After brief pastorates at Chilmark and Middleton, Massachusetts, however, he returned to Princeton as town teacher and "rendered good service" in a number of minor town offices during the mid-1780s. By 1788 "the ill feeling once so bitter against him appears to have given way to respect and warm feelings" to the degree that he was elected the town's representative to the Massachusetts ratifying convention, where he cast his vote against the Federal Constitution "on the ground of its recognition of slavery." Despite this ironic outcome, the Princeton parish remained vacant for ten years after Fuller's dismissal.[30] There as in other towns with Tory ministers, the political opposition between pastor and people severely weakened the corporate social bond which Congregationalism traditionally embodied and served. Similar weakening occurred widely in Shaysite areas where the clergy, if not outright Tory, were typically cautious about American independence, a view that reflected the opinion of New England's educated elite and stood in tension with the growing radicalism of their country parishioners after 1774.

A more long-standing Congregationalist dispute involved ritual norms, specifically the introduction of new techniques and texts for singing in public worship. Controversy first broke out over the quality of Congregational church song during the 1720s, when several Boston-area ministers including Cotton Mather protested against the "usual" way of singing the Psalms. Complaining that in some churches the traditional method of unison singing from *The Bay Psalm Book* had degenerated into "tunes . . . miserably tortured and twisted and quavered . . . into a horrid medley of confused and disorderly noises," the Boston reformers recommended "singing by rule" or "regular" singing according to the best available choral techniques. Their program included the elimination of "lining out"—the practice of precentors, who read or intoned each line of the psalm for the community to repeat—and the education of the laity to music literacy and choral techniques.[31]

During the Great Awakening a second dimension of the Singing Controversy erupted when New Light Congregationalists introduced the Evangelical poetics of Isaac Watts into their churches. Liturgically conservative older church members objected not only to Watts's theology but also to the audacity of New Lights in introducing "human composures" into divine worship, while the New Lights and their younger and heavily female constituency countered that their religious experience of the Holy Spirit entitled them to make new praise to God just as it had David and the Apostles.[32] The controversies over musical and textual innovation combined to produce complex and protracted argument throughout New England, a disagreement which easily spilled over into local membership, theological, gender, and generational disputes. Worcester County was the main battleground of the Singing Controversy in the 1780s, and parishes in at least two Shaysite towns—Princeton and Spencer—experienced major confrontations over the issue.

The most fundamental division within the house of Congregationalism, however, was theological. After the relative calm of the 1770s, the doctrinal controversies of the Great Awakening reappeared in a rapidly escalating debate between the New Divinity of Evangelical Calvinists in rural New England and the Arminianism of Boston-area Liberals. The New Divinity, now remembered, if at all, for extreme doctrinal claims, such as the damnation of infants and the demand that one "be willing to be damned for the glory of God," was an imposing construction of Evangelical Calvinism, grounded in the teachings of Jonathan Edwards, which was characterized by rigorous propositional logic and demanding moral standards. The New Divinity envisioned a determinate and hierarchic universe presided over by a righteous yet arbitrary God, who held sinners responsible for their sin even though they were incapable of not sinning. And they demanded the abrogation of the Half-Way Covenant whereby the unregenerate could obtain a qualified membership in the church of Christ and baptism for their infant children.[33]

Samuel Hopkins (1721–1803), the leading writer and educator of the New Divinity party, served twenty-four years at Great Barrington in Berkshire County before moving to Newport in 1775. For another thirty years Hopkins produced a constant stream of students and publications culminating in his *System of Doctrines* (1792), an achievement that lent his name to the most extreme form of the New Divinity. By the time of Shays's Rebellion, New Divinity ministers had created two major enclaves in rural Massachusetts, one in Berkshire County centered around Stephen West (1735–1819) of Stockbridge and one in western Suffolk County, led by David Sanford (1737–1810) of Medway and Nathaniel Emmons (1745–1840) of Franklin.[34]

On the other side of the debate, the Arminians countered that God presided benevolently over a sacred cosmos that was created good and intended for human happiness. Following their preeminent leader Charles Chauncy (1708–1787), senior minister of First Church, Boston, they advocated freedom of the will and tended strongly toward universal salvation. Accordingly they sustained the Half-Way Covenant as an appropriately inclusive ecclesiology that brought all citizens into the church to find their own eventual ways to salvation and morality. In Shaysite country Arminian pastors were settled almost exclusively in provincial centers that shared the cosmopolitan culture of the capital, including Robert Breck (1734–1784) and Bezaleel Howard (1784–1809) of Springfield, Aaron Bancroft of Worcester (1786–1839), and Ezra Ripley of Concord (1778–1841).[35]

Most ministers in rural Massachusetts were not members of either of these extreme parties. The great majority of them were more moderate Calvinists educated at Yale or, more rarely, at Harvard. Yet the extremes of New Divinity Evangelicalism and Arminian Liberalism did accurately define the theological spectrum, and the religious geography of Shaysite Massachusetts did correspond strikingly with political divisions between Regulators and Friends of Government. Arminians held forth in the very shire towns that were under political and military attack by Shaysites from smaller communities ministered to by various sorts of Calvinists, including New Divinity men. Indeed, the intellectual divisions between the two theological parties were at least as extreme, if not more so, than the political discontinuities between Shaysites and Friends of Government. By 1786 New Divinity advocates and Arminians taught what amounted to two different worldviews within the same ecclesiastical communion.

Under these circumstances the very idea of orthodoxy itself began to lose its hold. The Evangelical-Liberal tension had existed since the New Light–Old Light controversies of the Great Awakening, but for a generation the Standing Order had been able to contain the dispute in service of common cultural and political ties to the colonial regime and the Patriot cause. After the Revolution these ties were lost in a struggle for control of the new regime, and most Congregationalists in Shaysite country found themselves confusingly located between the two extremes. In rural Massachusetts towns of the 1780s, theology could not supply the personal assurance and collective security that was its traditional function to provide. The severe everyday problems of maintaining the parish system in fact demanded even more ideological reinforcement than normal. Instead it seemed that even the most basic ideas of God could be divisive.

THUS FAR WE HAVE concentrated on the internal institutional and intellectual problems of Congregationalism. All these difficulties, however, were compounded by the rise of religious dissent in rural Massachusetts. While Congregationalism languished, the dissenters enjoyed their most vigorous growth since the Great Awakening. The key to this expansion was a regional revival, called the New Light Stir by contemporaries, that in Massachusetts both benefited already established dissenting groups including Separate Baptists, Presbyterians, and Quakers and gave birth to new sects, particularly the Shakers and the Universalists.

Revivals were a constant religious factor in Massachusetts between the Great Awakening and the Revolution. On several occasions, notably during the early 1760s, the pace of revivalism rose to moderate peaks. These episodes helped maintain the momentum of Evangelical New Light parishes in western Massachusetts, but fewer and fewer Congregationalist revivals occurred in the years before and during the Revolution. Revivalism, however, remained a staple element in the religious appeal of the Separate Baptists, the chief rivals of the Congregationalist Standing Order.

Taking their origins from the combination of Calvinistic Particular Baptists from Rhode Island with schismatic New Light radicals—the Separate or Strict Congregationalists—after the Great Awakening, the Separate Baptists equated Christian evangelism with revivalism. Their evangelistic methods in the New Light Stir bore all the hallmarks of the Great Awakening—itinerancy, emotional preaching, charismatic gifts, dramatic conversions.[36] And while Congregationalism struggled to consolidate its expensive and divided parish system, Separate Baptists operated virtually without such institutional constraints. They did not require university training for ordination, and they stood absolutely opposed to the "hireling ministry," as they termed pastors of the Standing Order. They chose to support their elders by strictly voluntary contributions. In practice this meant that most Separate Baptist elders earned their living as farmers or artisans and received church contributions as income supplements. The farmer-preacher also enjoyed the advantage of mobility, able freely to relocate wherever a religious community could be gathered, ready to itinerate wherever a religious quickening seemed imminent.

In the five years before the Revolution, Baptist revivalism and church organization grew quickly, especially in Bristol and Berkshire counties. After the first shocks of the Revolution, Baptist revivals commenced first in Berkshire County, particularly in the northern part. The Separate Baptists founded churches at Cheshire in 1769 and Pittsfield in 1770, from which elders Peter Werden and Valentine Rathbun conducted extensive revivals in 1773 and again from 1779 to 1782. By the end of these revivals two more churches had been organized, and Separate Baptist strength in northwest Massachusetts had grown enough to help form the Shaftesbury, Vermont, Baptist Association in 1781. Another church was gathered in 1779 under Elder Joshua Morse at Sandisfield in southern Berkshire.[37]

The rest of Massachusetts Separate Baptists fell under the jurisdiction of the Warren, Rhode Island, Baptist Association, a zealous and politically active institution organized in 1767 and led by Elder Isaac Backus of Middleborough, Massachusetts. The revival spread eastward into Hampshire and Worcester counties, where again churches organized before the Revolution served as the base for renewed itinerant evangelism. By the first years of the 1780s, Separate Baptist revivalism was in full swing throughout Shaysite country, most heavily concentrated in Bristol, Middlesex, Worcester, and Hampshire counties. To place this first Baptist stage of the New Light Stir in perspective, the denomination in Massachusetts grew by nearly 60 percent between 1775 and 1782, adding twenty-two churches to the thirty-eight organized before the Revolution. Between 1780 and 1782 alone, Separate Baptists increased by nearly one-third. And each new congregation legally incorporated under the state constitution represented a commensurate loss to the Congregationalist parish tax base.[38]

The Baptist revival ceased abruptly during the next few years and growth remained weak during the period of Shays's Rebellion. It was during this brief hiatus that Massachusetts Congregationalists were able to capitalize on the Stir, organizing seven churches in 1785, their largest annual total since the 1760s. But almost immediately after the insurrection Baptist growth returned, bringing another 60 percent increase between 1788 and 1795, most of it concentrated in Hampshire and Berkshire counties. Another measure suggests the magnitude of this growth relative to the Standing Order: it was during the 1780s that Separate Baptists first surpassed Congregationalists in absolute growth, thirty-three churches to twenty-five.[39] Translating these aggregate patterns into specifically Shaysite terms, twelve of the forty-two principal Shaysite parishes (28.5 percent) had at least one organized Separate Baptist congregation. By 1790 the number had risen to fifteen—more than one-third of the total (35.7 percent).

The Separate Baptists, however, were themselves divided during the 1780s in ways not unlike the Congregationalists. In the first place, a cultural and political distinction subsisted between the more "cosmopolitan" denominational leadership around Boston and the rural majority. Samuel Stillman, minister of Boston's First Baptist Church epitomized the tendency of Separate Baptists to absorb some of the metropolitan culture. Arrayed in wig and waistcoat, college-trained and intimate with the intellectual and political elite of Boston, Stillman was the symbol of accommodation. He was the first non-Congregationalist ever to deliver the annual election sermon at Boston—in 1777—and supported both the state constitution of 1780 and the Federal Constitution.[40]

The other major eastern denominational leader was Isaac Backus, staunch Calvinist and revival preacher, whose Old Colony background kept him within the pale of cosmopolitan culture. His opposition to the state constitution gained him fame and loyalty among the rural western majority, but that same constituency was outraged when he joined Stillman in backing the proposed Federal Constitution without a specific guarantee of religious liberty. The rural Separate Baptist majority was represented by figures as diverse as Noah Alden of Bellingham, outspoken advocate of religious liberty and opponent of Federalism, and Valentine Rathbun of Pittsfield, political colleague of Thomas Allen and effective revivalist. More typical of the rural constituency, however, were local farmer-preachers like Samuel Bigelow of New Salem or Chileab and Ebenezer Smith, father and son who ministered to rival Baptist congregations in Ashfield.[41]

During the New Light Stir the Warren Association encountered difficulty establishing its discipline over the burgeoning Separate Baptist constituency. In 1786, for example, it listed forty-five member congregations in forty-two towns, but its published *Minutes* indicated that nineteen of them "did not send a messenger or letter" to the association meeting of 1785.[42] In addition, roughly a dozen independent churches existed in the Commonwealth unaffiliated with either the Warren or the Shaftesbury associations, and the former excluded Sutton in 1786 and Ashfield and Grafton in 1788. At the moment of Shays's Rebellion roughly half of the Baptist congregations in Massachusetts were out of regular or recent contact with the associations. Despite their impressive growth, therefore, the Baptists possessed little capacity effectively to regulate local churches. Their institutional weaknesses, combined with the rampant vacancy and destitution among Congregationalists, permitted an intense parochialism to prevail among rural believers of both persuasions.

Doctrinal and ecclesiological disputes also disturbed the Separate Baptist communion. The Boston circle of clergy sought and found a more philosophical theology of Evangelical Calvinism to do intellectual battle with the Edwardseans. This they found in the thought of the London Particular Baptist John Gill. Gill's systematic theology was as "hyper-Calvinist" as Samuel Hopkins's and argued in the same philosophical language, that of the British Enlightenment.[43]

Gillite views had the same controversial effect on ecclesiology for the Separate Baptists as Edwardseanism did for New Light Congregationalists. The merger of Separates and Baptists had been unstable, and one of their ongoing disagreements was the debate over "open" and "closed" communion. The open communion party, located primarily among former Separates in southeastern New England, conceived of the Separate Baptists as a confederation of different denominations and therefore advocated co-communion with congregations who had not joined their union, specifically the remaining Separate Congregationalist churches. The dominant closed communion group, represented by the Warren Baptist Association, insisted that adult baptism was a distinguishing mark of the true church. They therefore refused to commune with the Separates, who persisted in baptizing infants.[44]

Yet another issue divided Separate Baptists as it did Congregationalists, namely the support of ministers. Virtually all Baptists, of course, opposed public taxation for ministerial salaries, but they disagreed among themselves on the degree to which financial aid was beneficial to the ministry and mandated upon the congregation. Congregations with more Separate Congregationalist origins—extreme New Light piety, open communion, anti-Gillite, independent—questioned the propriety of paying salaries to their elders, arguing that any form of hire polluted the apostolic purity of the ministry. Adherents of the Warren and Shaftesbury associations took a more professionalized position on the ministry that reflected their desire to develop a clerical elite to rival the Congregationalist pastorate.

THE SEPARATE BAPTISTS WERE not the only dissenting communion well-represented in Shaysite territory. The Society of Friends organized a Quarterly Meeting in 1783 at Uxbridge which included Monthly Meetings from that town, Leicester, and Northbridge in Massachusetts and Richmond, New Hampshire.[45] More directly related to the Shaysite constituency were the Presbyterians, who were present in surprising numbers and at key locations. Eighteenth-century Scots-Irish immigration to New England had created a number of rural cultural enclaves in Massachusetts sufficiently large to sustain a Presbyterian church and settle a minister. The list of Presbyterian communities in Shaysite country is short but impressive, including some of the most important rebel centers—Groton, Colrain, and Pelham.

It appears that Presbyterianism in rural Massachusetts reached a historic peak of vitality during the New Light Stir, but it is difficult to gain a clear picture of these congregations in the 1780s for several reasons. Most of them were somewhere in the process of transition from Presbyterian to Congregationalist polity. At the same time, New England Presbyterianism was itself divided into a number of distinct constituencies. The New Side Presbytery of Boston was aligned with Princeton and Edwardsean New Divinity. The Presbytery of Londonderry, New Hampshire, represented the conservative ethnic constituency of the Merrimack Valley under the leadership of David Annan, minister at Londonderry. The independent Grafton Presbytery, centered at Hanover, New Hampshire, and Dartmouth College, followed the theology and polity of its founder Eleazar

Wheelock. All these groups vied with one another for leadership of New England Presbyterianism, and constant ecclesiastical reorganization was the norm of the 1780s. The only regional organization in Shaysite territory proper was a presbytery that briefly convened at Palmer from 1784 to 1786. Yet despite this diversity it is important to remember that Presbyterians shared a common Scottish heritage of revolutionary action in the name of a divinely covenanted people against what they took to be degenerate and profane royal leaders.[46]

Two other groups also played important roles in the religious culture of Shaysite Massachusetts, the Universalists and the Shakers. Unlike the denominations discussed earlier, these two religious communities were new sectarian movements produced by the New Light Stir. Two distinct varieties of Universalism existed in Massachusetts by 1786, one associated with John Murray in coastal cities, the other led by Caleb Rich in the Connecticut Valley. Murray arrived in America from England in 1770 already preaching the doctrine of universal salvation, combining the charismatic preaching style he learned as a disciple of George Whitefield with the theology of English Universalist James Relly. In 1779 Murray gathered a congregation in Gloucester, and after the war his ministry spread to Boston and Salem.[47]

The second variety of Universalism, however, was a product of the Shaysite environment. Its founder, Caleb Rich, was raised in the Worcester County town of Sutton, a community that during the 1770s had experienced a Congregationalist dispute over the Half-Way Covenant and a Baptist contest over open and closed communion. After returning from military service in the Revolution, Rich, member of an important extended family of Separate Baptists, experienced a series of charismatic visions that instructed him to preach a distinctive form of Universalism based on the finite nature of sin. Human sin was committed by finite creatures; therefore, he reasoned, it could not be reckoned as an infinite offense to God punishable by eternal damnation. Rather, sin was limited in its extent and would be punished in this finite and probationary life. After death, humans stand before God not as depraved sinners but in their original created state of innocence and will be exalted, not condemned. Rich took his new gospel to Separate Baptists in Worcester and Hampshire counties and gained a number of converts.

He formed his own congregations at Warwick, Massachusetts, and Richmond and Jaffrey, New Hampshire. He was soon joined by Separate Baptist elders Adams Streeter of Oxford, Elkanah Ingalls of Grafton, and Ebenezer Lamson of Sutton. By 1786 significant Universalist enclaves existed in southwestern Worcester County and northern Hampshire County, and individual Universalists were scattered across the Shaysite religious landscape.[48]

The most spectacular sectarian movement of the Shaysite environment was Shakerism, the charismatic, communal, celibate community gathered by Mother Ann Lee (1736–1784). Lee, leader of the "Shaking Quakers" of Manchester, England, emigrated with seven followers to America in 1774 and settled in 1776 at Niskeyuna near Albany. In the spring of 1780, after being imprisoned several times on suspicion of espionage, she undertook a missionary journey to central and southern New England that would consume four years and repeatedly traverse all of Shaysite country. Mother Ann taught that the Second Coming of Christ was a spiritual event, not a physical or historical one, and that it had already begun in the souls of herself and her colleagues who thereby had "travelled" into spiritual perfection. Her commanding presence and extraordinary charismatic gifts—including speaking in tongues, charismatic dance and song, prophecy, and spiritual discernment—drew thousands of converts, especially among the more extreme and apocalyptic Separate Baptists.[49]

By 1790 the Shakers had organized formal societies in three principal Shaysite towns, Harvard, Shirley, and Tyringham, and another in the Berkshire County town of Hancock. The "lead ministry" and largest society was set up at New Lebanon, New York, just across the Massachusetts line from Pittsfield. Under Father James Whittaker, Mother Ann's foster son, and Father Joseph Meacham, a Baptist lay exhorter and son of the Baptist elder at Enfield, Connecticut, the Shakers created a highly disciplined and hierarchic yet charismatically bonded community at New Lebanon during the very time that Shays's Rebellion raged.[50]

The picture that emerges from this survey of religion in Shaysite country suggests not homogeneity and orthodox stability but precisely their opposite, heterogeneity and unstable dissent. Whether examined in the aggregate or in the context of particular towns, the evidence clearly points to a condition of sudden and complex religious change. Combining all the factors of change we have reviewed—vacancy and destitution, financial distress, doctrinal controversy, and dissenting presence—only four of the forty-two principal Shaysite parishes did not experience a significant episode of crisis and change between 1776 and 1786.

Within this overall pattern of disruption there were some significant variations. At the county level, Worcester County was distinguished for its lack of dissent. Only two of ten Shaysite parishes of Worcester County—Harvard and Templeton—harbored dissenting congregations in 1786, while everywhere else dissent occurred at much higher levels: two of four Shaysite parishes in Middlesex County, two of three in Bristol County, seven of sixteen in Hampshire County, and five of nine in Berkshire County.

At the local parish level, no two cases were precisely the same in their permutations of dissent, vacancy, financial crisis, and doctrinal controversy. Congregationalist fiscal troubles along with Baptist and Shaker agitation at Rehoboth and Ashfield; Presbyterian dissent and a Tory minister at Groton; Baptist dissent along with a meetinghouse controversy and schism in the Presbyterian parish at Colerain; vacancy and an anti-Shaysite, Deist minister at Ware; anti-Shaysite ministers and Baptist dissent at Alford and Egremont—these and virtually every other possible combination of disruptions afflicted the Shaysite parishes of rural Massachusetts in 1786. Only a complete listing of religious conditions in the forty-two principal Shaysite parishes, provided in the Appendix to this chapter, can fully indicate the dimensions of religious change in the insurrectionary environment.

HAVING ESTABLISHED THE NATURE and extent of religious change in Shaysite communities, the remaining question concerns how, if at all, such unrest related to the Regulation. Some connections are obvious. Certainly the increasing public cost of ministerial salaries and meetinghouses added to the tax burdens of rural towns and thereby contributed to the economic causes of the insurrection. The breakdown of clerical authority can also be inferred from the evidence, though perhaps not so clearly as John Brooke's "deacon's orthodoxy" hypothesis argues. Beyond question, however, the almost universal weakening of Congregationalist institutions and the simultaneous rise of dissent indicates a lessened ability of ministers to perform their traditional functions as enforcers and legitimators of the social and political order.

The problem of legitimation is fundamental to understanding the religious context of the Regulation, because it was through this symbolic linkage of divine authority with government that Congregational ministers had helped to maintain the remarkable stability of New England public culture since the seventeenth century. In election, thanksgiving, anniversary, and fast day sermons, pastors stood before their communities as religious interpreters of contemporary politics. The intellectual vehicle they employed for this purpose was the same covenant or "Federal" theology that informed their teaching on matters of salvation and church membership. Its master concept was the idea that all individuals and communities related to God and to each other through a series of covenants, contracts that stipulated certain conditions and standards that, if observed, bound both parties to perform certain acts.[51]

The Federal political theology adopted a complex stance toward the state. On the one hand it promulgated divine standards for government, which was defined according to the Calvinist tradition as custodian of the earthly kingdom of God. Furtherance of the kingdom by good rulers was just cause for praise and was presumed to bring forth God's blessings; degeneracy in government, however, constituted violation of the divine covenant and would incur God's wrath and punishment. Federal political theology carried a concomitant covenant for the people. It required obedience to all properly constituted political authority, invoking St. Paul's doctrine of submission to higher powers in Romans 13. On the other hand, this Calvinist heritage also permitted resistance to the state, but only if it promoted a true tyranny whose evil acts explicitly violated the laws of God and persecuted the church.

During the Revolution, Congregationalist ministers claimed the divine right of revolution against British tyranny and corruption and invoked God's endorsement of the American cause. "The Black Regiment" of New England ministers also preached jeremiads demanding spiritual and moral purity as the indispensable precondition for political union and military victory. Shays's Rebellion, however, created a classic problem for Federal political theologians: how should they interpret internal conflict within the camp of the righteous victor? The iron logic of Federal theology could only interpret the rebellion as a symptom of spiritual declension somewhere in the body politic. The Congregationalist elite was faced with an obvious choice: either make that charge against the Regulators or implicate themselves in it.

The Great and General Court itself presented a classic Federal indictment of the Shaysites in its Address to the People of November 14, 1786:

> We feel in common with our neighbors the scarcity of money, but is not this scarcity owing to our own folly? . . . [I]mmense sums have been spent for what is of no value, for the gewgaws imported from Europe and the more pernicious produce of the West Indies. . . . It is said that [paper] currency would give us present relief. But like the pleasure of sin, it would be but for a season, and like that too, it would be a reproach to the community and would produce calamities without end. Without a reformation of manners we can have little hope to prosper in our public or private concerns.[52]

For the first time an independent Massachusetts government faced the reality of substantial and violent political division. In keeping with its ancient tradition in such matters, the General Court identified the disease of sin as the cause of the trouble and prescribed a strong dose of virtue as the cure.

The provincial election sermons of the mid-1780s registered most clearly the impact of Shays's Rebellion on Federal political theology. The prospect and eventual achievement of Revolutionary victory had suffused election sermons of the early 1780s with optimism and exaltation, whether delivered by Arminians Simeon Howard of Boston's West Church (1780), Henry Cumings of Billerica (1783), and William Symmes of Andover (1785) or by Calvinists like Moses Hemmenway of York, Maine (1784). All these ministers could rest confident in the capacity of "rational beings" to overcome all political differences through the exercise of common reason and common piety.[53]

In the aftermath of the insurrection, however, the General Court pointedly chose Joseph Lyman of Hatfield to preach the 1787 election sermon. A conservative pastor since 1772 at one of the chief Shaysite assembly points, Lyman was thoroughly qualified to speak to the civil unrest that had afflicted the Commonwealth during the past year. He did not mince words. He drew his text from the classic Pauline reference, selecting Romans 13:4 for closer exegesis: "For [the ruler] is a minister of God unto thee for good."

Grounding his teaching in the maxim "Order is Heaven's first law," Lyman outlined the Pauline argument for obedience to civil authority and offered a spirited apology for outgoing governor James Bowdoin's military suppression of the insurrection. Lyman retailed the public virtues requisite in good rulers and pointedly instructed the General Court: "Do rulers wish to be public blessings? Then let them keep good the public faith, sustain the credit of the state, and pay punctually the public contracts."[54] Lyman exhorted the magistracy "to protect good citizens and punish the wicked" on pain of suffering divine wrath. But Lyman reserved his most severe strictures for "wicked and disobedient subjects" like the Shaysites: "They who despise government are presumptuous, self-willed, and are not afraid to speak evil of dignities, and speak evil things which they know not, have little sense of their duty to magistrates, are disturbers of the public peace, and shall utterly perish in their own corruption."[55]

Lyman ably presented the Standing Order's Federal argument against the Shaysites. Their ignorance and overweening self-confidence have literally removed their ability to understand and perform their covenant duty of obedience to the magistrate. These moral disorders could have only one cause, Satan, and only one remedy, true repentance: "Men who resist lawful authority and are engaged in tumults and confusion, may be fit for the realms of anarchy, darkness, and despotism, but without repentance they shall never behold the seats of the blessed, where every man is content in his station."[56] Lyman's characterization of heaven as a place where "every man is content in his station," and his application of it as the norm for political society perfectly illustrated the election sermon's legitimating support of the Boston government.

Lyman's election sermon was a distant thundering from the capital urging the citizenry to return to spiritual and political union under the terms of the old Federal theology. His pronouncement clearly represented the conservative consensus of Congregationalist ministers. While there were a number of outspoken clerical opponents of the Regulation even in Shaysite towns—including Benjamin Judd of Ware, Joseph Avery of Alford, and Eliphalet Steele of Egremont—there is no evidence of any settled ministers who urged or supported insurrection.

THE EFFECTIVE MONOPOLY OF the Standing Order's clergy over the Federal political theology made it difficult for the Regulators to appropriate that tradition in their cause. Although Shaysite addresses and petitions did contain strong notes of moral outrage and condemnation of government injustice, they did not invoke the revolutionary codicil of the divine covenant against the government at Boston. If the Shaysites were indeed motivated at least in part by "a deacon's orthodoxy," that theological persuasion was not overtly expressed in their petitions and addresses. Deacon Daniel Gray of Pelham, for example, presented a moral indictment of debt collection, the suspension of habeas corpus, and the "revenge, hatred, and envy" of local justices and sheriffs, but neither he nor the other Regulator spokesmen elevated their complaints into a formal political countertheology.

There is circumstantial evidence, however, that religious categories did operate in Shaysite agitation. One of the key figures in the Regulation was Samuel Ely, Yale class of 1765, the "industrious fomentor" and "inveterate demagogue" of Shaysite unrest and the leader of the Regulators' April 1782 attack on the court at Northampton. Arrested and imprisoned at Springfield, he was released by mob action and fled to Vermont. There he was later convicted of "denying the authority of the state" and remanded to Massachusetts, where he finally served his prison term for insurrectionary activity.

Before his Shaysite career, however, Ely was a minister in Somers, Connecticut, a border town long claimed by Hampshire County. In 1767 the town voted to settle Ely by a narrow 58–42 vote, but soon after his opponents, citing "suspicions as to his character," gained a majority to rescind the offer. Ely's allies withdrew, formed a Separate church, and "set him aside" by lay ordination on June 13,

1770. Two of his sermons, preached on March 18, 1770, were published at Hartford in 1771. Even twelve years before his emergence as a Regulator leader, the sermons reveal the sort of religiopolitical sensibility that he successfully used later to provoke rebellion.[57]

"You may think it strange that I should appear in print," the thirty-year-old Ely wrote in his preface, "being young, and so much dispised by the great, and by the fashionable world. But since there have been sundry reports spread abroad . . . about me much to the prejudice of truth, I have got so reproach harden'd, that I have nothing to fear from any quarter, nor to hope for applause, which I hope I crave not, overmuch." By 1770 Ely was already alienated and "reproach harden'd" by his experience at Somers, and his sermons reflected an ability to manipulate religious rhetoric for his own advantage.

Somewhat disingenuously, Ely preached to the Somers Separates on the patience of Job. In the first sermon Ely taught the doctrine of submission to divine authority. Humans owe "a free and full obedience to all [God's] commands," he wrote, "and an entire, universal resignation to the orders of his providence." In words that prefigured the decades of war and insurrection to come, Ely proclaimed that "in whatsoever instance God's will is declared, either in misfortunes, in estate, pains in the body, or convictions in the mind; we must, with humility and meekness submit, as he has an equal empire in disposing of all things, whether mercies or afflictions which are equally his own."[58]

In the second sermon, however, Ely drew upon Job's example to justify an appeal to God against the injustices of men. Though ostensibly presenting a message of humility and peaceable obedience to circumstance, the last paragraph of Ely's sermon bespoke the spirit of righteous resistance of the innocent against oppressive authority: "We may infer the great necessity of all saints maintaining their own innocency, and the rights of conscience, in opposition to all the hard speeches, cruel charges and forgerous accusations, that may be brought from every quarter. Indeed, a concienciousness of innocency, should cause God's saints to withstand earth and hell, yea, they must not suffer the sincerity of their hearts to be baffled by the most bold accusations, nor must they give up the truth at the burning stake, but with Job they must protest and asseverate their integrity, whether they are credited or not, and even engage to vindicate and justify themselves."[59]

Ely's subsequent career demonstrated that he indeed did not possess the patience of Job, but from his earliest experiences in the pulpit he was manifestly equipped to use Scripture and religious rhetoric to justify his endemic hostility to traditional authority. Ely left Somers in 1773 for Vermont; he was arrested and eventually acquitted of looting after the Battle of Bennington, and a few years later he commenced his Regulator career. Literary evidence does not exist to confirm the sort of exhortations that Ely delivered to his Regulator comrades, but it seems safe to assume that his denunciation of state government was replete with biblical rhetoric and prophetic jeremiad, if not with a fully realized theology of revolution.

The only other publications ascribed to Ely certainly embodied this style. Ely eventually located in Lincolnville, Maine, and until 1797 he championed the cause of poor squatters there being driven off their farms by wealthy nonresident proprietors. Writing anonymously in 1797, for example, Ely compared the proprietors of the Waldo Patent, and specifically Henry Knox, to King Ahab, while he identified the squatters with the virtuous Naboth, whose vineyard Ahab usurped and for which usurpation Ahab was cursed by the prophet Elijah. Building upon this biblical reference, Ely urged the squatters to rise up against the government that protected the proprietors in words surely reminiscent of his Shaysite agitation:

> Shall we call this a land of liberty? Did we fight for such liberty? How may the Tories laugh at us and call us fools for our pains. While other parts of the union enjoy the great blessings of liberty and a very happy constitution, we are tied up and bowed down under oppression, our just rights are threatened to be taken from us, and we have no liberty to help ourselves; we are loth to fight for liberty again, we do not delight in war; but if it must be we will try it once more; we had as good die by the sword as by oppression; I say, if we must be destroyed we will stand as long as we can, and who can blame us if we are driven off of our possessions?[60]

The Regulation brought forth a powerful reassertion of Federal political theology from Congregational ministers and the General

Court and an ill-defined religious and moral protest from the Shaysite leaders. But political theology in 1786-87 was no longer limited to Congregationalism. Other religious voices—Baptist, Shaker, and New Light—also spoke to the reality of civil insurrection in Massachusetts. Scholars have concentrated on Isaac Backus's 1787 pamphlet, *An Address to the Inhabitants of New England concerning the Present Bloody Controversy Therein,* as representative of Separate Baptist opinion on the Regulation. Szatmary called this short work "a vitriolic denunciation of the Regulators," but McLoughlin described a more balanced position for Backus's political theology. Surprisingly, neither have noted several fundamental differences between Backus and his Congregationalist clerical brethren.[61]

The starting point for Backus seems to have been his critical response to American consumer behavior after the Peace of Paris. In his diary for December 28, 1783, Backus made this apprehensive assessment of the months after peace was declared on September 3d: "The great men of earth crowded in their fine wares upon us, which all ranks of people in America were fond of buying, to our unspeakable damage, in the sinking of public credit, and the most extravagant gratification of pride, intemperance, fraud, and cruel oppression. Rev. 18.2."[62] Backus's moral condemnation of conspicuous consumption preceded the General Court's by nearly three years, but there were significant differences in their analyses. The Court in 1786 would lay complete blame on a degenerate public for their succumbing to "the gewgaws of Europe" and rum from the Indies. Backus in contrast condemned mercantile interests for the phenomenon of overconsumption.

A closer look at the *Address* suggests that it is the product of a very different theological world than that of the Congregationalist Federal political theology. Backus certainly cited with approval the General Court's condemnation of the overconsuming public's "folly" and responsibility for the crisis. But he also admitted the great disappointment of some citizens who after the insurrection declared "their sorrow that we ever revolted from Great Britain." Anxious to prevent any such counterrevolutionary association with Separate Baptists, Backus hastened to condemn British paper currency, labeling it the vehicle whereby "the Court of England have been enabled to carry blood and slavery round the world and load the nation with debt."[63] Backus's opposition to paper currency and its Shaysite advocates derived not from his support of Boston's mercantile interests but from his conviction that it was the best way to fall into Britain's continuing moral corruption.

Like Lyman, Backus argued for the Calvinist doctrine of submission, urging citizens to acknowledge that "God's immutable plan of government determines the choice of the worst men without the least excuse for their wickedness."[64] There were, however, deeper and more fundamental differences between Backus and the Federal political theology. The clue to these lies in Backus's repeated citations of Revelation 18:2: "For thy merchants were the great men of earth, for by their sorceries were all nations deceived." From 1782 through 1787 Backus continued to use this passage as his master text for understanding the Commonwealth's woes. This biblical focus yielded not a Federal theological analysis of the Regulation but an apocalyptic one. The mundane problems of economic crisis and civil insurrection paled before their status as signs of the approaching end of the world.

For Backus, human history had one purpose only, the fulfillment of scriptural prophecy and the divine will therein revealed. The fact that great merchants had deceived the virtuous infant commonwealth was, for him, de facto proof that the Revolution had itself been an eschatological event, an earnest of Christ's imminent return. Now the corruption prophesied in the Book of Revelation was also coming to pass. Obedience to rulers remained a mandate for Christians, but now they should understand the corruption and violence of the revolutionary state as an instrument of God's purpose soon to bring in the Kingdom.

Another major sign of the End was the appearance of false prophets; and in concluding the *Address*, Backus blamed the corruption of citizens and magistrates alike on the false prophecy of Arminian Liberals. "The way wherein teachers have kept up these evils so long in the world has been by insisting upon it that self-determination in the will of man is essential to moral agency. This doctrine . . . is now carried further in London and Boston than it is in Rome."[65] Why have the citizens run amok in an orgy of consumption? Why have rulers abandoned their duty to moderation and justice? Because they have been taught by Arminians to trust their own reason and will rather than God's. Backus urged upon his Separate Baptist brothers and sisters a different kind of freedom, willful submission to God, "the only perfect law of liberty."

The *Address* located Backus, and the Separate Baptists he represented, somewhere between the two extremes of Federal political theology and Shaysite extremism. But there were other varieties of sectarian apocalyptic political theology, best represented by the Shakers, who believed they were already living in the millennial kingdom. The Shaker leadership denounced Shays's Rebellion on grounds of Christian pacificism. Perhaps more surprisingly, their tradition does indicate that some Massachusetts Believers "manifested some party spirit concerning that event." Father James Whittaker, the sect's leader in 1786, left no room for doubt where he stood on the matter: "Those who give way to a party spirit, and are influenced by the divisions and contentions of the world, so as to feel for one political party more than another, have no part with me. . . . The spirit of party is the spirit of the world, and whoever indulges it, and unites with one evil spirit against another, is off from Christian ground."[66] This is the only published reference to the Regulation in Shaker literature, but it is sufficient to show that the Shakers' apolitical apocalypticism attracted and held at least some proportion of the citizenry in Shaysite Massachusetts.

The most intriguing voice, however, may have belonged to those rural religious folk who stood with neither government nor the Shaysites; with neither Backus nor the Shakers. These people, overwhelmingly New Light in sympathy whether Congregationalist or Separate Baptist, liable to conversion by Shakers or Universalists, found a spokesman in Christopher Babbitt of Lanesborough, who published a broadside in 1787 addressed to John Hancock. Babbitt described how he went to visit General Lincoln at Pittsfield and asked him about "the reason of his hope" for salvation, but Lincoln "answered not a word." Turning to the Massachusetts governor, Babbitt asked point-blank: "How is it with you, Governor Hancock? Was you never born again?" Tracing the source of Shaysite unrest to the Revolution, Babbitt voiced the anti-Revolutionary sentiment that Backus had tried to shield the Separate Baptists against: "They say you and Mr. Adams, who first began the great difficulty, neglect[ed] the Scripture for your rule, so the Devil deceived you, and you the people." Waxing prophetic, Babbitt delivered his summary judgment on the "rich men" governing at Boston:

> Being faithful to my Heavenly Father, I declare it unto you rulers, ruling with tyrannical powers, oppressing the oppressed, refusing to hear their cries, slain a number of men, neglecting to take scripture for your rule. . . . Did you ever know God's penetrating eye, that looks through the secrets of the children of men? Robbing men of their arms by violence, to maintain your bloody laws, condemning and hanging men, advising the same things yourselves, yet think to be excused. . . . I must declare unto you, what is proclaimed in the dark, shall be proclaimed upon the housetop. You will call to the rocks and the mountains to fall on you, to hide you from the wrath of the Lamb.[67]

Here is the sentiment of one who could not in conscience embrace either party. "As for Shays, I condemn them for taking up the gun. Was any of you born again? 'except you be born again, you cannot see God in peace.'" Whatever Babbitt's religious affiliation, he was committed, like the Shakers, to Christian pacifism. Yet he could not like them be called apolitical. Furiously engaged in the political issues at hand, Babbitt delivered a radical New Light jeremiad against the rulers, the diametrical opposite of Lyman's establishmentarian jeremiad against the people: "My heart's desire in praying to God for the rulers is, that they may be saved, and if you would your sins must be set in order before you, you must exercise repentance before God, and make restitution to your fellow creatures." Christopher Babbitt represented yet another political theology, one embraced by dissenters more extreme than Isaac Backus and more political than the Shakers. To them Backus's apocalyptic perspective on the Regulation made sense, but they hoped for a simpler and more hopeful resolution of the crisis—may God save the rulers as God has already saved the people.

Just as the Congregationalist religious establishment was experiencing rapid changes under the pressure of vacancy, financial crisis, theological dispute, and dissent, so the correlative Federal political theology had lost its immemorial consensus in New England by 1786. No longer could ministers of the Standing Order speak with unquestioned authority on God's will for the people and their governors. From within Congregationalism itself, the Shaysites struggled unsuccessfully to articulate a theology of government corruption and godly justice to legitimate their cause. In response to the Regulation, Baptists, Shakers, and other dissenters developed their own political theologies that challenged the assumptions upon which settled ministers and the Friends of Government relied. Like the rebellion itself, these theological and ecclesiastical challenges failed to transform Massachusetts society in 1786–87; but in the process, the religious world of Daniel Shays had encountered a new reality of pluralism and dissent from which there was no turning back.

APPENDIX: RELIGION IN PRINCIPAL SHAYSITE TOWNS, 1770–1800

Town and ministers	Parish dispute	Dissenters
Middlesex County		
Groton		
Samuel Dana, 1761–75	Tory minister	Presbyterians, 1782
Daniel Chapin, 1776–1826		
Pepperell		
Joseph Emerson, 1747–75	Vacant 1775–79	
John Bullard, 1779–1821		
Shirley		
Phinehas Whitney, 1762–1819		Shakers, 1783
Townsend		
Samuel Dix, 1761–97		
Bristol County		
Easton		
Archibald Campbell, 1763–82	Vacant 1782–84	Presbyterians, 1750
William Reed, 1784–1809		
Rehoboth		
1st Parish		
Ephraim Hyde, 1766–83	Salary, 1784–96	Baptists, 1753
John Ellis, 1784–96		Shakers, 1783
2d Parish		
Robert Rogerson, 1759–99		Baptists, 1753
		Shakers, 1783
Worcester County		
Barre		
Josiah Dana, 1767–1801	Salary, 1785–88	
Harvard		
Daniel Johnson, 1769–77	Vacant 1777–82	Baptists, 1776
Ebenezer Grosvenor, 1782–88	Vacant 1788–92	Shakers, 1781
William Emerson, 1792–99		
Hubbardston		
Nehemiah Parker, 1770–92	Salary, 1785–92	
	Vacant 1792–1802	
Oakham		
Presbyterian		
John Strickland, 1767–73	Vacant 1773–86	
Reorganized Congregational		
Daniel Tomlinson, 1786–1828	Half-Way Covenant, 1786	

Town and ministers	Parish dispute	Dissenters
Paxton		
Alexander Thayer, 1770–82	Vacant 1782–85	
John Foster, 1785–89	Vacant 1789–94	
Daniel Grosvenor, 1794–1802		
Princeton		
Timothy Fuller, 1767–76	Tory minister	
Thomas Crafts, 1786–91	Vacant 1776–86	
Joseph Russell, 1796–1801	Singing, 1784–87	
Spencer		
Joseph Pope, 1773–1826	Singing, 1785–89	
Templeton		
1st Church		
Ebenezer Sparhawk, 1761–1805		Baptists, 1782
2d Church		
Ebenezer Tucker, 1788–99	Vacant 1785–88	
Ward		
Isaac Bailey, 1774–1814		
Hampshire County		
Ashfield		
Nehemiah Porter, 1774–1819	Salary, 1783–89	Baptists, 1761
		Shakers, 1781
Colrain		
Presbyterian		
Samuel Taggart, 1777–1818	Meetinghouse, 1779–88	Baptists, 1780
	Schism, 1784–86	
Conway		
John Emerson, 1769–1829		Baptists, 1788
Greenwich		
Robert Cutler, 1760–86		
Joseph Blodgett, 1786–1833		
Leverett		
Henry Williams, 1784–1811	Vacant 1774–84	Baptists, 1765
Leyden		
	Destitute to 1800	Baptists, 1780
		Dorrelites, 1794
Longmeadow		
Stephen Williams, 1716–82	Vacant 1782–85	
Richard Storrs, 1785–1819		
Ludlow		
Antipas Steward, 1793–1802	Meetinghouse 1780–88	
	Destitute to 1789	
	Vacant 1789–93	

Town and ministers	Parish dispute	Dissenters
Monson		
Jesse Ives, 1773–1805	Salary, 1783–87	Baptists, 1793
New Salem		
Joel Foster, 1752–1805		Baptists, 1770
Pelham		
1st Presbyterian		
Nathaniel Merrill, 1775–80	Salary, 1780	
Jabez Fisher, 1793–1805	Vacant 1780–93	
2d Presbyterian		
Matthias Crozier, 1791–98	Vacant 1786–91	
Shutesbury		
Abraham Hill, 1742–78	Tory minister	Baptists, 1780
	Vacant 1778–1806	
South Brimfield		
Ezra Reeves, 1765–1818		Baptists, 1736
		Revival, 1779–83
Ware		
Ezra Thayer, 1759–75	Vacant 1775–85	
Benjamin Judd, 1785–87	Deist, anti-Shays minister	
Reuben Moss, 1792–1809	Vacant 1787–92	
Whately		
Rufus Wells, 1771–1834		Baptists, 1789
Berkshire County		
Adams		
Samuel Todd, 1766–78	Vacant 1778–1800	Baptists, 1769
Alford		
Joseph Avery, 1779–87	Anti-Shays minister	Baptists, 1786
Dalton		
James Thompson, 1795–99	Vacant 1785–95	
Egremont		
Eliphalet Steele, 1770–94	Anti-Shays minister	Baptists, 1787
Lee		
Elisha Parmalee, 1783–84	Vacant 1780–83	
Alvan Hyde, 1792–1829	Vacant 1784–92	
New Ashford	Destitute to 1800	
Pittsfield		
Thomas Allen, 1764–1810		Baptists, 1772
		Shakers, 1780
Tyringham		
Adonijah Bidwell, 1750–84	Vacant 1784–89	Shakers, 1782
Joseph Avery, 1789–1808		
West Stockbridge		
Oliver Ayres, 1793–1807	Destitute to 1789	Baptists, 1780
		Shakers, 1781

PART FOUR
Consolidating the Republic

11

IN SHAYS'S SHADOW:
Separation and Ratification of the Constitution in Maine

James Leamon

In February 1788 William Widgery described the events surrounding the ratification of the Federal Constitution in Boston, where he had been a delegate to the ratifying convention from the town of New Gloucester in Maine. His letter reflected the feelings of relief and joyous harmony that prevailed once the tense, bitter debate ended. He described the celebratory procession led by a federal ship of state erected on a sled hauled by thirteen horses followed by tradesmen according to their crafts and professions. Merchants followed behind another replica of a full-rigged vessel drawn by thirteen more horses, and next in line a similar number of horses dragged still another sled carrying a miniature shipyard and several small vessels. After visiting the homes of Boston's convention delegates, the procession returned to Faneuil Hall to enjoy several hogsheads of punch, wine cakes, and cheese. The marchers then proceeded on to the State House, where they fired a thirteen-gun salute. Widgery went on to note that although he had been an outspoken, indeed a leading, opponent of ratification, "I most Tel you I was never Treated with So much politeness in my Life as I was afterwards by the Tradesmen of Boston[,] Merchants & every other Gentleman."[1] For virtually everyone, the fight was over and the issue closed. Widgery publicly proclaimed he would return to New Gloucester to point out that he had fought the good fight but had been overruled by a majority of "wise and understanding men."[2]

From a paper presented at the Bicentennial Conference on Shays's Rebellion and the Constitution, 1986, sponsored by Historic Deerfield, Inc.

One notable exception to this spirit of harmony and goodwill was a convention delegate from Topsham, Maine, named Samuel Thompson, who, along with Widgery, had played a leading part in opposing ratification. Widgery's letter, in fact, had expressed concern over Thompson's behavior, and several other persons echoed his misgivings. Thompson apparently had refused to accept the convention vote as final. He "had entered too deeply into the Opposition, to think he might be mistaken," wrote one; "his Zeal, to render it efficatious needs the Addition of good Sense, Lear[n]ing & prudence."[3] Another writer warned that Thompson, whom he called "Ursa Major," threatened to spread Antifederalist sentiment among the delegates to the ratifying convention in New Hampshire.[4] This rumor was corroborated by another who added the alarming news that Thompson was taking his Antifederalist campaign into the "western Counties," the very heart of the recent Shays's Rebellion, as well as to New Hampshire.[5] In genuine fear one of Thompson's acquaintances urged a mutual friend:

> Do for God's sake write him once more—he conducts as if the Devil has possessed him. His opposition to the New Constitution continues.—When he left Boston, his last words were—*I will throw the State into Confusion*—It is true, these were great *swelling words;* but he may do a great deal of mischief,—Can not you contrive a letter that will do him good?—For I do not believe Thompson to be a man of a bad heart—Should you tell him that the Constitution with the proposed *amendments,* which will certainly take place, will operate less injuriously than many suppose—that other amendments if found necessary will certainly take place—that you admire the submissive conduct of the minority etc. etc.—(richly interlarding the whole with Republicanism)—something of this kind might be serviceable.[6]

A portrait of Samuel Thompson begins to emerge: stocky and pugnacious (Ursa Major), outspoken to the point of belligerency, a man of violent action, convinced of his own rectitude, and ardently republican. Among the leaders of society, he seemed to arouse feelings of contempt and fear. Thompson symbolized turbulent, levelling, antiauthoritarian republicanism. In the late 1780s in Maine that meant "Shaysism." An awareness of potential violence hung heavy over Maine and tainted the political scene, especially the movement to separate Maine from Massachusetts and efforts to ratify the Federal Constitution. To opponents of separation and to Maine's Federalists, the political career of Samuel Thompson seemed to epitomize and even to link a triad of disunion: separation—state disunion, Antifederalism—national disunion, and Shaysism—social disunion.

From the beginning of the American Revolution Samuel Thompson had been a threat to conservative Whig leaders who were trying to conduct an orderly separation from Britain. Agitation preceding the war had provided Thompson with an opportunity to rise above merely local prominence as tavern keeper and officeholder in the town of Brunswick. Despite his lack of formal education and a pronounced tendency to stutter when excited, his fellow townsmen sent him as their delegate to county congresses and to the Provincial Congress in Boston, which appointed him lieutenant colonel, later colonel of militia, and named him chairman of the Committee of Safety for Cumberland County.[7] In 1774 and 1775 Thompson assumed a quasi-legitimate responsibility for enforcing the embargo against Britain, called the Solemn League and Covenant. He led his Brunswick militiamen into the towns of Wiscasset, Pownalborough, and then Georgetown, where he seized "contraband," humiliated suspected Tories, and even exacted oaths from the justices of the county court that they would reject British authority.[8]

He also intruded into the affairs of Falmouth, Maine's leading seaport. The town's chief men were engaged in delicate negotiations with a British merchant who, protected by the guns of a British man-of-war, was flouting the embargo. Impatient with Falmouth's lack of action, Thompson and his men captured the British naval commander while he was walking on the beach—and almost precipitated a civil war with the outraged townsmen fearful of British retaliation. Thompson eventually released his captive, who sailed away leaving the town unharmed and its leading men complaining bitterly to the Provincial Congress about Thompson's illegal actions. Falmouth's worst fears came true in October 1775, when a British fleet arrived and punished the town by destroying two-thirds of its buildings and virtually all of its merchant fleet. While

Falmouth burned, militia from Scarborough, Gorham, and Brunswick arrived on the scene, but rather than defend the town against the British, they proceeded to plunder the houses and possessions of those who had fled.[9]

With considerable justice, the citizens of Falmouth blamed Samuel Thompson for the destruction of their town. Shortly afterwards they were understandably dismayed to learn that Thompson had received a commission as brigadier general of militia for all Cumberland County—including Falmouth. When the new brigadier general appeared suspiciously slow in providing Falmouth with a garrison against British attack, the town tried to engineer his removal from office on grounds of incompetence. Thompson, however, led a charmed political life, and he emerged from the war unscathed though unpopular with the District's leading Whigs.[10]

After the war's end, General Thompson moved from Brunswick across the Androscoggin to Topsham, where he operated a ferry and ran a tavern and store, as well as several sawmills, while speculating in land. He continued his active political career by representing his new town in the state legislature, and in 1785 the townsmen of Topsham elected him as their delegate to a gathering in Portland to consider separation from Massachusetts—and to succeeding conventions as well.[11]

This first postwar movement to separate the District of Maine from Massachusetts began in 1785, when a group of residents prominent in the Falmouth-Gorham area initiated a newspaper campaign calling for a general meeting to discuss the matter. The instigators included a group of Falmouth merchants, notably Stephen Hall, Enoch Ilsley, Samuel Freeman, and Peleg Wadsworth (celebrated for his distinguished military record). They were joined by the editor of the *Falmouth* (later *Cumberland*) *Gazette*, Thomas Wait, two Congregational clergymen, and two leading citizens of nearby Gorham.

More than one commentator described the group as chiefly composed of men looking for positions of profit in the new state.[12] With the District's population expanding from 56,300 to 96,500 in the six years following the war, such motives seem reasonable.[13] Several newspaper articles even more pointedly suggested that Falmouth (renamed Portland in 1786) might be the capital of the new state. Following the Revolution, Falmouth/Portland reemerged very rapidly from its wartime devastation. In 1784 an inhabitant recorded in his diary that forty-one houses, eleven stores, six shops and four barns had been built that year alone, and "strangers (traders and others) crowd in among us surprisingly." The next year he reported thirty-three new dwellings.[14] The newspaper reflected the booster spirit by publishing an acrostic on the name Falmouth which included this last couplet:

> Till (what no doubt will be her prosp'rous fate)
> Herself's the mistress of a rising STATE.[15]

Maine and Falmouth would rise together.

The most immediate problem facing the secessionists was how to generate and organize popular support for their scheme. They seized upon the traditional means of popular expression sanctioned by the Revolution—the convention. After a planning conference in October 1785, the separatists organized what became a series of conventions from January 1786 to March 1789. Much opinion was expressed in the newspapers and private correspondence over the size and shape of the new government, and especially concerning the legality of separation and of the methods used to achieve it. The entire debate occurred within the context of unrest and violence leading to Shays's Rebellion in western Massachusetts, all faithfully reported in the local newspaper.

As early as December 1785, the town of York refused to participate in the convention on grounds of its prior loyalty to the state constitution and for fear of stirring up civil discord.[16] Opposition to separation and to conventions became more vehement as news from western Massachusetts grew more alarming. Late in August 1786, while mobs in Northampton and then in Worcester were closing courts, a Portland town meeting elected delegates to a separation convention, only to have a second meeting instruct them "to oppose every measure that might be taken to establish a new Government," for it was not a "proper time" to hold conventions with the western part of the state "but a step from anarchy—that we should but add to the confusion—that Conventions, at all times, were dangerous things, and always so considered by the General Court."[17]

The General Court, indeed, had expressed itself in no uncertain terms regarding the separation movement. Governor James Bowdoin called it "a design against the Commonwealth, of very evil tendency, being calculated for the purpose of effecting the dismemberment of it."[18] The legislature responded that it felt the "danger and impropriety of individuals, or bodies of men, attempting to dismember the state—The social compact solemnly entered into by the people of this Commonwealth, ought, we conceive, to be attended to and guarded with the utmost care; and it shall ever be the aim of this Legislature, to prevent any infraction upon it, and preserve it entire."[19]

Not all opinion from Massachusetts was hostile. Several letters in the *Falmouth Gazette,* presumably from Worcester and even Boston, suggested that separating Maine from the rest of the state would allow the legislature to be moved to a more central location, such as Worcester, "free from the hurry, noise, and confusion which necessarily disturb its deliberations in large and populous sea ports."[20] A writer from Boston declared emphatically that the state capital would have been moved westward long ago had it not been for Maine's distance from Boston and the injustice of moving it still farther. The entire state of Massachusetts twenty miles and more west of Boston was anxious for the removal of the General Court. "Their wish to be better accommodated is as ardent as yours," the author continued, "and they as well know that your Independence would accomplish it."[21] Such promises of support from western Massachusetts became counterproductive as protest in the western counties turned to mob violence and military confrontation. Then, opponents of separation eagerly resurrected these same arguments as a means of discrediting the movement and its die-hard supporters with the stigma of Shaysism.

Opinions tended to polarize between those who denounced conventions as dangerous and unconstitutional and their defenders, who tried to draw distinctions between legitimate conventions and those that were illegitimate. One commentator justified mobs and conventions against parliamentary tyranny during the Revolution but condemned the small minority of unredeemed Tories who were trying to subvert the present voluntary, sacred compact "which holds us in one society."[22] The editor of the *Cumberland Gazette,* Thomas Wait, agreed that the westerners were acting in an "unconstitutional, riotous, not to say treasonable manner," yet the separation movement in Maine was "moving with manly firmness towards the Grand Object in view, yet with all that precaution and prudence necessary to ensure the confidence of their constituents, the good will and attention of Government, and Success in the end." Wait pointed out that the movement in Maine differed from that in the western counties, and he warned his readers to keep their fingers out of that "State Pudding" and not "rush off to butcher their Berkshire Brethren."[23]

Another writer, who called himself "Senex," accepted the theoretical necessity of conventions to instruct delegates and to petition the government but condemned those gatherings downeast as well as in the west whose purposes were either to alter or dismember free government. Indeed, Senex went on to point out that the separation movement in Maine was even more dangerous than the unrest in western Massachusetts in that the westerners merely wanted an alteration of government and redress of grievances; by contrast, the so-called peaceable and orderly conventions in Portland sought to dissolve the government. The Shaysites, he pointed out, "declare certain parts" of the constitution are grievances; the separationists claim "it's very existence is one."[24]

The argument led Senex into a public debate with "Scribble-Scrabble" over whether Article 19 of the state's Declaration of Rights, which guaranteed the right of assembly and petition to instruct delegates and to seek redress of grievances, included the right to meet in convention. Senex urged a progressively narrower interpretation of the Massachusetts constitution. By late winter and early spring 1786, as western unrest erupted into rebellion, Senex was arguing that conventions were not specifically permitted by Article 19, and so were illegal and unconstitutional. In rejoinder, Scribble-Scrabble pointed out that the people had never surrendered their right to meet in conventions; therefore such gatherings were perfectly consistent with the constitution.[25]

Opponents of separation were not successful in preventing a convention in January 1786, another in September following, and an entire series of them down to 1789; yet concern over Shays's Rebellion had a divisive and dampening influence on delegates and their deliberations. The composition of the conventions took on a new ominous meaning in light of western unrest. The cause of separation held little attraction for Maine's coastal commercial centers. North Yarmouth, Scarborough, Wells, and York were adamantly opposed, and so too was a majority in Portland. In the January 1786 convention, for example, only four towns from York sent representatives and only six from Cumberland County.[26] The most populous, wealthiest areas of the District, containing the leading merchants, lawyers, and officeholders, opposed separation or were apathetic to it. On the other hand, the areas where separation gained popular support commanded little respect from political notables. Lincoln County, because of its poverty and alienation, had representation from ten towns.[27] The idea of statehood appealed to the newcomers settling the interior towns along the Kennebec River on lands claimed by the Kennebec Proprietors, the heirs of Clarke and Lake, the Pejepscot Company, and, farther downeast, on lands inherited by General Henry Knox, who would soon acquire millions of acres more. The Great Proprietors clashed with the newly arrived settlers, many of whom were squatters taking up and improving land they regarded as their own by virtue of the common effort in the Revolution. In the eyes of the downeast and interior inhabitants, grubbing out a precarious existence in the Maine woods, the Massachusetts legislature was wrong in granting to anyone tracts of land so vast as to create dangerous inequities in the republic. The government of a new state of Maine would be more responsive to the people occupying and improving the land than to the speculators who merely monopolized it.[28]

Well might the genteel promoters of separation in Portland view their allies with suspicion; they appeared to be the stuff from which Shaysites were made. Indeed, one of the participants later described his fellow delegates from the interior as imbued with the sentiments of genuine insurgents, who "did not hesitate to speak of the senate and the attorney-general as grievances" and sought relief through paper money and legal tender acts.[29] Furthermore, Samuel Thompson was among them as their spokesman. The conservative separationists were determined to keep control of the proceedings, and they succeeded in defeating a motion that voting should be by town rather than by head. The interior towns would have controlled the convention had the motion passed. As it was, the southern coastal towns with their more numerous delegates easily outvoted the interior towns, whose poverty limited them to single or even combined delegates.[30]

In this manner, the more conservative members of the convention controlled the proceedings and shaped the decisions. The results were so temperate as to be almost anticlimatic. The two conventions in 1786 did, indeed, submit to the towns a referendum on separation and an "Appeal to the People," which assured Mainers that "mysteries in politicks are mere absurdities invented entirely to gratify the ambitions of princes and designing men—to aggrandize those who govern, at the expense of those who are governed."[31] Such potentially radical rhetoric, however, failed to strike much of a spark; the referendum returns supported separation by a two-to-one margin, but only one-third of Maine's incorporated towns responded. The conservative influence was more evident in the list of grievances and petition to the General Court which the conventions produced. The grievances contained no demands for paper money or stay laws, no philosophical statement of rights to self-government; instead the conventions emphasized the physical difficulties arising from Maine's isolated location. Distance from Massachusetts made the administration of justice and political representation awkward and expensive and taxation discriminatory. Even if Maine received additional representation, the problems arising from a disadvantageous location would persist; the only solution was a separate state.[32] The petition to the General Court was equally restrained; it merely reiterated the list of grievances and humbly requested a separation from Massachusetts, promising an equitable division of public lands and public debt.[33]

Mild and peaceable the petition might have been, but conservative members of the convention pushed through a motion to withhold the petition for the present "as the commonwealth in general is at this time in a perplexed state, and this convention being unwilling to do anything that shall seem to lay any greater burthen on the General Court."[34] Newspaperman Thomas Wait, an early supporter of separation and defender of conventions, agreed. In an editorial he declared that it would be cruel under the present distressing circumstances "to perplex government with a request of this kind."[35]

The radical element did not give up without a struggle. They responded that on the contrary, now, if ever, was the "golden opportunity" to present the petition: "The legislature are now distracted with care and trouble; if we apply to them at this time, they will not dare to refuse our request; and if they do, we can drive them into a compliance, by threatening to join in the insurrection."[36] When one of the Portland delegates remonstrated against such disposition to "perplex the government," he was told he was "out of his senses."[37]

The convention finally compromised by placing the petition into the hands of a committee with discretionary power to submit it to the General Court when it saw fit. The chairman of the committee was Samuel Thompson. Yet even he could not buck the forces of moderation and the news of violence in western Massachusetts. On March 23, 1787, the *Cumberland Gazette* carried a notice over Thompson's signature as chairman that the committee had decided, "considering the peculiar embarrassments of government, and the alarming and distressed situation of the Western Counties," against submitting the petition at that time.[38] The conservative separationists clearly controlled the deliberations and actions of the conventions and were determined to keep the movement orderly and peaceable—uncontaminated by association with Shays's Rebellion.

Shays's Rebellion was not the only hindrance to separation; the debate over ratification of the Federal Constitution also divided and diverted the movement. Strictly speaking, separation and ratification were separate issues, but in actual fact they were closely intertwined. There was much speculation in Maine how the new constitution might affect separation and what the political consequences of ratification might be.[39] General Knox exaggerated somewhat when he declared that the majority in the District would adopt or reject the new constitution as it affected the erection of the new state, yet he saw the connection clearly. From Massachusetts, Christopher Gore urged an influential friend to write to "Eastern people" to relieve their fears that adopting the Constitution would prevent their separation.[40] Articles in the *Cumberland Gazette* also reflected this concern over the relationship between separation and ratification. One writer argued that now was the time to act on behalf of separation before the new government made it more difficult than ever.[41] A differing view came from a writer who acknowledged the need to delay separation until the Constitution was ratified. Then, he went on, not only Massachusetts but everyone "this side of Philadelphia" would support it in expectation of adding two more senators "in the northern interest."[42]

To the Federalists it became increasingly evident that separatists, Antifederalists, and Shaysites were united in an unholy trinity against political unity and social harmony. In correspondence with each other, Federalists acknowledged that a majority in the District opposed ratification and that Antifederalist sentiment seemed especially to prevail in the interior and eastern towns which had supported separation. One observer commented that the common people in general were opposed, and in Lincoln County in particular, the "middling & common sort," were "decidedly against" the Constitution.[43] Statistics from Van Beck Hall support the alignment: Of the eighteen Maine towns whose delegates voted against ratification, ten had sent representatives to separation conventions at Falmouth. On the other hand, only five of the twenty-one towns whose delegates favored the Constitution had been represented at the Falmouth conventions.[44]

Gradually distinctions among Antifederalists, separatists, and Shaysites blurred and disappeared. A conservative member of the separation convention referred to his more radically minded colleagues as "genuine insurgents."[45] A Federalist in York County used the terms "Shaysism" and "Antifederalism" interchangeably in describing widespread opposition to the Constitution.[46] Another York Federalist, Judge David Sewall, described his opponents as the sort of people who "would degrade a man of Sensibility and Integrity, if it were known and realized he was a *genuine* Representative of them."[47] By this time distinctions among separatists, Antifederalists, and Shaysites had disappeared. Sewall, who had long been fulminating against conventions and rebellions, tarred them all with the same brush when he described Antifederalists as those who favored paper money and canceling the state debt at depreciated value; as those who were for setting up a new state in Maine, "many of whom reside in Worcester County—for they Suppose if we are disunited *Worcester* will be the Seat of Government"; and finally as those who "were Shaysites in principle & practice, who are averse to any Government."[48]

Several of Maine's delegates to the ratifying convention in Boston seemed almost to confirm Sewall's stereotype, none more so than Samuel Thompson from Topsham, Revolutionary radical and veteran of the separation movement. In the ratifying convention he spoke frequently and violently against the proposed constitution. Occasionally he interrupted debate, and more than once he had to be called to order by the chair. His arguments comprise a classic statement of Antifederalism rooted in the conviction that the framers of the Constitution at Philadelphia had exceeded their authority in failing to amend the Confederation and in trying to replace it with a "national consolidation" which would inevitably lead to tyranny.[49]

Not only was the new consolidated frame of government unconstitutional, but, Thompson argued, it placed in the hands of fallible men unlimited power to legislate, tax, regulate trade, and maintain a standing army. Thompson expressed surprise that his Federalist colleagues had no fear of entrusting "our federal rulers" with such power. He reminded his listeners of the everyday message of the clergy, "who are continually representing mankind as reprobate and deceitful, and that we really grow worse day after day." To prove his point, Thompson drew examples from the Old Testament and then concluded with a flourish, "Sir, I suspect my own heart, and I shall suspect our rulers."[50]

At various times Thompson suggested ways to assure a more responsible Congress. One would be to require a property qualification for election, for he said, "when men have *nothing to lose*, they have *nothing to fear.*" One of the Federalists could not resist the opportunity to express surprise that someone who so vigorously advocated popular rights should wish to exclude from government "a *good* man because he was not a *rich* one."[51] Thompson was on sounder ground when he emphasized the need for a bill of rights, "which shall check the power of Congress, which shall say, *Thus far shall ye come, and no farther.*"[52] Annual elections would also serve to restrain even bad men in government. Thompson brushed away the examples from classical history to which his more learned colleagues alluded; "but I am, sir, acquainted with the history of my own country." He proceeded to point out how annual elections had saved the state of Massachusetts by declaring that if the previous state administration had remained in power one year more, "our liberties would have been lost, and the country involved in blood."⁵³ At this an outcry arose in the convention; the chair had to call Thompson to order and then permit a recess to allow tempers to cool.

The whole process of ratification aroused Thompson's ire. What would happen, he asked, if three or four states failed to ratify? Would the others use force, and would this not then break up the Union rather than bind it closer? He pleaded for several months' delay in accepting this new, dangerous frame of government, time to consider amendments to the old Confederation.⁵⁴ At least, he argued, ratification of the new constitution ought to have been submitted to the towns rather than to a convention so that the people themselves could express their minds. Had that been done, he clearly implied that public opinion would have run strongly against ratification, and would the convention then have dared to act contrary to the popular will?⁵⁵

Finally, Thompson expressed his abhorrence that the new constitution recognized the institution of slavery and even gave it political representation. How, he asked, could a people who had just won their freedom enslave others? George Washington was as bad as the rest. "O! Washington," Thompson exclaimed, "What a name has he had! How he has immortalized himself! But he holds those in slavery who have as good a right to be free as he has. He is still for self; and, in my opinion, his character has sunk fifty percent."⁵⁶

Although Thompson and his Antifederalist allies failed to block or even to delay ratification, their opposition did force the Federalists to propose ratification that would recommend several amendments—a compromise later followed by many other states. This strategy persuaded enough opponents to shift their position so the Federalists could manage a narrow victory of 187 to 168; by four votes, 25 to 21, the Maine delegation supported the majority. Thompson saw the danger and stoutly resisted the amendments, insisting the convention had no right to propose them. He himself would not vote in favor, even though some men might be persuaded to do so, men whom Thompson implied were no better than so many Judases.⁵⁷

The difference of only four votes was not especially representative of Maine's real sentiments. At least fourteen eligible towns failed to send delegates, probably registering their opposition to the constitution in this money-saving but self-defeating manner. Furthermore, at least one Antifederalist delegate, Nathaniel Barrell, of York, submitted to intense pressure from Federalist relatives and switched his vote at the last minute.[58] Federalist leaders had good reason to be concerned over the palpable Antifederalist groundswell in Maine, but through a combination of good fortune and good management, they carried the day.

Snarling and bitter, Thompson took no part in the celebration following ratification and the conclusion of the convention. Yet despite his threats and the fears of acquaintances, he never did go to the western counties to rekindle the embers of Shays's Rebellion or to New Hampshire to block ratification there. Instead, he resumed his seat in the General Court as representative from Topsham and tried to rekindle the movement to separate Maine from Massachusetts. In January 1789 the General Court finally took up the petition for separation—the very same petition which the committee, chaired by Thompson, had submitted almost two years before. As a member of the legislature, Thompson now could defend "his" petition and the idea of separation, aided by his old Antifederalist ally, William Widgery and other diehards. Defeat was a foregone conclusion; the most that the separatists could hope for was to have the petition tabled so that it might be taken up again at some later date. Opponents tried to have the petition killed outright by arguing the separation conventions and petition were not representative of the people.[59] To this, Maine separationists pointedly replied that the number of people in Maine supporting statehood probably exceeded the number supporting the Federal Constitution. Thompson added that by including Maine, the Commonwealth of Massachusetts was simply too large for effective administration, and the government could do its business more effectively without the eastern counties. Thompson went on to say that whereas he had formerly opposed the Federal Constitution, he now supported it and that under this new frame of government it made sense to separate Maine in order to increase the northern representation in the national congress: "and as we have the 'trumps' in our hands, we ought . . . to make the best possible use of them."[60] On January 22, 1789, Thompson and his allies enjoyed a victory of sorts when the General Court reluctantly accepted the recommendation that "the respectability of the Eastern

Counties demanded so much compliance as that the petition should lay on the files."[61]

Separation was all but dead; it expired at what proved to be the last of the Portland conventions in March 1789. Attendance had been dwindling at the previous conventions until at this final one only three delegates arrived. Having elected one of their number president, another one clerk, there was no one to second the motion made by the third to adjourn; the movement came to an end.[62] It would revive and subside several times more before finally reaching fruition in 1820, but for the time being it appeared to be over. Shays's Rebellion had tainted the movement and split the leadership, and ratification drove the wedge yet further.

Important as were Shays's Rebellion and ratification in the failure of the movement for Maine statehood, that movement actually was doomed from the very start. An economic dependency on Massachusetts, a General Court willing to make concessions for Maine, and an undeveloped sense of regional identity would have undermined the separation movement in any case. Shays and ratification were important chiefly as divisive and diversionary influences. The shadow of Shays's Rebellion, "Shaysism," provided a useful political tool and an epithet—an eighteenth-century version of Bolshevism. Federalists and those hostile to Maine statehood used "Shaysism" to discredit separation and Antifederalism, while supporters of an independent Maine used it to pressure the government.

Maine produced no Shaysites—least of all Samuel Thompson, despite his reputation for radicalism and his "great swelling words," which so alarmed his acquaintances. He never did advocate physical violence against the state or closing the courts, nor did he advocate radical economic measures such as paper money and stay laws. As the owner of a tavern, a store, and sawmills, as a speculator in land and even a canal, he must have found little attraction in economic radicalism.[63] He was a successful entrepreneur in a region growing in population and in potential. This set off the eastern counties of Massachusetts from the western ones. The western ones had enjoyed prosperity during the war only to see it disappear with the war's end, leading to frustration, despair, and armed violence. In Maine the war years brought suffering and devastation. The postwar years, despite depression and economic dislocation, held a promise of better times, as Thompson's career shows. Optimism in Maine's future was the basis for immigration into Maine and the separation movement. After the collapse of the initial effort in 1789, the movement revived and, with the continued participation of Samuel Thompson, produced more conventions and another referendum in the 1790s.[64] Thompson was never a Shaysite, but he was a persistent separationist until he died in 1798.

Maine's interior squatters and farmers, isolated, burdened with debt, harassed by proprietary agents and court officers, should have provided fertile ground for the seeds of Shaysism. For the time being, however, they found an alternative to radicalism and organized violence in the promise of separation and Maine's statehood. If Shaysism—and ratification—undermined the separation movement, so did that movement with its promise of statehood dilute the appeal of Shays. It is significant that once the interior settlers lost their faith and confidence in the movement for statehood, they drifted into their own brand of violence and radicalism during the 1790s—but by then, Shays's Rebellion no longer threatened. The first separation movement, although ultimately a failure, proved to be as much a deterrent to Shaysism in Maine as was the threat of Shays to separation.

12

THE CONFIDENCE MAN AND THE PREACHER:
The Cultural Politics of Shays's Rebellion

Robert A. Gross

Shays's Rebellion is noted for many things, but hardly for its humor. So polarized were government and insurgents in 1786–87, and so high were the stakes, that neither side was disposed to view its situation with the slightest detachment.

It was, after all, no laughing matter for a farmer to lose his land or go to jail for debt—and at the hands of the very government he had fought to erect. Or, so he thought. For many in the backcountry, the natural response was bitterness and fury that turned distant public officials into "a set of plunderers . . . rioting on the spoils of the industrious." "Come on my brave boys," the erstwhile minister Samuel Ely urged his followers, as they set out to close the Northampton court in April 1782, "we'll go to the wood Pile and get Clubs enough and knock their Grey Wiggs off and send them out of the World in an Instant." Government was not amused at the spectacle. Nor did the defenders of law and order harbor any self-doubts. Their characteristic tone was the sarcasm of the Connecticut Wits, whose mock-epic, *The Anarchiad,* snidely satirized the Regulators as dupes of demagogues and dishonest rogues. But as protest turned into insurrection and events moved to a bloody climax in January and February 1787, that assurance gave way to hysteria—and a grim resolve to smash Shays's "horrid and unnatu-

From a paper presented at the Bicentennial Conference on Shays's Rebellion, 1986, sponsored by the Colonial Society of Massachusetts.

ral rebellion," as it was called by the Massachusetts General Court. At Springfield armory and on Petersham field, nobody, neither insurgent nor government soldier, was tempted to agree with Thomas Jefferson that "a little rebellion, now and then," is a good thing.[1]

In this embattled setting, which has fixed the terms of historiographical debate for two hundred years, it may seem pointless, if not perverse, to explore the comic dimensions of Shays's Rebellion and the larger crisis of the 1780s, as I propose to do here. But I am entirely serious. For the disorders in Massachusetts ought not to be regarded narrowly in political or socioeconomic terms. They can tell us a great deal as well about the changing culture and society of post-Revolutionary New England. To that end, we have to shift the focus from the issues of the insurrection to the diverse personalities who brought it forth. And what a marvelous collection of Yankee types they are!

Think, for example, of Samuel Ely, the club-wielding ex-parson, Yale College 1764, who claimed to hold "in his Pockett" a constitution "that the Angel Gabriel could not find fault with," yet who vowed in 1782, while American independence was still at issue, that he "had rather fight against this Authority [of Massachusetts] than against the King of Great Britain." Then there is the incendiary Captain Nathan Smith from Shirley, Massachusetts, who became notorious for his part in stopping the courts at Concord in September 1786. Supposedly carried away by "intoxication" and "enthusiasm," Smith told an astonished crowd of spectators, gathered on the Concord common, that they risked divine wrath—carried out by himself—if they failed to join the insurrection: "As Christ laid down his life to save the world, so will I lay down my life to suppress the government from all tirrannical oppression, and you who are willing to join us in this hear affair may fall into our ranks. Those who do not after two hours, shall stand the monuments of God's sparing mercy." Captain Daniel Shays, the supposed "Generalissimo" of the insurgency, is himself a figure cloaked in mystery and contradiction: a seemingly reluctant rebel, who on the eve of the assault on Springfield armory announced that he would desert the "scrape" in a minute if he could get a pardon and in the next moment pledged to march on Boston and burn "the nest of devils" down. In such concern to save his own skin, Shays may have provided a model for his Pelham neighbor, the little-known Henry McCulloch, one of a handful of rebels sentenced to hang for treason. Petitioning the government for pardon, McCulloch, a married man in his thirties, denied any leadership in the uprising; he merely liked to ride his "good Horse" in front of a crowd, owing to a "foolish Fondness to be thought active and alert." Besides, his mother added in a supporting document, he was a good boy, though he drank too much and lacked a father to guide him.[2]

With their blunt, homespun speech, biblical idioms, and wily ways, their passions and their eccentricities, these insurgents resonate familiar themes in Yankee lore. Here, one is tempted to think, the provincial son of the Puritans steps forth, like Goffe and Whalley of old, in all the parochialism of his backcountry parish. He is a local amid the cosmopolitans, and that is exactly how enlightened Anglo-Americans perceived him. "The manners of the town and country are so very different," one writer opined in the *Massachusetts Centinel* of March 1784, "that I hardly know how to mention them together. The ideas of the country people are too often cribbed, narrow and confined: All their notions are little; their minds want the expanding peculiar to the education of the great world; their desire for reading extends no farther than *Robinson Crusoe* or *Mr. John Bunyan's Pilgrim's Progress;* and their converse the regular diurnal scandal of the neighborhood or village, for . . . there are no great and noble objects to amuse the mind." By contrast, the inhabitants of large towns have refined manners and large thoughts. Encountering a diversity of business and amusements, they "keep the mind employed" and become "citizens of the world."[3]

Such contrasts between the cosmopolitan and the local, born of Enlightenment ideology, have rattled down the centuries to our own time, to be accepted uncritically by some historians of Shays's Rebellion. But the "citizen of the world"—the educated gentleman of New England—had his peculiarities and eccentricities, too, and it is upon two such figures, viewed in relation to the countryside, that this essay focuses. The first is Stephen Burroughs, an early American rogue, who turned up in Pelham, Massachusetts—the home of Daniel Shays—in the spring of 1784 to seek employment as a preacher. Dressed in a light gray coat with silver-plated buttons, a green vest, and red velvet breeches, the young man, age nineteen, made a very unlikely candidate. In fact, despite his years, he had already run a riotous course through life. The son of a minister in Hanover, New Hampshire, Burroughs was thrown out of Dartmouth College for his numerous pranks, after which he first kept school, then sailed as physician on a privateer to France. He arrived in Pelham nearly penniless and on the lam, having fled from Hanover in order to avoid punishment for stealing a beehive and for courting a "widow" whose husband had just returned. His principal resource was his wits—supplemented by a secret cache of sermons he pilfered from his father before departing home. But that and a recommendation from a minister who barely knew him were enough to persuade Pelham to overlook the lad's apparel and give him a chance to "supply" preaching for the town's vacant pulpit.

For several months, it was all smooth sailing for Parson "Davis" —his mother's name—who won a quick reputation for always being prepared to preach. Then, somebody smelled a rat when the youth was detected reading from an old, faded manuscript. His credentials in doubt, Burroughs accepted a challenge to preach from any passage in the Bible, sight unseen, and in a hilarious episode, offered an improvisation on Joshua 9:5 ("old shoes and clouted on their feet"). Why shoes in the text? "We are all . . . sojourners in this world but for a season," en route to our eternal fates. Why old? "The old shoes represent old sins"—like "the spirit of jealousy and discord" that had been tearing Pelham apart. And why "clouted"? To patch over their sins with "false and feigned pretenses, to hide their shame and disgrace." It was, as Burroughs tells it, a convincing performance, simultaneously a parody of evangelical preaching and a sly hit at the petty squabbles of the Pelhamites. Accused of fraud, Burroughs turned the tables on his accusers, shamelessly preaching a sermon on their hypocrisy. That inspiration saved his job, but not for long. He was soon recognized by a passing clergyman and exposed as a fraud. Burroughs fled Pelham with a mob on his heels. Even so, he had spent enough time in the troubled town to get caught up in alchemy and counterfeiting schemes, which eventually proved his ruin. In late 1785 he was convicted of passing fake money in Springfield and sentenced to three years in jail. It was clearly riskier to counterfeit money than sermons.

Out of this web of deceit and a host of other escapades, including jailbreaks, a trial for attempted rape, and speculation in the Yazoo land frauds in Georgia, Burroughs fashioned an early American best-seller, *Memoirs of Stephen Burroughs,* first issued in 1798 by a publisher in Hanover, New Hampshire, with the wonderfully inappropriate name of Benjamin True, that went through more than twenty printings over the next half century and established his place as a pioneer of the "confidence man" tradition in American literature and life. In the process, he took his revenge on the Scots-Irish people of Pelham, whose violent passions, jealousy, and gullibility he painstakingly satirized for the readers. Through the deftness of his prose, Pelham became the credulous town that supported both Stephen Burroughs and Daniel Shays.[4]

Now for the second "citizen of the world," a better-known figure, the jurist and playwright Royall Tyler. Eight years Burroughs's senior, Tyler was also casting about for his future on the eve of Shays's Rebellion, though on a far grander scale. The heir of a rich Boston merchant, Tyler graduated from Harvard College in 1776, then studied law, and served on one brief military expedition. But his real energies went into pursuing a career in "dissipation." Among other things, he was arrested for creating a drunken disturbance at Harvard in 1777 and was suspected of fathering an illegitimate child, Royall Morse, by a chambermaid at the College. By the 1780s he had settled down and devoted himself to the practice of law and the courtship of John Adams's daughter. Unfortunately, his potential father-in-law did not welcome a "reformed rake" into the family, no matter how hard Tyler tried to be "regular" at his office and to improve an expensive farm he had bought in Braintree in anticipation of the marriage. That was never to be: by 1786 Tyler had been jilted, his legal practice was faltering, and he was £200 in debt for his farm, on which, as if symbolically, he had just tried and failed to build a windmill. "Courtship," he would one day write, "is ever a state of deception," wherein "the sexes deceive each other upon the most praiseworthy motives."[5]

At this ebb in his fortunes, Tyler remade his life out of the opportunities cast up by Shays's Rebellion. Despite his slight military experience, Tyler gained appointment as aide-de-camp to General Benjamin Lincoln and was dispatched by Massachusetts to seek extradition of the fugitive rebels from Vermont and New York.

Tyler relished the assignment, especially the room it afforded for playing not only diplomat but spy in quest of Daniel Shays. The rebel leader traveled about the countryside under false names; Tyler followed suit by wearing disguises and using secret passwords, such as "I have a great cold." In one instance, he dispatched a spy to "Chesterfield it" with Mrs. Shays in Bennington. None of this amounted to much. But when Tyler carried his mission to New York City, he was able to indulge his taste for playacting to the full.[6]

The story goes that after seeing a professional play, Sheridan's *School for Scandal,* for the first time in his life, Tyler decided to try writing his own. The result was *The Contrast,* the first American play to be professionally produced on the stage. Presented in April 1787, it was an overnight success. Tyler took the stock themes of the eighteenth-century theater—appearance and reality, deception and sincerity—and adapted them to the needs of the new republic. His characters were all conventional figures on the stage—rakes, gentlemen, and coquettes—except for one, and that one seized the show. In the comic figure of Jonathan, a servant to the hero, Colonel Manly, Tyler created full-blown an authentic American type, the Yankee on the stage, who would emerge as "a genuine folk figure" over the next half century. A provincial New Englander, instantly recognizable for his vernacular speech, homely wit, resourcefulness, independence, and tribal ways, Jonathan would prove Tyler's lasting mark on American culture. Thanks to the play, Tyler, who would go on to a distinguished career as the chief justice of Vermont, would be remembered mainly as the cosmopolitan gentleman who captured the archetypal Yankee yeoman, instead of Daniel Shays.[7]

The stories of Stephen Burroughs and Royall Tyler afford an intriguing vantage point from which to view Shays's Rebellion and the crisis of the new republic. Burroughs, to be sure, never played a direct part in the tumultuous events—the public auctions, the county conventions, the court closings, the militia trainings, and so on—that unsettled Pelham and the other Regulator towns. But he moved in, without compunction, to exploit the unhappy financial circumstances behind the rebellion. What better trade in a currency crisis than the secret arts of engraving money and minting coin? By contrast, Royall Tyler had a few principles. Though he aimed to make his name in the government army, he did believe, or so he told the public officials of Vermont, that "the Persons whom we seek your Aid in apprehending are not merely Rebels against the Wholesome Government of the Commonwealth of Massachusetts but under the Influence of the most Pernicious Principles which ever Blackened the Human Heart and are the Common Professed Enemies of Civil Society."[8] Still, the two men have a lot in common. They share the characteristic sentiments of the self-styled cosmopolitan gentleman, and they embody the fundamental paradox of the type. They claim to idealize the man of feelings, whose every act and gesture vibrate to the spontaneous promptings of the heart. Yet, their lives are obsessed with self-created duplicity and disguise. In their polished manners, secretive ways, and eye on the main chance, they appear to fit the stereotype of the insincere, self-interested elite—exactly what the Shaysites feared. They are the very opposite of the plainspoken, honest Yankee farmer, whose cultural image they did so much to create.

Why such preoccupation with fraud and masquerade? These concerns were hardly unique to Burroughs and Tyler. They formed the common currency of Shays's Rebellion, circulated throughout all the charges and countercharges of the rancorous public debate, without ever losing any value. In Massachusetts of the 1780s, nothing was what it seemed. The spokesmen for government were sure that artful, designing men—perhaps agents of British power—were planting lies among the people in order to stir up disaffection and put themselves in power. In preparation against popular violence, state and federal officials secretly connived to raise troops for possible deployment in Massachusetts; concealing this purpose, Congress adopted the ruse that soldiers were needed against restive Indians on the Confederation's western frontier. The Shaysites were equally suspicious of the governing elite. Inverting the claims of their opponents, the insurgents maintained that a conspiracy of merchants, lawyers, and magistrates meant to impose "lordships" and "slavery" upon the people. Every act of the leading participants came under question. Did Daniel Shays sign the call to arms, summoning the people of western Massachusetts to fight? "I never did," he declared; "it was a cursed falsehood." Someone put his name on the document without his permission. Nor was he the leader of the insurgents. "I at their head! I am not," he told General Rufus Putnam. "You are deceived." In post-Revolutionary New England, that was a condition one could scarcely escape.⁹

The widespread fears of deceit reflected more than the political moment. They sprang from a society in change, experiencing profound upheaval in every aspect of its life. That unsettlement had been going on for a long time, precipitated by such forces as population pressures on land and the growth of markets and heightened by the radical currents of the Great Awakening and the Revolution. It was simultaneously a political, economic, religious, and cultural crisis. It brought fluidity and instability to a people who had been raised to idealize fixity as their governing norm. It shattered conventional social roles and obliged people to confront contradiction and ambiguity in their daily lives. It ended the isolation of backwoods communities, gathering up town and country alike in a common process. And it cast up splendid opportunities for the sharpsters like Stephen Burroughs and the ambitious like Royall Tyler to move into the social vacuum and invent their own self-dramatizing parts.¹⁰

It is unlikely that Stephen Burroughs had such notions in mind, nor even any literary ambitions, the day he walked into Pelham in hopes of work. Friendless, penniless, exiled from his father's home as a result of his constant defiance of authority, he was driven to impersonate a preacher out of sheer desperation. As Burroughs recounted his dialogue with himself, the decision to trade on his father's sermons went this way: "There is one thing, said contrivance, which you may do, and it will answer your purpose;—preach! Preach! What a pretty fellow am I for a preacher! A pretty character mine, to tickle the ears of a grave audience." Then again, what else could he do, since he had no money to study medicine or law and no capital for trade; he was unable to keep a school—the head tutor at Dartmouth got him fired, wherever he started up; and most importantly, it never occurred to him to step outside the narrow circle of learned professions and take up the usual resort of the landless, young man: day labor on a farm! One hundred and fifty miles from home, and he had never left the social orbit of Dartmouth.¹¹

Even so, Burroughs's exigency met Pelham's needs. The Scots-Irish Presbyterian town was notoriously hard on its ministers. It had dismissed its first pastor after nine years, had driven the second to an early grave, and had gotten rid of the third after a protracted salary dispute during the Revolutionary War. In fact, the town had gone without a settled minister for half of its entire existence down to 1786. And the pulpit had been vacant for some five years when Stephen Burroughs sauntered into town. Given the town's reputation, hardly anyone wanted the job. The Pelhamites prided themselves on evaluating the theological niceties of their preachers, and when they didn't like what they heard, they were free with their opinions. They were, said Burroughs, "a people generally possessing violent passions, which once disturbed, raged, uncontrolled by the dictates of reason; unpolished in their manners, possessing a jealous disposition; and either very friendly or very inimical, not knowing a medium between those two extremes." Passionate, jealous, impulsive: this was the standard cosmopolitan indictment of backcountry folk. In the realm of religion, the Pelhamites fit the bill.[12]

But the sorry situation of Pelham's church was not unique in the world of the 1780s. More than a third of the parishes of New England were "destitute" of a pastor, according to an estimate by the Reverend Ezra Stiles. In the strong Regulator towns of Hampshire County, Massachusetts, the situation was even more extreme: close to half of the pulpits were vacant. The vacuum of clerical leadership had its immediate roots in the Revolution: the army had enlisted many pastors as chaplains; the war had cut down on college enrollments and therefore the supply of new preachers; the financial troubles of the 1780s sapped the capacity of communities to pay ministerial salaries. But beyond these forces lay the vast expansion of New England's population, spreading into the backcountry faster than institutions could follow, and the religious upheaval of the Great Awakening and the succeeding "stirs" that reverberated throughout the hill country in the decades of the Revolutionary conflict.[13]

The spiritual upheaval in the backcountry shattered the religious unity of New England for good, fracturing society into diverse cultures and forcing ministers to compete with new sects—Separates, Strict Baptists, Universalists, Shakers, Free-Will Baptists, and a host of other short-lived faiths emerging in the years of the Revolution. Evangelical piety posed a powerful challenge to the legitimacy of the established clergy. In the intense fervor of the day, traditional ministers, reading cold, formal sermons from the pulpit, struck many parishioners as "dead dogs," who knew only the letter and not the Spirit. Congregations began demanding visible piety from their pastors and insisting on authentic, spontaneous preaching, such as they had witnessed in the histrionics of George Whitefield and his followers. It was hard to get around that test. Once Congregational clergy had enjoyed a monopoly over their parishes; but increasingly they had to fend off itinerant preachers, who invaded ministerial bailiwicks and offered their own spiritual lines. In a typical lament, the shepherd of Westfield, Massachusetts, the Reverend John Ballantine, complained that Separates were "grievous wolves" devouring his flock. But there was no way to hold back the forces of dissent.[14]

If a minister tried to keep the competition out, he could lose his job, once considered a sacred trust for life. The Old Light pastor William Rand of Sunderland, Massachusetts, not far from Pelham, suffered that fate after he refused to let itinerants preach in his church. Publicly denouncing those who "cry out against the ministers of Christ, reproach them, and treat them with Contempt . . . as unconverted, dead, carnal, etc." Rand spurned any interference with his office. For such adamancy, he forfeited the post, but Rand was lucky: he soon found another with a congregation that had fired its preacher for excessive enthusiasm for George Whitefield. The rude dismissal of ministers became an increasingly common fact of life in Hampshire County in the two decades before the Revolution. More than a dozen pastors lost their offices owing to quarrels with their parishes. Deference to the clergy, the traditional mainstay of social order, was fast on the wane, especially in backcountry towns. When Grindall Rawson of South Hadley tried to hang onto his post after being sacked, he was physically hauled out of the pulpit, roughed up, and thrown out of the church.[15]

Even when a minister retained his job, he had to meet the new standards of authentic performance. No longer could he get by with formal recital of a prepared text, rehearsing the strict logic—firstly, secondly, thirdly—of the Puritan sermon. Congregations demanded the visible display of a sanctified heart, in spontaneous harmony with the inner spirit. For such purposes, a minister needed both a new rhetoric and a new style. The model preacher was, of course, the charismatic George Whitefield, whose dramatic gestures—"a protean face, a penchant for the histrionic, and an almost perfect sense of timing"—aroused envy in the great English actor David Garrick. Lesser performers felt only resentment. The minister Ebenezer Turrell of Medford, Massachusetts, was notorious for his hatred of competition; it was said that "whenever he appeared in the pulpit, he chose to be the sole speaker, and would never listen to the performances of others." Yet, even Turrell could not escape comparison to his colleagues, many of whom he claimed to despise. Defensively, he announced that he disliked equally the ornate "flourishes of Rhetoric" on the part of genteel preachers and the resort to "indecent and homely Phrases, such as savour of the Mobb or Playhouse," by vulgar ones. Turrell made his comments in 1740, when the demands of the lay audience were still new. By the Revolutionary War, no minister could pretend to ignore his reviews. New Englanders in the Continental army were sophisticated critics of chaplains—popularly called "pulpit drums"—whom they measured by the new standard of spontaneity. One soldier waxed enthusiastically about the Reverend William Emerson, on leave from his parish in Concord, Massachusetts: "This was preaching he had no not[e]s." Another gauged sermons by their emotional effects. "He reads," it was said forgivingly of one chaplain, "but is very pathetic." In short, the revival spirit was converting the meetinghouse into a theater of piety, where the successful actor never revealed his script.[16]

In the popular zeal for spiritual purity, there arose a new sensitivity to plagiarism in the pulpit. Some ministers were charged not only with being "dead dogs" but of not even whimpering in their own voice. In Philadelphia, a few years before George Whitefield swept into town and electrified thousands with his evangelical message, a Presbyterian pastor named Samuel Hemphill came under severe attack for preaching "Good Works," instead of the Calvinist doctrine of election. Pro- and anti-Hemphill factions waged a bitter war of words in the press, with Benjamin Franklin taking a prominent part in the minister's defense. Unfortunately, Hemphill proved an embarrassment to his friends when it was revealed that he had been extracting his sermons from the British reviews. Virtually everybody abandoned his cause—except for the freethinking Franklin. "I stuck by him . . . ," the liberal printer later explained, "as I rather approv'd his giving us good Sermons compos'd by others, than bad ones of his own manufacture." A similar controversy rocked the Connecticut Valley at the height of the Great Awakening. In South Hadley the obstinate Grindall Rawson was ousted chiefly for his opposition to the revival. But among the counts against him was the charge of stealing his sermons from other preachers.[17]

On the other hand, thanks to the new emphasis upon affecting oratory, any unlettered, uncertified individual could impersonate a minister, if he could perform well enough. Indeed, in 1780, only a few years before Stephen Burroughs strolled into Pelham, another "imposter" was upsetting the Hampshire County town of West Springfield (not incidentally, the home of the prominent Regulator Luke Day). It happens that an Englishman named John Watkins suddenly appeared in the parish of the Reverend Joseph Lathrop at a moment when the pastor was seriously ill. Watkins quickly filled the void. Hired to supply preaching, he "showed every characteristic of a genuine imposter," we are told: "made professions of the most extraordinary sanctity; maintained that saints certainly know each others' hearts; and that all whom they cannot fellowship are unregenerate." Watkins aimed to draw the parish away from Lathrop, but no luck. The Congregational community stuck to its regular preacher. "Watkins rendered himself so odious to the community at large, that he was glad to seek some other field on which he might more successfully practice his imposture." In his wake, the Reverend Mr. Lathrop returned to the pulpit and preached a set of sermons on "the marks of false teachers." Published under the title *Wolves in Sheep's Clothing*, the warning clearly spoke to the times; it went through more than a dozen editions.[18]

The problem of religious imposters reflected the larger unsettlement of society. From the 1750s on, as the Atlantic economy prospered, growing numbers of middling Americans aspired to the trappings of gentility—fine homes, china, portraits, books, college educations—for themselves and their children. This quest for social mobility reached new heights in the upheaval of war and revolution. The conflict with Britain offered numerous opportunities to get rich, from army contracts and privateering to speculation in paper money and in Loyalist estates. It drove Tory placeholders from posts of honor and profit and set off a scramble for political and military office. At the same time, the rhetoric of republicanism legitimated the pursuit of personal advancement. In the new society, top honors would go to "natural gentlemen," distinguished by virtue and talents, and not to the favorites of privilege and power. But who was to judge individual merit? Seizing the promise of the Revolution, many men of humble origin pressed for recognition, despite their lack of genteel style. In the fluid circumstances of the era, it proved impossible to maintain social boundaries, to separate the worthy few from the vulgar mass.[19]

Indeed, the rise of the "fake" gentleman obsessed social critics. The Massachusetts politician James Warren, a self-styled apostle of virtue, complained to his good friend John Adams in 1779 that "fellows who would have cleaned my shoes five years ago, have amassed fortunes, and are riding in chariots. Were you to be set down here you . . . would think you was upon enchanted Ground in a world turned topsy turvy." In an essay for the *American Museum* in 1786, Timothy Dwight retailed the story of a recent immigrant to America who palmed himself off as a lawyer and immediately obtained an important office. Not long after, the man's wife arrived and exposed him as a "tallow chandler." This was doubtless an apocryphal tale—Dwight related it in a fictional sketch—but it bespoke the same concerns that led members of the elite to denounce Daniel Shays as a social upstart. Though born poor, the son of a laborer, Shays had climbed to the rank of captain in the Continental army and could thus claim the status of gentleman. In that capacity, he was entitled to deference from ordinary folk and to a hearing among leading men. To discredit such pretensions, the Boston press branded Shays a "mushroom General," sprung up overnight in the dark soil of rebellion. Shays, it was said, had gotten his officer's rank by "duplicity," recruiting men for the Continental service on the condition he should be their captain. Having risen through fraud, he soon betrayed his lack of honor. The story was told that back in 1780, the marquis de Lafayette had bestowed ornamental swords upon the Continental officers under his command as a mark of personal esteem. Captain Shays was one of the fortunate few. But did he treasure this gift, this "elegant sword," as a "pledge of [Lafayette's] affection, which a man of honour and spirit would have sacredly preserved, and handed down to his posterity as a jewel of high price?" Not at all. Shays sold the sword for a "trifling consideration." Utterly insensitive to the compliment he had received, caring more for money than friendship, he was no officer and gentleman. He belonged back where he started in the lower orders.[20]

Yet, the Patriot gentry was not above masquerades of its own. In the face of the militant egalitarianism that was unleashed by the Revolution, spokesmen for authority were put on the defensive. No longer could they assert the values of deference and hierarchy in a confident, directive voice. That tone would only arouse popular resentment. Instead, in the newspapers and periodicals of the day, members of the elite dropped the authoritative stance and posed as simple, independent farmers, offering the wit and wisdom of the countryside. The Reverend Timothy Dwight, a scion of the Connecticut Valley River Gods, assumed the persona of "John Homely," a patriotic farmer, to expose his archetypal confidence man, the chandler-turned-lawyer. In another essay in the *Massachusetts Centinel,* a shrewd literary gentleman, claiming to be an "honest farmer," presented a parable for the times in his sad descent from sturdy self-sufficiency into luxury and debt. Supposedly born poor and put out to a farmer, the author had "married me," at age twenty-two, "a very good working young woman." Together, through industry and frugality, they had gradually built up a substantial farm, which comfortably took care of their needs. "Nothing to wear, eat, or drink was purchased," the "Farmer" boasted, "as my farm provided all. With this saving, I put money to interest, bought cattle, fatted and sold them, and made great profit." With that money, he acquired more land to provide for his children. But then the love of luxury crept into his happy home. The hardworking wife turned into a conspicuous consumer: there must be silk gowns for the daughters, a looking glass in the bedchamber, tea and sugar on the table. Such tastes absorbed all the income from the farm—and more. "Now, this has gone on a good many years," he advised, "and has brought hard times into my family: and, if I can't reform it, ruin must follow—my land must go. I am not alone. Thirty in our parish have gone hand in hand with me: and they all say, 'hard times.'" The solution was obvious: return to the simple ways of the past. "The tea-kettle shall be sold." This was, of course, a political message, designed for the Massachusetts crisis of 1786.

In the guise of a fellow victim of illusion, the literary gentleman blamed the troubles of farmers on themselves and served up the Federalist prescription for "hard times." Whether he fooled anybody is unknown—though he has successfully duped twentieth-century historians of rural *mentalité*.[21]

A man of many faces—college dropout, quack physician, fake clergyman, lewd schoolmaster, benevolent counterfeiter—Stephen Burroughs was the archetypal confidence man of the age. Through a life that was "one continued course of tumult, revolution and vexation," he acquired—and exploited—a reputation as a devil in disguise, endlessly changing his shape to achieve his ends. Appropriately, it was in the realm of religion that he first discovered his calling. Burroughs knew intimately the conflicts and contradictions of the evangelical world—not, we may presume, from his own conversion, but from his family background. His father, Eden Burroughs, Yale 1757, was an ardent New Light, who ministered to a little church of Separates in rural Connecticut before moving to Hanover, where he presided over a standing Presbyterian church and labored in support of Dartmouth College. Noted as "an extemporaneous preacher," the Reverend Mr. Burroughs was a contentious figure, constantly embroiled in church disputes, owing to his zeal in regulating the moral lives of parishioners. The minister freely denounced the hypocrisy of "professing Christians" who betrayed their pledges of "mutual confidence" by "bit[ing] and devour[ing] one another" in the everyday conduct of trade. But to his critics, Burroughs ran a high-handed moral inquisition, and they soon overthrew his leadership. At the height of the controversy, the uncompromising parson revived his early stance of dissent. With his salary in arrears, he made a virtue of necessity and denounced the practice of religious taxation. He was back in the sectarian world from which he had sprung, exchanging pulpits with Baptists, and embracing the principle of voluntary religious choice.[22]

In this family ethos of dissent, Stephen Burroughs spent his formative years. His uncle, Ebenezer Davis, was a prominent Universalist layman in Charlton, Massachusetts. (Interestingly, he was also chair of the Worcester County convention of 1784, in protest against state financial policies.) And he was tutored for college by a close family friend, the Reverend Mr. Joseph Huntington of Coventry,

Connecticut, who, his pupil detected, "conformed to the established modes and forms [of Congregationalism], but internally despised them." Popular for his spontaneous sermons, Huntington kept a tight lid on his inner convictions. At his death, he left behind a manuscript that shocked his colleagues: an embrace of the doctrine of universal salvation for all mankind.[23]

Out of this dissenting culture, then, Stephen Burroughs developed a keen sense of spiritual fraud and an irrepressible delight in puncturing the pretenses of the self-righteous. His first lessons in hypocrisy came at home. While Eden Burroughs was denouncing the pharisees of Hanover, he was unwittingly providing a model of insincerity to his son. "Our actions are as strong a language, and perhaps stronger, than our words," Stephen Burroughs advised readers, "and . . . children . . . discover at once, whether our words and our actions speak the same language; and when they find them interfering, they immediately conclude, that deception is the object of the parent . . . a view of which insensibly leads the child into the practice of dissimulation." In that moment of disillusion, young Burroughs was born again; the dutiful son became the irreverent prankster, determined to turn parental authority on its head. But not directly. All in the name of fun, the lad got revenge by tormenting his elders—the more pious, the better. In their "sanctimonious self-importance," they were clearly proxies for the humbug at home.[24]

Even as he made sport of his father's piety, Burroughs absorbed its inner spirit. Projecting himself as an enemy of coercion, he treasured the dissenters' voluntary ideal. "This one thing I fully believe," he observed, "that our happiness is in our power more than is generally thought. . . . No state or condition of life, but from which we may (if we exercise that reason which the God of Nature has given us) draw comfort and happiness." In that faith, which would be severely tested in the course of his *Memoirs,* Burroughs carried forward the rejection of Calvinism that was rapidly advancing on the frontier. In matters of the soul, everyone must look to his own resources. That is certainly what Stephen Burroughs did when he was forced to make his own way in the world: he impersonated a minister. All it took was an impassioned spirit and an eloquent tongue.[25]

In the account of his short relation with the Pelhamites, Burroughs cast himself as a man of sensibility, forced to endure the petty jealousies, the harsh tempers, the confined minds of the Scots-Irish congregation and triumphing over them by the sheer resourcefulness of his speech and the power of his mind. In every episode of the book, he emerges as an heroic figure, resisting coercion. Ironically, in this embattled stance, he bears a striking resemblance to the very people in Pelham who would march under the command of Daniel Shays. Burroughs was a young, propertyless transient, on the margins of the town—exactly like the typical insurgent. Echoing the refrain of the rebellion, he saw himself as an injured innocent, under constant siege from artful, designing men. But Burroughs never made these connections; instead, he pointedly dissociated himself from his surround. In his telling, he is a lone "man of feeling" in an unsympathetic world, expressing not the piety of a converted sinner but the natural sentiments of a benevolent heart. Burroughs claims to idealize the bonds of equality and fraternity, but in practice, he elevates himself far above the crowd; he is intimate with only a few souls, superior in their refinement and knowledge. His is an enlightened elect of sensibility, secularizing the evangelical creed, while retaining a sense of superiority to both ordinary and orthodox folk. He repudiates equally the bigotry of his father's faith and the superstitious parochialism of the backcountry. His motives, he announces, are always pure; at worst, he has been too "volatile," too impulsive in expressing his feelings. The heart must be its own judge. "We cannot discern the operations of the human heart in man, until we are in such a situation, as to prevent his wearing a disguise."[26]

By such self-dramatization, Burroughs recreated himself as "a citizen of the world" and fixed upon the backcountry all the scorn of the cosmopolitan gentlemen in Boston. Yet it was all a ruse. In a separate publication of the sermon he supposedly offered up to the Pelhamites when they cornered him atop a haymow in a barn in Rutland, Massachusetts, Burroughs acknowledged that he had been engaged in a charade all along. Purporting to be the prophet of Pelham, he conjured up the voice of the Lord, "which crieth against the Pelhamites" for driving each of their ministers away. "'Then,' said the Lord, 'I will give them a Minister like unto themselves, full of deceit, hypocricy, and duplicity. But whom, among all the sons of men shall I send?' Then there came forth a lying Spirit, and stood before the Lord, saying, 'I will go forth, and be a spirit in the mouth of Stephen the Burrowite.'" In short, a deceitful, lying congregation deserved a deceitful, lying preacher—a "hoaxster" like himself. It was all humbug, and P. T. Barnum, another Universalist turned confidence man, would have appreciated the joke.[27]

But Burroughs could not let well enough alone. He poured out his anger at the townspeople in scurrilous verse and bad jokes. Playing upon the ethnic prejudice of Yankees against the Scots-Irish, he invented a psalm for the Pelhamites to remember their origins: the conjoining of the devil and a sow. And in an outright fabrication upon his experience in Pelham, he offered a malicious satire of Shays's Rebellion, which had occurred, in fact, two years after his sojourn in the town. The center of the event was, naturally, Stephen himself. It seems that the Pelhamites were in hot pursuit of their false prophet, Stephen the Burrowite, who "sorely oppressed [them], taking from them ten shekels of silver, a mighty fine horse, and changes of raiment, and ran off to Rutland." Suddenly, out of nowhere, they encountered the army of the "Lincolnites" at the ford of the river "Jourdan." "They sought by guile to deceive the army of the Lincolnites; therefore, they say unto the Lincolnites, 'We be strangers from a far country, with old shoes, and clouted on our feet.' Then said the Lincolnites unto the men of Pelham, 'Say Faith!' Then the Pelhamites said 'fath,' for they could not say faith. Then the Lincolnites knew them to be Pelhamites and fell upon them and slew them so that not one was left to lean against the wall." Captured by the invading host, the Pelhamites were driven into exile in the "city of *Dan*." There they begged mercy from "Jammy the Bostonian, saying 'We be evil men, dealing in lies and wickedness; we have sought to destroy the goodness of the land! we have trusted to St. Patrick to deliver us, but he has utterly forsaken us,'" and pledging, in exchange for pardon, to forget about affairs of state. "We will leave assembling ourselves together to talk politics, and follow our occupation of raising potatoes." In that satire lay a familiar worldview: government belonged in the hands of the virtuous few. Despite his repeated imprisonment by the same government that had suppressed the backcountry, the Dartmouth dropout never shed his identification with the cosmopolitan elite.[28]

Yet Burroughs missed his true calling for the stage. The consummate role-player, who delighted in amusing the crowd, he adapted himself perfectly to the "broad theatre of the world." In the *Memoirs* he portrayed his life as an unfolding series of "characters" and "scenes" on a constantly changing "stage." His ideal part was that of Guy, earl of Warwick, "at head of armies, rushing with impetuosity into the thickest of embattled foes, and bearing down all who dared to oppose me." But he settled for whatever role was available—prankster, preacher, defendant, escape artist, philanthropist—constantly preparing his character in dialogues with himself. To judge by one review, Burroughs was especially effective in the courtroom, where he enacted the part of injured innocent with a fine sense of the dramatic gesture. As a teenager in Northampton, Daniel Stebbins witnessed Burroughs's trial for counterfeiting in 1785 and still recalled the event vividly sixty years later: "He stood forth in the attitude of an Orator—gracefully bowed to the Court and audience and addressed them." After attacking the witnesses against him, "he then turned and pointed with the fingers of severe contempt . . . and with gestures perfectly easy and natural—his very look was withering. They blushed—they were crimson and quailed under his severe rebuke. . . . He was indeed eloquent in his native language and could speak the Latin and Greek with great purity, freedom and fluency." It hardly mattered that his case was doomed. Burroughs was determined to make the most of his moment on stage. Like his fictional contemporary Arthur Mervyn, whose character he uncannily anticipated, Burroughs was a model of the performing self amid the slippery circumstances of a Revolutionary age.[29]

Royall Tyler was equally alert to the theatrical quality of eighteenth-century life, but in the construction of his play proved far better disposed than Burroughs to the backcountry folk. Pelhamites everywhere would never have believed it. For Tyler created his comedy of Shays's Rebellion for the stage, which most rural New Englanders knew was the devil's workshop, a lure to spread luxury, dissipation, and vice and to distract people into an idle world of the imagination, where fact and fiction were blurred and pleasant fancies could become frightening realities. "What is the talent of an actor?" one minister asked, but "the art of counterfeiting himself, of putting on another character than his own, of appearing different than he is"—all for mercenary gain. To such critics, the theater epitomized the dangerous fluidity of the age.[30]

Not so for Tyler. He was already comfortable with a world of fictions and invented selves. Besides, he shared with other genteel, educated Americans a desire to spread the larger world of Atlantic culture. In accord with this sentiment, educated gentlemen began to sponsor the publication of weekly newspapers in the countryside, as carriers of "correct" information to a misguided people. So, too, the refinement of the theater could improve the republic. "What does all this anarchy proceed from?" one writer asked in 1786. "From the want of theatres, dances, shows, and other public amusements."[31]

Such benign hopes for the stage as a school of popular morality were a minority sentiment in the depressed 1780s. A symbol of luxury and inequality, the theater catered primarily to the rich, who turned the playhouse into a setting for their own conspicuous display. Not surprisingly at a time of austerity, the parade of luxury stirred class resentments among the lower orders. On this issue, backcountry farmers and urban artisans could join hands. Pennsylvania banned the theater, along with swearing, cockfighting, and Sabbath breaking, in an "Act for the Prevention of Vice and Immorality." Boston did the same in 1784 and every year thereafter until 1791. Royall Tyler had to go to New York City to taste the delights of the stage.[32]

Designed for a comfortable, urban audience, *The Contrast* is, seemingly, a play by the elite, for the elite, and about the elite. But it reaches beyond British drawing-room comedy to replay the central issues of the rural rebellion Tyler had just been engaged in suppressing and to frame a republican solution for the twin ills of the day: aristocratic vices at the top and popular anarchy in the lower orders. The formal contrast in the play opposes Dimple, the snobbish, Frenchified American, to Colonel Henry Manly, a New England Patriot-gentleman. Dimple scorns his own country for fashionable European tastes, indulges the game of seduction, and sets about winning a rich wife to support his gambling and lavish tastes. But he is more than a mere bounder and rake. He is the type of the fake gentleman, the artful, scheming designer, whom conservatives blamed for rousing the masses into rebellion in order to advance himself. Once a simple American Van Dumpling, Dimple has altered his name and character through addiction to luxury and vice. He has dissipated his inheritance in the pursuit of pleasure, but no matter; he will break any promise, abuse any sentiment to gain his way. Engaged to a woman he doesn't want, he wants a woman he can't afford, and so courts a third woman whose fortune he craves. There is no restraining his desires. Dimple refuses to choose among his conflicting drives and needs; like a late twentieth-century consumer, he wants it all. In pursuit of his insatiable ends, he keeps up a false front and practices the art of insinuation, as explained in his ever-handy copy of Chesterfield. Upon meeting Manly, his first response is, "I ought, according to every rule of Chesterfield, to wait on him and insinuate myself into his good graces." That strategy involves more than flattery; it requires a hidden, subtle adaptation of the self to others, for the sake of exploiting their trust. Driven by greed, indifferent to public good, Dimple will counterfeit whatever beliefs, blast whatever sentiments serve his needs. He is, in short, the epitome of the popular demagogue in the new republic.[33]

On the other hand, Manly is a blunt, sincere, patriotic sentimentalist, who freely wears the feelings of his heart on his worn regimental coat. Manly, we may guess, stands in part for Tyler's ideal self. He has just arrived in New York after serving in the army against the insurgents. He offers a Federalist speech warning of the dangers of "pernicious, foreign luxury" and of the ruin that comes from indulging petty jealousies, "the vices of little minds." For Manly, the ideal republic is a great family, bound together by mutual affection and common sacrifice. Grown poor in his country's service, he declines to speculate in army certificates: "I may be romantic," he says, "but I preserve them as a sacred deposit." He is equally loyal to his old soldiers—"my family," he calls them—and to the authority of his elders. With such devotion to family, Manly naturally foils Dimple's plots against female virtue. Ironically, he is obliged to play spy—like Royall Tyler himself—to catch his prey. But at the end of the play, in a gesture that was meant to identify Dimple with Daniel Shays, he draws his "Lafayette sword" against the rake. Surely, nobody missed the reference.[34]

Yet, Manly is so sincere and so mawkishly sentimental that it is hard to believe that Tyler found him a complete surrogate. Indeed, in his utter selflessness and simplicity, the character is a world apart from the wily playwright, who knew, from his own experience, that even authentic gentlemen look out for their own ambitions and self-interest in a good cause. It was perhaps for this reason that Tyler could not introduce much life into Manly. No sophisticated realist in the Federalist ranks could ever believe in such uncalculating devotion to the common good.[35]

The vibrancy of the play comes, instead, from Jonathan's few appearances on the stage. When Jonathan—a Tory name for the New Englander—struts on stage, singing "Yankee Doodle Dandy," the anthem of the Revolution, it is an important moment in the self-assertion of American culture. In an inversion of English snobbery, popular culture in the new republic embraces the ways of the common folk. Well, not exactly. That is the common reading. But it is important to note that Tyler, too, rewrites the rural New Englander into a reassuring part.[36]

In the play Jonathan is a figure of comic relief: the clownish, country bumpkin in the city. He is easily deceived by appearances: he mistakes a whorehouse for a meetinghouse, a harlot for a deacon's daughter, and like the critics of theater, he cannot tell the difference between a play and real life. Even so, he can conjure his own tricks with words and things. No innocent in his own rural sphere, he searches out hidden purposes in the most respectable magistrates. "Mr. Joseph . . . talked as sober and as pious as a minister," he observes of an actor he has seen on stage; "but, like some ministers that I know, he was a sly tike in his heart for all that." Although he does the duties of servant to Colonel Manly, even blackening his boots, Jonathan resists the name: "Sir, do you take me for a neger,— I am Colonel Manly's waiter." "A true Yankee distinction," comes the response from Dimple's servant, "egad, without a difference." Jonathan boasts of his independence: his father has a farm as good as the colonel's. No man will "master" him. He has accompanied the colonel on this trip as a way of seeing the world. Being a servant is the common Yankee's cosmopolitan project.[37]

As the character develops, Jonathan displays all the mother wit, the play of language, and the feisty spirit that we have come to associate with the Yankee. He is also a closet Shaysite. Like his counterparts in the backcountry, he can be easily led astray from his obligations. Under the prodding of Jessamy, the servant of Dimple, Jonathan forgets about his betrothed back home, Tabitha Wymen with her twenty acres of rocky land, Bible, and cow, and briefly becomes a fortune hunter himself. He is equally unreliable in politics. Asked his views of the insurgents, Jonathan at first demurs: "Why, since General Shays has sneaked off and given us the bag to hold, I don't care to give my opinion." But he does, anyway: "But you'll promise not to tell—put your ear this way—you won't tell?—I vow I did think the sturgeons [insurgents] were right." Why, then, didn't he grab his gun and join the fight? Jonathan, it turns out, was loyal to the colonel, a member of the Cincinnati, who said "it was a burning shame for the true blue Bunker-Hill sons of liberty, who had fought Governor Hutchinson, Lord North, and the Devil to have any hand in kicking up a cursed dust against a government which we had, every mother's son of us, a hand in making."[38]

In this resolution, Jonathan becomes what elite New Englanders needed urgently to imagine him in 1786–87: full of grievances perhaps, yet still deferential to the gentry. In the theater of New York, Royall Tyler muted the backcountry radicalism he had witnessed in his travels through western Massachusetts and Vermont in quest of Daniel Shays. The social tension embodied in the real Jonathans of New England was drained off in the comic figure on the stage. Jonathan is independent, a little wily, and maybe a bit of a confidence man himself. But under the tutelage of brave Colonel Manly, he remains loyal to the dominant order.

Except for one thing: on stage, as in life, Jonathan upstaged everyone else. And in the succeeding decades, this popular model of the Yankee eventually became a heroic figure in his own right, commanding the theater and sending the cosmopolitan gentleman to the wings. Offstage, he may have merged entirely with the commercial humbug, P. T. Barnum, or with that literary "hoaxster," Henry David Thoreau. Whatever his destiny, we ought to remember the long, complicated process that gave him birth. The invention of the Yankee owed a great deal to the defeat of Shays's Rebellion. He came to be celebrated on stage and in prose, precisely because he had lost out in life. In the process, his qualities of radicalism were cut out of their political context and made the stuff of American myth.

NOTES
CONTRIBUTORS
INDEX

NOTES

ABBREVIATIONS

AAS   American Antiquarian Society, Worcester, Mass.
Feer   Robert Arnold Feer, *Shays's Rebellion* (New York and London: Garland Publishing, 1988)
Hall   Van Beck Hall, *Politics without Parties: Massachusetts, 1780–1791* (Pittsburgh: Univ. of Pittsburgh Press, 1972)
MA   Massachusetts Archives, Boston
MHS   Massachusetts Historical Society, Boston
Minot   George Richards Minot, *History of the Insurrections in Massachusetts*, 2d ed. (Boston: James W. Burditt & Co., 1810)
Starkey   Marion L. Starkey, *A Little Rebellion* (New York: Knopf, 1955)
Szatmary   David P. Szatmary, *Shays' Rebellion: The Making of an Agrarian Insurrection* (Amherst: Univ. of Massachusetts Press, 1980)
WMQ   *William and Mary Quarterly*

INTRODUCTION. THE UNINVITED GUEST: Daniel Shays and the Constitution

1. Fred Somkin, *Unquiet Eagle: Memory and Desire in the Idea of American Freedom, 1815–1860* (Ithaca, N.Y.: Cornell Univ. Press, 1967), 137.

2. Robert A. Gross, "Daniel Shays and Lafayette's Sword," *OAH Newsletter* 15 (Nov. 1987): 8–9; *Massachusetts Centinel*, Dec. 2, 1786; Gregory H. Nobles and Herbert L. Zarov, eds., *Selected Papers from the Sylvester Judd Manuscript* (Northampton, Mass.: Forbes Library, 1976), 581–82; Elmer S. Smail, "The Daniel Shays Family," *New England Historical and Genealogical Register* 140 (1986): 301–2; *Acts and Laws of the Commonwealth of Massachusetts . . .* , 13 vols. (Boston: Wright and Potter, 1890–97), 4:424–26.

3. *New York Evening Post*, Oct. 15, 1825; George B. Forgie, *Patricide in the House Divided: A Psychological Interpretation of Lincoln and His Age* (New York: Norton, 1979).

4. *Hampshire Gazette*, Oct. 19, 26, 1825 (rept. from the *Boston Commercial Gazette*); *Concord Yeoman and Middlesex Gazette*, Oct. 22, 1825; *Boston Columbian Centinel*, Oct. 19, 1825.

5. Forrest McDonald and Ellen Shapiro McDonald, *Requiem: Variations on Eighteenth-Century Themes* (Lawrence: Univ. Press of Kansas, 1988), chap. 4, "On the Late Disturbances in Massachusetts."

6. Novels: [Ralph Ingersoll Lockwood], *The Insurgents* (Philadelphia: Carey, Lea and Blanchard, 1835); Edward Bellamy, *The Duke of Stockbridge: A Romance of Shays' Rebellion* (New York: Silver, Burdett, 1900); Walter A. Dyer, *Sprigs of Hemlock* (New York and London: Century Co., 1931); William Degenhard, *The Regulators* (New York: Dial Press, 1943); Robert Muir, *The Sprig of Hemlock: A Novel about Shays' Rebellion* (New York: Longmans, Green, 1957); James L. and Christopher Collier, *The Winter Hero* (New York: Four Winds Press, 1978); Harvey Wasserman, "The Secret Life of Daniel Shays," *Valley Advocate*, Feb. 16, 23, Mar. 2, 9, 16, 23, Apr. 6, 1987. Plays: Royall Tyler, *The Contrast* (1787), in Montrose J. Moses, ed., *Representative Plays by American Dramatists*, 3 vols. (New York: E. P. Dutton, 1918–25), 1:433–98. In 1936, at the commemoration of the 150th anniversary of Shays's Rebellion in Pelham, several boys from New York City performed a play written by eleven-year-old David Granet; the previous summer the children had attended the Pioneer Youth Camp, where they had learned about the Massachusetts insurrection from a teacher, Shays enthusiast Walter Ludwig (see *Springfield Union and Republican*, Sept. 20, 1936). Films: *The People vs. Job Shattuck* (1975); *A Little Rebellion* (1986). Murals: Diego Rivera, *Portrait of America: With an Explanatory Text by Bertram D. Wolfe* (New York: Covici, Friede, 1934); Edward Bruce and Forbes Watson, *Art in Federal Buildings: An Illustrated Record of the Treasury Department's New Program in Painting and Sculpture*, vol. 1, *Mural Designs, 1934–1936* (Washington, D.C.: Art in Federal Buildings, 1936). Music: Gurdon Barrows, "The Ballad of Daniel Shays" (1793), in Charles H. Barrows, ed., *The Poets and Poetry of Springfield in Massachusetts from Early Times to the End of the Nineteenth Century* (Springfield, Mass.: Connecticut Valley Historical Society, 1907), 26–29; *Daniel Shays Highway*, album by Shays' Rebellion, Flying Fish Records, 1987. Official opening of Daniel Shays Highway, 1937. President Reagan, quoted in *Springfield Union*, Jan. 15, 1986. Gore Vidal, *Homage to Daniel Shays: Collected Essays, 1952–72* (New York: Random House, 1973).

7. Anson E. Morse, *The Federalist Party in Massachusetts to the Year 1800* (Princeton, N.J.: Univ. Library, 1909), 40; Joseph T. Buckingham, *Specimens of Newspaper Literature: With Personal Memoirs, Anecdotes, and Reminiscences*, 2 vols. (Boston: C. C. Little and J. Brown, 1850), 2:40–56;

Richard D. Brown, "Shays's Rebellion and the Ratification of the Federal Constitution in Massachusetts," in Richard Beeman, Stephen Botein, and Edward C. Carter II, eds., *Beyond Confederation: Origins of the Constitution and American National Identity* (Chapel Hill: Univ. of North Carolina Press, 1987), 113–27.

8. Interestingly, Robert J. Taylor made a similar point years ago. Noting the inconsistent course taken by the Massachusetts legislature in funding state securities, Taylor observed that "with respect to redemption, the General Court pursued a confused policy which satisfied neither creditor nor debtor classes" (*Western Massachusetts in the Revolution* [Providence: Brown Univ. Press, 1954], 132).

9. Taylor draws the concept of the "protection covenant" from Richard L. Bushman, *King and People in Provincial Massachusetts* (Chapel Hill: Univ. of North Carolina Press, 1985), 37–46.

10. Paul Boyer and Stephen Nissenbaum, *Salem Possessed: The Social Origins of Witchcraft* (Cambridge, Mass.: Harvard Univ. Press, 1974).

11. I owe this splendid turn of phrase to Edward Countryman of the University of Warwick.

12. For a similar argument, see Gregory H. Nobles, *Divisions throughout the Whole: Politics and Society in Hampshire County, Massachusetts, 1740–1775* (New York and Cambridge: Cambridge Univ. Press, 1983).

13. Peter S. Onuf observes that Shays's Rebellion confirmed and crystallized conservative anxieties about the dissident movements gathering on the frontiers of every state. "Shays's Rebellion assumed the stature of a national event," he writes, "because it offered a model for domestic dissidence in every state. New state movements in frontier areas were irritating and even potentially dangerous. . . . But Shays's Rebellion struck at the authority of the leading northern state within its universally recognized boundaries" (*The Origins of the Federal Republic: Jurisdictional Controversies in the United States, 1775–1787* [Philadelphia: Univ. of Pennsylvania Press, 1983], 178). See also Thomas P. Slaughter, *The Whiskey Rebellion: Frontier Epilogue to the American Revolution* (New York: Oxford Univ. Press, 1986), 46–60.

14. For more on cultural politics in the 1780s, see Kenneth Silverman, *A Cultural History of the American Revolution* (New York: Thomas Y. Crowell, 1976), 484–567; Emory Elliott, *Revolutionary Writers: Literature and Authority in the New Republic, 1725–1810* (New York: Oxford Univ. Press, 1982), 19–54.

15. Robert H. Wiebe, *The Search for Order, 1877–1920* (New York: Hill and Wang, 1967); John Higham, *From Boundlessness to Consolidation: The Transformation of American Culture, 1848–1860* (Ann Arbor, Mich.: William L. Clements Library, 1969).

16. Richard D. Brown, "Shays's Rebellion and Its Aftermath: A View from Springfield, Massachusetts, 1787," *WMQ*, 3d ser., 40 (1983): 598–615; Brown, "Shays's Rebellion and the Ratification of the Federal Constitu-

tion in Massachusetts," 113–37; Grindall Reynolds, "Concord during the Shays Rebellion," *A Collection of Historical and Other Papers* (Concord, Mass.: Privately printed, 1895), 195–244.

17. Louis Hartz, *The Liberal Tradition in America* (New York: Random House, 1955).

1. THE PUBLIC CREDITOR INTEREST IN MASSACHUSETTS POLITICS, 1780–86

1. Oscar Handlin and Mary Flug Handlin, *Commonwealth: A Study of the Role of Government in the American Economy: Massachusetts, 1774–1861* (New York: New York Univ. Press, 1947), 41–48; Whitney K. Bates, "The State Finances of Massachusetts, 1780–1789" (M.A. thesis, Univ. of Wisconsin, 1948); Paul Goodman, *The Democratic-Republicans of Massachusetts: Politics in a Young Republic* (Cambridge, Mass.: Harvard Univ. Press, 1964), 14; Hall, 167, 204; Szatmary, xiii, 4–46, 70–76.

2. E. James Ferguson, *The Power of the Purse: A History of American Public Finance, 1776–1790* (Chapel Hill: Univ. of North Carolina Press, 1961), 26.

3. See Congress's "Address to the States," Apr. 26, 1783, in W. C. Ford, ed., *Journals of the Continental Congress, 1774–1789*, 34 vols. (Washington, D.C.: GPO, 1904–47), 24:277–83.

4. See Benjamin Lincoln to James Warren, Apr. 5, 1783, MHS *Collections* 73 (1925): 200.

5. See James Warren to John Adams, Oct. 27, 1783, Jan. 28, 1785, ibid., 230, 248.

6. Lincoln to Warren, Apr. 5, 1783, James Warren to John Adams, June 24, 1783, ibid., 203, 220. See also Nicholas Brown to Nathaniel Appleton, Dec. 13, 1784, Brown Papers, John Carter Brown Library, Brown Univ.

7. Warren to Adams, Oct. 27, 1783, MHS *Collections* 73 (1925): 232.

8. Hall, 154–57. See also Nicholas Brown to David Howell, Aug. 26, 1782, Brown Papers.

9. *The Acts and Resolves, Public and Private, of the Province of the Massachusetts Bay . . .* , 21 vols. (Boston: Wright and Potter, 1869–1922), 20:588.

10. Nicholas Brown to Moses Hayes, Oct. 31, 1782, Brown Papers.

11. See Roxbury's response to Wrentham's and Medway's instructions, *Independent Chronicle*, Mar. 25, 1784.

12. Richard Buel, Jr., "Samson Shorn: The Impact of the Revolutionary War on Estimates of the Republic's Strength," in Ronald Hoffman and Peter J. Albert, eds., *Arms and Independence: The Military Character of the American Revolution* (Charlottesville: Univ. Press of Virginia, 1984), 164–65. See also Ralph Volney Harlow, "Economic Conditions in Massachu-

setts during the American Revolution," *Colonial Society of Massachusetts Publications* 20 (1920): 183–84.

13. John Hancock to Elias Boudinot, Oct. 23, 1783, Papers of the Continental Congress, Library of Congress. See also Richard Buel, Jr., *Dear Liberty* (Middletown, Conn.: Wesleyan Univ. Press, 1980), 244; Bates, "State Finances," 83, 143.

14. Congress did print a report of a grand committee recommending compensatory measures for the old Continentals, but these proposals were never enacted. See *The Grand Committee to Whom Was Referred a Letter of the Governor of Massachusetts of the 28th of October 1783 Relative to the Continental Bills of Credit of the Old Emissions* . . . (Annapolis: Printed by John Dunlap, 1784); *Journal of the Continental Congress* 37:395–96; *Independent Chronicle*, Apr. 22, 1784; Report of the Committee considering the Congressional Requisitions, ibid., Dec. 29, 1785. Massachusetts did finally receive credit against the Continent for its expenses in the Penobscot expedition in 1784; see report in ibid., July 7, 1784. I have found no reference to this in the *Journals of the Continental Congress*, which appear to be incomplete for this period.

15. Bates, "State Finances," 85, 144.

16. On the commercial revival and the influx of bullion, see James Warren to John Adams, Oct. 12, 1780, MHS *Collections* 73 (1925): 141. James Swan, *National Arithmetick* . . . (Boston, 1786), 82, estimated that by the end of the war Massachusetts had accumulated two to three times the gold and silver that had been present in 1774. See also Bates, "State Finances," 73, 79.

17. See "Honorius" in *Independent Chronicle*, Oct. 9, 1783; *Boston Magazine*, Mar. 1786, 139.

18. See Eaton and Benson to Nicholas Brown, Aug. 8, 1781, Brown Papers.

19. *Acts and Laws of the Commonwealth of Massachusetts* . . . , 13 vols. (Boston: Wright and Potter, 1890–97), 1:525–33, 573–79, 2:152–53. The resulting measure was really a combined excise-impost.

20. Delays were normal; see Nicholas Brown to Thomas Ives, Dec. 29, 1784, Feb. 9, 1786, George Benson to Nicholas Brown, Mar. 23, 1785, Brown Papers; "A.B." in *Massachusetts Centinel*, Feb. 22, 1786.

21. Benjamin M. Stillman to Nicholas Brown, Dec. 16, 1783, Brown Papers.

22. The difficulties that creditors could face in getting paid the interest due on their consolidation notes are documented in Nicholas Brown to Thomas Ives, June 23, Oct. 20, 1784, Brown to George Benson, Oct. 12, 1785, Brown to Thomas Ives, Feb. 20, June 23, 1786, Brown Papers. See also Hall, 115.

23. See Nicholas Brown to Moses Hayes, Oct. 31, 1782, Brown to James

Walker, June 17, 1784, Brown to Ephraim Willard, Apr. 2, 1785, George Benson to Nicholas Brown, Mar. 14, 1785, Eaton and Benson to Nicholas Brown, Nov. 13, 23, 1782, Brown Papers.

24. Ferguson, *Power of the Purse,* chap. 12, has a good account of this. Hall cites evidence suggesting that ownership of the Massachusetts state debt had become highly concentrated; see Hall, 43 n.46.

25. The traders in the eastern towns had engrossed most of the Massachusetts consolidated notes (*Boston Magazine,* Mar. 1786, 139–40, and Nov.–Dec. 1786, 437). See also "Excise" from the *Hampshire Herald* in *Massachusetts Centinel,* Feb. 15, 1786.

26. See "Free Republican," *Independent Chronicle,* Dec. 22, 1785.

27. See "An Address from the General Court to the Commonwealth of Massachusetts," Nov. 14, 1786, *Acts and Laws* 3:47. See also petition of the public creditors to the legislature of Pennsylvania, rept. in *Independent Chronicle,* Jan. 25, 1785; Pennsylvania General Assembly Address to the Council, ibid., Feb. 3, 1785; "Honestus," ibid., Mar. 10, 1785. There was also a tendency to moralize the creditor-debtor relationship, of which modern commentators have been critical; see Hall, 79, 83, 96.

28. "Public Faith," rept. from a Springfield paper in *Massachusetts Centinel,* Feb. 8, 1786, and *Independent Chronicle,* Feb. 16, 1786, forcefully advanced such a position. It was greeted by a chorus of denunciations, including "A Friend to the Community," *Massachusetts Centinel,* Feb. 11, 1786; "An American," ibid., Feb. 18, 1786; "A.B.," ibid., Feb. 22, 1786. See also Hall, 119.

29. "Address from the General Court," *Acts and Laws* 4:146; *Boston Magazine,* Nov.–Dec. 1786, 435.

30. See James Warren to Elbridge Gerry, Jan. 11, 1785, in C. Harvey Gardiner, *A Study in Dissent: The Warren-Gerry Correspondence, 1776–1792* (Carbondale: Southern Illinois Univ. Press, 1968), 182; James Warren to John Adams, Jan. 28, Sept. 4, 1785, Apr. 30, 1786, MHS *Collections* 73 (1925): 249, 264, 272. See also *Independent Chronicle,* Mar. 18, 1783; Hall, 189, 192–93; Minot, 11–14; Swan, *National Arithmetick,* 82.

31. *Journal of the Continental Congress* 29:765–71.

32. Hunter Miller, ed., *Treaties and Other International Acts of the United States of America,* 8 vols. (Washington, D.C.: GPO, 1931–47), 2:48–56.

33. See James Bowdoin's address, Oct. 24, 1785, *Acts and Laws* 3:602–3.

34. See "A.B." in *Independent Chronicle,* Dec. 29, 1785; *Acts and Laws* 3:602–3.

35. See *Boston Magazine,* Dec. 1785, 475.

36. *Acts and Laws* 3:453–57; *Independent Chronicle,* July 29, 1785.

37. See "A Friend of Commerce" in *Independent Chronicle,* Aug. 12, Oct. 14, 1784. See also ibid., Mar. 2, 1786.

38. Though only the House was supposed to represent population proportionately, in effect the Senate did also; see Oscar Handlin and Mary Flug Handlin, eds., *The Popular Sources of Political Authority: Documents on the Massachusetts Constitution of 1780* (Cambridge, Mass.: Harvard Univ. Press, 1966), 451, 454; Hall, 69, 72. Bates, "State Finances," 66, emphasizes the disproportionate influence the seacoast towns exercised by virtue of their proximity to the capitol at Boston. For the attempt to divert the funds raised from the excise and impost to other purposes, see *Boston Magazine,* Mar. 1788, 139–40, and Nov.–Dec. 1788, 437. See also "S" in *Massachusetts Centinel,* Mar. 8, 1786. The utility of partial funding had been amply demonstrated when the supply of specie had dwindled in the mid-1780s. The consolidated notes had then provided a substitute medium of exchange, being collateral for loans. In addition, merchants were able to discount their duties at the customshouse with them. See N. S. B. Gras, *The Massachusetts First National Bank of Boston, 1784–1934* (Cambridge, Mass.: Harvard Univ. Press, 1937), 50–51, 246, 272; see also *Boston Magazine,* Mar. 1786, 139–40, and Nov.–Dec. 1786, 437.

39. See MA, vol. 161.

40. The evaluation procedures are discussed in *Boston Magazine,* Mar. 1785, 175, and Mar. 1786, 138.

41. The regressive aspect of relying on a poll tax has been emphasized by modern commentators. See Bates, "State Finances," 56, 99, 146, and Handlin, *Commonwealth,* 37. But if labor was indeed the principal source of wealth in the rural economy, as has been recently argued by Fred Anderson, *A People's Army: Massachusetts Soldiers and Society in the Seven Years' War* (Chapel Hill: Univ. of North Carolina Press, 1984), 29, 33, failure to assess it at some fixed rate would seem less fair than what was actually done.

42. The process is documented in MA, vols. 162–63.

43. The political process is best followed through newspaper allusions. See *Independent Chronicle,* Apr. 8, Nov. 10, Dec. 16, 22, 1785, Jan. 26, Feb. 9, Mar. 8, 1786. Suffolk County's share of the state's direct taxes dropped from 17.5% in 1780 to 14.9% in 1786; Essex County's from 19.9% to 14.1%. On the other hand, Hampshire's rose from 7.9% to 10.9%, Worcester's from 10.9% to 13.8%, and Berkshire's from 3.9% to 5.7%. Though the coastal counties succeeded in reducing their own share of the grand list, they felt it was only proper that areas that had seen the growth of new settlements during the war should begin to bear some of the public burden. Criticism of the evaluation process was voiced by "Public Faith" in *Independent Chronicle,* Feb. 16, 1786, on the grounds that the western towns' consent had been extracted through exhaustion rather than persuasion.

44. *Boston Magazine,* Mar. 1786, 141–42.

45. See Governor Bowdoin's address to the legislature in May 1785,

Independent Chronicle, June 2, 1785; "A Friend to America" and "H," ibid., Feb. 9, 1786.

46. See "Letter from a Gentleman in a Southern State," ibid., Mar. 25, 1784. See also Address of L. J. Brutus, ibid., Oct. 26, 1786; Stephen Higginson to John Adams, Dec. 30, 1785, in J. Franklin Jameson, ed., "Letters of Stephen Higginson, 1784–1804," *Annual Report of the American Historical Association for the Year 1896* (Washington, D.C.: GPO, 1897), 1:732. Massachusetts citizens were reminded of the state's relative size in the *Massachusetts Register* (1786), appended to T. & J. Fleet, *Pocket Almanac for the Year of Our Lord 1787* . . . (Boston: T. & J. Fleet, 1787), 15.

47. "A Republican" in *Independent Chronicle,* Oct. 6, 1785; "Honestus," ibid., Feb. 2, 1786. See also "Correspondent," ibid., June 8, 1786. A fear that the state was losing ground to Virginia also played a role in its vanguardism; see "Portius," ibid., Sept. 7, 1786; "Speech of a Member of the General Court of Massachusetts," *American Museum* 1 (1787): 361; Hall, 143.

49. Warnings against the dangers of a consolidated government frequently found their way into the public prints; see "Jonathan of the Valley" in *Independent Chronicle,* June 16, Oct. 20, 1785. These sentiments were shared by the eastern leadership; see Stephen Higginson to John Adams, July 1786, "Letters of Higginson," 734–35. The preservation of the Articles of Confederation seemed to be very much on the mind of the public creditor interest in the state; see "An American" in *Independent Chronicle,* Jan. 26, 1786.

49. See "Honestus" and "Solon" in *Independent Chronicle,* Mar. 10, 1785, Feb. 23, 1786; "Speech of a Member of the General Court of Massachusetts," *American Museum* 1 (1787): 360.

50. Thomas Paine, "Dissertation on Government: The Affairs of the Bank and Paper Money," rept. in *Massachusetts Centinel,* Mar. 22, 1786, and in William M. van der Weyde, ed., *The Life and Works of Thomas Paine* (New Rochelle, N.Y.: Thomas Paine Historical Association, 1925), 4:234.

51. These sentiments were those of the national leadership; see Alexander Hamilton, "To the Public Creditors of the State of New York," Sept. 30, 1782, in Harold C. Syrett, ed., *The Papers of Alexander Hamilton,* 27 vols. (New York: Columbia Univ. Press, 1961–79), 3:176; James Madison, "Notes on Debates," Feb. 27, 1783, and "Congress's Address to the States," Apr. 25, 1783, in William T. Hutchinson et al., eds., *The Papers of James Madison,* 17 vols. (Chicago: Univ. of Chicago Press and Charlottesville: University Press of Virginia, 1962–91), 6:298, 494; George Washington to John Jay, May 18, 1786, in John C. Fitzpatrick, ed., *The Writings of George Washington,* 39 vols. (Washington, D.C.: GPO, 1937–44), 28:431–32. But they were echoed by many others of less exalted station; see Nathaniel Hazard, *Observations on the Peculiar Case of Whig Merchants* . . . (New York: By a citizen, 1785), 13, 20, 25. And they repeatedly surfaced in the Massa-

chusetts press; see, for instance, the reprinting of Paine's "Dissertation on Government" in *Massachusetts Centinel,* Mar. 15 and 22, 1786.

52. See Hall, 227–28, 232, 235, 246, 252; Bates, "State Finances," 12, 107, 131, 134. In its May session the General Court had finally granted Congress the supplemental funds it had been requesting since 1783 to service the federal debt, but since this law became operative only when all the other states had passed similar laws, it remained a dead letter. See *Boston Magazine,* Nov.–Dec. 1786, 439.

53. See Szatmary, 78–79, 124–26. For agitation outside the Northeast, see Freeman H. Hart, *The Valley of Virginia in the American Revolution, 1763–1789* (Chapel Hill: Univ. of North Carolina Press, 1942), 125; Philip A. Crowl, *Maryland during and after the Revolution* (Baltimore: Johns Hopkins Univ. Press, 1943), 92–94, 106–7.

54. Virginia leaders reacted with extreme sensitivity to developments in Massachusetts; see Henry Lee to James Madison, Oct. 28, 1786, Madison, "Notes on Debates," Feb. 19, 1787, Madison to James Madison, Sr., and to James Monroe, Feb. 25, 1787, Edmund Randolph to Madison, Mar. 1, 7, 1787, Madison to Monroe, Apr. 19, 1787, and to Edmund Pendleton, Apr. 22, 1787, *Papers of James Madison* 9:145, 277, 278, 297, 301, 303, 391, 394–95. See also James Madison to James Madison, Sr., May 27, Sept. 4, 1787, Joseph Jones to Madison, July 6, 1787, James McClurg to Madison, Aug. 22, 1787, and Madison to Thomas Jefferson, Sept. 6, 1787, ibid., 10:10, 161, 98, 155, 164. For reactions elsewhere, see *American Mercury,* Feb. 5, 1787, and "Harrington" from the *Independent Gazette* in Philadelphia, both in ibid., June 11, 1787; *American Museum* 1 (1787): 278, 430, 443, 445. See also Alexander Hamilton, "Notes for a Speech on a Plan of Government," June 8, 1787, *Papers of Alexander Hamilton* 4:179.

55. New York enjoyed such advantages and managed to fund not only its own debt but the Continental debt held by its citizens in 1786. See Forrest McDonald, *E Pluribus Unum: The Formation of the American Republic, 1776–1790* (Boston: Houghton Mifflin, 1965), 59–61, 63.

56. Stephen Higginson to Henry Knox, Nov. 25, 1786, "Letters of Higginson," 743; Hall, 161, 191, 256–57, 264.

2. SHAYS'S REBELLION IN LONG PERSPECTIVE: The Merchants and the "Money Question"

The present essay is from a work in progress concerned with the money question in eighteenth-century New England. I found the work of Leslie V. Brock, Marc Egnal, Ronald Michener, and William D. Metz and the theses and dissertations written at the University of Wisconsin following World

War II that are cited below especially useful. A York University research grant facilitated the essay's completion.

1. John Adams identifies the "Merchantile Interest" in a letter to James Warren, Oct. 20, 1775, in Robert J. Taylor et al., eds., *Papers of John Adams*, 6 vols. (Cambridge, Mass.: Harvard Univ. Press, 1977–83), 3:217. Spelling and punctuation in all quotations in this essay have been changed to conform to modern usage.

2. See the recent discussion of ideological "languages" in Isaac Kramnick, "The 'Great National Discussion': The Discourse of Politics in 1787," *WMQ*, 3d ser., 45 (1988): 3–32.

3. Libertarian opposition to "government by money" is developed at length in Rodger D. Parker, "The Gospel of Opposition: A Study of Eighteenth-Century Anglo-American Opposition" (Ph.D. diss., Wayne State University, 1975). See also the recent discussions by Lance Banning, "Jeffersonian Ideology Revisited: Liberal and Classical Ideas in the New American Republic," and Joyce Appleby, "Republicanism in Old and New Contexts," *WMQ*, 3d ser., 43 (1986): 3–34.

4. Nov. 14, 1786, *Acts and Laws of the Commonwealth of Massachusetts . . .* , 13 vols. (Boston: Wright and Potter, 1890–97), 4:142–64.

5. Peter G. M. Dickson, *The Financial Revolution in England: A Study in the Development of Public Credit, 1688–1756* (London: Macmillan, 1967), 16.

6. The introduction of paper currency is discussed in Andrew M. Davis, *Currency and Banking in the Province of the Massachusetts-Bay*, pt. 1, *Currency* (1839; rept. New York: Augustus M. Kelley, 1968), 11–64. Leslie V. Brock, *The Currency of the American Colonies, 1700–1764: A Study in Colonial Finance and Imperial Relations* (New York: Arno Press, 1975), 591–92, is the source throughout this chapter for currency figures before 1776.

7. For the view of a breakdown in de facto convertibility and its connection with specie exports and paper currency issues, see Ronald Michener, "Fixed Exchange Rates and the Quantity Theory in Colonial America," in Karl Brunner and Allan Metzler, eds., *Empirical Studies of Velocity, Real Exchange Rates, Unemployment, and Productivity* 27 (Amsterdam: North-Holland, 1987): 233–305. The increasing price of silver in Massachusetts, or the depreciation of the currency, is the subject of great controversy among some economists and economic historians; see, for instance, Bruce Smith, "Money and Inflation in Colonial Massachusetts," *Federal Reserve Bank of Minneapolis Quarterly Review* 8 (1984): 1–14, and Smith, "American Colonial Monetary Regimes: The Failure of the Quantity Theory and Some Evidence in Favor of an Alternative View," *Canadian Journal of Economics* 18 (1985): 531–65. Compare Roger C. West, "Money in the Colonial American Economy," *Economic Inquiry* 16 (1978): 1–15; Elmus Wicker, "Colonial Monetary Standards Contrasted: Evidence from the Seven Years' War,"

Journal of Economic History 45 (1985): 869–84; Ronald Michener, "A Neoclassical Model of the Balance of Payments," *Review of Economic Studies* 51 (1984): 651–64; Leslie V. Brock, "The Colonial Currency, Prices, and Exchange Rates," Leslie V. Brock Collection, Univ. of Virginia Library, Charlottesville.

Economic conditions in Massachusetts at the time are considered in Curtis P. Nettels, *The Money Supply of the American Colonies before 1720* (1934; rept. New York: Augustus M. Kelley, 1964), 67–98, 128–61, 179–201, 251–58, and William D. Metz, "Politics and Finance in Massachusetts, 1713–1741" (Ph.D. diss., Univ. of Wisconsin, 1945), 44–56, 70–73. Silver prices for the colonial period are listed in John J. McCusker, *Money and Exchange in Europe and America, 1600–1775: A Handbook* (Chapel Hill: Univ. of North Carolina Press, 1978), 151. For Massachusetts currency issues, see the Brock references cited above; cf. Davis, *Currency and Banking*, pt. 1, *Currency*, 443.

8. In his history of Massachusetts, Thomas Hutchinson, Jr., claimed that the controversy over the currency in 1714 shattered nearly six years of relative political peace and divided the House of Representatives, "towns, parishes and particular families" into those supporting the private bank and those supporting the public bank. Hutchinson declared the "very numerous" backers of the private scheme to be persons "in difficult or involved circumstances in trade, or such as was possessed of real estates, but had little or no ready money at command, or men of no substance at all"; still others probably joined "out of mistaken principles," he went on, or "in apprehension" that the plan benefited the public, presumably by helping to enliven an ailing economy. Public bankers in contrast were said to represent two factions: one "very small," which included among others Hutchinson's own father, threw in with the public bank as the lesser of two evils; the other, headed by the "principal men of the Council," viewed a public bank where the interest went into the treasury as an "easy way" of paying government charges.

According to William Metz, while none of the private bankers were great merchants and a few were traders in shaky circumstances, the vast majority were men of some means who "optimistically aspired to improve their standing by use of capital borrowed from the bank." Similarly, six of the nine sponsors of the Bank of Credit were ambitious commercial men, entrepreneurs and property holders, but not great merchants. The other three were prominent politicians and members of the Popular party. Metz's conclusions rest on his scrutiny of a surviving list of 200 bank supporters. See Thomas Hutchinson, Jr., *The History of the Colony and Province of Massachusetts-Bay*, ed. Lawrence S. Mayo, 3 vols. (Cambridge, Mass.: Harvard Univ. Press, 1936), 2:154–56, and Metz, "Politics and Finance," 73–82.

Other studies of these and related events include Bernard Bailyn, *The New England Merchants in the Seventeenth Century* (Cambridge, Mass.: Harvard Univ. Press, 1957), 188–89; Joseph B. Felt, *Historical Account of Massachusetts Currency* (1839; rept., New York: Burt Franklin, 1968), 64–68; Gary Nash, *The Urban Crucible: Social Change, Political Consciousness, and the Origins of the American Revolution* (Cambridge, Mass.: Harvard Univ. Press, 1975), 62–65, 112–13; William Pencak, *War, Politics, and Revolution in Provincial Massachusetts* (Boston: Northeastern Univ. Press, 1981), 62–65; Robert F. Seybolt, *The Town Officials of Colonial Boston, 1634–1775* (Cambridge, Mass.: Harvard Univ. Press, 1939), 122, 130 n. 32; G. B. Warden, *Boston, 1689–1776* (Boston: Little, Brown, 1970), 68–79.

9. For a general discussion of party at the time, see Stephen E. Patterson, *Political Parties in Revolutionary Massachusetts* (Madison: Univ. of Wisconsin Press, 1973), 3–62; Pencak, *War, Politics, and Revolution*, 4–6. A specific discussion of the relationship between party and the money question is to be found in Metz, "Politics and Finance," as indicated in the many references already cited; but see as well Robert Zemsky, *Merchants, Farmers, and River Gods: An Essay on Eighteenth-Century American Politics* (Boston: Gambit, 1971), esp. 265–75; Marc Egnal, *A Mighty Empire: The Origins of the American Revolution* (Ithaca, N.Y.: Cornell Univ. Press, 1988), 6–8, 20–37.

10. Adam Smith, *An Inquiry into the Nature and Causes of the Wealth of Nations*, ed. Roy H. Campbell and Andrew S. Skinner, 2 vols. (1776; rept. Oxford: Clarendon Press, 1979), 1:428.

11. *The Present Melancholy Circumstances of the Province, Considered . . . , The Distressed State of the Town of Boston, Considered . . . , A Letter from One in the Country to His Friend in Boston . . .* , and *The Distressed State of the Town of Boston Once More Considered . . .* , in Andrew McFarland Davis, ed., *Colonial Currency Reprints, 1682–1751*, 4 vols. (1910–11; rept. New York: Augustus M. Kelley, 1964), 1:351–63, 397–409, 416–42, 2:65–90.

See the brief but suggestive discussion in Michener, "Fixed Exchange Rates and the Quantity Theory in Colonial America," 277 n. 35.

12. *A Word of Comfort to a Melancholy Country . . .* , and *A Letter to an Eminent Clergy-Man . . .* , in Davis, *Colonial Currency Reprints* 2:159–223, 227–42.

Other scholars have placed this debate in a larger ideological framework but with little or no interest in the interplay between language, or discourse, and the social and political-economic environment; see, for instance, J. E. Crowley, *"This Sheba Self": The Conceptualization of Economic Life in Eighteenth-Century America* (Baltimore: Johns Hopkins Univ. Press, 1974), 34–116; Timothy H. Breen, *The Character of a Good Ruler: A History of Political Ideas, 1630–1730* (New Haven: Yale Univ. Press, 1970), 203–69. On the other hand, E. James Ferguson asserts that colonial Americans never had occasion to "reflect upon the connection between currency finance and their conceptions of liberty"; such matters confronted the nation for the first time following the end of the Revolution and the rise of the nationalist movement, according to Ferguson; see Ferguson, "Political Economy, Public Liberty, and the Formation of the Constitution," *WMQ*, 3d ser., 40 (1983): 389–412. The present chapter rejects both the abstracted ideological views of Crowley and Breen and the interpretation of Ferguson.

See also Davis, *Colonial Currency Reprints* 1:352, and Benjamin Franklin, *The Autobiography . . . A Genetic Text*, ed. J. A. Leo Lemay and Paul M. Zall (Knoxville: Univ. of Tennessee Press, 1981), 30. I am indebted to Ronald Michener for these citations and for sharing with me results of his own research.

13. See Brock, *Currency of the American Colonies*, 28–32; Felt, *Massachusetts Currency*, 73–78; Metz, "Politics and Finance," 190–231, 290–97; William B. Weeden, *Economic and Social History of New England, 1620–1789*, 2 vols. (1890; rept. New York: Hillary House, 1963), 2:480–81.

14. For varying analyses of Belcher's uneasy political relations during his early years as governor, compare Davis, *Currency and Banking*, pt. 1, *Currency*, 109–20; Hutchinson, *History of Massachusetts-Bay* 2:280–87; Metz, "Politics and Finance," 360–442; Pencak, *War, Politics, and Revolution*, 91–108; Joel A. Shufro, "Boston in Massachusetts Politics, 1730–1760" (Ph.D. diss., Univ. of Wisconsin, 1976), 56–76; Zemsky, *Merchants, Farmers, and River Gods*, 99–128.

15. John B. MacInnes, "Rhode Island Bills of Public Credit, 1710–1755," 2 vols. (Ph.D. diss., Brown Univ., 1952), 1:71–209, offers an excellent analysis of that colony's currency practices during this period. See also Sydney V. James, *Colonial Rhode Island: A History* (New York: Scribner's, 1975), 157, 171, 176; Christian McBurney, "The Rise and Decline of the South Kingston Planters, 1660–1783" (B.A. honors thesis, Brown Univ., 1981).

16. Davis, *Colonial Currency Reprints* 2:439–41. Compare Davis, *The Merchants' Notes of 1733* (Cambridge, Mass.: Harvard Univ. Press, 1903); Shufro, "Boston in Massachusetts Politics," 92–97; Zemsky, *Merchants, Farmers, and River Gods*, 102–14; John A. Schutz, "Succession Politics in Massachusetts, 1730–1741," *WMQ*, 3d ser., 15 (1958): 508–20.

17. See Shufro, "Boston in Massachusetts Politics," 24–34, 37–55, for a suggestive analysis of party alignments based upon the money question during Belcher's governorship. See also Davis, *Currency and Banking*, pt. 1, *Currency*, 131–51; Metz, "Politics and Finance," 453–94.

18. The best published study of the Land Bank controversy is George A. Billias, *The Massachusetts Land Bankers of 1740* (Orono: Univ. of Maine Press, 1959). Metz, "Politics and Finance," 495–540, displays a better understand-

ing of the political-economic background of the struggle, however. Other important accounts include: Hutchinson, *History of Massachusetts-Bay* 2:298–300; Zemsky, *Merchants, Farmers, and River Gods*, 117–41, 273–76; Davis, "Provincial Banks: Land and Silver," Colonial Society of Massachusetts *Transactions* 3 (1896): 2–40; Pencak, *War, Politics, and Revolution*, 103–8, 116–19; Cathy Mitten, "The New England Paper Money Tradition and the Massachusetts Land Bank of 1740" (M.A. thesis, Columbia Univ., 1979); Herman Belz, "Paper Money in Colonial Massachusetts," *Essex Institute Historical Collections* 51 (1965): 159–62.

19. Compare the modern accounts cited in notes 16 and 18 above with the contemporary *Account of the Rise, Progress, and Consequence of the Two Late Schemes Commonly Called the Land Bank, or the Manufacturing Scheme, and the Silver Scheme* in Davis, *Colonial Currency Reprints* 4:237–351. See also Davis, "List of Subscribers to the Silver Bank," Colonial Society of Massachusetts *Publications* 3 (1910): 199–200.

20. See Mitten, "The New England Paper Money Tradition," 60–80; John A. Schutz, *William Shirley: King's Governor of Massachusetts* (Chapel Hill: Univ. of North Carolina Press, 1961), 33–44, 70–72, 82–85, 90–92, 107, 115, 124, 132–33, 142–43; Brock, *Currency of the American Colonies*, 244–70; Shufro, "Boston in Massachusetts Politics," 213–21, 235–57; Malcolm Freiberg, "Thomas Hutchinson and the Province Currency," *New England Quarterly* 30 (1957): 197–204; Pencak, *War, Politics, and Revolution*, 309–15; Hutchinson, *History of Massachusetts-Bay* 2:334–35.

21. 24 Geo. II, c. 53, *Statutes at Large . . . of Great Britain. Anno 1701 Continued to 1806*, ed. Danby Pickering (Cambridge: J. Bentham, 1762–1807), 20:277–90. See also the extensive discussion in MacInnes, "Rhode Island Bills of Public Credit," 511–26, and Brock, *Currency of the American Colonies*, 201–43.

22. Hutchinson, *History of Massachusetts-Bay* 2:335–37; Thomas Hancock to Christopher Kilby, May 5, 1750, to Kilby and Bernard, June 21, 1750, Letter Book of Thomas Hancock, New-England Historical and Genealogical Society, Boston.

For a careful and well-written analysis of the economic situation in the northern colonies in the years 1750–54, see William Sachs, "The Business Outlook in the Northern Colonies, 1750–1775" (Ph.D. diss., Columbia Univ., 1957), 28–63. Both politics and economics in relation to the money question are discussed in Shufro, "Boston in Massachusetts Politics," 258–68. Also see the suggestive study by Gloria L. Main, "The Standard of Living in Southern New England," *WMQ*, 3d ser., 45 (1988): 124–34.

23. Hutchinson, *History of Massachusetts-Bay* 3:7. An informed consideration of the treasury notes is to be found in Brock, "The Colonial Currency, Prices, and Exchange Rates" and *Currency of the American Colonies*, 270–89;

note especially Brock's changing and mature views on the subject. See also Anne Rowe Cunningham, ed., *Letters and Diary of John Rowe, Boston Merchant, 1759–1762, 1764–1779* . . . (Boston: W. B. Clarke, 1903), 339. The study by Sachs, "Business Outlook in the Northern Colonies," 64–127, has an excellent discussion of both monetary and general economic conditions during the French and Indian War.

24. In addition to the references in note 23 above, see Andrew M. Davis, "Emergent Treasury-Supply in Massachusetts in Early Days," AAS *Proceedings* 14 (1905): 45–46.

25. The political dimensions of these matters are taken up in Shufro, "Boston in Massachusetts Politics," 275–351. For contrasting analyses of divisions within the merchant ranks in the Revolutionary movement, see Stephen E. Patterson, "Boston Merchants and the American Revolution to 1776" (M.A. thesis, Univ. of Wisconsin, 1960), and John W. Tyler, "The First Revolution: Boston Merchants and the Acts of Trade, 1760–1774" (Ph.D. diss., Princeton Univ. 1980).

26. See the tables, references, and discussion in William B. Norton, "Paper Currency in Massachusetts during the Revolution," *New England Quarterly* 7 (1934): 45–55. See also James Warren to John Adams, May 7, 1775, and William Tudor to John Adams, May 1, 1775, *Papers of John Adams* 3:3, 6, 65, 161. The government did actually try taxation and borrowing, but they had proven too uncertain and slow in their effect. Currency finance was the only alternative.

27. For contemporary responses to these developments, see, for example, entries for Jan. 1 and 30, 1776, in Oliver E. Fitch, ed., *The Diary of William Pynchon of Salem: A Picture of Salem Life, Social and Political, A Century Ago* (Boston: Houghton, Mifflin, 1890), 1, 3; Josiah Quincy to John Adams, Oct. 25, 1775, William Tudor to John Adams, Oct. 28, 1775, James Warren to John Adams, Nov. 5, 1775, Joseph Hawley to John Adams, Dec. 18, 1775, *Papers of John Adams* 3:249–50, 259, 280–81, 369–70. See also *The Acts and Resolves, Public and Private, of the Province of Massachusetts Bay* . . . , 21 vols. (Boston: Wright and Potter, 1869–1922), 5:669 and nn. These and related matters are discussed at length and with great clarity in a chapter about "The War, the Government, and the Massachusetts Economy, 1774–1776," in Marc Egnal, "Society and Politics in Massachusetts, 1774 to 1778" (M.A. thesis, Univ. of Wisconsin, 1967), 85–115.

28. James Sullivan to John Adams, May 9, 1776, John Adams to William Gordon, June 23, 1776, *Papers of John Adams* 4:179, 329; Abigail Adams to John Adams, June 3, Aug. 25, 1776, in L. H. Butterfield et al., eds., *Adams Family Correspondence*, 4 vols. (Cambridge, Mass.: Harvard Univ. Press, 1963–), 2:5, 107. Compare Ralph Volney Harlow, "Economic Conditions in Massachusetts during the American Revolution, 1775–1783," Colonial

Society of Massachusetts *Publications* 20 (1920): 166–67; Robert A. East, *Business Enterprise in the American Revolutionary Era* (1938; rept. Gloucester, Mass.: Peter Smith, 1965), 49–65; Patterson, *Political Parties in Revolutionary Massachusetts*, 144–46, 155–60; and the Egnal reference in note 27 above.

29. See especially Aug. 29, Dec. 4, 1776, *Journal of the Honourable House of Representatives of . . . Massachusetts-Bay, 1776–1780*, in William S. Jenkins, ed., *Records of the States of the United States of America: A Microfilm Compilation* (Washington, D.C.: microfilmed by the Library of Congress Duplication Service, 1949), and the Patterson reference in note 28 above. Treasury notes and bills of credit are compared in Norton, "Paper Currency in Massachusetts," 46–51, and in Brock, *Currency of the American Colonies,* 278, 279 n. 56; but see Brock, "Colonial Currency, Prices, and Exchange Rates" for his later views on this subject. See also Oscar Handlin and Mary F. Handlin, "Revolutionary Economic Policy in Massachusetts," *WMQ,* 3d ser., 4 (1947): 8–9; Felt, *Massachusetts Currency.*

For economists the core difference is that treasury notes, as interest-bearing securities, would not have the high velocity of circulation that lawful currency would have. The economist and student of Massachusetts's monetary system, Ronald Michener, notes that the distinction is "somewhat arbitrary" and that in Massachusetts "many instruments were used from time to time to extinguish debt" (letter to author, Sept. 1, 1986).

30. New Hampshire Historical Society *Collections* 9 (1889): 245–71; *Acts and Resolves . . . of Massachusetts Bay* 5:669–70nn.; James Sullivan to John Adams, Oct. 11, 1776, Adams to unknown, Nov. 5, 1776, *Papers of John Adams* 5:51–53; *Independent Chronicle,* Dec. 13, 1776.

See the discussion in Kenneth Scott, "Price Control in New England during the Revolution," *New England Quarterly* 19 (1948): 453–58; another matter at issue was the impact of depreciation on military recruitment. No doubt a contributing factor to the growing sense of crisis in Massachusetts at the time was the treasury's failure to find lenders who would subscribe to the enormous government loans in late 1776. As one historian has aptly remarked, the treasury note loans of 1775 and early 1776 for which there were subscribers represented "an investment in public securities yielding interest"; the forced loans of December 1776 were simply payments "to soldiers, furnishers of supplies for the army, and others who had financial claims on the treasury." Both kinds of treasury notes were negotiable; see Norton, "Paper Currency in Massachusetts," 48.

For a contemporary view of the critical importance of government borrowing, a view which both supported commercial and monied interests and reflected a larger moral vision of the role of money in commercial society, see John Adams to James Warren, Feb. 12, 1777, *Papers of John Adams* 5:80–83; cf. Adams to unknown, Nov. 5, 1776, ibid., 5:51–53.

31. James Warren to Samuel Adams, Feb. 24, 1777, in Worthington C.

Ford, ed., *Warren-Adams Letters . . . John Adams, Samuel Adams, and James Warren, 1743–1814*, 2 vols. (1917–25; rept. New York: Arno Press, 1972), 2:446; *Acts and Resolves . . . of Massachusetts Bay* 5:564–89, 669–73. Massachusetts also banned exports of most foodstuffs, cloth, and leather (ibid., 19:808–10; William Tudor to John Adams, Mar. 16, 1777, *Papers of John Adams* 5:113). See also Norton, "Paper Currency in Massachusetts," 50.

Compare the extended discussion in Egnal, "Society and Politics in Massachusetts," 108–13, 121–26, and Richard B. Morris, "Labor and Mercantilism in the Revolutionary Era," in Richard B. Morris, ed., *The Era of the American Revolution* (1939; rept. Gloucester, Mass.: Peter Smith, 1971), 94–98. See also Barbara Clark Smith, "The Politics of Price Control in Revolutionary Massachusetts, 1774–1780" (Ph.D. diss., Yale Univ., 1983), 380–404, for a general discussion of these and related events in Boston in 1777.

32. James Warren to John Adams, Mar. 23, 1777, *Papers of John Adams* 5:127. Adams shared Warren's views, as did most of Adams's correspondents at the time; see, for instance, ibid., 5:182–83, 201–11; *Adams Family Correspondence* 2:156–57, 172–73, 201, 210–12, 214–15, 217–19. See as well Samuel Adams to Mrs. Adams, Mar. 19, 1777, to John Scollary, Mar. 20, 1777, in Harry A. Cushing, ed., *The Writings of Samuel Adams*, 4 vols. (1904–7; rept. New York: G. P. Putnam's Sons, 1968), 3:364–66; Feb. 31, 1777, *Pynchon Diary*, 24.

33. *Papers of John Adams* 5:127; Abigail Adams to John Adams, Apr. 20 and 21, 1777, *Adams Family Correspondence* 2:217–19; *Acts and Resolves . . . of Massachusetts Bay* 5:642–47. See also Apr. 21, 26, 28, 1777, *Pynchon Diary*, 29; *Independent Chronicle*, Apr. 3, 1777.

Extended treatments of these events are given in Albert Matthews, "Joyce Junior" and "Joyce Junior Again," Colonial Society of Massachusetts *Transactions* 8 (1906): 90–104 and 11 (1910): 280–94; Egnal, "Society and Politics in Massachusetts," 127–43; Patterson, *Political Parties in Revolutionary Massachusetts*, 166. For some information concerning the "doing away" with the currencies of the other states on the grounds of widespread counterfeiting, see *Acts and Resolves . . . of Massachusetts Bay* 5:639–40; Abigail Adams to John Adams, May 6, 1777, *Adams Family Correspondence* 2:232. Kenneth Scott's study of *Counterfeiting in Colonial America* (New York: Oxford Univ. Press, 1957), 256–61, is also useful, although this subject is in the process of being revised by historian John Brooke.

34. *A Report of the Record Commissioners of the City of Boston Containing the Boston Town Records . . .* (Boston, 1887), 285; Samuel Cooper to Samuel Adams, June 12, 1777, Samuel Adams Papers, New York Public Library; see also James Warren to John Adams, June 11, 1777, *Papers of John Adams* 5:223.

For a more detailed analysis, see Egnal, "Society and Politics in Massachusetts," 152–56, and Morris, "Labor and Mercantilism," 105–6, and compare "A Countryman" in *Independent Chronicle*, Aug. 29, 1777. Evidence of merchant control of Boston's town meeting is discussed in Egnal, "Society and Politics in Massachusetts," 102–4, 122–23.

35. James Warren to Samuel Adams, June 16, 1777, *Warren-Adams Letters* 2:449. See also June 10, 19, 24, 27, 1777, *Journal of House of Representatives*; James Warren to John Adams, June 22, Aug. 10, 1777, *Papers of John Adams* 5:230, 271. For what appears to have been personal and political reasons, Orne did not attend the conference. A sense of the problems of price controls and currency inflation at this time is conveyed in the letters of Abigail Adams to John Adams, June 10, 15, 23, July 1777, *Adams Family Correspondence* 2:265–66, 269–70, 278–79; see as well June 30, 1777, *Pynchon Diary*, 33.

36. *Public Records of the State of Connecticut* (1894), 1:599–606. See also Aug. 12, 13, Sept. 19, 20, 23, 26, Oct. 9, 10, 13, 1777, *Journal of House of Representatives*; *Acts and Resolves . . . of Massachusetts Bay* 5:733–37, 720–58; Samuel Freeman to John Adams, Sept. 4, 25, 1775, *Papers of John Adams* 5:282, 294–95.

Whitney K. Bates, "The State Finances of Massachusetts, 1780–1789" (M.A. thesis, Univ. of Wisconsin, 1948), 44–58, and Egnal, "Society and Politics in Massachusetts," 157–79, 248, treat these matters at greater length. Contemporary descriptions of the out-of-doors violence appear in Abigail Adams to John Adams, July 30, 1777, *Adams Family Correspondence* 2:296–97 n.3, and *Independent Chronicle*, Sept. 18, 1777. See also John Adams to Elbridge Gerry, Dec. 6, 1777, *Papers of John Adams* 5:345–47, for an instructive response to the question of inflation and taxation, and Gerry to Adams, Jan. 25, 1778, ibid., 5:394–97, to the question of inflation and price controls.

37. *Acts and Resolves . . . of Massachusetts Bay* 5:816–17nn; Nov. 28, Dec. 1–2, 4–5, 12, 15, 1777, *Journal of House of Representatives*; Samuel Adams to unknown, Jan. 10, 1778, *Writings of Samuel Adams* 5:6–7; John Adams to Abigail Adams, Dec. 13, 1777, *Adams Family Correspondence* 2:369–70.

Further analysis of these issues is to be found in E. James Ferguson, *The Power of the Purse: A History of American Public Finance, 1776–1790* (Chapel Hill: Univ. of North Carolina Press, 1961), 28–32; Patterson, *Political Parties in Revolutionary Massachusetts*, 181–82; Egnal, "Society and Politics in Massachusetts," 179–86.

38. *Acts and Resolves . . . of Massachusetts Bay* 5:759–60.

39. *Independent Chronicle*, Jan. 1, 1778. John Adams described these "monied men" in a letter to James Warren of Feb. 12, 1777, *Papers of John Adams* 5:82.

40. See, for instance, "Letter from a Gentleman in the Country . . . , VI, VII," *Independent Chronicle*, Apr. 2, May 7, 1778; Samuel Adams to Francis Lightfoot Lee, Apr. 1778, *Writings of Samuel Adams* 4:19–20. Discussions

of economic conditions appear in Egnal, "Society and Politics in Massachusetts," 201–10; Robert J. Taylor, *Western Massachusetts in the Revolution* (Providence: Brown Univ. Press, 1954), 91–92; Morris, "Labor and Mercantilism," 107–9. See also Smith, "Politics of Price Control," 405–46, for a general analysis of events in 1778.

41. *Boston Town Records* . . . (Boston, 1895), 9, 13; James Warren to John Adams, June 7, 1778, *Papers of John Adams* 5:188n; see also "Record of the Commissioners' Meeting at New Haven, Jan. 1778," New Hampshire Historical Society *Collections* 9 (1889): 272–95.

Compare the analyses in Scott, "Price Controls in New England," 458–65; Morris, "Labor and Mercantilism," 110; Harlow, "Economic Conditions in Massachusetts," 175–78; Jonathan Grossman, "Wage and Price Controls during the American Revolution," *Monthly Labor Review* 66 (1973): 3–10.

42. Sept. 18, 1778, *Pynchon Diary*, 57. See Ferguson, *Power of the Purse*, 44–46; James L. Cooper, "Interests, Ideas, and Empires: The Roots of American Foreign Policy, 1763–1789" (Ph.D. diss., Univ. of Wisconsin, 1964), 533. Some comments concerning comparative inflationary rates appear in Egnal, "Society and Politics in Massachusetts," 189–91, 195.

43. *Independent Chronicle*, Apr. 15, June 17, 1779. See as well Abigail Adams to John Adams, Mar. 20, June 8, 1779, in Charles Francis Adams, ed., *Familiar Letters of John Adams and His Wife Abigail Adams, during the Revolution* . . . (Boston: Houghton, Mifflin, 1875), 361, 364; William H. Whitmore et al., eds., *A Report of the Records Commission of the City of Boston Continuing the Selectmen's Minutes from 1776 through 1786* (Boston, 1894), 96–98; James Warren to John Adams, June 13, 1779, *Warren-Adams Letters* 2:104–5.

Ferguson, *Power of the Purse*, is the standard work on congressional monetary and fiscal policies; see especially p. 32. For a detailed discussion of events in Massachusetts during 1779, see Smith, "Politics of Price Control," 447–96.

44. *Independent Chronicle*, June 17, 1779.

45. Ibid., June 24, 1779.

46. Ibid., July 29, Aug. 19, 1779; *Boston Town Records*, 78–79, 100–101; Warren to Adams, July 29, 1779, *Warren-Adams Letters* 2:112. See the discussion in Morris, "Labor and Mercantilism," 112–14; see also William Lincoln and Charles Hersey, *History of Worcester, Massachusetts* (Worcester: C. Hersey, 1862), 107–9.

47. *Independent Chronicle*, Sept. 9, 1779, and Morris, "Labor and Mercantilism," 112–14; cf. Harlow, "Economic Conditions in Massachusetts," 181–82.

48. See Ferguson, *Power of the Purse*, 46–53; Norton, "Paper Currency in Massachusetts," 49, 58–59.

49. *Independent Chronicle*, Apr. 27, Oct. 12, 19, 1780, Jan. 25, 1781. The

most frequently proposed solution to the currency crisis was increased taxation. The debate over this subject is a matter for separate investigation, though it should be noted that Charles Beard could easily have discerned a distinction between "Realty" and "Personalty" interests from reading contemporary newspaper accounts; see, for instance, "To Squaretoes" in *Independent Chronicle*, Feb. 8, 1781. See also Ferguson, *Power of the Purse*, 32.

50. *Independent Chronicle*, Jan. 25, May 29, June 2, July 8, 1781; *Pynchon Diary*, 96, 97, 100; Felt, *Massachusetts Currency*, 190. See also *Independent Chronicle*, Jan. 11, Feb. 1, Mar. 22, Apr. 12, July 5, 12, 1781; Abigail Adams to John Adams, Jan. 28, 1781, *Familiar Letters*, 390. A discussion of some of these events is to be found in Taylor, *Western Massachusetts*, 104–9, and E. James Ferguson ed., *The Papers of Robert Morris, 1781–1784* (Pittsburgh: Univ. of Pittsburgh Press, 1973–), 2:135–38; see also note 52 below.

Van Beck Hall uses the analytical category "commercial-cosmopolitan," as opposed to mercantile interest. I would add that the two are closely, and functionally, related.

51. Bates, "State Finances of Massachusetts," 85–93, and Hall, 104–2; see also Norton, "Paper Currency in Massachusetts," 67–69.

52. See Timothy Dwight, *Travels in New England and New York*, ed. Barbara M. Solomon, 4 vols. (Cambridge, Mass.: Harvard Univ. Press, 1969), 4:261–62. Cf. the general discussion in Crowley, *"This Sheba Self,"* 76–95, and Joyce Appleby, "The Social Origins of American Revolutionary Ideology," *Journal of American History* 64 (1978): 935–38.

53. See Minot and Szatmary.

3. "DEBT LITIGATION AND SHAYS'S REBELLION"

1. John J. McCusker and Russell R. Menard estimate that the per capita GNP for the period 1774–90 declined approximately 46%. Comparing this to the 48% decline for 1929–30, they believe the colonial figures underestimate the actual situation (McCusker and Menard, *The Economy of British America, 1607–1789* [Chapel Hill: Univ. of North Carolina Press, 1985], 373–75). Winifred Rothenberg asserts that farm prices fell approximately 30% in Massachusetts between 1783 and 1784. Prices rebounded slightly in 1785, only to drop below 1784 levels the following year (Rothenberg, "A Price Index for Rural Massachusetts, 1750–1855," *Journal of Economic History* 39 [1979]: 983). See also Ruth Crandall, "Wholesale Commodity Prices in Boston during the Eighteenth Century," *Review of Economic Statistics* 16 (1934): 127. Crandall argues wholesale prices for 1785–86 in Boston were at a high in March and April 1785. The prices, however, were lower than

they had been the previous year and did not reach comparable levels until winter 1791.

2. Charles A. Beard's classic statement of this theme used Worcester County as the principal buttress of the argument; see *An Economic Interpretation of the Constitution of the United States* (1913; rept. New York: Free Press, 1965), 59, 262–64. Szatmary, esp. 1–13, 33–36, is the most recent reiteration of this theme. See also Barbara Karsky, "Agrarian Radicalism in the Late Revolutionary Period (1780–1795)" in Erich Angermann, Marie-Luise Frings, and Hermann Wellenreuther, eds., *New Wine in Old Skins: A Comparative View of Socio-Political Structures and Values Affecting the American Revolution* (Stuttgart: Klett, 1976), 92. Even Jonathan Smith, who argued that legal costs were not excessive, still saw the twin polarities of rural-urban and yeoman-merchant divides. See "Some Features of Shays' Rebellion," Clinton Historical Society *Publications* 1 (1905): 11, 13, 15, and "The Depression of 1785 and Daniel Shays' Rebellion," *WMQ*, 3d ser., 5 (1948): 84–85. Hall, 167–68, modifies the geographical but largely retains the economic polarities of the traditional explanation. For an example of the way in which scholarship moves from this presumption of class distinctions in the courts to other attributes of post-Revolutionary Massachusetts, see J. R. Pole, "Shays's Rebellion: A Political Interpretation," in Jack P. Greene, ed., *The Reinterpretation of the American Revolution, 1763–1789* (New York: Harper and Row, 1968), 415–16, 429–30.

3. Bruce H. Mann describes this process for eighteenth-century Connecticut; see Mann, *Neighbors and Strangers: Law and Community in Early Connecticut* (Chapel Hill: Univ. of North Carolina Press, 1987), 12–27. See also Margaret Martin, "Merchants and Trade of the Connecticut River Valley, 1750–1820," Smith College *Studies in History* 24 (1939): 156, 162; Fred Anderson, *A People's Army: Massachusetts Soldiers and Society in the Seven Years' War* (Chapel Hill: Univ. of North Carolina Press, 1984), 29–32; Michael A. Bellesiles, "The Establishment of Legal Structures on the Frontier: The Case of Revolutionary Vermont," *Journal of American History* 73 (1987): 906.

4. Promissory note, Jan. 15, 1785, Salisbury Family Papers, box 5, folder 1, AAS. The turnover of the note would seem to indicate that it was negotiable. William E. Nelson points out that the holder of a nonnegotiable note only had recourse against the maker (Nelson, *Americanization of the Common Law: The Impact of Legal Change on Massachusetts Society, 1760–1783* [Cambridge, Mass.: Harvard Univ. Press, 1975], 43). A nonnegotiable note, however, could easily be made negotiable. The recipient of an endorsed note could obtain recognition of the original writer's obligation by demanding immediate payment as part of the process of accepting the note. See, for example, *Stevens* v. *Sterne*, Supreme Judicial Court (hereafter cited as SJC) Records, Feb.–June 1785, 120–21, and *Gates* v. *Hillhouse*, Suffolk

Files, nos. 154214, 154220, SJC Archives, MA. See also Mann, *Neighbors and Strangers,* 39–41.

5. Since the notes were fixed, the requirement for payment in lawful money, specie, thereafter meant a dramatic decrease in the purchasing power of even relatively secure notes. James Sullivan estimated that property on which a note of £100 was given in 1783 had declined in value to £40 (Robert J. Taylor, *Western Massachusetts in the Revolution* [Providence: Brown Univ. Press, 1954], 134).

6. Creditors could have the debtor's goods or land appraised and then seized to the specific amount of his debt or have the goods sold at auction and obtain their satisfaction out of the proceeds of the sale (Nelson, *Americanization,* 41–45).

7. Peter Coleman, *Debtors and Creditors in America* (Madison: State Historical Society of Wisconsin, 1974), 8–11, 42–43. Pennsylvania in 1785 discharged both the debt and the debtor; see S. Lawrence Shaiman, "The History of Imprisonment for Debt and Insolvency Laws in Pennsylvania as They Evolved from the Common Law," *American Journal of Legal History* 4 (1960): 207. See also Robert Feer, "Imprisonment for Debt in Massachusetts," *Mississippi Valley Historical Review* 48 (1961–62): 256.

8. Feer, "Imprisonment for Debt in Massachusetts," 267–68. Louis Edward Levinthal notes a minor, tertiary objective of bankruptcy is the protection of honest debtors from their creditors after the discharge of the debts—something the Massachusetts law clearly does not do—"but this is by no means a fundamental feature of the law" (Levinthal, "The Early History of Bankruptcy Law," *University of Pennsylvania Law Review* 66 [1918]: 225–26). See also Thomas H. Jackson, *The Logic and Limits of Bankruptcy Law* (Cambridge, Mass.: Harvard Univ. Press, 1987), 3, 7–15. See especially Jackson's perspective on the proper role of bankruptcy law: "Bankruptcy law, at its core, is debt-collection law."

9. Salisbury Family Papers, box 5, folder 2. Also see Julian Hoppit's observations on eighteenth-century bankruptcy in England in *Risk and Failure in English Business, 1700–1800* (Cambridge: Cambridge Univ. Press, 1987), 18, 27.

10. Feer, "Imprisonment for Debt in Massachusetts," 256. Note that only in the event that the sale of a debtor into servitude produced an amount greater than or equal to the indebtedness would there be any discharge of the debt (Shaiman, "The History of Imprisonment for Debt," 207).

11. Salisbury Family Papers, box 5, folder 1. Jennison subsequently would be committed for a debt of £138 in Jan. 1786 by Benjamin Lee (A Register of All Persons Committed to the Worcester Gaol, Worcester County, Massachusetts, MSS Collection, box 2, folder 1, AAS).

12. See, for example, the problem as explained by Samuel Corey, who petitioned the Supreme Judicial Court for his release after a year's con-

finement for being unable to pay the remainder of his sentence of £7. 15. 8. Corey had a wife and two children, ages 3 and 1 ½ (Suffolk Files, no. 15418).

13. Committee to Review the Jail, Dec. 8, 1785, Worcester County, Mass., MSS Coll., box 2, file 2; Feer, 62, 67; Feer, "Imprisonment for Debt in Massachusetts," 260–61.

14. List of Prisoners, Dec. 6, 1785, box 2, folder 1, Petition Complaining of Poor Jail Conditions, Dec. 7, 1785, Committee to Review Jail, Dec. 8, 1785, box 2, folder 2, and Register of All Prisoners Committed to Gaol, box 2, folder 1, Worcester County, Mass., MSS Coll. The closing date for the list is presumed to be Mar. 16, 1786, the last entry provided.

15. Aaron Hunt wrote Stephen Salisbury on Jan. 25, 1786, that two small executions had kept him confined to his house (Salisbury Family Papers, box 5, folder 3). In the town of York, imprisoned debtors were allowed access to the village center in 1785. After 1799, the definition was extended to include a quarter-mile radius from the center. In Boston, the Suffolk County Court received a petition to include the entire city of Boston plus a hundred yards into the water (Feer, "Imprisonment for Debt in Massachusetts," 261).

16. Wiser entered on June 21, 1784, and was released June 14, 1785 (Register of All Persons Committed to Gaol, box 2, folder 1). His name does not appear on the state treasurer's sheriff's account book as a tax collector. Four other men from Southborough, Paul Newton, Ezekiel Collins, Jotham Bellows, and John Richards, were held responsible for over £800 in uncollected executions relating to three state taxes dating back to 1781 and still outstanding in October 1785. (Sheriff's Account Book 1781–85, Massachusetts Treasurer's Records, MA).

17. Richardson was also listed on the Dec. 7, 1785, petition and the Dec. 6, 1785, list of prisoners. Feer notes that frequently a debtor's fate depended upon the whims of the justices before whom the case was heard, the reputation of the debtor, and the willingness of the jailer to support his prisoners ("Imprisonment for Debt in Massachusetts," 253).

18. Oscar Handlin and Mary Flug Handlin, *Commonwealth: A Study in the Role of Government in the American Economy: Massachusetts, 1774–1861* (New York: New York Univ. Press, 1947), 42–43. For a detailed description of the implications of public policy and redemption for the money supply, see Taylor, *Western Massachusetts*, 105–8. See also Minot, 28.

19. Twenty served in excess of 100 days, four had terms of nearly a year, and eight of the prisoners were released within the 50-day limit. When only a month and a year are provided, I have assumed that release occurred on the last day of the month. Assuming the first of the month made no difference; in each case, the prisoner was released within the 50-day statutory limit (Register of All Prisoners Committed to Gaol, box 2, folder 1).

20. Suffolk Files, no. 154255; SJC Records, Feb.–June 1785, 129. Raw-

son alleged the amount in dispute was £600. The files suggest that Cogswell may have satisfied part of the note but that the amount was subject to dispute; hence the suit.

21. SJC Records, Feb.–June 1785, 166.
22. Suffolk Files, no. 154336; SJC Records, Feb.–June 1785, 158.
23. SJC Records, Feb.–June 1785, 143, 144, 170, 171, 176.
24. SJC Records, Feb.–June 1785, 171; Suffolk Files, no. 154388. On the appeal bond, Rawson is listed as being the major surety and responsible for the first £6 on the appeal.
25. SJC Records, Feb.–June 1785, 143, 144, 170, 176.
26. Ibid., 129, 158; Register of All Persons Committed to Gaol, box 2, folder 1.
27. SJC Records, Feb.–June 1785, 170; Suffolk Files, no. 154384. Note that Weson could have submitted the action to the June session of the Worcester Court of Common Pleas, but then one would have to consider why would Weson have acquired a note he knew was probably unsound. The note was for £12.14 and was payable on demand with interest. The court assessed 12s. 4d. in interest and an additional £3.10.10 in costs. Also note that Rawson was present at the two cases in which he was the plaintiff.
28. Register of All Prisoners Committed to Gaol, box 2, folder 1.
29. Ibid., SJC Records, Feb.–June 1785, 122.
30. SJC Records, Feb.–June 1785, 146, 163. See also Albert Farnsworth, "Shays's Rebellion in Worcester County, Massachusetts" (Ph.D. diss., Clark Univ., 1927), 16.
31. SJC Records, Feb.–June 1785, 122.
32. Prisoner's Bonds, Aug. 10, 1785, and Sept. 14, 1785, box 2, folder 3, Worcester County, Mass., MSS Coll. Stearn's own bond was for £98.18.8. The Shaysite confrontation at the Sept. 1786 session of the Worcester Court of Common Pleas took place at Patch's tavern (Farnsworth, "Shays's Rebellion in Worcester County," 3–18).
33. Mar. 1786, Salisbury Oversize Manuscript. See generally Salisbury's collection problems in the correspondence to be found in box 5 of the Salisbury Family Papers.
34. Feer counted 700 cases at the December session of the Worcester Common Pleas (Feer, 60). The 2-to-7 ratio would understate the number of cases actually appealed since a number of cases were continued or never called; see, for example, *Legate* v. *Parsons*, *Legate* v. *Downing*, and *Stevens* v. *Porter*, SJC Records, Feb.–June 1785, 122, 125. See also *Legate* v. *Porter*, Worcester Minute Book of the SJC, Sept. 1784–Apr. 1786, no. 15, SJC Archives.
35. See the fee schedule in *Acts and Laws of the Commonwealth of Massachusetts, 1782–83*, (Boston: Wright and Potter, 1890), 16–21; ibid., *1786–87*

(Boston: Wright and Potter, 1893), 226–35. For the rate of interest, see *Bancroft* v. *Wiser* and *Lee* v. *Frost,* Suffolk Files, nos. 154262, 154342.

36. John Adams collected a flat rate of two days per diem for every default judgment. The papers for the Worcester session of the SJC do not indicate a consistent practice. In some instances the lawyers' fees are included in the cost of drafting the writ; in others they are given as a separate charge (L. Kinvin Wroth and Hiller B. Zobel, eds., *The Legal Papers of John Adams,* 3 vols. [Cambridge, Mass.: Harvard Univ. Press, 1965], 1:lxx).

37. The judgments for *White* and *Alexander* were £16.5.10 and £74.16.5, respectively (Suffolk Files, no. 154286; SJC Records, Feb.–June 1785, 144, 146, 171).

38. Promissory note and copy of the lower court judgment in Suffolk Files, no. 154221; SJC Records, Feb.–June 1785, 133. Note too that an execution of judgment would not necessarily have made the creditor whole. If the debtor was insolvent, the judgment would remain unsatisfied, and the creditor's only remedy was to hope that the debtor would ultimately become solvent and discharge the obligation.

39. Nelson, *Americanization,* 41. See also Shaiman, "History of Imprisonment for Debt," 207.

40. Minot, 32; David Grayson Allen et al., eds., *Diary of John Quincy Adams,* 2 vols. (Cambridge, Mass.: Harvard Univ. Press, 1981), 2:92. See also Caleb Strong to Theodore Sedgwick, June 27, 1786, Theodore Sedgwick Papers, MHS.

41. Taylor, *Western Massachusetts in the Revolution,* 130–31; Hall, 60–61.

42. The bonds for each case list the primary and secondary sureties and may be found in the Suffolk Files for the pertinent cases.

43. Suffolk Files, nos. 154209, 154210, 154211, 154213, 154222, 154255, 154338 (the four attorneys in these eleven cases were Dwight Foster, Nathaniel Paine, John Sprague, and Caleb Strong), and nos. 154225–27, 154238, 154241, 154252, 154279, 154292–93, 154302, 154327.

One of the actions was *Stearn* v. *Johnson,* described above in the action involving £10.12.6 (SJC Records, Feb.–June 1785, 122). In this case, Lincoln would have been subsidizing the creditor interest.

44. *Legal Papers of John Adams* 1:xlvi; Register of All Prisoners Committed to Gaol, box 2, folder 1; Levi Lincoln Family Papers, octavo 5, AAS.

45. Moreover, the granting of services indicates lawyers had something to gain from subsidizing appeals. One could argue that Bangs collected no fees from these bonds, but that would, of course, leave two unanswered questions: what was the extent of the oppression suffered by defaulting debtors and why would he put money at risk for no return?

46. He had fifty-seven plaintiffs, twenty-five defendants, and one client in both capacities.

47. D. Hamilton Hurd, comp., *History of Worcester County, Massachusetts, with Biographical Sketches of Many of Its Pioneers and Prominent Men*, 2 vols. (Philadelphia: J. W. Lewis, 1889), 1:xxiv–xxv.

48. Kenneth J. Moynihan, "Meetinghouse vs. Courthouse: The Struggle for Legitimacy in Worcester, 1783–1788," in Martin J. Kauffman, ed., *Shays' Rebellion: Selected Essays* (Westfield, Mass.: Institute for Massachusetts History, 1987), 34–36, 43–47. See Lauren Abramson's table, "Members of the Second Parish Society, 1787," in her essay, "A New World View," typescript, in AAS 1980 American Studies Seminar Papers.

49. Gerard W. Gawalt, *The Promise of Power: The Emergence of the Legal Profession in Massachusetts, 1760–1840* (Westport, Conn.: Greenwood Press, 1979), 44–45, 51–55, 63. See also "Honestus" [Benjamin Austin], *Some Observations of the Pernicious Effects of Lawyers* (Worcester, Mass.: Isaiah Thomas, 1786), 6–7.

50. To be distinguished from the above-mentioned William Jennison Stearn.

51. Suffolk Files, no. 154198; SJC Records, Feb.–June 1785, 111–12.

52. SJC Records, Feb.–June 1785, 126–28.

53. Andrews to Salisbury, Jan. 5, Feb. 21, 1786, Salisbury Family Papers, box 5, folder 3. Despite a number of delinquent debtors during 1784–86, Salisbury did not commit anyone to jail in 1785–86 or have any cases before the Supreme Judicial Court in April 1785. See, in addition, his correspondence from Aaron Hunt, Peter Rowell, and John Coburn in box 5, ibid.

54. Wetmore to Salisbury, Apr. 6, 1786, ibid., box 5, folder 3. On Salisbury's business, see especially the correspondence between him and his brother in Boston, ibid. See also Account Book, 1783–1810, General Merchandise, Salisbury Family Ledger, ibid.

55. Jennison to Sewall, Mar. 4, 1786, ibid., box 5, folder 3. Jennison, in Mar. 1784, was responsible for committing John Taylor to jail for a debt of over £913.

56. See, for example, Deputy Sheriff Levi Thayer's inability to obtain an execution on £94.15.9 at the Worcester Court of Common Pleas. The Supreme Judicial Court ordered him to pay damages for that amount plus interest and costs (*Pearce* v. *Thayer*, SJC Records, Feb.–June 1785, 125, and Suffolk Files, no. 154241).

57. Maxwell Bloomfield, *American Lawyers in a Changing Society, 1776–1876* (Cambridge, Mass.: Harvard Univ. Press, 1976), 44. For an opposing view, see Hall, 181–82.

58. "Honestus," *Some Observations of Lawyers*, 4–6. Austin's critics seemed to have recognized the implications of this point. Indeed, they were somewhat mystified by Honestus's identification with the debtor interest. Sidney Kaplan points out that Austin's vilification of lawyers is the link

that paradoxically made him a favorite of debtors (" 'Honestus' and the Annihilation of the Lawyers," *South Atlantic Quarterly* 48 [1949]: 412–14).

59. Demand determined the frequency of the justice of the peace sessions. In Worcester County, justice of the peace courts met almost continuously. See, for example, Benjamin Read, Judicial Records, 1786–1800, and Joseph Allen, Justice Trials before Joseph Allen, 1786–1794, Allen Family MS Coll., both in AAS.

60. Courts of Common Pleas met quarterly while the sessions of the Supreme Judicial Court were, depending upon the population of the county, annual or semiannual (Michael Hindus, "Guide to the Court Records of Early Massachusetts," in Daniel Coquillette et al., eds., *Law in Colonial Massachusetts, 1630–1800*, Colonial Society of Massachusetts *Publications* 62 [Boston, 1984], 522–23).

61. Minot, 13–15, 39–40. See also *Diary of J. Q. Adams* 2:93, and Gordon S. Wood, *The Creation of the American Republic, 1776–1787* (Chapel Hill: Univ. of North Carolina Press, 1969), 411–13, 417–19. Rawson was one of the leaders of a group of insurgents in Leicester on Feb. 2, 1787 (Deposition of Samuel Flagg, Suffolk Files, no. 133939).

4. The Federalist Reaction to Shays's Rebellion

1. Jonathan Smith, "The Depression of 1785 and Daniel Shays' Rebellion," *WMQ*, 3d ser., 5 (1948): 77–94, esp. 77–78. First published as a pamphlet in 1905, this article was republished by the *WMQ* because it was, in the view of the editor, "the best single article on the causes for the rebellion" (77).

2. William B. Weeden, *Economic and Social History of New England, 1620–1789*, 2 vols. (Boston: Houghton, Mifflin, 1890), 2:779–81; Ralph Volney Harlow, "Economic Conditions in Massachusetts during the American Revolution," Colonial Society of Massachusetts *Publications* 20 (1920): 163–90.

3. Hall, 96–110, 122–27, 192.

4. Gerald W. Gawalt, *The Promise of Power: The Emergence of the Legal Profession in Massachusetts, 1760–1840* (Westport, Conn.: Greenwood Press, 1979), 45.

5. For a slightly later period and in different ways, Richard D. Brown has written about similar changes in "The Emergence of Urban Society in Rural Massachusetts, 1790–1820," *Journal of American History* 61 (1974): 29–51.

6. Stephen E. Patterson, *Political Parties in Revolutionary Massachusetts* (Madison: Univ. of Wisconsin Press, 1973), 249; Hall, 166–89; James Sulli-

van to Benjamin Lincoln, Jan. 16, 1782, in Thomas C. Amory, *Life of James Sullivan, with Selections from His Writings*, 2 vols. (Boston: Phillips, Sampson, 1859), 2:384; *Massachusetts Spy*, Jan. 31, 1782; Joseph Hawley to Ephraim Wright, Apr. 16, 1782, "Documents: Shays's Rebellion," *American Historical Review* 36 (1931): 776–78.

7. Hall, 256, 263–65, 286–93; Jackson Turner Main, *Political Parties before the Constitution* (Chapel Hill: Univ. of North Carolina Press, 1973), 111–13, 119, 366, 396–97; Merrill Jensen, *The Making of the American Constitution* (New York: D. Van Nostrand, 1964), 142.

8. Stephen E. Patterson, "The Roots of Massachusetts Federalism: Conservative Politics and Political Culture before 1787," in Ronald Hoffman and Peter J. Albert, eds., *Sovereign States in an Age of Uncertainty* (Charlottesville: Univ. Press of Virginia, 1981), 31–61, 44–45, 48–50; Robert A. East, "The Massachusetts Conservatives in the Critical Period," in Richard B. Morris, ed., *The Era of the American Revolution* (New York: Columbia Univ. Press, 1939), 359–60.

9. Hawley to Ephraim Wright, Apr. 16, 1782, "Documents: Shays's Rebellion," 776–78.

10. *Independent Chronicle*, Apr. 5, 1784; *Massachusetts Spy*, Feb. 26, Mar. 25, 1784; *[Thirty-First] Report of the Records Commissioners of the City of Boston Containing the Boston Town Records, 1784–96* 31 (1903): 3, 12–14.

11. Minot, 9–10, 20–22; "An honest and chearful Citizen" and a column headed "Boston," *Independent Chronicle*, Sept. 7, 1786; Circular Letter of the town of Boston, Sept. 8, 11, 1786, *Boston Gazette*, Sept. 18, 1786; "Charge of the Chief Justice to the Grand Jury of the County of Middlesex," *Independent Chronicle*, Nov. 16, 1786; William Plumer to John Hale, Sept. 18, 1786, "Letters of William Plumer, 1786–1787," Colonial Society of Massachusetts *Publications* 11 (1910): 387–90.

12. See, for example, Alden Vaughan, "Shays' Rebellion," in John A. Garraty, ed., *Historical Viewpoints*, 2 vols. (New York: Harper & Row, 1970), 1:152–65; E. James Ferguson, *The American Revolution: A General History, 1763–1790* (Homewood, Ill.: Dorsey Press, 1979), 284–85.

13. "An American," *Boston Gazette*, June 19, 1786; "Seneca," *Independent Chronicle*, June 29, 1786; "An honest and chearful Citizen," *Independent Chronicle*, Sept. 7, 1786; "Political Paragraphs," *Boston Gazette*, Dec. 4, 1786.

14. See, for example, "A letter signed N.T.," *Independent Chronicle*, June 29, 1786, which purports to be "an extract of a letter from a gentleman at W[est]t S[pringfiel]d, to his friend in a remote part of the country." The letter discusses the plot in which both the author and correspondent are presumably engaged to restore British control of America. See also "Publicus" and "Boston," *Independent Chronicle*, Sept. 7, 1786; Boston Circular Letter, *Boston Gazette*, Sept. 18, 1786; "Justice," *Boston Gazette*, Oct. 9, 1786.

15. Arthur Meier Schlesinger, *Colonial Merchants and the American Revolution, 1763–1776* (1918; rept. New York: Frederick Ungar, 1957), 308–9, 311–25, 359, 604; Robert A. East, *Business Enterprise in the American Revolutionary Era* (New York: Columbia Univ. Press, 1938), 219–20; Patterson, *Political Parties*, 65–70, 75–86.

16. Patterson, *Political Parties*, 148–50, 158–61, 162, 179–80; Patterson, "The Roots of Massachusetts Federalism," 45–46.

17. Pickering to Mrs. Mehitible Higginson, June 15, 1783, Pickering Papers, MHS, as quoted by Merrill Jensen, *The New Nation: A History of the United States during the Confederation, 1781–1789* (New York: Knopf, 1950), 267.

18. See, for example, the advertisement of Samuel Eliot of Boston, *Massachusetts Spy*, July 19, 1784.

19. Weeden, *Economic and Social History* 2:819–20; Edmund C. Burnett, ed., *Letters of Members of the Continental Congress*, 8 vols. (Washington, D.C.: Carnegie Institution, 1921–36), 8:xv.

20. Neil McKendrick, John Brewer, and J. H. Plumb, *The Birth of a Consumer Society: The Commercialization of Eighteenth-Century England* (London: Europa Publications, 1982), pt. 1: Neil McKendrick, "Commercialization and the Economy," 9–194.

21. *Massachusetts Spy*, May 20, June 3, July 1, Aug. 26, Sept. 2, 9, 1784.

22. Szatmary, esp. 29–36.

23. *Massachusetts Spy*, Oct. 7, 14, 1784.

24. Ibid., Mar. 31, 1785.

25. Typical of the attacks on British factors in the Massachusetts press was one appearing under the heading "Worcester," ibid., June 16, 1785.

26. *Boston Gazette*, Apr. 18, 1785. See also "To all whom it may concern," ibid., Apr. 11, 1785.

27. Ibid., May 9, 1785.

28. Merchants & Traders of Boston to Gov. Bowdoin, June 4, 1785, Committee of Tradesmen & Manufacturers to Gov. Bowdoin, June 7, 1785, Bowdoin-Temple Papers, MHS.

29. Nathan Dane to Rufus King, Oct. 8, 1785, in Charles R. King, ed., *Life and Correspondence of Rufus King; Comprising His Letters, Private and Official, His Public Documents, and His Speeches*, 6 vols. (New York: Putnam, 1894–1900), 1:67–69.

30. Stephen E. Patterson, "After Newburgh: The Struggle for the Impost in Massachusetts," in James Kirby Martin, ed., *The Human Dimensions of Nation Making* (Madison: State Historical Society of Wisconsin, 1976), 218–42.

31. *Massachusetts Spy*, Nov. 24, 1785.

32. Samuel Eliot Morison, *The Maritime History of Massachusetts, 1783–1860* (1921; rept. Boston: Houghton, Mifflin, 1961), 44–46.

33. Theodore Sedgwick to Caleb Strong, Aug. 6, 1786, *Letters of Members of Continental Congress* 8:415.

34. James Monroe to Thomas Jefferson, July 16, 1786, Charles Thomson's Minutes of Congress, Aug. 16, 1786 (Rufus King's speech), ibid., 8:403–4, 427–30.

35. James Monroe to James Madison, July 26, 1785, Richard Henry Lee to Madison, Aug. 11, 1785, David Howell to Gov. William Greene of Rhode Island, Aug. 23, 1785, ibid., 8:171–72, 180–81, 198–200.

36. John W. Tyler, *Smugglers and Patriots: Boston Merchants and the Advent of the American Revolution* (Boston: Northeastern Univ. Press, 1986), 100–107, 230–31, 238.

37. Massachusetts delegates to Gov. Bowdoin, Sept. 3, 1785, Rufus King to Nathan Dane, Sept. 17, 1785, Massachusetts delegates to Gov. Bowdoin, Nov. 2, 1785, *Letters of Members of Continental Congress*, 8:206–10, 218–19, 245–46.

38. King to John Adams, Nov. 2, Dec. 4, 1785, ibid., 8:247–48, 268–69.

39. Among the most vociferous antilawyer spokesmen was "Honestus," Boston ropemaker Benjamin Austin, Jr., who wrote in Boston's *Independent Chronicle*, Mar. 9, 30, May 25, 1786. See also "An Elector," "One of the People," and "Agrippa," *Boston Gazette*, Apr. 3, June 12, 19, 1786, and "Equity," *Independent Chronicle*, Apr. 27, 1786. For a full discussion of the antilawyer campaign, and especially of Austin, see Sidney Kaplan, " 'Honestus' and the Annihilation of the Lawyers," *South Atlantic Quarterly* 48 (1949): 401–20.

40. *Boston Gazette*, May 1, 1786. For the prolawyer view, see "Zenas," *Independent Chronicle*, Apr. 27, 1786.

41. Caleb Strong to Theodore Sedgwick, June 24, 1786, Theodore Sedgwick Papers, MHS.

42. Rufus King warned Jonathan Jackson that the persons organizing the convention were opposed to a general regulation of trade and sought only to promote new state regulations (King to Jackson, June 11, 1786, *Letters of Members of Continental Congress* 8:389–90).

43. Theodore Sedgwick to Caleb Strong, Aug. 6, 1785, James Monroe to Gov. Patrick Henry, Aug. 12, 1786, ibid., 8:415, 421–25.

44. The mood of Federalists is indicated in Nathan Dane to Theodore Sedgwick and [Timothy?] Dwight, Feb. 11, 1786, Nathan Dane Papers, Library of Congress; Theodore Sedgwick to Nathan Dane, Feb. 24, 1786, Livingston Papers, ser. 2, box 2, (1784–87), New-York Historical Society.

45. Artemas Ward wrote Gov. James Bowdoin that the insurgents' demands could be easily satisfied, while most of the inhabitants of the interior were not very sympathetic to the Shaysites (Ward to Bowdoin, Dec. 7, 1786, Shays' Rebellion Papers, MHS).

46. The material in this paragraph derives from a reading of the *Boston Gazette* and the *Independent Chronicle* for the fall and winter of 1786–87.
47. "Consideration," *Boston Gazette,* Apr. 17, 1786.
48. Stephen Higginson to [Henry Knox], Nov. 25, 1786, Henry Knox Papers, MHS.
49. Knox to Stephen Higginson, Feb. 25, 1787, ibid.
50. Patterson, "Roots of Massachusetts Federalism," 44–45.

5. "THE FINE THEORETIC GOVERNMENT OF MASSACHUSETTS IS PROSTRATED TO THE EARTH": The Response to Shays's Rebellion Reconsidered

Research for this chapter was funded by a grant from the American Philosophical Society. I wish to thank Richard D. Brown, William Fowler, Robert Gross, Shirley Marchalonis, Barry Shain, Robert J. Taylor, and Conrad Edick Wright for their criticisms. The quotation in the title is from Henry Knox to George Washington, Oct. 23, 1786, Henry Knox Papers, MHS.

1. Minot, 149, 192; Feer, 412–19.
2. Josiah Gilbert Holland, *History of Western Massachusetts,* 2 vols. (Springfield: S. Bowers, 1855), 297; see also John Fiske, "The Paper Money Craze of 1786 and the Shays's Rebellion," *Atlantic Monthly* 58 (1886), 376–85; Seth Chandler, *History of the Town of Shirley, Massachusetts* (Shirley: For the author, 1883), 707; *Poets and Poetry of Springfield* (Springfield: Conn. Valley Hist. Soc., 1902), 26–27.
3. *Springfield Republican,* Sept. 14, 1936, Daniel Shays file, Springfield City Library (hereafter cited as SCL); AAS *Proceedings* 15 (1902): 115, 118–20.
4. Joseph Parker Warren, "Shays's Rebellion" (Ph.D. diss., Harvard Univ., 1905), 31, copy at AAS; Feer, 101, 94, 434, 352, 265; Barbara Karsky, "Agrarian Radicalism in the Late Revolutionary Period (1780–1795)," in Erich Angermann, Marie-Luise Frings, and Hermann Wellenreuther, eds., *New Wine in Old Skins: A Comparative View of Socio-Political Structures and Values Affecting the American Revolution* (Stuttgart: Klett, 1976), 89, 98; Szatmary, 70, 83, 95.
5. Vernon Louis Parrington, *Main Currents in American Thought,* 3 vols. (New York: Harcourt, Brace, 1930), 1:277; Merrill Jensen, *The New Nation: A History of the United States during the Confederation, 1781–1789* (New York: Knopf, 1950), 56, 365; Pauline Maier, *From Resistance to Revolution: Colonial Radicals and the Development of American Opposition to Britain, 1765–1776* (New York: Knopf, 1972), esp. 22; Gordon Wood, "A Note on Mobs in the American Revolution," *WMQ,* 3d ser., 23 (1966): 641, quoted in Szatmary, 76.

6. Cecilia M. Kenyon, "Men of Little Faith: The Anti-Federalists on the Nature of Representative Government," *WMQ*, 3d ser., 12 (1955): 3–43; John P. Roche, "The Founding Fathers: A Reform Caucus in Action," *American Political Science Review* 55 (1961): 799–816; Gordon S. Wood, *The Creation of the American Republic, 1776–1787* (Chapel Hill: Univ. of North Carolina Press, 1969); proclamation in MA, 189:3–4.

7. C. O. Parmenter, *History of Pelham, Mass., from 1738 to 1898, Including the Early History of Prescott* . . . (Amherst: Carpenter and Morehouse, 1898), 366; various petitions, Shays's Rebellion Papers, AAS; Stephen T. Riley, "Dr. William Whiting and Shays's Rebellion," AAS *Proceedings* 66 (1957): 157; a good discussion of conventions generally is in J. R. Pole, *Political Representation in England and the Origins of the American Republic* (New York: St. Martin's, 1966), 227–44.

8. Adam Wheeler declaration, Nov. 17, 1786, petitions folder, Shays's Rebellion Papers, AAS; Samuel Buffinton narrative, 102, Caleb Strong Papers, Forbes Library, Northampton (hereafter cited as FLN); *Massachusetts Centinel*, Jan. 17, 1787; Samuel Holden Parsons to Benjamin Lincoln, Sept. 29, 1786, Benjamin Lincoln Papers, MHS.

9. Peter Shaw, *American Patriots and the Rituals of Revolution*, (Cambridge, Mass.: Harvard Univ. Press, 1981), 21; *Massachusetts Centinel*, Dec. 13, 1786; Daniel Stebbins Notebook, 45, FLN.

10. See note 7 above; Feer, 142–56, 530–39; Warren, "Shays's Rebellion," 37.

11. *Massachusetts Centinel*, Nov. 11, 1786.

12. MA, 189:3–4; "Proceedings of the Mob at Worcester," MA, 318:7; Loammi Baldwin to James Bowdoin, Sept. 26, 1786, MA, 318:13; *Massachusetts Centinel*, Sept. 6, 1786; "Rumors from the Country" (William Pynchon probable author) and Testimony of Robert Fowler, AAS trial folder, Shays's Rebellion Papers, AAS; Daniel Stebbins Notebook, 46.

13. Parmenter, *History of Pelham*, 373–74, 395–96; *Worcester Magazine*, second week of Oct. 1786; rank of prisoners in Worcester jail, Apr. 10, 1787, Robert Treat Paine Papers, box 23, MHS; Buffinton narrative, 102, Caleb Strong Papers.

14. Justus Forward Diary, Sept. 27, 1786, AAS; Charles Royster, *A Revolutionary People at War: The Continental Army and the American Character, 1775–1783* (Chapel Hill: Univ. of North Carolina Press, 1979), 237; Henry Van Schaack to Theodore Sedgwick, Feb. 15, 1787, Theodore Sedgwick Papers, MHS; Silas Tyson to Benjamin Lincoln, Feb. 20, 1787, anonymous letter to Lincoln, Apr. 2, 1787, Lincoln Papers.

15. Holland narrative reprinted in appendix to Warren, "Shays's Rebellion"; see also Jonathan Smith, "The Depression of 1785 and Daniel Shays' Rebellion," *WMQ*, 3d ser., 5 (1948): 88 (rept. of 1905 paper).

16. Parmenter, *History of Pelham*, 391–96; signed note dated Feb. 24, 1777, and Edward Phelan to Benjamin Russell, Dec. 27, 1786, misc. folder, Shays's Rebellion Papers, AAS; James Avery Smith, "Families of Amherst, Massachusetts," Reuben Dickinson, entry no. 1584, Jones Library, Amherst (hereafter cited as JL); warrants for "principal abettors," Feb. 9, 1787, MA, 189:121; Wheeler listed in Massachusetts, Secretary of the Commonwealth, *Massachusetts Soldiers and Sailors of the Revolutionary War*, 17 vols. (Boston: Wright and Potter, 1896–1908), 16:959.

17. Lee cited in Sidney Kaplan, "Veteran Officers and Politics in Massachusetts, 1783–1787," *WMQ*, 3d ser., 9 (1952): 52 (see also Henry Knox to Marquis de Lafayette, Feb. 13, 1787, Knox Papers: "the great body of officers, and all those of proper grade, were firm to good government"); Szatmary, 64–65, 176; Paul Guzzi, *Historical Data Relating to Counties, Cities, and Towns in Massachusetts* (Boston: Commonwealth of Massachusetts, Office of the Secretary of State, 1975); Hopkinton petition, Feb. 1, 1787, petitions folder, Shays's Rebellion Collection, AAS; Robert Treat Paine Papers, box 23; government warrants in MA, 189:36, 75, 100, 121–22; men traced in *Massachusetts Soldiers and Sailors in the Revolutionary War*.

18. Royster, *Revolutionary People at War*, 239; Daniel Stebbins Notebook, 46–47; "Rumors from the Country" (William Pynchon?), Shays's Rebellion Papers, AAS; Walter A. Dyer, "Embattled Farmers," *New England Quarterly* 4 (1931): 467.

19. Szatmary, 60, 66; Karsky, "Agrarian Radicalism," 90; Jackson Turner Main, *The Social Structure of Revolutionary America* (Princeton, N.J.: Princeton Univ. Press, 1965), 273, 274; for farm sizes, see various tax lists in MA; letters for 1786 in box 5, Salisbury Family Papers, AAS; Caleb Strong to Theodore Sedgwick, Mar. 13, 1786, Sedgwick Papers; Ebenezer Mattoon to Major Cushing, May 8, 1787, JL.

20. Barnabas Bidwell to David Daggett, June 16, 1787, AAS *Proceedings*, new ser., 4(1887): 368; Lemuel Tyler to (?) Maltbie, Sept. 26, 1786, SCL; Forward Diary, Sept. 27, 1786; *Worcester Magazine*, fourth week of Dec. 1786.

21. E. Haskell letter of Feb. 1787, SCL; Holland narrative in appendix to Warren, "Shays's Rebellion"; Benjamin Lincoln Orderly Book, Jan. 31, Feb. 21, 1787, Shays's Rebellion manuscripts at the Pittsfield Atheneum, copies at FLN.

22. Jedidiah Baldwin to Benjamin Lincoln, Jan. 19, 1787, Lincoln Papers, for Brookfield volunteers; Springfield volunteers listed in Shays's Rebellion Papers, SCL; "Newbury Men in Shays's Rebellion," Essex Institute *Historical Collections* 77 (1941): 103–4; men traced in *Massachusetts Soldiers and Sailors;* Holland narrative, Warren, "Shays's Rebellion"; Daniel Stebbins Notebook, 48; *Massachusetts Centinel*, Jan. 17, 1787; petition of army

officers, Oct. 11, 1786, Lincoln Papers; proclamation of Feb. 4, 1787, MA, 189:108; *Independent Chronicle,* Aug. 17, 1786; Samuel Salisbury to Stephen Salisbury, Sept. 8, 1786, Salisbury Family Papers, box 5.

23. Data compiled by Philip Swain, seminar paper, Tufts Univ., 1979; Royster, *Revolutionary People at War,* 134; Ralph Volney Harlow, "Economic Conditions in Massachusetts during the American Revolution," Colonial Society of Massachusetts *Publications* 20 (1920): 176–83; E. Wayne Carp, *To Starve the Army at Pleasure: Continental Army Administration and American Political Culture, 1775–1783* (Chapel Hill, Univ. of North Carolina Press, 1984).

24. Harlow, "Economic Conditions," 176; Oscar Handlin and Mary Flug Handlin, *Commonwealth: A Study of the Role of Government in the American Economy, Massachusetts, 1774–1861* (1947; rept. Cambridge, Mass.: Harvard Univ. Press, 1969), 12–13.

25. *Independent Chronicle,* Aug. 24, 1786; Noah Webster to Timothy Pickering, Aug. 10, 1786, Timothy Pickering Papers, vol. 19, MHS; *Diary of John Quincy Adams,* David Grayson Allen et al., eds., 2 vols. (Cambridge, Mass.: Harvard Univ. Press, 1981), 2:92, 150; farmer's quotation from Harlow, "Economic Conditions," 189; "An Address to the People of the Commonwealth of Massachusetts," *Acts and Resolves of the Commonwealth of Massachusetts, 1786–1787* (Boston: Wright and Potter, 1893), 142–64.

26. For the problems of eastern Massachusetts, see William Pencak and Ralph J. Crandall, "Metropolitan Boston before the American Revolution: An Urban Interpretation of the Imperial Crisis," Bostonian Society *Proceedings* (1985): 57–79; *Massachusetts Centinel,* Aug. 19, Sept. 6, 1786; "An Address to the People," 146.

27. *Independent Chronicle,* Sept. 7, 1786; *Massachusetts Centinel,* Sept. 13, 1786, Jan. 7, 1787; *Worcester Magazine,* last week of Aug. and second week of Oct. 1786.

28. Robert J. Taylor, *Western Massachusetts in the Revolution* (Providence: Brown Univ. Press, 1954), 52.

29. Handlin, *Commonwealth,* 27–31, 247–48.

30. Taylor, *Western Massachusetts,* 32, 82.

31. Richard L. Bushman, *King and People in Provincial Massachusetts* (Chapel Hill: Univ. of North Carolina Press, 1985), 40–46; Handlin, *Commonwealth,* 27–31.

32. MA, 189:108.

33. *Acts and Resolves, 1786–1787,* fall session, ch. 32, 38, 39, 40, 41, 43, 45; "Address to the People," 142–64; statement of Dr. Dix relative to case of Dr. Isaac Cheney, Shays's Rebellion Collection, AAS; *Worcester Magazine,* third week of Jan. 1787.

34. MA, 189:64, subscription for funds dated Jan. 4, 1787; Braintree Petition dated Oct. 23, 1786, Shays's Rebellion Collection, AAS; Peter Thacher to Thomas Cushing, Sept. 15, 1786, misc. MSS, MHS; John Pickering to

Timothy Pickering, Oct. 27, 1786, Pickering Papers, vol. 19, MHS; Thomas Cabot to Benjamin Lincoln, Feb. 13, 1787, Lincoln Papers; Winthrop Sargent to Henry Knox, Jan. 30, 1787, Knox Papers.

35. Petition to John Brooks, Sept. 10, 1786, MA, 189:18–19; Peter Thacher to Thomas Cushing, Sept. 15, 1786, misc. MSS, MHS; town of Rowe, "To all it may concern," Lincoln Papers.

36. Jackson Turner Main, *Political Parties before the Constitution* (Chapel Hill: Univ. of North Carolina Press, 1973), 105; Taylor, *Western Massachusetts*, 151–67. Shepherd had about 1,200 men at Springfield, and Patterson an equal number in Berkshire, in addition to General Lincoln's 4,400 men, justifying Colonel Henry Jackson's estimate of 10,000 men in arms throughout the state, including 3,000 insurgents (Jackson to Henry Knox, Jan. 28, 1787, Knox Papers; Kaplan, "Veteran Officers and Politics in Massachusetts," 30; Minot, 104; Benjamin Lincoln to James Bowdoin, Feb. 27, 1787, Lincoln Papers).

37. Levi Lincoln to ?, Dec. 28, 1786, Emmett Collection, New York Public Library, quoted in Feer, 345; Jonas Cummins testimony relative to Caleb Cushing, Jan. 1, 1787, Robert Treat Paine Papers, box 23; Daniel Stebbins Notebook, 48; Holland narrative, Warren, "Shays's Rebellion"; William Shepherd to James Bowdoin, Jan. 26, 1787, in *American Historical Review* 2 (1896–97): 694–95; James Bowdoin to William Shepherd, Jan. 30, 1787, SCL.

38. General Lincoln's orders for Jan. 19, 21, Feb. 5, 1787, materials relating to Shays's Rebellion at the Pittsfield Atheneum, copy at FLN; Benjamin Lincoln to John Patterson, Feb. 6, 1787, Walker-Rockwell Papers, box 1, New-York Historical Society; Benjamin Lincoln to James Bowdoin, Feb. 27, Mar. 1, 1787, with copies to General Knox, Knox Papers. Park Holland writes of a similar attitude on the part of a Captain Foote, who captured a group of Shaysites who only wanted to return home. He said: "That is the very best thing you can do, I earnestly wish it also. . . . If you need provision, or sleighs to carry you, I will furnish them, you are now at liberty to depart. They bade the General and all of us a friendly farewell, with their eyes filled with tears of joy and gratitude. I believe it is very seldom that we see so many men so completely happy as they were. They would be the last men that would raise their hands a second time against government" (Holland narrative, Warren, "Shays's Rebellion").

39. Henry Jackson to Henry Knox, Jan. 28, 1787, Knox Papers.

40. *Boston Magazine*, Dec. 5, 1786, quoted in appendix to Warren, "Shays's Rebellion"; Henry Jackson to Henry Knox, Jan. 21, 1787, Knox Papers; *Massachusetts Centinel*, Nov. 8, 18, 1786; *Diary of J. Q. Adams* 2:150.

41. *Massachusetts Centinel*, Dec. 9, 1786, Jan. 13, 1787; Minot, 169–70; Henry Van Schaack to Theodore Sedgwick, Feb. 16, 1787, Sedgwick Papers.

42. *Federalist Papers no. 14* and *No. 10;* Jonathan Elliot, ed., *The Debates of*

the *Several State Conventions on the Adoption of the Federal Constitution*, 5 vols. (Washington, D.C.: For the editor, 1830), 2:116; Minot, 192.

6. REGULATORS AND WHITE INDIANS: Forms of Agrarian Resistance in Post-Revolutionary New England

I am grateful to the National Endowment for the Humanities and to the Institute of Early American History and Culture for their financial support during the preparation of this essay. The essay extends the analysis in my book, *Liberty Men and Great Proprietors: The Revolutionary Settlement on the Maine Frontier, 1760–1820* (Chapel Hill: Univ. of North Carolina Press for the Institute of Early American History and Culture, 1990). I appreciate the generous assistance afforded me by Gil Kelly, Michael McGiffert, Thad Tate, Fredrika Teute, and the late Stephen Botein of the Institute. I especially wish to thank the editor of this volume for his help in improving my work.

1. Szatmary, 101–5.
2. Alan Taylor, "'Stopping the Progres of Rogues and Deceivers': A White Indian Recruiting Notice of 1808," *WMQ*, 3d ser., 42 (1985): 90–103; A. Mann to Gov. James Sullivan, Feb. 15, 1808, Lemuel Paine to Sullivan, Feb. 15, 1808, Henry Johnson's deposition, Feb. 15, 1808, Pitt Dillingham's deposition, Feb. 15, 1808, Council Files, box 16 (Aug. 1807–May 1808), MA.
3. William Plumer to John Hale, Sept. 20, 1786, "Letters of William Plumer, 1786–1787," Colonial Society of Massachusetts *Publications* 11 (1910): 390–92; see also Jeremy Belknap, *The History of New Hampshire*, vol. 2, *Comprehending the Events of Seventy-five Years, from MDCCXV to MDCCXC* (Boston: For the author, 1791), 470–73; Lynn Warren Turner, *The Ninth State: New Hampshire's Formative Years* (Chapel Hill: Univ. of North Carolina Press, 1983), 50–52.
4. William Plumer to John Hale, Sept. 20, 1786, in "Letters of William Plumer," 392; "An Account of the Insurrection in New Hampshire in 1786 . . . ," New Hampshire Historical Society *Collections* 3 (1832): 120; Jeremy Belknap to Col. Josiah Waters, Sept. 24, 1786, MHS *Collections*, 6th ser., 4 (1891): 315; Belknap, *New Hampshire* 2:473.
5. Jeremy Belknap to Col. Josiah Waters, Sept. 24, 1786, MHS *Collections*, 6th ser., 4 (1891): 315–16; William Plumer to John Hale, Sept. 21, 1786, "Letters of William Plumer," 392; Belknap, *New Hampshire* 2:473–74.
6. Lynn W. Turner, *William Plumer of New Hampshire, 1759–1850* (Chapel Hill: Univ. of North Carolina Press, 1962), 24; William Plumer to John Hale, Sept. 21, 1786, "Letters of William Plumer," 393–94.
7. William Plumer to John Hale, Sept. 26, 1786, "Letters of William Plumer," 394–96; Belknap, *New Hampshire* 2:475–76; Turner, *The Ninth State*, 55.

8. Belknap, *New Hampshire* 2: 474–75; William Plumer to John Hale, Sept. 21, 1786, "Letters of William Plumer," 392; "An Account of the Insurrection," 121.

9. John L. Brooke, *The Heart of the Commonwealth: Society and Political Culture in Worcester County, Massachusetts, 1713–1861* (New York: Cambridge Univ. Press, 1989), 215–24. For the logic of elite leniency to defeated rebels, see also chapter 8 below, by Gregory H. Nobles.

10. For the limited impact of republican notions on the Regulators, see Richard D. Brown, "Shays's Rebellion and Its Aftermath: A View from Springfield, Massachusetts, 1787," *WMQ*, 3d ser., 40 (1983): 598–99; Brooke, *The Heart of the Commonwealth*, 222–24. For the protection covenant, see Richard L. Bushman, *King and People in Provincial Massachusetts* (Chapel Hill: Univ. of North Carolina Press, 1985), esp. 37–46, 235–37. For the nature of political leadership in eighteenth-century New England towns, see Robert Zemsky, *Merchants, Farmers, and River Gods: An Essay on Eighteenth-Century American Politics* (Boston: Gambit, 1971), 28–38; Edward M. Cook, Jr., *The Fathers of the Towns: Leadership and Community Structure in Eighteenth-Century New England* (Baltimore: Johns Hopkins Univ. Press, 1976), 23–118; Robert A. Gross, *The Minutemen and Their World* (New York: Hill and Wang, 1976), 10–15; Charles S. Grant, *Democracy in the Connecticut Frontier Town of Kent* (New York: Columbia Univ. Press, 1961), 10–15; Christopher M. Jedrey, *The World of John Cleaveland: Family and Community in Eighteenth-Century New England* (New York: Norton, 1979), 121–23; Turner, *The Ninth State*, 60–61. For the older Progressive interpretation of the Regulators as egalitarian democrats, see James Truslow Adams, *New England in the Republic, 1776–1850* (Boston: Little, Brown, 1926), 136–66.

11. John Howe, "Attitudes toward Violence in the Pre-War Period," in John Parker and Carol Urness, eds., *The American Revolution: A Heritage of Change* (Minneapolis: Associates of the James Ford Bell Library, 1975), 84–95. For the King confrontation, see Silas Burbank's deposition, June 28, 1773, and Jonathan Wingate's deposition, June 16, 1773, in L. Kinvin Wroth and Hiller B. Zobel, eds., *The Legal Papers of John Adams*, 3 vols. (Cambridge, Mass.: Harvard Univ. Press, 1965), 2:121, 125; James T. Leamon, "The Stamp Act Crisis in Maine: The Case of Scarborough," *Maine Historical Society Newsletter* 11 (Winter 1971): 74–93.

12. Brooke, *The Heart of the Commonwealth*, 189–92. In contrast to my interpretation, Szatmary, 97–100, interprets alleged talk of marching on Boston as a new commitment to actually overthrowing their rulers. There is reason to doubt that any Regulators actually talked of marching on Boston, and there is reason to believe that if they did, it was more bluff than intent.

13. William Plumer to John Hale, Sept. 21, 1786, "Letters of William Plumer," 394. For the evolving attitudes of Whig gentlemen, see Pauline

Maier, "Popular Uprisings and Civil Authority in Eighteenth-Century America," *WMQ*, 3d ser., 27 (1970): 33–35; Gordon S. Wood, *The Creation of the American Republic, 1776–1787* (Chapel Hill: Univ. of North Carolina Press, 1969), 319–21, 403–13.

14. Brooke, *The Heart of the Commonwealth*, 224–29, 234–38. Richard D. Brown, "Shays's Rebellion and the Ratification of the Federal Constitution in Massachusetts," in Richard Beeman, Stephen Botein, and Edward C. Carter II, eds., *Beyond Confederation: Origins of the Constitution and American National Identity* (Chapel Hill: Univ. of North Carolina Press, 1987), 113–27.

15. Pitt Dillingham to Arthur Lithgow, Jan. 30, 1808, Related papers filed with Resolve 55 (June 19, 1809), MA; Dillingham to Nathan Weston, Feb. 4, 1808, Council Files, box 16 (Aug. 1807–May 1808). This section summarizes the discussion in my *Liberty Men and Great Proprietors*, 181–208.

16. John O. Webster's deposition, Feb. 12, 1808, Council Files, box 16 (Aug. 1807–May 1808); James W. North, *The History of Augusta from the Earliest Settlement to the Present Time* (Augusta, Me.: Clapp and North, 1870), 358, 373; Charles Vaughan to the Kennebeck Proprietors, Mar. 9, 1806, Kennebeck Proprietors Papers, box 6, Maine Historical Society.

17. Ephraim Ballard to the Kennebeck Proprietors, Jan. 1, 1796, Kennebeck Proprietors Papers, box 4; Elliot G. Vaughan to Col. Thomas Cutts, Oct. 30, 1810, misc. box 24 ("Papers Relating to Lands in Lincoln County . . ."), MA. For the blasphemous style in English crowds, see E. P. Thompson, "The Crime of Anonymity," in Douglas Hay et al., eds., *Albion's Fatal Tree: Crime and Society in Eighteenth Century England* (New York: Pantheon Books, 1975), 306.

18. Henry Johnson's deposition, Feb. 15, 1808, Pitt Dillingham's deposition, Feb. 15, 1808, Council Files, box 16 (Aug. 1807–May 1808); Abraham Welch to George Ulmer, July 11, 1801, Thurston Whiting and Benjamin Brackett to Henry Knox, Aug. 28, 1801, Henry Knox Papers, MHS.

19. Gov. James Sullivan to John Chandler, Apr. 2, 1808, House File (unpassed) no. 6311, MA; Sullivan to Chandler, Apr. 29, 1808, House File (unpassed) no. 6380, MA; Thomas C. Amory, *Life of James Sullivan, with Selections from His Writings*, 2 vols. (Boston: Phillips, Sampson, 1859), 2:273–75; Charles Hayden to Sullivan, Feb. 13, 1808, George Bender's deposition, Feb. 13, 1808, Council Files, box 16 (Aug. 1807–May 1808).

20. John Chandler to Gov. James Sullivan, Apr. 25, 1808, House File (unpassed) no. 6381, MA.

21. Amory, *Life of James Sullivan* 2:273–75; Gov. James Sullivan to Edmund Bridge, June 24, 1808, Eastern Lands Committee Papers, box 45, MA; Samuel Titcomb to Sullivan, Feb. 14, 1808, Council Files, box 16 (Aug. 1807–May 1808), MA.

22. Henry Knox to George Ulmer, July 11, 1801, to Ulmer and Robert Houston, Aug. 23, 1801, Knox Papers; [John Merrick], *Remarks on Some of*

the Circumstances and Arguments Produced by the Murder of Mr. Paul Chadwick, at Malta, on the East Side of the Kennebec, on the 7th [sic] *of September, 1809* (Hallowell, Me.: n.p., 1810), 19; North, *Augusta*, 354. Maine's agrarian unrest is briefly addressed in Gordon Kershaw, *The Kennebeck Proprietors, 1749–1775: "Gentlemen of Large Property and Judicious Men"* (Somersworth, N.H.: New Hampshire Publishing Co., 1975), 290–95; Robert E. Moody, "Samuel Ely: Forerunner of Shays," *New England Quarterly* 5 (1932): 105–34; Richard E. Ellis, *Jeffersonian Crisis: Courts and Politics in the Young Republic* (New York: Oxford Univ. Press, 1971), 224–29; Frederick S. Allis, Jr., ed., *William Bingham's Maine Lands, 1790–1820,* Colonial Society of Massachusetts Publications 36 (Boston, 1954), 3–34.

23. James M. Banner, Jr., *To the Hartford Convention: The Federalists and the Origins of Party Politics in Massachusetts, 1789–1815* (New York: Knopf, 1970), 183, observes "many of the subsistence farmers of Worcester and 'Old Hampshire' [Regulator centers] were Federalists, while similarly circumstanced men in Maine exhibited a tenacious Republicanism."

24. Brooke, *The Heart of the Commonwealth,* 247–68; Joyce Appleby, *Capitalism and a New Social Order: The Republican Vision of the 1790s* (New York: New York Univ. Press, 1984), 59; David Hackett Fischer, *The Revolution of American Conservatism: The Federalist Party in the Era of Jeffersonian Democracy* (New York: Harper and Row, 1965), 1–28.

25. In his study of Worcester County, John Brooke concludes that the Jeffersonians found their constituency among the Baptists and artisans—groups that overlapped considerably—in the county's larger, more commercial, more cosmopolitan towns, people and places that had been indifferent or hostile to the Regulation (Brooke, *The Heart of the Commonwealth,* 252–59). Similarly, James Banner observes that in Berkshire County, Massachusetts, the larger, more commercial towns voted Jeffersonian while the smaller, more isolated towns (that had been the Regulator strongholds) voted Federalist (Banner, *To the Hartford Convention,* 176). On New Hampshire's Regulators lapsing back into their normal deference, see Turner, *The Ninth State,* 61. Middlesex County, Massachusetts, a haven of Regulators in 1786 and of Jeffersonians after 1790, was an anomaly to the general pattern; see Paul Goodman, *The Democratic-Republicans of Massachusetts: Politics in a Young Republic* (Cambridge, Mass.: Harvard Univ. Press, 1964), 82–83.

26. In 1803, of the 75 mid-Maine communities detected by the 1800 federal census, 55 voted, 20 did not; 29 of 55 towns cast 90% of their ballots for one candidate, 26 of those 29 for the Federalist Caleb Strong. The Federalists won majorities in 44 of 55 towns and 2,861 of the 4,005 votes (71%). I define "mid-Maine" as Kennebec County (excluding the northern towns set off to Somerset County), Lincoln County, and Hancock County west of the Penobscot River and south of Hampden. See Abstract of Votes for Governor and Lieutenant Governor, 1785–1819, MA; James Shurtleff, *The*

Substance of a Late Remarkable Dream in Which Was Presented the Celestial Worlds and the Infernal Regions . . . (Hallowell, Me.: Peter Edes, 1800), 15, 19.

27. Ronald F. Banks, *Maine Becomes a State: The Movement to Separate Maine from Massachusetts, 1785–1820* (Middletown, Conn.: Wesleyan Univ. Press, 1970).

28. Ibid., 55–56; Amory, *Life of James Sullivan* 2:277; "The Betterment Act," chap. 74 (Mar. 2, 1808), in *Acts and Laws of the General Court of the Commonwealth of Massachusetts* (Boston, 1808), 290–92; North, *Augusta*, 373–76; John Merrick, *Trial of David Lynn, Jabez Meigs, Elijah Barton, Prince Cain, Nathaniel Lynn, Ansel Meigs, and Adam Pitts for the Murder of Paul Chadwick at Malta in Maine on September 8, 1809* (Hallowell, Me.: Ezekiel Goodale, 1810), 1–11; Robert Hallowell Gardiner, "History of the Kennebeck Purchase," *Maine Historical Society Collections* 2 (1847): 290–94.

7. REINTERPRETING REBELLION: The Influence of Shays's Rebellion on American Political Thought

1. James MacGregor Burns, J. W. Peltason, and Thomas E. Cronin, *Government by the People*, 13th ed. (Englewood Cliffs, N.J.: Prentice Hall, 1989), 2. See Richard D. Brown, "Shays's Rebellion and the Ratification of the Federal Constitution in Massachusetts," in Richard Beeman, Stephen Botein, and Edward C. Carter II, eds., *Beyond Confederation* (Chapel Hill: Univ. of North Carolina Press, 1987), 113–27. The most important exception to the consensus is Feer.

2. Ronald E. Pynn, *American Politics: Changing Expectations*, 2d ed. (Monterey, Calif.: Brooks/Cole Publishing Co., 1984), 53; John C. Shea, *American Government and Politics*, 2d ed. (New York: St. Martin's Press, 1987), 68; G. Calvin Mackenzie, *American Government: Politics and Public Policy* (New York: Random House, 1986), 24; Henry Knox to George Washington, Dec. 21, 1784, cited in Szatmary, 127. On the place of conceptual history in political science, see James Farr, "Historical Concepts in Political Science: The Case of 'Revolution,'" *American Journal of Political Science* 26 (1982): 688–708.

3. Isaac Kramnick, "The 'Great National Discussion': The Discourse of Politics in 1787," *WMQ*, 3d ser., 45 (1988): 3–32. On keywords, see Raymond Williams, *Keywords: A Vocabulary of Culture and Society*, rev. ed. (New York: Oxford Univ. Press, 1985), and on contested concepts, see W. B. Gallie, "Essentially Contested Concepts," *Aristotelian Society Proceedings* 56 (1955–56): 167–98; John N. Gray, "On the Contestability of Social and Political Concepts," *Political Theory* 5 (1977): 331–48; Terence Ball, *Transforming Political Discourse: Political Theory and Critical Conceptual History* (Oxford: Basil Blackwell, 1988), 6–14. On the relationship between conceptual con-

flict and political reform, see William E. Connolly, *The Terms of Political Discourse* (Lexington, Mass.: D. C. Heath, 1974), 1–7, 180–210. On transformation, see Ball, *Transforming Political Discourse*, 6–17. See also Terence Ball and J. G. A. Pocock, eds., *Conceptual Change and the Constitution* (Lawrence: Univ. Press of Kansas, 1988), 1–4. On the relation between transformation and tradition, see Russell L. Hanson, *The Democratic Imagination in America: Conversations with Our Past* (Princeton, N.J.: Princeton Univ. Press, 1985), 22–53.

4. "A Citizen," "From the Massachusetts Gazette. On Conventions," *Worcester Magazine*, Aug. 1786; "A New Hampshire Freeman," letter to the *New Hampshire Mercury*, Sept. 6, 1786; "A Countryman," letter to ibid., Sept. 6, 1786; "Not a Mobb man," letter to the *Worcester Magazine*, Jan. 1787. For background on the political economy of the protests, see Szatmary, 1–36.

5. "Modestus," "To the Member of the Convention," *Worcester Magazine*, Oct. 1786.

6. "A Freeman," letter to ibid., Oct. 1786; "Monitor," letter to ibid., Nov. 1786; "A Friend to Humanity and Good Government," letter to ibid., Feb. 1787; "Camillus," letter to the *Independent Chronicle*, Mar. 8, 1787. The "Camillus" letters were written by Fisher Ames.

7. "Suffolk," "To Honestus," *Independent Chronicle*, Jan. 18, 1787.

8. "Camillus," letter to ibid., Mar. 8, 1787; "A Citizen of Philadelphia" [Peletiah Webster], "The Weakness of Brutus exposed . . .," 1787, in Paul Leicester Ford, ed., *Pamphlets on the Constitution of the United States* (Brooklyn, N.Y.: n.p., 1888), 130; "Camillus," letter to the *Independent Chronicle*, Mar. 8, 1787. See also Brown, "Shays's Rebellion and the Ratification of the Federal Constitution in Massachusetts," 121–27.

9. "A Member of the Convention," letter to the *Worcester Magazine*, Oct. 1786. On radical Whig republicanism, see Bernard Bailyn, *The Ideological Origins of the American Revolution* (Cambridge, Mass.: Harvard Univ. Press, 1967), 283–84. For background on the concept of resistance, see Pauline Maier, *From Resistance to Revolution: Colonial Radicals and the Development of American Opposition to Britain, 1765–1776* (New York: Knopf, 1972), 27–48.

10. "A Freeman," letter to the *Worcester Magazine*, Oct. 1786. On popular protests, see J. R. Pole, "Shays's Rebellion: A Political Interpretation," in Jack P. Greene, ed., *The Reinterpretation of the American Revolution, 1763–1789* (New York: Harper and Row, 1968), 416–34.

11. "Attleborough," letter to the *Independent Chronicle*, Aug. 31, 1786; "A Freeman," letter to the *Worcester Magazine*, Oct. 1786.

12. "Petition of a committee from several towns in the county of Worcester . . . under the command of Capt. Shays and Capt. Wheeler . . . ," *New Hampshire Mercury*, Dec. 20, 1786; Luke Day, "To the Commanding Officer at Springfield," *Worcester Magazine*, Feb. 1787; Francis Stone, Daniel

Shays, and Adam Wheeler, "To the Honorable General Lincoln," *Independent Chronicle,* Feb. 8, 1787; "A Member of the Convention," letter to the *Worcester Magazine,* Oct. 1786; Daniel Shays, "To the Honourable Major-General Lincoln," ibid., Feb. 1787; "Attleborough," letter to the *Independent Chronicle,* Aug. 31, 1786.

13. "Jonathan of the Valley," letter to the *Independent Chronicle,* Oct. 5, 1786; Rev. James Madison to Jefferson, Mar. 28, 1787, in Julian P. Boyd et al., eds., *The Papers of Thomas Jefferson,* 23 vols. to date (Princeton, N.J.: Princeton Univ. Press, 1950—), 11:252; "Ploughjogger," letter to the *Worcester Magazine,* Nov. 1786; Alexander Hamilton, *Federalist No. 28,* in Clinton Rossiter, ed., *The Federalist Papers* (New York: New American Library, 1961), 178.

14. "One of the People," letter to the *Worcester Magazine,* Dec. 1786; "A Worcester County Man," letter to ibid., Jan. 1787; Knox to George Washington, Oct. 23, 1786, cited in Szatmary, 71; "Cassius," letter to the *Worcester Magazine,* Jan. 1787.

15. "A Member of Society," "To Mr. Adam Wheeler," *Worcester Magazine,* Jan. 1787; "Nestor," letter to ibid., Jan. 1787; "Extract from a Thanksgiving Sermon, Delivered in the County of Middlesex," ibid., Jan. 1787; "A Bostonian," letter to the *Independent Chronicle,* Aug. 10, 1786.

16. "An Other Citizen," "On Conventions," *Worcester Magazine,* Sept. 1786.

17. George Washington to Henry Lee, Oct. 31, 1786, in Worthington Chauncey Ford, ed., *The Writings of George Washington,* 14 vols. (New York: G. P. Putnam's Sons, 1889–93), 11:76; Henry Lee to James Madison, Oct. 25, 1786, in William T. Hutchinson et al., eds., *The Papers of James Madison,* 17 vols. (Chicago: Univ. of Chicago Press and Charlottesville, Univ. Press of Va., 1962–91), 9:145; "Extract from a Sermon preached in a neighbouring town, on the late Thanksgiving Day," *Worcester Magazine,* Jan. 1787; "Camillus," letter to the *Independent Chronicle,* Mar. 1, 1787; Ames to the Massachusetts ratifying convention, Jan. 15, 1788, in Jonathan Elliot, ed., *The Debates in the Several State Conventions on the Adoption of the Federal Constitution . . . ,* 5 vols., 2d ed. (Philadelphia: J. B. Lippincott Co., 1861–63), 2:10. For background, see Edmund S. Morgan, *Inventing the People: The Rise of Popular Sovereignty in England and America* (New York: Norton, 1988), 237–87.

18. "Brutus," letter to the *New York Journal,* Jan. 24, 1788, in Herbert J. Storing, ed., *The Complete Anti-Federalist,* 7 vols. (Chicago: Univ. of Chicago Press, 1981), 2:416; Richard Henry Lee to Henry Lee, Sept. 13, 1787, cited in Szatmary, 126; "A Columbian Patriot," "Observations on the new Constitution . . . ," *Pamphlets,* 22; James Warren to John Adams, May 18, 1787, in Worthington C. Ford, ed., *Warren-Adams Letters . . . John Adams,*

Samuel Adams, and James Warren, 1743–1814, 2 vols., MHS *Collections* 72–73 (Boston, 1917–25), 2:292.

19. Shays et al. to Luke Day, Jan. 20, 1787, and rebel enlistment form, 1787, both cited in Szatmary, 97.

20. "A Member of the Convention," letter to the *Worcester Magazine*, Oct. 1786. For background on the concept of revolution, see Bailyn, *Ideological Origins*, 94–143; Gordon S. Wood, *The Creation of the American Republic, 1776–1787* (Chapel Hill: Univ. of North Carolina Press, 1969), 28–36; and for its role in the mid-1780s, Michael Lienesch, "Historical Theory and Political Reform: Two Perspectives on Confederation Politics," *Review of Politics* 45 (1983): 95–99.

21. "Candidus," letter to the *Independent Chronicle*, Dec. 6, 1787, in *Complete Anti-Federalist* 4:125; "Centinel," letter to the Philadelphia *Independent Gazetteer*, Jan. 16, 1788, ibid., 2:185; "Petition... of Shays and... Wheeler," *New Hampshire Mercury*, Dec. 20, 1786; Jefferson to Madison, Jan. 30, 1787, *Papers of James Madison* 9:247; Jefferson to Ezra Stiles, Dec. 24, 1786, *Papers of Thomas Jefferson* 10:629. In one of Jefferson's most famous letters, he would explain to Abigail Adams why he hoped that Shays and his supporters would be pardoned: "I like a little rebellion now and then. It is like a storm in the Atmosphere" (Feb. 22, 1787, ibid., 11:174).

22. Madison to Washington, Feb. 21, 1787, in Edmund Burnett, ed., *Letters of Members of the Continental Congress*, 8 vols. (Washington, D.C.: Carnegie Institution, 1921–36), 8:546; Massachusetts General Court, Feb. 4, 1787, cited in Szatmary, 106; "Camillus," letter to the *Independent Chronicle*, Mar. 1, 1787. See John Adams to Benjamin Rush, May 21, 1807, in Charles Francis Adams, ed., *The Works of John Adams*, 10 vols. (Boston: Charles E. Little and James Brown, 1851–65), 9:598.

23. "Brutus," letter to the *Independent Chronicle*, July 13, 1786; "Landholder," letter to the *Connecticut Courant*, Nov. 26, 1787, in Paul Leicester Ford, ed., *Essays on the Constitution of the United States* (Brooklyn, N.Y.: Historical Printing Club, 1892), 151; "Cassius," letter to the *Massachusetts Gazette*, Nov. 23, 1787, ibid., 15.

24. Hamilton, *Federalist No. 9*, in *Federalist Papers*, 71; Adams, "A Defence of the Constitutions of Government of the United States...," *Works of John Adams* 4:285, 287.

25. "Caesar," letter to the New York *Daily Advertiser*, Oct. 17, 1787, *Essays*, 289; Adams, "Defence," *Works of John Adams* 6:151; "Landholder," letter to the *Connecticut Courant*, Dec. 3, 1787, in *Essays*, 157.

26. John Dickinson to the Federal Convention, June 2, 1787, Hamilton to the Federal Convention, June 26, 1787, in Max Farrand, ed., *The Records of the Federal Convention of 1787*, 4 vols. (New Haven: Yale Univ. Press, 1911), 1:87, 432.

27. John Jay to John Adams, Nov. 1, 1786, in Henry P. Johnston, ed., *The Correspondence and Public Papers of John Jay*, 4 vols. (New York: G. P. Putnam's Sons, 1890–93), 3:214; "Cassius," letter to the *Massachusetts Gazette*, Sept. 18, 1787, in *Essays*, 6, 7.

28. Hamilton to the New York ratifying convention, June 28, 1788, *Debates* 2:360.

29. "Cato Uticensis," letter to the *Virginia Independent Chronicle*, Oct. 17, 1787, in *Complete Anti-Federalist* 5:121; "Cato," letter to the *New York Journal*, Nov. 22, 1787, in *Essays*, 267. On Clinton, see Szatmary, 117.

30. Shays, "To the honourable Major-General Lincoln," *Worcester Magazine*, Feb. 1787.

31. "A Countryman," letter to the *New York Journal*, Dec. 20, 1787, in *Complete Anti-Federalist* 6:82.

32. Patrick Henry to the Virginia Convention, June 24, 1788, *Debates* 3:595; "Federal Farmer," "Observations leading to a fair examination of the system of government, proposed by the late Convention . . . ," Oct. 8, 1787, *Pamphlets*, 280. On the Antifederalist concept of reform, see Storing, "What the Anti-Federalists Were For," *Complete Anti-Federalist* 1:71–76. See also Michael Lienesch, "In Defence of the Antifederalists," *History of Political Thought* 4 (1983): 65–87.

33. "A Plebian," "An Address to the People of the State of New York," 1788, *Pamphlets*, 94; "Agrippa," letter to the *Massachusetts Gazette*, Nov. 27, 1787, in *Essays*, 57; "Vox Populi," letter to the *Massachusetts Gazette*, Nov. 9, 1787, in *Complete Anti-Federalist* 4:50.

34. "Federal Farmer," "Observations," Oct. 8, 1787, *Pamphlets*, 279; "An Old Whig," letter to the Philadelphia *Independent Gazetteer*, 1787, in *Complete Anti-Federalist* 3:39; "Brutus, Jr.," letter to the *New York Journal*, Nov. 8, 1787, in *Complete Anti-Federalist* 6:39; S. Thompson to the Massachusetts ratifying convention, Jan. 23, 1788, *Debates* 2:80.

35. Madison to James Madison, Sr., Feb. 25, 1787, *Papers of James Madison* 9:297; Jay to Jefferson, Apr. 24, 1787, *Papers of Thomas Jefferson* 11:313; Washington to Henry Lee, Oct. 31, 1787, *Writings of Washington* 11:78. On the election of Hancock, and its relation to the rebellion, see Brown, "Shays's Rebellion and the Ratification of the Federal Constitution in Massachusetts," 120–21.

36. "Phineas," "From the Hampshire Gazette," *Worcester Magazine*, Feb. 1787; "The Republican," letter to the *New Hampshire Mercury*, Mar. 14, 1787; "From the Massachusetts Centinel," *Worcester Magazine*, Mar. 1787; Washington to Madison, Mar. 31, 1787, *Papers of James Madison* 9:343.

37. David Humphreys, Joel Barlow, John Trumbull, and Lemuel Hopkins, *The Anarchiad: A New England Poem, 1786–1787*, ed. Luther G. Riggs (New Haven: Thomas H. Pease, 1861), 6, 20, 37.

38. "Camillus," letter to the *Independent Chronicle*, Mar. 15, 1787.

39. Rev. Thomas Thacher to the Massachusetts ratifying convention, Feb. 4, 1788, *Debates* 2:144; Josiah Smith to the Massachusetts ratifying convention, Jan. 25, 1788, ibid., 2:102, 103; Rev. Thomas Thacher to the Massachusetts ratifying convention, Feb. 4, 1788, ibid., 2:146.

40. "Cassius," letter to the *Massachusetts Gazette*, Nov. 16, 1787, in *Essays*, 14, 13; "Caesar," letter to the *Daily Advertiser*, Oct. 17, 1787, ibid., 290; "A Plain Dealer," letter to the *Virginia Independent Chronicle*, Feb. 13, 1788, ibid., 391. On Shays's exile, see Szatmary, 119.

41. Uriah Foster to Jefferson, Dec. 11, 1787, *Papers of Thomas Jefferson* 12:416; "Centinel," letter to the Philadelphia *Independent Gazetteer*, Apr. 5, 1788, in *Complete Anti-Federalist* 2:204–5; "Federal Farmer," "Observations," Oct. 15, 1787, *Pamphlets*, 321; "Agrippa," letter to the *Massachusetts Gazette*, Jan. 20, 1788, in *Essays*, 113.

42. Ames to George Richards Minot, July 23, 1789, in Seth Ames, ed., *Works of Fisher Ames*, 2 vols. (Boston: Little, Brown, 1854), 1:66; Minot, iii, 192.

43. Mercy Warren, "History of the Rise, Progress, and Termination of the American Revolution," 1805, *Complete Anti-Federalist* 6:203, 204, 205, 207. On reports of Shays's last days, see Brown, "Shays's Rebellion and the Ratification of the Federal Constitution in Massachusetts," 126–27.

44. Adams to Jefferson, June 30, 1813, *Works of John Adams* 10:47.

8. SHAYS'S NEIGHBORS: The Context of Rebellion in Pelham, Massachusetts

Earlier versions of this essay were also presented at the annual meeting of the American Historical Association (1984) and the History Department Colloquium at the University of Tennessee, Knoxville (1987). I am grateful to all the participants in those gatherings—especially Alfred L. Young, Richard D. Brown, and Robert A. Gross—for their comments and suggestions. None of them, of course, bears responsibility for any weaknesses that remain in this final version. I am also extremely grateful to the National Endowment for the Humanities, the American Association for State and Local History, and the Georgia Tech Foundation for the generous financial assistance that made the research possible.

1. "The Confession of Capt. Shays," in C. O. Parmenter, *History of Pelham, Mass., from 1738 to 1898, Including the Early History of Prescott . . .*, (Amherst: Carpenter and Morehouse, 1898), 399–402.

2. Szatmary; Barbara Karsky, "Agrarian Radicalism in the Late Revolutionary Period (1780–1795)," in Erich Angermann, Marie-Luise Frings,

and Hermann Wellenreuther, eds., *New Wine in Old Skins: A Comparative View of Socio-Political Structures and Values Affecting the American Revolution* (Stuttgart: Klett, 1976), 87–114.

3. For recent critiques of the New England community studies, see Gregory H. Nobles, "The New England Town: The Past Fifteen Years," *Journal of Social History* 19 (1985): 131–38; Marcus Rediker, "Toward a 'Real, Profane History' of Early American Society," *Social History* 10 (1985): 367–81.

4. The differences among Massachusetts towns at the time of Shays's Rebellion are analyzed in Hall, esp. chaps. 6–8.

5. The standard sources for identifying insurgents are the lists of men who surrendered their arms and took the oath of loyalty in the spring of 1787, in MA, vol. 190. Of these men, 103 gave their residence as Pelham, but that number is too high. After comparing the list of Pelham insurgents against Pelham's 1771, 1780, and 1784 valuation lists, the 1790 federal census, a 1795 tax list, and a 1799 voter list, I have excluded 15 of the alleged Pelhamites because neither they nor their family names ever appeared on a town list. If they lived in Pelham, they did so only briefly, and I suspect their identification with Pelham in 1787 was probably a matter of administrative convenience or confusion. The remaining 88 Shaysites who did have some definite connection with the town can be joined with Daniel Shays and Henry McCulloch—two Pelham insurgents who did not take the loyalty oath in 1787—to make a total of 90. They represent 41.5% of the 217 polls on the 1784 valuation.

6. Pelham's state tax for 1786 was £605.12.6, and the town's place among other county towns is shown in the following table.

State Tax, Hampshire County Towns, 1786

Tax	No. of towns in range	($N = 58$)
Over £1,000	6	
£710–1,000	10	
£401–700	20	
£100–400	22	
Mean tax = £564		
Median tax = £529		

Source: Joseph Barlow Felt, *Collections of the American Statistical Association* 1 (1847): 458–60.

The population estimate for Pelham is based on multiplying the number of polls in the 1784 valuation, 217, by four, which yields a total of 868. (The use of the multiplier of four is suggested by Evarts B. Greene and

Virginia D. Harrington, *American Population before the Federal Census of 1790* [New York: Columbia Univ. Press, 1932], xxiii.) The 1790 census lists 246 polls for Pelham and a total population of 1,040, which reflects about the same 1:4 ratio. The median number of polls per town in Hampshire County in 1784 was 183, and the median population in 1790 was 873. Population figures are taken from Felt, *Collections* 1:167, 564–66.

7. A brief discussion of the Pelham settlers' previous experience in Worcester is in William Lincoln, *History of Worcester, Massachusetts, from Its Earliest Settlement to September, 1836* (Worcester: C. Hersey, 1837), 47–48.

8. For the history of Pelham's settlement, see Parmenter, *History of Pelham*, 7–37.

9. Gregory H. Nobles, *Divisions throughout the Whole: Politics and Society in Hampshire County, Massachusetts, 1740–1775* (New York and London: Cambridge Univ. Press, 1983), 195–96.

10. For an overview of backcountry protest, see James A. Henretta and Gregory H. Nobles, *Evolution and Revolution: American Society, 1600–1820* (Lexington, Mass.: D. C. Heath, 1987), 118–21.

11. Sylvester Judd Manuscript, "Northampton Vol. 1," 482–83, Forbes Library, Northampton, Mass.

12. Timothy Dwight, *Travels in New England and New York*, ed. Barbara M. Solomon, 4 vols. (Cambridge, Mass.: Harvard Univ. Press, 1969), 1:238–39.

13. Charles S. Grant, *Democracy in the Connecticut Frontier Town of Kent* (New York: Columbia Univ. Press, 1961), chaps. 3 and 4.

14. Ibid., 98–103, 172–73. See also Robert A. Gross, *The Minutemen and Their World* (New York: Hill and Wang, 1976), chap. 4.

15. See the 1745 tax list in Pelham Town Record, 1743–79, Univ. of Massachusetts-Amherst Library, microfilm.

16. Grant, *Kent*, 34–39. There is a more refined version of Grant's estimate in his doctoral dissertation, "A History of Kent, 1738–1796: Democracy on Connecticut's Frontier" (Ph.D. diss., Columbia Univ., 1957), app. 3:323–31. See also Gross, *Minutemen*, 213–14n, for a similar estimate of the amount of land needed for "a middle class standard of living."

17. The figures for 1746 are in the 1746 tax list in Pelham Town Record, 1743–79. For later population growth in Pelham and other towns in the region, see Nobles, *Divisions throughout the Whole*, 195–96.

18. The economic development of Pelham is discussed in Gregory H. Nobles, "Hardship in the Hilltowns: Agricultural Development and Economic Conditions in Pelham, Massachusetts, 1740–1790," paper presented at the annual meeting of the Organization of American Historians, 1980.

19. Bettye Hobbs Pruitt, "Self-Sufficiency and the Agricultural Economy of Eighteenth-Century Massachusetts," *WMQ*, 3d ser., 41 (1984): 354.

20. For a general discussion of early economic conditions in the western Massachusetts hill towns, see Nobles, *Divisions throughout the Whole,* 119–20. For information on grain and cattle production, see Pruitt, "Self-Sufficiency," 357–61. For a detailed discussion of the role of cattle production, see J. Ritchie Garrison, "Farm Dynamics and Regional Exchange: Connecticut Valley Beef Trade, 1670–1850," *Agricultural History* 61 (1987): 1–17. It should be noted that in the early part of the nineteenth century, Pelham farmers did discover a marketable surplus commodity—the soil itself. Housekeepers in Northampton and other valley towns used sand to clean their floors, and Pelham's fields provided more than an adequate supply to meet the demand of the whole region. See Christopher Clark, "Household, Market, and Capital: The Process of Economic Change in the Connecticut Valley of Massachusetts, 1800–1860" (Ph.D. diss., Harvard Univ., 1981).

21. Nobles, "Hardship in the Hilltowns."

22. Edward M. Cook, Jr., *The Fathers of the Towns: Leadership and Community Structure in Eighteenth-Century England* (Baltimore: Johns Hopkins Univ. Press, 1976), 73. For a similar categorization compared to Massachusetts towns in general, see Bettye Hobbs Pruitt, "Agriculture and Society in the Towns of Massachusetts, 1771: A Statistical Analysis" (Ph.D. diss., Boston Univ., 1981).

23. Szatmary, chap. 2. The Conway petition is quoted on pp. 33–34.

24. Of thirty-one insurgents for whom some birth information is known, sixteen (51%) were born between 1752 and 1762, inclusive, which would make them between twenty-five and thirty-five at the time of the rebellion. Another four (13%) were born between 1763 and 1767, inclusive, and were therefore at least in their twenties. Five Shaysites (16%) were younger than twenty, and the remaining six—including Daniel Shays—were over thirty-five. Still, the paucity of the evidence makes any conclusions based on birth information alone only tentative at best. I have also consulted the *Vital Records of Pelham, Massachusetts, to the Year 1850* (Boston: New-England Historic Genealogical Society, 1902) in order to find the Shaysites listed either as new husbands in the marriage records or as new fathers in the birth records; in the latter case I have assumed that most men married within two years before the birth of their first child.

I have consulted Massachusetts, Secretary of the Commonwealth, *Massachusetts Soldiers and Sailors of the Revolutionary War,* 17 vols. (Boston: Wright and Potter, 1896–1908), and the Revolutionary War Pension Records in the National Archives, Washington, D.C., to determine the military service of Pelham's ninety Shaysites. Thirty-nine (43%) were listed in one source or the other.

Daniel Shelton, in "'Elementary Feelings': Pelham Massachusetts, in

Rebellion" (Honors thesis, Amherst College, 1981), 119–20, has counted some seventy-two debt cases in the Hampshire County Court of Common Pleas between 1782 and 1786 that involved Pelham men. In thirty of those cases, however, Pelham men were plaintiffs, and in only forty-two were they defendants; more important, only three future insurgents were sued for debt. My own examination of the court records has yielded similar results. Between 1781 and 1784 the county court records contain warrants for twenty-seven executions for debt—that is, the confiscation of property or imprisonment of debtors—but none involved Pelham residents. See Hampshire County Court of Common Pleas, vol. A/20 (1715–90), 54–80, Forbes Library, Northampton, Mass., microfilm.

25. Szatmary, 60. In describing Brookfield as a "market town," Szatmary overstates the town's economic development. For a detailed economic analysis of Brookfield, see Susan Geib, "Changing Works: Agriculture and Society in Brookfield, Massachusetts, 1785–1820" (Ph.D. diss., Boston Univ., 1981).

26. Parmenter, *History of Pelham*, 410–12.

27. James Russell Trumbull, *History of Northampton, Massachusetts, from Its First Settlement in 1654*, 2 vols. (Northampton: Press of Gazette Printing Co., 1898–1902), 2:373–74.

28. Ibid.

29. Stephen Burroughs, *Memoirs of the Notorious Stephen Burroughs* (1798; rept. New York: Cornish, Lamport, 1851), 53–54. For a discussion of the religious context of Pelham, see chapter 10 below, by Stephen A. Marini.

30. The term "generalissimo" comes from the "Black List" in the Robert Treat Paine Papers, MHS.

31. Edward W. Carpenter and Charles Frederick Morehouse, *The History of the Town of Amherst, Massachusetts* . . . (Amherst: Carpenter and Morehouse, 1896), 124.

32. Minot, passim.

33. Mason A. Green, *Springfield, 1636–1886: History of Town and City* (Springfield, Mass.: C. A. Nichols, 1888); Carpenter and Morehouse, *History of Amherst*, 135–36.

34. Gregory H. Nobles, "The Politics of Patriarchy in Shays's Rebellion: The Case of Henry McCulloch," in Peter Benes, ed., *Families and Children*, Dublin Seminar for New England Folklife Annual Proceedings 1985 (Boston: Boston Univ., 1987), 37–47.

35. For a brief biographical sketch of Shays, see Parmenter, *History of Pelham*, 391–402.

36. Robert J. Taylor, *Western Massachusetts in the Revolution* (Providence: Brown Univ. Press, 1954), 156–58.

37. For overviews of political behavior in western Massachusetts in the

early stages of the American Revolution, see ibid., chaps. 4 and 5, and Nobles, *Divisions throughout the Whole,* chap. 7.

38. For a discussion of local politics in the western counties in the Revolutionary era, especially the rise of the Berkshire Constitutionalists and the responses to the 1778 constitution, see Taylor, *Western Massachusetts,* chap. 5; Ronald Peters, *The Massachusetts Constitution of 1780: A Social Compact* (Amherst: Univ. of Mass. Press, 1978), 18–23; Stephen E. Patterson, *Political Parties in Revolutionary Massachusetts* (Madison: Univ. of Wisconsin Press, 1973), 204–8; Theodore M. Hammett, "Revolutionary Ideology in Massachusetts: Thomas Allen's 'Vindication' of the Berkshire Constitutionalists," *WMQ,* 3d ser., 33 (1976): 514–27; John L. Brooke, "To the Quiet of the People: Revolutionary Settlements and Civil Unrest in Western Massachusetts, 1774–1789," ibid., 46 (1989): 425–62.

39. For the returns of Pelham and Greenwich, see Oscar Handlin and Mary Flug Handlin, eds., *The Popular Sources of Political Authority: Documents on the Massachusetts Constitution of 1780* (Cambridge, Mass.: Harvard Univ. Press, 1966), 212–13, 321–22.

40. For a discussion of the Ely riots and other local disturbances, see Taylor, *Western Massachusetts,* 111–27.

41. Trumbull, *History of Northampton,* 2:346–48.

42. Justus Forward Diary, Sept. 28, 1786, AAS.

43. Taylor, *Western Massachusetts,* 158–67; Szatmary, chap. 6.

44. Nobles, "Politics of Patriarchy," 45.

45. For a discussion of the political identification of former Shaysites after 1790, see Richard D. Brown, *Massachusetts: A Bicentennial History* (New York: Norton, 1978), 125; and Ronald P. Formisano, *The Transformation of Political Culture: Massachusetts Parties, 1790s–1840s* (New York: Oxford Univ. Press, 1983), 167.

9. A Deacon's Orthodoxy: Religion, Class, and the Moral Economy of Shays's Rebellion

Portions of this chapter have appeared in John L. Brooke, *The Heart of the Commonwealth: Society and Political Culture in Worcester County, Massachusetts, 1713–1861* (New York: Cambridge University Press, 1989), and are reprinted with the permission of the publisher.

1. Shays's Rebellion Collection, 1786–87, folder 5, AAS.

2. Witness list, Robert Treat Paine Papers, box 23 (box on Shays's Rebellion), MHS. On Caleb Curtis, see Anson Titus, Jr., *Charlton, Historical Sketches* (Southbridge, Mass.: G. M. Whitaker, 1877), 14; L. Kinvin Wroth et al., eds., *Province in Rebellion: A Documentary History of the Founding of the*

Commonwealth of Massachusetts, 1774–1775 (Cambridge, Mass.: Harvard Univ. Press, 1975), 2821–23n.

3. Robert J. Taylor, *Western Massachusetts in the Revolution* (Providence: Brown Univ. Press, 1954); Feer; Hall. The most important discussions of the relationship between the Great Awakening and eighteenth-century politics include Alan Heimert, *Religion and the American Mind from the Great Awakening to the Revolution* (Cambridge, Mass.: Harvard Univ. Press, 1966); Philip Greven, *The Protestant Temperament: Patterns of Child-Rearing, Religious Experience, and the Self in Early America* (New York: Knopf, 1977); Gary Nash, *The Urban Crucible: Social Change, Political Consciousness, and the Origins of the American Revolution* (Cambridge, Mass.: Harvard Univ. Press, 1979); Harry S. Stout, "Religion, Communications, and the Ideological Origins of the American Revolution," *WMQ*, 3d ser., 34 (1977): 519–41. For critiques of this literature, see Jon Butler, "Enthusiasm Described and Decried: The Great Awakening as Interpretive Fiction," *Journal of American History* 69 (1982): 305–35; John M. Murrin, "No Awakening, No Revolution? More Counterfactual Speculations," *Reviews in American History* 11 (1983): 161–71.

4. William G. McLoughlin, *New England Dissent, 1630–1833: The Baptists and the Separation of Church and State*, 2 vols. (Cambridge, Mass.: Harvard Univ. Press, 1971), 2:777–78; Stephen A. Marini, *Radical Sects of Revolutionary New England* (Cambridge, Mass.: Harvard Univ. Press, 1982), 34–39.

5. Szatmary, 60–61; Ruth H. Bloch, *Visionary Republic: Millennial Themes in American Thought, 1756–1800* (New York: Cambridge Univ. Press, 1985), 111.

6. For ministerial support for the government, see Taylor, *Western Massachusetts*, 147–48; Szatmary, 89 n. 164; Emory Washburn, *Historical Sketches of the Town of Leicester, during the First Century from Its Settlement* (Boston: John Wilson and Son, 1860), 331; David D. Field and Chester Dewey, eds., *A History of the County of Berkshire, Massachusetts* (Pittsfield, Mass.: S. W. Bush, 1829), 216–17, 237, 301; Anson E. Morse, *The Federalist Party in Massachusetts to the Year 1800* (Princeton, N.J.: Univ. Library, 1909), 219.

7. Williston Walker, ed., *The Creeds and Platforms of Congregationalism* (1893; rept. Boston: Pilgrim Press, 1960), 22, 212–14, 221; William E. Barton, *The Law of Congregational Usage* (Chicago: Puritan Press, 1916), 173–75; William T. Youngs, *God's Messengers: Religious Leadership in Colonial New England, 1700–1750* (Baltimore: Johns Hopkins Univ. Press, 1976), 96–97, 160 n. 14.

8. The economic causes of the Regulation have been treated in detail in Taylor, *Western Massachusetts*; Hall; Szatmary; and E. James Ferguson, *The Power of the Purse: A History of American Public Finance, 1776–1790* (Chapel Hill: Univ. of North Carolina Press, 1961). I use the term "moral econ-

omy" in broadly the same spirit as it was originally defined by Edward P. Thompson, in "The Moral Economy of the English Crowd in the Eighteenth Century," *Past and Present* 50 (1971): 76–136, of corporate tradition of interference with private property and contract in times of economic crisis. For a parallel analysis of orthodoxy and dissent in this region, see John L. Brooke, "For Civil Worship to Any Worthy Person: Burial, Baptism, and Community on the Massachusetts Near Frontier, 1730–1790," in Robert B. St. George, ed., *Material Life in America, 1600–1860* (Boston: Northeastern Univ. Press, 1988), 463–85; also published as "Enterrement, Bapteme et Communaute en Nouvelle-Angleterre (1730–1790)," *Annales: Economies, Sociétés, Civilisations* 42 (1987): 653–86.

9. See, for example, Joseph S. Clark, *A Historical Sketch of the Congregational Churches in Massachusetts, from 1620 to 1858* (Boston: Congregational Board of Publication, 1858), 217–20. The rise and fall of Congregational revivalism between 1774 and the late 1770s is discussed in Brooke, *The Heart of the Commonwealth*, 151–52, 177.

10. Figures based on an analysis of the presence of orthodox ministers listed in *Fleeming's Register for New England and Nova Scotia . . . 1773* (Boston: Fleeming, 1773), 69–72; *Pocket Almanack for 1787 . . . Massachusetts Register* (Boston: Fleets, 1786), 57–60. More generally, see Taylor, *Western Massachusetts*, 68; Paul R. Lucas, *The Valley of Discord: Church and Society along the Connecticut River, 1636–1725* (Hanover, N.H.: Univ. Press of New England, 1976); Gregory H. Nobles, *Divisions throughout the Whole: Politics and Society in Hampshire County, Massachusetts, 1740–1775* (New York and London: Cambridge Univ. Press, 1983); Masonic affiliations for Daniel Shays, Luke Day, and Elijah Day from William R. Denslow, *10,000 Famous Freemasons*, 4 vols. (Independence: Missouri Lodge of Research, 1957–61), 4:127; for Daniel Shays, see also Rebecca D. Symmes, ed., *A Citizen-Soldier in the American Revolution: The Diary of Benjamin Gilbert in Massachusetts and New York* (Cooperstown: New York State Historical Association, 1980), 22–23, 27–29.

11. Marini, *Radical Sects*, 44ff.; see also Douglas H. Sweet, "Church Vitality and the American Revolution: Historiographical Consensus and Thoughts toward a New Perspective," *Church History* 45 (1976): 341–57. For the expansion of Baptist churches during this revival, compare the lists in *Minutes of the Warren [Baptist] Association, in Their Meeting at Middleborough, Sept. 9, & 10, 1777* (Boston: E. Draper, 1777), 1–2, and *Minutes of the Warren [Baptist] Association, Convened at Providence, the 10th of Sept. 1782* (Providence: Carter, [1782]), 1–3. The role of the Baptists in the constitution-making process is discussed in Elisha P. Douglas, *Rebels and Democrats: The Struggle for Equal Rights and Majority Rule during the Revolution* (Chapel Hill: Univ. of North Carolina Press, 1955), 138–41, 192–94, and in Brooke, *The Heart of the Commonwealth*, 158–88.

12. Marini, *Radical Sects*, 40–54, 63–101, and passim.
13. Stephen Burroughs, *Memoirs of the Notorious Stephen Burroughs of New Hampshire* (1798; rept. New York: Dial Press, 1924), 52–53.
14. Charles Tilly, *The Vendée*, 2d ed. (Cambridge, Mass.: Harvard Univ. Press, 1976), 323ff.
15. For sources, see Appendix B to this chapter.
16. On the hierarchy of towns, see Edward M. Cook, Jr., *The Fathers of the Towns: Leadership and Community Structure in Eighteenth-Century New England* (Baltimore: Johns Hopkins Univ. Press, 1976); Hall, 3–22. The cultural and economic geography of this region is described in detail in Brooke, *The Heart of the Commonwealth*. The estimate that 23.5% of the population of these towns was affiliated with dissenting societies is based on an analysis of church records and tax valuations. It assumes that the proportion of the top quintile of the valuation affiliated with dissenting societies was typical of the entire population.
17. Hall, 195; Szatmary, 29.
18. On deference in the Federalist era, see James M. Banner, Jr., *To the Hartford Convention: The Federalists and the Origins of Party Politics in Massachusetts, 1789–1815* (New York: Knopf, 1970); David Hackett Fischer, *The Revolution of American Conservatism: The Federalist Party in the Era of Jeffersonian Democracy* (New York: Harper and Row, 1965), 211ff.; and esp. Ronald P. Formisano, *The Transformation of Political Culture: Massachusetts Parties, 1790s–1840s* (New York: Oxford Univ. Press, 1983), 128ff.
19. James Draper, *History of Spencer, Massachusetts* . . . (Worcester: H. J. Howland, 1860), 62; Oakham Evidence, Robert Treat Paine Papers, box 23; MA, 190:107, 165–66; Henry B. Wright and Edwin D. Harvey, *The Settlement and History of Oakham, Massachusetts* (New Haven: n.p., 1947), 285. The debt cases are from Suffolk Files Collection, files no. 155016, 155133, 155148, and Worcester County Court of Common Pleas Record Book, 13 (1785–86): 62, 67, 76, 127, 175, 191, 200, 217, 223, 240, 259, 268, 273 (both sources in the Judicial Archives, located at the Massachusetts State Archives building, Columbia Point, Boston).
20. Jail Committee Report, Dec. 1785, Worcester County Papers, box 2, folder 2, AAS. I am indebted to Lou Mazur for this reference.
21. An episode involving Justice Percival Hall of New Braintree provides a further perspective on the sympathies of some of the lesser gentry for the Regulators. Justice Hall, accused of aiding the insurgents, printed a spirited defense in the *Worcester Magazine* 2 (1787): 587ff. Hall admitted to having attended "a meeting of the principal officers of the insurgents . . . to dissuade [them] from their purposes of taking up arms and rising against the government" and defended his transcribing a petition at this meeting by noting that he "could write faster than others there." Hall also defended his allowing a Regulator company to be quartered in his household, declaring

that he was "possessed with too tender feelings of humanity to drive them from shelter in such a cold and bitter season." Declaring himself "a firm supporter of the laws and government of the land," Justice Hall counterbalanced his sympathy for the Regulators by sending his son to serve with the government militia. Such men could hold firmly patriarchal assumptions. Worrying that his son might join the government militia, Major Francis Willson of Holden swore that "he should have not marched alive," and that "the Elderly people ought to take the matter up & not the youth." His fears were ultimately unwarranted, as his son would be taunted as a "Mob boy" as he was a "Mob man." Overall, in these six towns, thirty-five Regulators were the sons of other Regulators, and in only two instances were fathers and sons on the opposition side of the confrontation. Testimony taken from Sturbridge laborers in 1787 indicates that their masters had supplied them with arms and provisions to join the Regulators (testimony of John Dodd and Ann Webb against Francis Willson of Holden, Shays's Rebellion Collection, folder 5, AAS; Sturbridge evidence, Robert Treat Paine Papers, box 23). On the basis of this evidence I have assumed that men in the propertyless 9th and 10th deciles of the 1783 valuation were acting as members of other men's households, and I have arbitarily assigned them to their fathers' wealth quintile. See table 9.2.

22. The oaths of allegiance were overwhelmingly administered by justices who had some involvement in the economic politics of the 1780s.

Justices and oaths of allegiance in southwest Worcester County
(sixteen towns total)

	justices	Justices administering oaths	Total oaths administered
Friend of Government	9	2	5
Position unknown	9	3	76*
Regulator sympathies†	8	8	400

*Sixty of these 76 oaths were administered by Justice Paul Mandell of Hardwick.

†Justice of the peace was a convention leader, voted against consolidation in January 1781, was a brother of a Regulator, or represented debtors in the Court of Common Pleas between December 1785 and July 1786.

23. Investigations of the religious affiliations of Regulators in the Berkshire towns of Pittsfield and West Stockbridge and the Hampshire towns of Ashfield, Conway, Colerain, and Pelham also indicate that dissenters were less likely to be drawn into the insurgency. On wealth stratification and town officeholding, see Cook, *The Fathers of the Towns*, 80–84.

24. Stephen Burroughs's description of the electioneering by Israel Waters of Charlton is particularly revealing (Burroughs, *Memoirs*, 192–93). Several of the Charlton dissenters who served with the government light horse married into orthodox gentry families in the 1790s, and several were awarded judicial placeholdings, steps on the path toward a dissenting gentry.

25. The dissenter Regulators had, on average, almost twice the debt load as the nominally-orthodox Regulators from Oakham and Spencer, but the dissenter Friends of Government, with obligations to coastal merchants, owed the greatest amount of money.

Levels of indebtedness: dissenters from the six towns vs. the nominally orthodox in Spencer and Oakham

	Regulator	No evidence	Friend of Govt.	Total
Oakham/Spencer (All nondissenters)*				
Debtors	23	14	0	37
% in wealthiest quintile	39.1	28.6		35.1
Mean debt	£22.9	£23.7		£22.8
Mean indebtedness	£29.9	£36		£31.4
Dissenters				
Debtors	7	16	6	29
% in wealthiest quintile	0	41.1	50	34.5
Mean debt	£20	£42.9	£59	£34.6
Mean indebtedness	£51	£48.9	£73.7	£47.7

Sources: 1783 valuations, and material cited in Appendix B.

*There were no dissenting societies in these two towns, but there were a number of dissenters living in Spencer affiliated with societies in Charlton and Leicester. They are included in the "Dissenter" category.

26. Dudley and Charlton testimony, Robert Treat Paine Papers, box 23. None of the testimony against the Leicester, Charlton, or Sturbridge Regulators indicates that they were active before the December court closings. Four of the six dissenting creditors who sided with the Regulators were among the group mobilized by Caleb Curtis in Charlton, including David Dresser's cousin Richard Dresser, Jr.

27. Testimony against Asa Sprague, folder 5, Shays's Rebellion Collection; New Braintree evidence, Robert Treat Paine Papers, box 23; John

Noble, *A Few Notes on Shays Rebellion* (Worcester, Mass.: Charles Hamilton, 1903), 16–25; Leicester Articles of Agreement, MA, 318:20 (152 in light pencil).

28. Among sixty some rioters from Worcester County towns for which evidence for religion is available, fully one-half were affiliated with Baptist meetings or would join a Universalist society in 1785. This Universalist connection was very extensive, involving rioters from seven different towns, and at least two Universalist notables provided sureties for rioters. Of these sixty rioters, five can be connected to the Regulation, and six to the government militia. More impressionistic evidence suggests that such small riots in Hampshire and Berkshire counties were similarly situated in the Baptist neighborhoods. Rioters in all three western counties are listed in Massachusetts Supreme Judicial Court Docket Books, 1783: 212–20, 232, 239–41, 1784: 265, 1785: 177, Judicial Archives; see also Dudley Riot evidence, Robert Treat Paine Papers, box 23. Universalists in southwest Worcester are listed in The Second Religious Society in Oxford and Adjacent Towns (Called Universalist), Record Book, 1785–1845, Andover Harvard Theological Library; Mabel C. Coolidge, *The History of Petersham, Massachusetts* (Petersham: Petersham Historical Society, 1948), 56–57, 234. Sources for Berkshire County include J. E. A. Smith, *History of Pittsfield, Massachusetts* . . . (Boston: Lee and Shepherd, 1969), 459–60; Rollin C. Cooke, transcriber, "Pittsfield, Mass., Church and Other Records," 2 vols., 1:310–13, typescript, Berkshire Athenaeum. On the distinction between the tax riots and the court closings, see Hall, 184ff.

29. On the distinction between private and public mobs, see Gordon S. Wood, *The Creation of the American Republic, 1776–1787* (Chapel Hill: Univ. of North Carolina Press, 1969), 320–21.

30. Greenville (Leicester, Mass.) Baptist Church Records, vol. 1, minutes, 17–31, letters, 9–27, Andover-Newton Theological School, Newton, Mass. See Bealls to Backus, Sept. 4, 1787, Isaac Backus Papers, Andover-Newton Theological School, quoted in McLoughlin, *New England Dissent* 1:778.

31. First Congregational Church of Spencer Records, A:30–32 (MSS, church vault); Arthur Chase, *History of Ware, Mass.* (Cambridge, Mass.: Harvard Univ. Press, 1911), 95–96.

32. For Wheeler's statement, see Shays's Rebellion Collection, folder 1; for biography of Wheeler, see John M. Stowe, *The History of Hubbardston, Worcester County, Mass.* (Hubbardston: Charles Hamilton, 1881), 57–60, 87, 209, 213, 367–68.

10. The Religious World of Daniel Shays

1. Minot; Starkey; William G. McLoughlin, "The Role of Religion in the American Revolution," in Stephen Kurtz and James Hutson, eds., *Essays on the American Revolution* (Chapel Hill: Univ. of North Carolina Press, 1969), 206.
2. Szatmary, 60–61.
3. John L. Brooke, "Society, Revolution, and the Symbolic Uses of the Dead: An Historical Ethnography of the Massachusetts Near Frontier, 1730–1820" (Ph.D. diss., Univ. of Pennsylvania, 1982).
4. See William G. McLoughlin, *Isaac Backus and the American Pietistic Tradition* (Boston: Little, Brown, 1967), and *New England Dissent, 1630–1833: The Baptists and the Separation of Church and State*, 2 vols. (Cambridge, Mass.: Harvard Univ. Press, 1971).
5. Sydney E. Ahlstrom, *A Religious History of the American People* (New Haven: Yale Univ. Press, 1972), 365–66.
6. Nathan O. Hatch, *The Sacred Cause of Liberty: Republican Thought and the Millennium in Revolutionary New England* (New Haven: Yale Univ. Press, 1977); McLoughlin, *New England Dissent* 2:751–53.
7. Second Parish–Pelham and Prescott, Mass., Congregational Church Records, 1786–1851, Quabbin Towns Collection, box 3, 3:1, AAS.
8. Commonwealth of Massachusetts, *The Laws of the Commonwealth of Massachusetts*, 2 vols. (Boston: Manning and Loring, 1801), 1:19–20.
9. Robert Ellis Thompson, *A History of the Presbyterian Churches in the United States*, American Church History Series, 6 (New York: Christian Literature Co., 1895), 22–23.
10. Robert L. Merriam, "The Reverend Robert A. Abercrombie," 21, typescript, 1964, AAS.
11. C. O. Parmenter, *History of Pelham, Mass., from 1738 to 1898, Including the Early History of Prescott* . . . (Amherst: Carpenter and Morehouse, 1898), 297–300.
12. See Robert Abercrombie, *An Account of the Proceedings of the Presbytery . . . against the Rev. Mr. Robert Abercrombie* (Boston: Edes and Gill, 1754).
13. Parmenter, *History of Pelham*, 309–10, 312–17.
14. Ibid., 261–63.
15. Ibid., 317–20.
16. Prescott, Mass., Congregational Church Records, 1823–54, and Pelham, Mass., East Church Records, 1786–98, Quabbin Towns Collection, box 3, vol. 2.
17. Second Parish–Pelham and Prescott, Mass., Congregational Church Records, 1786–1851, Quabbin Towns Collection, box 3, 3:1.
18. Ibid., 8.

19. D. Hamilton Hurd, comp., *History of Worcester County, Massachusetts, with Biographical Sketches of Many of Its Pioneers and Prominent Men*, 2 vols. (Philadelphia: J. W. Lewis, 1899), 1:473.

20. Shakers, *The Testimonies of the Life, Character, Revelations, and Doctrines of Our Ever Blessed Mother Ann Lee, and the Elders with Her* (Hancock, Mass.: J. Tallcott and J. Deming, Jr., 1816), 93–98.

21. Dana, Mass., Baptist Church Records, 1786–1882, folder 1, AAS.

22. Shakers, *Testimonies of . . . Mother Ann Lee*, 155–58.

23. Dana, Mass., Baptist Church Records, 1768–1821, folder 1, AAS.

24. Hurd, *History of Worcester County* 2:1130–31.

25. See chapter 9 above, by John Brooke.

26. Franklin Bowditch Dexter, ed., *The Literary Diary of Ezra Stiles*, 3 vols. (New York: Charles Scribner's Sons, 1901), 2:412.

27. Nathaniel B. Sylvester, ed., *The History of the Connecticut Valley in Massachusetts*, 2 vols. (Philadelphia: L. H. Everts, 1879), 1:256.

28. Ibid.

29. Alice Mary Baldwin, *The New England Clergy and the American Revolution* (Durham, N.C.: Duke Univ. Press, 1928), 158–59; Caleb Butler, *History of the Town of Groton, Mass., including Pepperell and Shirley* (Boston: T. R. Marvin, 1848), 184; Francis Everett Blake, *History of the Town of Princeton, Massachusetts* (Princeton, Mass.: Published by the town, 1915), 1:148–50; Hurd, *History of Worcester County* 1:473, 522.

30. Blake, *History of Princeton* 1:145–57.

31. Stephen A. Marini, "Rehearsal for Revival: Sacred Singing and the Great Awakening in America," in Joyce Irwin, ed., *Sacred Sound: Music and Religion in Theory and Practice* (Chico, Calif.: Scholars Press, 1983), 73.

32. On the psalmody question, see ibid., and Isaac Watts, "A Short Essay toward the Improvement of Psalmody," *The Work of the Rev. Isaac Watts, D.D.*, 9 vols. (Leeds: Edward Baines, 1813), 9:1–26.

33. On late eighteenth-century New England Calvinism, see Frank Hugh Foster, *A Genetic History of the New England Theology* (Chicago: Univ. of Chicago Press, 1907), 107–272; Joseph Haroutunian, *Piety versus Moralism: The Passing of the New England Theology* (New York: Henry Holt, 1932).

34. Conrad Wright, *The Beginnings of Unitarianism in America* (Boston: Starr King Press, 1955), 288–91.

35. The best treatment of New England Arminianism is ibid. Ministerial data are taken from ibid., 281–88.

36. On the Separates and Separate Baptists, see C. C. Goen, *Revivalism and Separatism in New England, 1740–1800* (New Haven: Yale Univ. Press, 1962); McLoughlin, *New England Dissent*.

37. Isaac Backus, *A Church History of New England . . . with a Particular History of the Baptist Churches* (Boston: Manning and Loring, 1796), 3:190–

96. On the Shaftesbury Association, see Stephen Wright, *History of the Shaftesbury Baptist Association* (Troy, N.Y.: A. G. Johnson, 1823), 1–23.

38. Backus, *Church History* 3:93–96; Stephen A. Marini, *Radical Sects of Revolutionary New England* (Cambridge, Mass.: Harvard Univ. Press, 1982), 40–62.

39. Backus, *Church History* 3:93–96; Joseph S. Clark, *A Historical Sketch of the Congregational Churches in Massachusetts, from 1620 to 1858* (Boston: Congregational Board of Publication, 1858), 215–23.

40. Samuel Stillman, *A Sermon Preached before the Honorable Council* (Boston: Fleets and Gill, 1779).

41. Backus, *Church History* 3:186–89.

42. *Minutes of the Warren (Baptist) Association, at Their Annual Convention, Held at Mr. Blood's Meetinghouse in Newton, 1786* (Charlestown, Mass.: John W. Allen, 1786).

43. McLoughlin, *New England Dissent* 1:501–2, 2:1114–15.

44. See Thomas Baldwin, *Open Communion Examined* (Windsor, Vt.: Spooner, 1789) and *A Brief Vindication of . . . Particular Communion* (Boston: Manning and Loring, 1794).

45. Hurd, *History of Worcester County* 1:164.

46. Thompson, *History of the Presbyterian Churches*, 10.

47. See John Murray, *The Life of John Murray, Written by Himself* (Boston: Munroe and Francis, 1816).

48. Marini, *Radical Sects*, 68–69, 72–75.

49. Ibid., 75–80, 88–94, 127–32.

50. Ibid., 127–35.

51. On covenantalism, see Perry Miller, *The New England Mind: The Seventeenth Century* (New York: Macmillan, 1939).

52. William G. McLoughlin, ed., *Isaac Backus on Church, State, and Calvinism: Pamphlets, 1754–1789* (Cambridge, Mass.: Harvard Univ. Press, 1968), 443–44.

53. Simeon Howard, *A Sermon Preached before the Honorable Council* (Boston: Gill, 1780); Henry Cumings, *A Sermon Preached before His Honor Thomas Cushing* (Boston: Fleets, 1783); William Symmes, *A Sermon Preached before His Honor Thomas Cushing* (Boston: Adams and Nourse, 1785); Moses Hemmenway, *A Sermon Preached before His Excellency John Hancock* (Boston: Edes, 1784).

54. Joseph Lyman, *A Sermon Preached before His Excellency James Bowdoin* (Boston: Adams and Nourse, 1786), 25.

55. Ibid., 36.

56. Ibid., 38.

57. On Samuel Ely, see Franklin Bowditch Dexter, ed., *Biographical Sketches of the Graduates of Yale College*, 6 vols. (New York: Holt, 1885–

1912), 3:67–69; Robert E. Moody, "Samuel Ely: Forerunner of Shays," *New England Quarterly* 5 (1932): 105–34.

58. Samuel Ely, *Two Sermons Preached at Somers, March 18, 1770, When the Church and People Were under Peculiar Trials* (Hartford: Ebenezer Watson, 1771), iii, 13.

59. Ibid., 62.

60. Samuel Ely, *The Deformity of a Hideous Monster, Discovered in the Province of Maine* (Boston: n.p., 1797), 13.

61. Szatmary, 61; William G. McLoughlin, ed., *The Diary of Isaac Backus*, 3 vols. (Providence: Brown Univ. Press, 1979), 2:1133.

62. *Diary of Isaac Backus* 2:1133.

63. McLoughlin, *Isaac Backus on Church, State, and Calvinism*, 443–44.

64. Ibid., 444.

65. Ibid., 445.

66. Shakers, *The Testimonies of . . . Mother Ann Lee*, 371–72.

67. Christopher Babbitt, *To His Excellency John Hancock* (n.p., 1787).

11. IN SHAYS'S SHADOW: Separation and Ratification of the Constitution in Maine

1. William Widgery to George Thatcher, Boston, Feb. 8, 1788, William Goodwin, ed., "Thatcher Papers," *Historical Magazine*, 2d ser., 6 (1869): 270–71.

2. Jonathan Elliot, ed., *The Debates in the Several State Conventions on the Adoption of the Federal Constitution*, 2d ed., rev., 5 vols. (1888; rept. New York: Burt Franklin, 1968), 2:182.

3. Samuel P. Savage to George Thatcher, Weston, Feb. 17, 1788, "Thatcher Papers," 338.

4. David Sewall to George Thatcher, York, Feb. 11, 1788, ibid., 271.

5. Jeremiah Hill to George Thatcher, Biddeford, Feb. 28, 1788, ibid., 342.

6. Thomas B. Wait to George Thatcher, Portland, Feb. 29, 1788, ibid., 343.

7. For background on Samuel Thompson, see Nathan Goold, "General Samuel Thompson of Brunswick and Topsham, Maine," *Maine Historical Society Collections*, 3d ser., 1 (1904): 423–58; George A. and Henry W. Wheeler, *History of Brunswick, Topsham, and Harpswell, Maine* (Boston: Alfred Mudge & Son, 1878), 811–16.

8. Charles E. Allen, *History of Dresden, Maine* (Augusta, Me.: *Kennebec Journal*, 1931), 290–93; James H. Maguire, ed., "A Critical Edition of Edward Parry's Journal, Mar. 28, 1775, to Aug. 23, 1777" (Ph.D. diss., Indiana Univ. at Bloomington, 1970).

9. Donald Yerxa, "Admiral Samuel Graves and the Falmouth Affair: A Case Study in British Imperial Pacification, 1775" (M.A. thesis, Univ. of Maine at Orono, 1974). For a much shorter version, see Donald Yerxa, "The Burning of Falmouth, 1775: A Case Study in British Imperial Pacification," *Maine Historical Society Quarterly* 14 (Winter 1975): 119–61. For the Whig sack of Falmouth, see "Letter from Rev. Jacob Bailey in 1775, Describing the Destruction of Falmouth, Maine," *Maine Historical Society Collections*, 1st ser., 5 (1857): 449; also Gorham Town Records, Oct. 28, 30, 1775, Maine State Archives, Augusta.

10. Compare Cumberland County Convention to the General Court, Falmouth, Sept. 17, 1779, and Representation of the Committees of Cumberland County, Cumberland, Oct. 21, 1779, James P. Baxter, ed., *Documentary History of the State of Maine*, 24 vols. (Portland: Maine Historical Society, 1913), 17:143–46, 401–2 (hereafter cited as *Doc. Hist. Me.*).

11. Goold, "Samuel Thompson," 456–57.

12. Jonas Clark[, Jr.,] to Jonas Clark[, Sr.], Falmouth, Oct. 17, 1785, Jonas Clark Papers, MS Division, Library of Congress; [Daniel Davis], "The Proceedings of Two Conventions, Held at Portland, to Consider the Expedience of a Separate Government in the District of Maine," MHS *Collections* 4 (1795): 25.

13. Ronald F. Banks, *Maine Becomes a State: The Movement to Separate Maine from Massachusetts, 1785–1820* (1970; rpt. Middletown, Conn.: Wesleyan Univ. Press, 1970), 5.

14. William Willis, ed., *Journals of the Rev. Thomas Smith and the Rev. Samuel Deane* (Portland, Me.: Joseph S. Bailey, 1849), 252–54.

15. *Falmouth Gazette*, Feb. 5, 1785 (name changes to *Cumberland Gazette*).

16. Ibid., Dec. 10, 1785.

17. *Cumberland Gazette*, Aug. 31, 1786.

18. *Doc. Hist. Me.* 21:49–50.

19. *Falmouth Gazette*, Dec. 17, 1785.

20. Ibid., July 9, 1785.

21. Ibid., Sept. 3, 1785. The *Cumberland Gazette*, Apr. 18, 1788, carried an article reprinted from a Worcester paper with the news that if Maine's separation movement was successful the new state would be named "Columbia" in honor of Christopher Columbus, after whom the continent should have been named, rather than "Americanus"—a mere "adventurer after riches."

22. *Cumberland Gazette*, Sept. 28, 1786.

23. Ibid., Sept. 14, 1786.

24. Ibid., Sept. 21, Nov. 24, 1786.

25. Ibid., Nov. 1786–Mar. 1787 passim.

26. [Davis], "Proceedings of Two Conventions," 28.

27. Ibid.

28. Gordon Kershaw, *The Kennebec Proprietors, 1749–1775: "Gentlemen of*

Large Property and Judicious Men" (Somersworth, N.H.: New Hampshire Publishing Co., 1975), 290–93; Alan Taylor, "Liberty-Men and White Indians: Frontier Migration, Popular Protest, and Pursuit of Property in the Wake of the American Revolution" (Ph.D. diss., Brandeis Univ., 1986), chap. 4.

29. [Davis], "Proceedings of Two Conventions," 33.
30. Ibid., 29.
31. Ibid., 39.
32. Ibid., 36–37.
33. Ibid., 40.
34. Ibid., 32–33.
35. *Cumberland Gazette,* Feb. 9, 1787.
36. [Davis], "Proceedings of Two Conventions," 33.
37. Ibid.
38. *Cumberland Gazette,* Mar. 23, 1787.
39. Jackson Turner Main, *The Anti-Federalists: Critics of the Constitution, 1781–1788* (1961; rept. Chicago: Quadrangle Press, 1964), 207 n.56.
40. Christopher Gore to George Thatcher, Boston, Jan. 9, 1788, "Thatcher Papers," 263.
41. *Cumberland Gazette,* Sept. 13, 1787.
42. Thomas B. Wait to George Thatcher, Portland, Feb. 29, 1788, "Thatcher Papers," 342–43; see also *Falmouth Gazette,* May 14, 1785.
43. Silas Lee to George Thatcher, Biddeford, Jan. 23, 1788, "Thatcher Papers," 267.
44. Hall, 178 n.26.
45. [Davis], "The Proceedings of Two Conventions," 33.
46. Jeremiah Hill to George Thatcher, Jan. 1, 1788, "Thatcher Papers," 260–61.
47. David Sewall to George Thatcher, York, Feb. 11, 1788, ibid., 271.
48. Ibid.
49. Elliot, *Debates* 2:61, 80.
50. Ibid., 2:33–34.
51. Ibid., 2:35.
52. Ibid., 2:80.
53. Ibid., 2:15.
54. Ibid., 2:61, 80.
55. Ibid., 2:96.
56. Ibid., 2:107.
57. Ibid., 2:140.
58. Adele E. Plachta, "The Privileged and the Poor: A History of the District of Maine, 1771–1793" (Ph.D. diss., Univ. of Maine at Orono, 1975), 170–74; Main, *The Anti-Federalist,* 203–4.
59. *Cumberland Gazette,* Jan. 22, 29, 1789.

60. Ibid., Jan. 22, 1789.
61. Ibid., Jan. 29, 1789.
62. Banks, *Maine Becomes a State*, 24.
63. Goold, "Samuel Thompson," 456. Thompson is listed as part owner of a vessel in William A. Baker, *A Maritime History of Bath, Maine and the Kennebec River Region* (Bath: Maine Research Society of Bath, 1973), 1:121, and among the incorporators of a canal linking the New Meadows River to Merry Meeting Bay (*Doc. Hist. Me.*, 22:339).
64. Banks, *Maine Becomes a State*, chap. 2.

12. THE CONFIDENCE MAN AND THE PREACHER: The Cultural Politics of Shays's Rebellion

1. Szatmary, 67; Robert E. Moody, "Samuel Ely: Forerunner of Shays," *New England Quarterly* 5 (1932): 109; David Humphreys et al., *The Anarchiad*, in Vernon L. Parrington, ed., *The Connecticut Wits* (New York: Harcourt, Brace, 1926); Massachusetts General Court, Proclamation, "A Horrid and Unnatural Rebellion Exists within This Commonwealth," Feb. 4, 1787, in *Acts and Laws of the Commonwealth of Massachusetts . . .* , 13 vols., (Boston: Wright and Potter, 1890–94), 4:424–26; Thomas Jefferson to Abigail Adams, Feb. 22, 1787, in Julian P. Boyd et al., eds., *The Papers of Thomas Jefferson*, 23 vols. to date (Princeton, N.J.: Princeton Univ. Press, 1950–), 11:174.

2. Massachusetts Supreme Judicial Court Docket Book, 1781–82: 179–81, Case of *Commonwealth of Massachusetts* v. *Samuel Ely*, Apr. 1782, Northampton Session, Judicial Archives, at Massachusetts State Archives building, Columbia Point, Boston; Moody, "Samuel Ely," 108; "Some particulars of the proceedings of the Mob, at Concord," *Massachusetts Centinel*, Sept. 1786; *Hampshire Gazette*, Sept. 27, 1786; "Hampshire County Black List," Robert Treat Paine Papers, box 23, MHS; General Rufus Putnam to Governor James Bowdoin, Jan. 8, 1787, in C. O. Parmenter, *History of Pelham, Mass., from 1738 to 1898, Including the Early History of Prescott . . .* (Amherst: Carpenter and Morehouse, 1898), 384–90, 397; "Miscellany," *Massachusetts Centinel*, Jan. 17, 1787; Gregory H. Nobles, "The Politics of Patriarchy in Shays's Rebellion: The Case of Henry McCulloch," in Peter Benes, ed., *Families and Children*, Dublin Seminar for New England Folklife Annual Proceedings 1985 (Boston: Boston Univ., 1987), 37–47.

3. Constance Rourke, *American Humor: A Study of the National Character* (New York: Harcourt, Brace, 1931), 3–32; Douglas C. Wilson, "Goffe, Whalley, and the Legend of Hadley," *New England Quarterly* 60 (1987): 515–18; "An Essay on the Difference of Manners in the Town and the Country," *Massachusetts Centinel*, Mar. 24, 1784.

4. Stephen Burroughs, *Memoirs of Stephen Burroughs*, 2 vols. (Hanover,

N.H.: Benjamin True, 1798; rept. of 1924 ed., Boston: Northeastern Univ. Press, 1988, with a foreword by Philip F. Gura). For the publication history of Burroughs's *Memoirs*, see the *National Union Catalog of Pre-1956 Imprints*, briefly summarized in Gura's foreword, xx–xxii. Burroughs went through several waves of popularity. First issued in 1798, his book was reprinted in some ten editions, both complete and abridged, around the War of 1812, when Burroughs, then a resident of Canada, gained notoriety as an enemy of his homeland. Putting his skill at counterfeiting into the service of the British government, Burroughs flooded the Northeast with bogus American money. His fame continued throughout the antebellum era. Boston publishers issued three editions from 1832 to 1840; another three came out in New York City during the decade before the Civil War. The Connecticut Valley remembered the scoundrel, too; an Amherst printer reprinted the book in 1858. Burroughs was then forgotten until the 1920s, when the poet Robert Frost, who knew a confidence man when he saw him, resuscitated the *Memoirs*, writing a preface to an edition issued by Dial Press in 1924. For brief studies of Burroughs, see Lawrence Buell, *New England Literary Culture: From Revolution through Renaissance* (Cambridge and New York: Cambridge Univ. Press, 1986), 339–40; Jay Fliegelman, *Prodigals and Pilgrims: The American Revolution against Patriarchal Authority, 1750–1800* (Cambridge and New York: Cambridge Univ. Press, 1982), 245–47; Daniel E. Williams, "Rogues, Rascals and Scoundrels: The Underworld Literature of Early America," *American Studies* 24 (1983): 5–19. See also Gary H. Lindberg, *The Confidence Man in American Literature* (New York: Oxford Univ. Press, 1982).

    5. G. Thomas Tanselle, *Royall Tyler* (Cambridge, Mass.: Harvard Univ. Press, 1967), 1–19; Marius B. Péladeau, ed., *The Prose of Royall Tyler* (Montpelier: Vermont Historical Society, 1972), 453.

    6. Tanselle, *Royall Tyler*, 19–22; Royall Tyler to Major General Lincoln, Feb. 20, 1787, in "Bowdoin and Temple Papers," MHS *Collections*, 7th ser., 6 (1907): 144; Royall Tyler to Major General Lincoln, Feb. 18, 1787, MA, 318:232 (I am grateful to Sidney Kaplan of Northampton, Mass., for loaning me his photostatic copies of Tyler's letters); Michael Bellisles, "Shays in Exile," paper given at the Amherst College–Historic Deerfield Conference on Shays's Rebellion, Nov. 1986, 4.

    7. Royall Tyler, *The Contrast* (1787), in Montrose J. Moses, ed., *Representative Plays by American Dramatists*, 3 vols. (New York: E. P. Dutton, 1918–25), 1:433–98; Constance Rourke, *The Roots of American Culture and Other Essays* (New York: Harcourt, Brace, 1942), 114–24; Richard M. Dorson, "The Yankee on the Stage—A Folk Hero of American Drama," *New England Quarterly* 13 (1940): 467–93.

8. Royall Tyler to the Governor and Council of Vermont, Feb. 17, 1787, Royall Tyler Collection, MSS 8-9787167, Vermont Historical Society.

9. "Charge of the Chief Justice [William Cushing] to the GRAND-JURY of the County of MIDDLESEX," *Hampshire Gazette,* Nov. 29, 1786; Massachusetts General Court, *Address from the General Court to the People of the Commonwealth of Massachusetts, November 14, 1786* (Boston: Adams and Nourse, 1786); Szatmary, 57, 75; Peter S. Onuf, *The Origins of the Federal Republic: Jurisdictional Controversies in the United States, 1775–1787* (Philadelphia: Univ. of Pennsylvania Press, 1983), 182–83; Joseph Parker Warren, "The Confederation and the Shays Rebellion," *American Historical Review* 11 (1905): 42–67; General Rufus Putnam to Governor James Bowdoin, Jan. 8, 1787, in Parmenter, *History of Pelham,* 395–98. On the obsession of late eighteenth-century Americans with deceit and hypocrisy, see Gordon S. Wood, "Conspiracy and the Paranoid Style: Causality and Deceit in the Eighteenth Century," *WMQ,* 3d ser., 39 (1982): 401–42.

10. Edward Countryman, *The American Revolution* (New York: Hill and Wang, 1985), 214–45; Robert A. Gross, *The Minutemen and Their World* (New York: Hill and Wang, 1976), 68–108; Gregory H. Nobles, *Divisions throughout the Whole: Politics and Society in Hampshire County, Massachusetts, 1740–1775* (New York and Cambridge: Cambridge Univ. Press, 1983); Stephen A. Marini, *Radical Sects of Revolutionary New England* (Cambridge, Mass.: Harvard Univ. Press, 1982).

11. Burroughs, *Memoirs,* 45–50.

12. Parmenter, *History of Pelham,* 297–320; Burroughs, *Memoirs,* 52–54.

13. John L. Brooke, chapter 9 above, table 9.1; Stephen A. Marini, chapter 10 above; Marini, *Radical Sects,* 35–37; Sydney E. Ahlstrom, *A Religious History of the American People* (New Haven: Yale Univ. Press, 1972), 442–59.

14. Marini, *Radical Sects,* 11–24; Nobles, *Divisions throughout the Whole,* 36–58, 75–106.

15. Nobles, *Divisions throughout the Whole,* 54–56, 81–84; Marini, chapter 10 above; James W. Schmotter, "The Irony of Clerical Professionalism: New England's Congregational Clergy and the Great Awakening," *American Quarterly* 31 (1979): 148–68.

16. Marini, *Radical Sects,* 14–15; Donald Weber, *Rhetoric and History in Revolutionary New England* (New York: Oxford Univ. Press, 1988), 26–28; Harry S. Stout, *The New England Soul: Preaching and Religious Culture in Colonial New England* (New York: Oxford Univ. Press, 1986), 190–91; William B. Sprague, *Annals of the American Pulpit; or Commemorative Notices of Distinguished American Clergymen of Various Denominations, from the Early Settlement of the Country to the Close of the Year Eighteen Hundred and Fifty Five.*

With Historical Introduction, vols. 1–2, *Trinitarian-Congregational* (New York: R. Carter and Brothers, 1857), 2:73; William T. Youngs, *God's Messengers: Religious Leadership in Colonial New England, 1700–1750* (Baltimore: Johns Hopkins Univ. Press, 1976), 57; Charles Royster, *A Revolutionary People at War: The Continental Army and American Character, 1775–1783* (Chapel Hill: Univ. of North Carolina Press, 1979), 162–63.

17. Benjamin Franklin, *Autobiography,* ed. Leonard W. Labaree (New Haven: Yale Univ. Press, 1964), 167–68; Nobles, *Divisions throughout the Whole,* 52–53.

18. Sprague, *Annals* 1:530–31.

19. Richard L. Bushman, "American High-Style and Vernacular Cultures," in Jack P. Greene and J. R. Pole, eds., *Colonial British America: Essays on the New History of the Early Modern Era* (Baltimore: Johns Hopkins Univ. Press, 1984), 345–83; Stephanie G. Wolf, "Rarer than Riches: Gentility in Eighteenth-Century America," paper delivered at conference on "The Portrait in Eighteenth-Century America," National Portrait Gallery, Oct. 16, 1987; Robert A. East, *Business Enterprise in the American Revolutionary Era* (New York: Columbia Univ. Press, 1938); Richard B. Morris, *The Forging of the Union, 1781–1789* (New York: Harper & Row, 1987), 164–65; Gordon S. Wood, *The Creation of the American Republic, 1776–1787* (Chapel Hill: Univ. of North Carolina Press, 1969), 65–82, 393–403; Gordon S. Wood, "Interests and Disinterestedness in the Making of the Constitution," in Richard Beeman, Stephen Botein, and Edward C. Carter II, eds., *Beyond Confederation: Origins of the Constitution and American National Identity* (Chapel Hill: Univ. of North Carolina Press, 1987), 77–81.

20. Kenneth Silverman, *A Cultural History of the American Revolution* (New York: Thomas Y. Crowell, 1976), 504–9; James Warren to John Adams, Boston, June 23, 1779, Worthington C. Ford, ed., *Warren-Adams Letters . . . John Adams, Samuel Adams, and James Warren, 1743–1814,* 2 vols., MHS *Collections,* 72–73 (Boston, 1917–25), 1:105; Emory Elliott, *Revolutionary Writers: Literature and Authority in the New Republic, 1725–1810* (New York: Oxford Univ. Press, 1982), 64–65; "Anecdotes of Daniel Shaise, Leader of the Insurgents," *Massachusetts Centinel,* Dec. 2, 1786; Robert A. Gross, "Daniel Shays and Lafayette's Sword," *OAH Newsletter* 15 (Nov. 1987): 8–9.

21. Elliott, *Revolutionary Writers,* 47–48, 64–65; "A Farmer," "Cause of, and cure for, hard times," *American Museum* 1 (1787): 11–13, rept. from *Massachusetts Centinel,* June 24, 1786; James A. Henretta, "Families and Farms: *Mentalité* in Pre-Industrial America," *WMQ,* 3d ser., 35 (1978): 22–23; Carole Shammas, "How Self-Sufficient Was Early America?" *Journal of Interdisciplinary History* 13 (1982): 247–49.

22. Burroughs, *Memoirs,* 1; Franklin Bowditch Dexter, ed., *Biographical Sketches of the Graduates of Yale College,* 6 vols. (New York: Holt, 1885–

1912), 2:454–56; Frederick Chase, *A History of Dartmouth College and the Town of Hanover, New Hampshire* (Cambridge, Mass.: J. Wilson, 1891), 195–204; William G. McLoughlin, *New England Dissent, 1630–1833: The Baptists and the Separation of Church and State*, 2 vols. (Cambridge, Mass.: Harvard Univ. Press, 1971), 2:846–48.

23. Brooke, chapter 9 above; Dexter, *Biographical Sketches* 2:750–54; Sprague, *Annals* 1:602–6; Burroughs, *Memoirs*, 14.

24. Burroughs, *Memoirs*, 6, 24.

25. Ibid., xv, 1–2; Marini, *Radical Sects*.

26. Burroughs, *Memoirs*, 1, 3, 52–54, 58–60, 129; Daniel Shelton, "'Elementary Feelings': Pelham, Massachusetts, in Rebellion" (Honors thesis, Amherst College, 1981), 94–118.

27. Stephen Burroughs, *Sermon, Delivered in Rutland, on a Hay Mow, to His Auditory the Pelhamites, at the Time When a Mob of Them . . . Shut Him into a Barn . . . When He Ascended a Hay Mow . . . and Delivered to Them the Following Sermon*, appendix to his *Memoirs* (Hanover, N.H.: Benjamin True, 1798), rept. in Parmenter, *History of Pelham*, 336–40; Neil Harris, *Humbug: The Art of P. T. Barnum* (Boston and Toronto: Little, Brown, 1973). Although Burroughs operated on the rule that "there is a sucker born every minute," he never received notice in P. T. Barnum's compendium of first-class frauds, *The Humbugs of the World. An Account of Humbugs, Delusions, Impositions, Quackeries, Deceits, and Deceivers Generally. In All Ages* (New York: Carleton, 1865).

28. Burroughs, *Sermon*, in Parmenter, *History*, 338–40. Later in the *Memoirs*, Burroughs printed a letter from "an old practitioner of the law" in Massachusetts, in support of the view that Burroughs's trial in 1790 for attempted rape was a travesty of justice. According to Philip Gura, that lawyer was Robert Treat Paine, attorney general of the Commonwealth in 1787, who drew up the notorious "Black List" against the Shaysite leaders and spearheaded the prosecution of the rebels in the courts. Burroughs found his friends in the enemies of the backcountry (Burroughs, *Memoirs*, xvi).

29. Burroughs, *Memoirs*, 3–5, 30; Daniel E. Williams, "In Defense of Self: Author and Authority in the *Memoirs of the Notorious Stephen Burroughs*," *Early American Literature* 25 (1990): 96–122; Daniel A. Cohen, "Pillars of Salt: The Transformation of New England Crime Literature, 1674–1860" (Ph.D. diss., Brandeis Univ., 1988), 298–304; Jean-Christophe Agnew, *Worlds Apart: The Market and the Theatre in Anglo-American Thought, 1550–1750* (Cambridge and New York: Cambridge Univ. Press, 1986), 159–69; Daniel Stebbins Notebook, 44–45, Forbes Library, Northampton, Mass.; Charles Brockden Brown, *Arthur Mervyn; or Memoirs of the Year 1793* (Philadelphia: H. Maxwell, 1799).

30. Joseph J. Ellis, *After the Revolution: Profiles of Early American Culture* (New York: Norton, 1979), 129–33; Silverman, *Cultural History*, 545–56.

31. James Russell Trumbull, *History of Northampton, Massachusetts, from Its Settlement in 1654*, 2 vols. (Northampton, Mass.: Press of Gazette Printing Co., 1898–1902), 1:479–82; Richard D. Birdsall, *Berkshire County: A Cultural History* (New Haven: Yale Univ. Press, 1959), 180–81; Silverman, *Cultural History*, 552–53.

32. Silverman, *Cultural History*, 555–57.

33. Tyler, *The Contrast*, 471; Silverman, *Cultural History*, 560–62; Michael T. Gilmore, "The Drama of the Early Republic," in *Cambridge History of American Literature*, vol. 1 (forthcoming).

34. Tyler, *The Contrast*, 460, 462, 478–79, 496.

35. My interpretation differs from that of Richard S. Pressman, who views Tyler's satire of Manly as a way of subordinating the rural patriot-gentleman to the sophisticated, urban, mercantile class that constitutes the audience for the play. See Pressman, "Class Positioning and Shays' Rebellion: Resolving the Contradictions of *The Contrast*," *Early American Literature* 21 (1986): 87–102. See also Silverman, *Cultural History*, 563.

36. Albert Mathews, "Brother Jonathan," Colonial Society of Massachusetts *Publications* 7 (1901): 111; Dorson, "Yankee on the Stage," 478–80; Rourke, *Roots of American Culture*, 117–23; Tanselle, *Royall Tyler*, 71–72.

37. Tyler, *The Contrast*, 464–65, 472–75.

38. Ibid., 465.

CONTRIBUTORS

JOHN L. BROOKE is Associate Professor of History at Tufts University. His first book, *The Heart of the Commonwealth: Society and Political Culture in Worcester County, Massachusetts, 1713–1861* (1989), received the Merle Curti Prize from the Organization of American Historians. He is currently working on a book examining the intellectual origins of Mormon cosmology.

RICHARD BUEL, JR., teaches at Wesleyan University, where he is Professor of History and associate editor of *History and Theory*. He is the author of *Securing the Revolution* (1972), *Dear Liberty* (1980), and, with the late Joy D. Buel, *The Way of Duty* (1984).

JONATHAN M. CHU is Associate Professor of History at the University of Massachusetts-Boston. Author of *Neighbors, Friends, or Madmen: Quakers and the Puritan Adjustment to Heterodoxy in Seventeenth-Century Massachusetts* (1985), he is currently writing on law and lawyers in colonial Massachusetts.

JOSEPH A. ERNST is Professor of History at York University. He is the author of *Money and Politics in America, 1755–1775: A Study in the Currency Act of 1764 and the Political Economy of Revolution* (1973).

ROBERT A. GROSS is Director of American Studies and Professor of American Studies and History at the College of William and Mary. His first book, *The Minutemen and Their World* (1976), won the Bancroft Prize in American History. Author of *Books and Libraries in Thoreau's Concord: Two Essays* (1988), he is completing a community study of Concord, Massachusetts, during the era of Emerson and Thoreau, entitled *The Transcendentalists and Their World*.

JAMES LEAMON is Professor of History at Bates College. Coeditor of *Maine in the Early Republic* (1989), he is currently completing a history of the American Revolution in Maine.

MICHAEL LIENESCH is Associate Professor of Political Science at the University of North Carolina at Chapel Hill. He is the author of *New Order of the Ages: Time, the Constitution, and the Making of American Political Thought* (1988) and coeditor of *Ratifying the Constitution* (1989).

STEPHEN A. MARINI is Professor of Religion at Wellesley College and Adjunct Professor of Church History at Weston School of Theology in Cambridge, Massachusetts. Author of *Radical Sects of Revolutionary New England* (1983), he is currently completing a large-scale study of religion and politics in the era of the American Revolution.

GREGORY H. NOBLES is Associate Professor of History at the Georgia Institute of Technology. His first book, *Divisions throughout the Whole: Politics and Society in Hampshire County, Massachusetts, 1740–1775* (1983), and much of his subsequent research dealt with the social and economic development of rural society in western Massachusetts, ca. 1700–1850. He is now working on a broader study of American frontier regions.

STEPHEN E. PATTERSON is Professor in History at the University of New Brunswick. The author of *Political Parties in Revolutionary Massachusetts* (1973), he continues to explore the making of the new republic in two works in progress, *The Origins of American Conservatism* and *American Revolution*.

WILLIAM PENCAK is Professor of History at Penn State University at Ogontz. He is the author of *War, Politics, and Revolution in Provincial Massachusetts* (1981), *America's Burke: The Mind of Thomas Hutchinson* (1982), and *For God and Country: The American Legion, 1919–1941* (1989).

ALAN TAYLOR is Associate Professor of History at Boston University. He recently published his study of agrarian settlement and popular protest on the Maine frontier, *Liberty Men and Great Proprietors: The Revolutionary Settlement on the Maine Frontier, 1760–1820* (1990). He is currently at work on a study of Cooperstown, New York, and the Cooper family, entitled *William Cooper's Town: Power and Persuasion on the Early American Frontier*.

INDEX

Abercrombie, Robert, 243
"Act for the Prevention of Vice and Immorality," 316
Adams, Abigail, 178
Adams, Charles Francis, 122
Adams, John: on government, 172, 173; and James Warren, 76, 170, 309; and Jefferson, 182; on "Mercantile Interest," 58; as president, 159; and Royall Tyler, 301; on Shays's Rebellion, 182
Adams, John Quincy, 134
Adams, Samuel, 20, 124, 141, 169, 170
Adams (family), 138, 301
Adams, Mass., 129, 232, 277
Address to the Inhabitants of New England concerning the Present Bloody Controversy Therein, 270–73
"Address to the People," 59, 135, 137, 265
Advertising, 103, 107–8, 109
Agriculture, 61, 192–93, 207
Ahlstrom, Sydney, 240
Albany, N.Y., 262
Albion, Maine, 152–53
Alden, Noah, 258
Alexander, Elijah, 88
Alexander v. Taft, 91
Alford, Mass., 232, 263, 267, 277
Allen, Thomas, 258, 277
American Antiquarian Society, 122
American Museum, 309
Ames, Fisher, 169, 181
Amherst, Mass.: Am Rev. in, 209; clergy in, 209; Friends of Government in, 202, 233; Loyalists in, 209; political culture of, 199; religion in, 233, 251–52; Shaysites in, 129, 130, 233
Amherst College, 6
Ammidowns (militia officer), 206
Anarchiad, The, 177–78, 297
Anarchy: conservative republicans / Friends of Government on, 12, 143, 152, 171–72, 177, 179; Federalists on, 179; radical republicans on, 170, 174; and republicanism, 316
Andover, Mass., 265
Andrews, Thomas, 95–96

Androscoggin River, 284
Anglicans, 188
Annan, David, 260
Annapolis, Md., 114, 179
Antifederalism, 19, 152, 206, 240
Antifederalists: on Confederation, 175, 180, 292, 293; on Congress, 292; on Daniel Shays, 180, 181–82; on elections, 292–93; and Federalists, 291, 292, 294, 295; Friends of Government as, 4; Henry Knox on, 102; and Jefferson, 180; in Maine, 281–83, 291–94; in Mass., 102, 176, 179, 294; in N.Y., 176; on paper money, 291; radical republicans as, 175; on rebellion (concept), 180–81; and republicanism, 282–83; and Shays's Rebellion, 175–76, 180–82; on slavery, 293; on state debt, 291; and U.S. Constitution, 176, 180–81, 292, 293
Apocalypticism, 271
"Appeal to the People," 289
Aristocracy, 142, 166, 172
Aristocrats, 113, 168. *See also* Elites
Arminianism, 254–55
Arminians, 265, 271–72
Army, Continental: Bostonians in, 133; chaplains in, 307; Daniel Shays in, 1, 2–3, 309; Friends of Government in, 13; mentioned, 132; officers of, 48–49, 103; clothing of, 128–29; payments for, 48–49, 72, 103; provisions for, 102, 133; and religion, 209, 210; soldiers of, 72, 95, 103
Army, standing, 292
Arsenal, federal. *See* Shays's Rebellion: in Springfield, Mass.
Articles of Confederation, 4, 8, 48, 54, 113–14, 175
Artisans: in backcountry, 190; and banks, 65; in Boston, 110–11, 281; as clergy, 256; and culture, 316; and debt, 86, 145; employment of, 103; and Federalism, 113, 114; interests of, 58, 70; as Jeffersonians, 361 n.25; and merchants, 113; and paper money, 61; as

393

Artisans (*continued*)
  Shaysites, 145; and taxes, 145; and U.S. Constitution, 281; in Worcester Co., Mass., 94
Ashburnham, Mass., 234
Ashfield, Mass., 233, 259, 276
Atholl, Mass., 234
Augusta, Maine, 153, 154, 156
Austin, Benjamin, 97–98
Avery, Joseph, 267, 277
Ayres, Oliver, 277

Babbitt, Christopher, 272–73
Backcountry: advertising in, 103, 107–8; agriculture in, 14, 192–93; and Am. Rev., 13–14, 20, 22, 102, 134–35, 203; artisans in, 102–3, 190; bankers in, 65; Baptists in, 17, 210–11, 262, 272, 305; British factors in, 106; change in, 16, 18, 22, 102; class in, 16, 136, 150, 189, 199; clergy in, 200, 249, 250; community in, 16, 18, 186; Congregationalism in, 17, 210–11, 241, 272, 312; of Conn., 190–91; consumers in, 107; county conventions in, 104, 135, 200; courts in, 74, 135, 199, 200–202; culture of, 7, 19–20, 103, 299, 316; debt in, 74, 104, 134–36, 193–94, 306; and eastern Mass., 12; economy of, 6, 16, 22, 134–35, 189, 199, 295; factions in, 16, 17; farmers in, 22, 123, 134, 188, 190; in literature, 19–20; Loyalists in, 199; and magistrates, 12; of Maine, 14–16, 153–60; of Mass., 187–88; and Mass. constitutions, 135–36; and Mass. government, 13, 14, 22, 71, 103, 199–200; and merchants, 9, 12, 107, 190, 217; money in, 9, 11, 109; of N.C., 188; newspapers in, 103, 107; occupations in, 102–3; of Pa., 188; political culture of, 12–16, 135, 136, 199–200, 203, 306; politics in, 7, 103, 189; and prices, 13, 70; Protestantism in, 206, 255; scholarship on, 135, 136; sects in, 16, 17–18, 210–11, 241, 305; Separates in, 17, 305; settlement of, 18, 187–88, 305; Shakers in, 17, 18, 210–11, 262, 272, 305; and Shays's Rebellion, 12–13, 20, 282; society in, 6, 13–14, 15, 16, 186, 189; specie in, 134, 136; stereotypes of, 299, 305; taxes in, 14, 74, 135, 136; towns in, 17, 20, 103, 104, 187–88, 199; trade with, 75, 106, 190; Universalists in, 17, 210–11, 262, 272, 305; and U.S. Constitution, 282; of Va., 188; wealth in, 13, 134, 190. *See also* specific places
Backus, Isaac, 257, 258, 270–73
Bailey, Isaac, 276
Baldwin, Moses, 244
Ballantine, John, 306
Ballard, Ephraim, 154
Balltown, Maine, 154
Bancroft, George, 161
Banditti. *See* Shaysites
Bangs, Edward, 82, 93–94
Bankers, 65
Bankruptcy, 10, 84
Banks, 60–66, 80, 333 n.8
Baptist Association, Shaftesbury, 259, 260
Baptist Association, Warren, 209, 213, 257, 258–59, 260
Baptists: in Bristol Co., Mass., 275; in Conn., 262; as Friends of Government, 221–22, 223, 226; in Hampshire Co., Mass., 263, 276–77; as Jeffersonians, 361 n.25; and Mass. Constitution of 1780, 222; in N.H., 311; and political theology, 270, 274; in Rehoboth, Mass., 263; and Separates, 259, and Shakers, 262; as Shaysites, 206, 221–22, 225, 226; in Shaysite towns, 17; and Shays's Rebellion, 20, 274; as Universalists, 210; in Va., 188; in Worcester Co., Mass., 224, 225, 261, 275, 277
Baptists, Calvinistic Particular, 256
Baptists, Free Will, 210, 305
Baptists, Particular, 259
Baptists, Separate, 209, 213, 239–40, 246–48, 256–62, 270–73
Baptists, Strict, 305
Barnum, P. T., 314, 319
Barre, Mass., 234, 275
Barrell, Nathaniel, 294
Bay Psalm Book, The, 253
Beals, Isaac, 226
Becket, Mass., 232
Belcher, Jonathan, 63–65
Belchertown, Mass., 131, 233
Belknap, Jeremy, 149
Bellingham, Mass., 258
Bellows, Jon, 84
Bemiss, Benjamin, 219
Bemiss (family), 219
Bender, George, 155
Bennington, Battle of, 269
Bennington, Vt., 302
Berkshire Co., Mass.: Baptists in, 209, 257, 258, 263, 277; class in, 213;

INDEX | 395

clergy in, 209, 211, 248, 250, 267, 277; Congregationalism in, 211, 248–49, 254, 277; and county conventions, 125, 127; Friends of Government in, 277; Jeffersonians in, 361 n.25; and Mass. constitution of 1778, 199–200; sects in, 209, 211, 262; Shakers in, 262, 277; Shaysites in, 277; Shays's Rebellion in, 174, 199, 287; and taxes, 329 n.43; towns in, 213, 232, 277
Berlin, Mass., 234
Bernardston, Mass., 233
Betterment Act, 159–60
Bicknell, Thomas, 87
Bidwell, Adonijah, 277
Bigelow, Daniel, 94
Bigelow, Samuel, 258
Billerica, Mass., 265
Billings, John, 130
Bill of rights (U.S. Constitution), 181, 292, 293
Bills, loan office, 63, 64
Birth of a Consumer Society, The, 107
Bisco, John, 220
Black Regiment, 205, 264
Blackstone Valley, 225
Blandford, Mass., 233
Block, Ruth, 207
Blodgett, Joseph, 276
Board of Trade, 64, 65, 66
Board of War, 73
Bolton, Mass., 234
Bonds, 67
Boston, Mass., 271, 298; and Am. Rev., 13, 106, 133, 141, 210, 246; Antifederalists in, 176; artisans in, 110–11, 281; bankers in, 65; banks in, 61; British in, 52, 68; clergy in, 253, 259; Colonial Society of Mass. in, 64; creditors in, 131, 215, 218; culture of, 14, 213, 255, 316; Daniel Shays on, 126; elections in, 114; elites in, 258, 313; ideology in, 133, 135; importers in, 108; laborers in, 62; leaders of, 61, 64; and Maine statehood, 286; Mass. legislature in, 103, 125–26, 241, 283, 286; merchants in, 69, 71, 75, 106, 110, 124, 131, 138, 301; money in, 75, 109; newspapers in, 2, 3, 107, 309; population of, 133; prices in, 62, 70, 74, 75; protests in, 70; radical republicans in, 169–70; religion in, 241, 243, 253–54, 258, 260–61, 265, 271; representation of, 114; and Shays's Rebellion, 115, 124, 138; as state capital, 1, 21, 73, 156, 213, 266–67; stores in, 96, 107; town meetings in, 71, 75; tradesmen in, 110–11; trade with, 74, 75, 192; and U.S. Constitution, 281, 282, 291–92; wholesalers in, 11
Boston Commercial Gazette, 2–3
Boston Gazette, 110
Boston Magazine, 141
Bowdoin, James: administration of, 137; Benjamin Lincoln and, 140–41; and elections of 1787, 139; and Friends of Government, 21; on Maine statehood, 285–86; merchants and, 110–11; petitions to, 138; proclamation of, 128; salary of, 117; and Shaysites, 124, 126, 127, 140–41; and Shays's Rebellion, 115, 266
Bowdoin, James, Sr., 64
Bowman, William, 95
Boylston, Mass., 234
Braintree, Mass., 138, 301
Breck, Robert, 255
Bridge, Edmund, 156, 157
Brimfield, Mass., 233
Bristol Co., Mass.: clergy in, 250; conventions in, 127; and Gov. Bowdoin, 138; petitions from, 68; religion in, 257, 263, 275
Bristol, Maine, 154
British, 68, 105–6, 116, 117, 118, 151
Broad, Aaron, 128, 205
Broad, Wilder, 153
Bromfield, Edward, Jr., 64
Brooke, John L., 16–18, 239–41, 248–51, 361 n.25
Brookfield, Mass., 213; creditors in, 218, 220, 221, 223; Daniel Shays in, 194; debtors in, 218; economy of, 194–95; elites in, 17, 217–18, 220, 221; Friends of Government in, 17, 132, 194–95, 214, 234; religion in, 214, 218, 221, 223, 234; Rev. veterans in, 194; Shaysites in, 214, 234
Brooks, John, 133
Brown, Richard, 161
Brunswick, Maine, 283, 284
Buckland, Mass., 233
Bullard, John, 275
Bullard, Jonathan, 220
Bullion, 49, 327 n.16. *See also* Currency; Money; Money, paper; Specie; *specific types of money*
Bunker Hill, Battle of, 130
Bunyan, John, 299
Burgoyne, John, 130
Burns, James MacGregor, 161

Burroughs, Eden, 243, 244, 300, 304, 311, 312
Burroughs, Mrs Eden, 300
Burroughs, Stephen, 303, 308; capture of, 244, 313–14; as "clergyman," 19, 212, 243–44, 299–300, 304–5, 312–13; as counterfeiter, 19, 302, 315; education of, 19, 300, 311; family of, 243, 244, 300, 304, 311; flight of, 244, 300; imprisonment of, 19, 300, 314–15; life of, 311–12; memoirs of, 301, 312–13, 315; on Pelham, Mass., 196, 212, 313–14; on Shays's Rebellion, 314; trial of, 300, 315; wealth of, 300, 313
Bushman, Richard L., 136, 325 n.9
Butler, Ephraim, 95

Cabot, Thomas, 138
Calvinism, 243, 259, 264, 271, 307, 312
Calvinists, 254, 255, 258, 265
Cambridge, Mass., 115, 215, 218
Cambridge Platform, 208
Campbell, Archibald, 275
Cape Breton campaign, 66
Capitalism, 4, 6, 16, 17, 22. *See also* Economy
Carp, E. Wayne, 133
Certificate, Continental, 107, 109
Certificates of indebtedness, 67
Certificates, treasury, 71
Chaddock, Joseph, 219–20
Chadwick, Paul, 160
Chapin, Daniel, 275
Charles I, king of Eng., 70
Charlmont, Mass., 233
Charlton, Mass., 213; Am. Rev. in, 209; clergy in, 209; creditors in, 214; debtors in, 214; Friends of Government in, 205–6, 214, 221, 224, 234; religion in, 221, 222, 234, 311; Shaysites in, 205–6, 214, 224, 234
Charter of 1692 (Mass.), 135, 222
Chauncy, Charles, 254
Chenery, Isaac, 137, 205, 227
Cheshire, Mass., 257
Chester, Mass., 233
Chesterfield, Mass., 233
Chileab, Mass., 258
Chilmark, Mass., 252
China, 112
Choate, Isaac, 226
Cilly, Joseph, 148
Cities, 109, 261, 316. *See also* Seaports; Towns
Clarke (family), 288. *See also* Great Proprietors

Clarks (family), 189
Clary, Elisha, 95
Class: in backcountry, 150, 189; in Berkshire Co., Mass., 213; challenges to, 20; clergy and, 212; courts and, 10, 11; and debt, 81–82; Federalists and, 218; Friends of Government and, 217–21, 223; in Hampshire Co., Mass., 212, 213; and ideology, 59; Minot on, 104–5; and religion, 213–21; and republicanism, 15; Shaysites and, 217–21, 223; and Shays's Rebellion, 15, 20, 79–81, 117, 123, 212–16; and theater, 316; in Worcester Co., Mass., 213, 217–21
Clemons, Jonathan, 220
Clergy: in Amherst, Mass., 209; and Am. Rev., 205–6, 249–50, 252–53, 261, 305, 307; artisans as, 256; in backcountry, 200, 249, 250; and banks, 65; in Berkshire Co., Mass., 211, 248, 250, 267, 277; in Boston, 253, 258, 259; in Bristol Co., Mass., 250, 275; in Charlton, Mass., 209; in Chilmark, Mass., 252; and class, 18, 207, 212, 258, 310; in Concord, Mass., 255, 307; of Congregationalists, 260, 267; and congregations, 209, 306–7; in Conn., 267–69, 311–12; on culture, 316; in Deerfield, Mass., 209; and deference, 228, 306; employment of, 242, 248, 273, 305, 306; farmers as, 256, 258; as Friends of Government, 263, 266, 267, 277; in Great Britain, 261; in Greenfield, Mass., 209; in Hampshire Co., Mass., 211, 250, 305, 306; in Hatfield, Mass., 266; on human nature, 292; ideology of, 274; imposters as, 308; as local leaders, 249, 263–64; Loyalists as, 209, 252–53, 263, 275, 276, 277; in Maine, 269, 284; and Mass. government, 205, 258, 298; in Medford, Mass., 307; in Middlesex Co., Mass., 250, 252; in Middleton, Mass., 252; in N.H., 149, 260–61, 300, 311; in Northampton, Mass., 196, 267; in Northfield, Mass., 209; in Pelham, Mass., 212, 242–44, 245, 300, 304–5; and plagiarism, 307–8; and politics, 263–64; and popular protest, 269; in Princeton, Mass., 252; and property, 242, 249; on protesters, 169; on religious decline, 208, 240; role of, 207–8; salaries of, 207–8, 226, 242–43, 251, 256, 259–60, 275–

77, 304–5; as Shaysites, 267–69; and Shays's Rebellion, 205–7, 210, 220, 224, 227, 264–65, 270; in Shutesbury, Mass., 209, 252; in South Hadley, Mass., 308; in Springfield, Mass., 255; in Sunderland, Mass., 306; and U.S. Constitution, 258; in Vt., 269; in Ware, Mass., 267; in Warwick, Mass., 209; in Westfield, Mass., 306; in West Springfield, Mass., 308; in Worcester Co., Mass , 209, 211, 248, 250, 252, 255, 275
Clinton, DeWitt, 174
Clinton Historical Society, 101
Cochrane, James, 148–49
Cogswell, Benjamin, 87, 88, 90, 91
Colman, John, 62, 65
Colonial Society of Massachusetts, 6
Colrain, Mass., 233, 260, 276
Commerce, 61, 69, 70, 169
Committees of correspondence, 70, 196, 246
Committees of safety, 283
Communitarianism, 124
Community: and agriculture, 207; and Am. Rev., 186, 187; in backcountry, 186; concept of, 16; Daniel Shays and, 185; and debt relationships, 83–84; in eastern Mass., 186; Friends of Government and, 223; leaders of, 65, 208; in New England, 186, 193; and political behavior, 195; political culture of, 203, 207; and political theory, 141; and religion, 207–8; scholarship on, 190–91, 193, 203; Shaysites and, 185, 217, 219–21; and Shays's Rebellion, 186–87, 207, 208, 212, 228, 248–49
Commutation, 48
Concord, Battle of, 10, 21, 81, 130, 252
Concord, Mass.: clergy in, 255, 307; courts in, 298; on Daniel Shays, 2; prices in, 75–76; religion in, 255, 307; Shaysites in, 128; and Shays's Rebellion, 20–21, 138
Concord, N.H., 109
Concord Gazette and Middlesex Yeoman, 3
Confederation: Antifederalists on, 175, 180, 292, 293; capital of, 117; conservative republicans on, 175; Federalists and, 101, 181; finances of, 47, 48; frontier of, 303; members of, 54; radical republicans on, 175; reform of, 180, 292, 293; scholarship on, 143; and trade regulation, 111; and U.S. Constitution, 181

Congregationalism: challenges to, 18, 240–41, 245, 248–56, 260, 273; change in, 273; decline of, 240–41; and Shays's Rebellion, 207–10, 212, 226–27, 248–49, 250
Congregationalists. in backcountry, 272; and Baptists, 258; before Am. Rev., 242; clergy of, 259, 260, 269, 270, 305–6, 308; decline of, 264; divisions among, 226–27, 258; and finance, 263; in folklore, 189; as Friends of Government, 267; in Hampshire Co , Mass., 188, 227, 308; institutions of, 242, 264; in Maine, 284; and New Light Stir, 257; and political theology, 263–74; and Presbyterians, 187; and Scots-Irish, 187; and sects, 305–6; and Shaysites, 149, 207, 239; in Shaysite towns, 17; wealth of, 259; in Worcester Co., Mass., 187, 220–24, 226–27, 245, 247
Congregationalists, Reorganized, 275
Congregationalists, Separate, 260
Congress, Continental, 68
Congress, U.S.: and Am. Rev., 47–48, 74; Antifederalists on, 292; and army, 48–49; and currency reform, 74; and economy, 112; Federalists and, 113, 116–17, and Mass., 49–50, 51–52, 53; and Mass. General Court, 74; members of, 111, 291, 294; merchants and, 110; and militias, 303; and monetary policy, 47–50, 52–53, 72, 77, 101; and price controls, 74, 76; requisitions of, 8, 49, 51–55, 73, 327 n. 14, 331 n 52; and revenue, 111, 113; and sectionalism, 112; and trade, 110, 113, 116; and U.S. bill of rights, 292
Congresses, provincial (Mass.), 68, 127, 283
Conkey, William, Jr., 198, 244
Conkey (family), 244, 245
Connecticut. backcountry of, 190–91; and border disputes, 267; clergy in, 267–69, 311–12; conservative republicans in, 172; economy of, 193; farms in, 191, 192; and fiscal policy, 69, 71, 76; reformation men in, 225; religion in, 262, 267–68, 311–12; scholarship on, 190–91; Shays's Rebellion in, 190; towns in, 190–91; and U.S Constitution, 6; wealth in, 190–91
Connecticut Valley, 187; agriculture in, 190, 192; elites in, 195, 310; Loyalists in, 195; religion in, 261, 308; towns in, 14

Consensus, 141, 164
Conservatives: on county conventions, 104; and farmers, 103, 104; lawyers as, 114; and Mass. government, 103, 104; merchants as, 105, 114; and paper money, 115; and property, 104, 127; and radical republicans, 162; and Shaysites, 123, 127; and Shay's Rebellion, 18–19, 101, 115; as traders, 105. *See also* Republicans
Conspiracy, 21, 303
Constitution, U.S.: Antifederalists and, 162, 175, 176, 180–81; artisans and, 281; Bicentennial of, 6; clergy and, 258; debate over, 5; and elections, 292–93; Federalists and, 179–80, framers of, 4, 19, 162, 176, 179, 292; Hamilton and, 6; Henry Knox on, 290; Jay and, 6; Madison and, 6, 142–43; and Maine, 290–91, 296; Mass. and, 5, 169; merchants and, 281; Minot on, 181; N.Y. and, 6; ratification of, 152, 176, 179–81, 252, 281–83, 290–96; and religion, 258; and republicanism, 282; scholarship on, 4, 6, 7, 124, 161–62; and Shays's Rebellion, 3–5, 7, 102, 105, 143, 161–62; and slavery, 252, 293; supporters of, 162, 176, 180; as symbol, 182; and U.S. bill of rights, 181, 282, 292, 293
Constitution of 1778 (Mass.), 135–36, 199–200, 222
Constitution of 1780 (Mass.): "Attleborough" on, 167; backcountry and, 13, 135–36, 200; Benjamin Lincoln and, 141; clergy and, 258, 298; conservatives on, 104; and county conventions, 104, 127; and courts, 136; and creditors, 55, 105; and debtors, 105; Declaration of Rights of, 242, 247, 287; eastern Mass. and, 135, 136; framing of, 127; Friends of Government and, 223; and Mass. Senate, 136; Minot on, 105, 143; Pelham, Mass., and, 14; radical republicans on, 170; ratification of, 49, 54, 200; and religion, 217, 222, 241–42, 245, 247; and representation, 53; and restricted franchise, 136; Shaysites and, 125, 133, 135–36, 141; and Shays's Rebellion, 102; supporters of, 241
Consumer goods, 11, 22, 69, 308, 310
Consumerism, 51, 310
Consumers, 22, 103, 107, 109, 270
Contrast, The (play), 19, 302, 316–19
Convention, Annapolis, 114, 179

Convention, constitutional (Mass., 1780), 127
Convention, Constitutional (U.S., 1787), 4, 6, 56, 173, 175, 178–79, 185–86; Conn. and, 6; Henry Knox, 102; merchants and, 113; N.J. and, 6; and Shays's Rebellion, 105, 161; Va. and, 6
Conventions, county: in backcountry, 104, 135, 200; in Berkshire Co., Mass., 125–26; conservatives and, 104; Daniel Shays and, 198; debates in, 162; delegates to, 165; demands of, 125–26, 127; during Am. Rev., 75–76, 104; Federalists and, 114; and fiscal policy, 163; in Hampshire Co., 137; in Hampshire Co., Mass., 125–26, 244; in Maine, 284, 285, 286–92, 294, 295, 296; in Mass., 104, 127; opponents of, 163, 286–92; petitions of, 163, 165; and property, 104; response to, 163; Samuel Adams on, 169; Shaysites and, 125, 127, 219–20, 244; and Shays's Rebellion, 2, 13, 114, 123, 127; significance of, 127; supporters of, 163, 286–87; in towns, 104; in Worcester Co., Mass., 94, 219–20, 311
Conventions, state ratifying (U.S. Constitution): Maine and, 282, 291–94; in Mass., 130, 176, 179, 252, 281, 282; in N.H., 282; in N.Y., 174
Conventions of 1782 (Mass.), 127
Conventions of 1784 (Mass.), 127
Conway, Mass., 194, 233, 276
Corruption: and Am. Rev., 264; Congregationalists on, 264, 274; and national debt, 60; paper money opponents on, 271; paper money supporters on, 59, 63; rulers and, 166; Shaysites on, 5, 274
Council (Mass.), 61, 68, 71, 157
Counterfeiting, 19, 73, 74, 300, 302, 315
Counterprotest, 163
Counterrevolution, 173–74, 270
Court of Common Pleas: in Berkshire, Mass., 130; debt cases in, 10, 87–91, 94, 221; opponents of, 97–98, 125; Shaysites and, 213, 227; in Worcester Co., Mass., 10, 87–91, 94, 213, 227
Court of General Sessions, 125, 227
"Court Party," 59, 73, 165
Courts: Adam Wheeler on, 227–28; and Am. Rev., 199, 201; appeals in, 93, 114; in backcountry, 74, 135, 199, 200–202; and class, 10, 11; closings

of, 55, 81, 123, 135, 139, 145, 151, 163, 199–202, 205–6, 213, 217, 224–25, 227, 285, 297–98; in Concord, Mass., 21, 298; and Constitution of 1780 (Mass.), 136; costs in, 11, 81, 87, 90–91, 94, 97–98; creditors and, 10–11, 83–85, 94–99, 137, 201; debtors and, 10, 82–99, 108–9, 113–14, 137; efficiency of, 10, 11; farmers and, 102, 117; Federalists and, 103, 114, 117, in Hampshire Co., Mass., 200, 201–2; lawyers and, 201; in Maine, 157, 283, 296; merchants and, 10–11; in N.H., 149, 163; in Northampton, Mass., 104, 267, 285, 297; reform of, 11, 97–98, 99, 114, 127; Samuel Thompson on, 295; scholarship on, 10, 81, 93, 97; in Shirley, Mass., 298; structure of, 82; in Worcester Co., Mass., 81–82, 205–6, 224, 227, 285
Covenant political theology. *See* Political theology
Coventry, Conn., 311–12
Cowden, Capt., 198
Cozier, Matthias, 245
Crafts, Thomas, 276
Credit: in 1780s, 11; and Articles of Confederation, 54; Commonwealth of Mass. and, 49, 50; and consumer purchases, 108; during Am. Rev., 51, 54, 58, 68; federal government and, 56; in Great Britain, 54; and ideology, 58–59; merchants and, 11, 58, 71, 131; Province of Mass. and, 9, 58, 67; and republican government, 55, 56; and specie, 82; and taxes, 69, 72
Credit, bills of, 47, 67, 70, 72
Credit, foreign, 52, 54, 106, 109
Creditors: and Am Rev., 47, 48; in Boston, 131, 215, 218; in Cambridge, Mass., 215; and class, 218, 219–221; Daniel Shays as, 129; and debt litigation, 10–11, 81–99, 131, 137, 213, 219; as debtors, 11, 87, 105, 131; diversity of, 47; and economy, 83, 92; and federal debt, 52–53; as Federalists, 104, 114; as Friends of Government, 218–21; interests of, 47, 54; and Mass. state debt, 48, 50, 52–53; Minot on, 105; and monetary policy, 50, 53, 66, 76, 78, 104; number of, 51; occupations of, 10–11, 82, 87, 90; petitioners and, 166; in Plymouth, Mass., 215; and property, 105; in Province of Mass., 67; and religion, 226; and republican government, 55, 59; in R.I., 215; as Shaysites, 16–17, 219–20; and taxes, 54, 55; wealth of, 10, 81, 83; in Worcester Co., Mass., 85–99, 218–21
Creditors, foreign, 52, 58, 60, 65–66, 147
Critical Period. *See* Confederation
Cromwell, Oliver, 152
Cronin, Thomas E., 161
Crozier, Matthias, 277
Culture: and Am. Rev., 255; of backcountry, 103, 299; of Boston, 255; change in, 103; elites and, 22, 188; and ethnicity, 245; of farmers, 103, 188; and religion, 241, 258; and Shays's Rebellion, 103, 298; and social structure, 19; spread of, 316; and theater, 318; in towns, 299
Culture, folk, 154
Culture, political. *See* Political culture
Cumberland Co., Maine, 283, 284, 288
Cumberland Gazette, 284, 286–87, 290
Cumings, Henry, 265
Cummington, Mass., 233
Cunningham, John, Jr , 109
Currency, 57–59, 61, 63, 66, 68–69, 72
Currency Act of 1751, 66
Currency finance, 58, 60, 68–92, 334 n.12
Curtis, Caleb, 205–6, 207, 209, 224
Cushing, Thomas, Jr., 64, 69, 71
Cushing, William, 81, 82
Cutler, Robert, 276

Dalton, Tristan, 69
Dalton, Mass., 232, 277
Dana, Josiah, 275
Dana, Samuel, 252, 275
Dane, Nathan, 111, 113
Danforth, Asa, 86
Dartmouth College, 19, 260–61, 300, 304, 315
Davis. *See* Burroughs, Stephen
Davis, Ebenezer, 311
Day, Elijah, 209
Day, Luke, 129, 166, 209, 308
Deacons, 207–8, 218–24, 226–27, 240
Debt: in 1780s, 47; Antifederalists on, 291; arbitration of, 220; artisans and, 86, 145; in backcountry, 74, 136, 193–94; British and, 106; certificates for, 79; and class, 81–82; and community, 83–84; concentration of, 51; consolidation of, 49, 50, 52, 78; Continental officers and, 132; courts and, 81–82; and currency, 66; depreciation of, 51, 78; and economy, 83, 101; elites and, 73; farmers and, 11, 117, 145, 194, 297; federal government and,

Debt (*continued*)
8, 48, 50, 52, 115; Federalists on, 115, 117; Friends of Government and, 132; in Great Britain, 60; and ideology, 59; imprisonment for, 126; of individuals, 51; laborers and, 11; laws on, 194; and luxury, 134, 137; in Maine, 296; Mass. government and, 22, 59, 60, 67, 73, 137; merchants and, 71; payment of, 60, 65–66, 77–78, 125, 137, 194, 217, 267, 344 n.6; protests against, 19; public opinion on, 11; relief from, 22; scholarship on, 78, 81, 193–94; Shaysites and, 123, 145, 224; and Shays's Rebellion, 7, 22, 55, 78; and society, 82, 225; and specie, 60, 86; speculation in, 50–51; and taxes, 60, 78, 125, 217; towns and, 72–73; women and, 86

Debtors, 1; aid for, 220, 225; in backcountry, 104, 217; bankruptcy of, 84; and banks, 62; Baptists and, 226; character of, 82; and class, 228; and Commonwealth of Mass., 105; and Mass. Constitution of 1780, 105; and courts, 10, 81–99, 108–9, 113–14, 137; and creditors, 10, 105, 131, 166; creditors as, 11, 87, 105, 131; default by, 10; and economy, 82; financial support of, 85; as Friends of Government, 17, 218–21; and lawyers, 93, 113, 137; legal appeals by, 91–92, 95, 114; merchants and, 10; Minot on, 105; and monetary policy, 76; in N.H., 149; occupations of, 11, 87, 89; as petitioners, 166; punishment of, 84–87, 93, 194, 217, 297; and republican government, 55; scholarship on, 97, 98–99; in seaports, 217; as Shaysites, 16–17, 108–9, 131, 194, 219–21, 223; state legislatures and, 124; in Worcester Co., Mass., 85–99, 217, 218–21

Deerfield, Mass., 209, 233

Defence of the Constitutions of Government of the United States, 172

Deference: in backcountry, 189, 306; collapse of, 223, 224; creditors and, 228; Daniel Shays and, 309; debtors and, 228; elites and, 228, 310, 319; Federalists and, 158, 159; in Maine, 159

Deflation, 81, 82, 83, 99. *See also* Economy

Deism, 263

Deists, 277

Democracy, 142, 172, 173

Dennis, Samuel, 246, 247

Denny, Samuel, 226

Denny (family), 226

Depreciation: Congress and, 74; of debts, 51, 78; ideology and, 69; and military recruitment, 338 n.30; of paper money, 49, 60, 68, 74, 76–77, 126; and price controls, 76–77; in R.I., 64; of treasury notes, 79

Depression, economic: courts and, 10; creditors and, 82, 83, 99; and debt, 81; and debt cases, 81; elites and, 11; Mass. government and, 3, 7; and public loans, 64; response to, 17, 21. *See also* Economy

Despotism, 12

Development, economic, 57–58, 64. *See also* Economy

Dickinson, Reuben, 129

Dictatorship, 173

Dillingham, Pitt, 153, 155, 156

Discourse, political, 162–65

Disorder, 150

Dissent, religious, 16, 17–18, 20, 225. *See also* Religion; Sects, evangelical; *specific denominations*

District of Maine. *See* Maine

Dix, Elijah, 89–90, 91

Dix, Samuel, 275

Dollars, Continental. *See* Money, Continental

Dollars, Spanish, 67, 77

Dorrelites, 276

Dorrell, William, 210

Douglass, Mass., 234

Dresser, David, 224

Dudley, Mass., 234

Dutch, 52

Dwight, Timothy, 190, 309, 310

Easthampton, Mass., 233

Easton, Mass., 275

East Pelham parish (Mass.), 241–43, 244–45. *See also* Pelham, Mass.

Economy: in 1780s, 7, 217; and Am. Rev., 18, 22, 58, 68, 79, 133–35, 241; of backcountry, 14, 16, 22, 189–90, 192–93, 199, 295; and capitalism, 6; change in, 18, 208; Congress and, 112; of Conn., 193; courts and, 10; and debt, 101; of eastern Mass., 189; elites and, 8; farmers and, 186; Federalists on, 117; and foreign credit, 54; growth of, 59, 62, 65, 112; Henry Knox on, 169; Henry Lee on, 169;

ideology and, 62; and King George's War, 66; and loans, 65; of Maine, 295–96; of Mass., 3, 7, 133, 193–94; Mass. General Court and, 135; merchants and, 58; and money supply, 62; and political culture, 14, 169; and religion, 251–52; scholarship on, 7; and Shays's Rebellion, 7–8, 79, 194–95, 208, 217, 241; and society, 304; state role in, 59; of towns, 134, 190; of U.S., 54
Edwards, Jonathan, 243, 254
Edwardseanism, 259, 260
Egalitarianism, 57–58, 310
Egremont, Mass., 232, 263, 267, 277
Ejectment suits, 146, 159
Election (Calvinist doctrine), 307
Elections: in 1776, 69; Antifederalists and, 292–93; in backcountry, 70; Bowdoin administration and, 21, 139; Federalists and, 113–114; Friends of Government on, 12; in Maine, 157–58
Elites: and Am. Rev., 199; in backcountry, 16, 136, 199; in Boston, 258, 313; and change, 18; and class, 189; clergy and, 207, 310; and commerce, 157; in Conn. Valley, 310; as creditors, 218, 228; and culture, 22, 188, 316; and deception, 309, 310–11; and economy, 8, and education, 150, 216, 223; factions among, 22; and farmers, 311; and Freemasonry, 209; and government, 7, 150; and government 8; in Hampshire Co., Mass., 189, 195–96; in literature, 19; in Maine, 156; and militias, 224; in N.C., 188; in N.H., 218; occupations of, 8, 113; in Pa., 188; and political culture, 15, 22, 146, 150–52, 157–58, 310; and political office, 22, 216; and religion, 188, 216, 253; scholarship on, 8; as Shaysites, 130, 156; and Shays's Rebellion, 15, 22, 146, 152, 206; stereotypes of, 303; in Va., 188; values of, 157; wealth of, 22, 150, 151; in Worcester Co., Mass., 218
Ellis, John, 275
Ely, Samuel, 200, 267–69, 297, 298
Embargoes, 283
Emerson, John, 276
Emerson, Joseph, 275
Emerson, William, 275, 307
Emmons, Nathaniel, 254
Enfield, Conn., 262
Enlightenment, 259, 299

Essex Co., Mass., 68, 106, 138, 329 n.43
Europe, 70, 75, 111, 112, 270
Excise, 52–53, 103. *See also* Taxes
Exeter, N.H., 145–48, 150, 153, 157

Factors, British, 11, 52, 106, 110, 116
Fairfax, Maine, 152–53, 156
Falmouth, Maine, 283–85, 291. *See also* Portland, Maine
Falmouth Gazette, 284, 286, 290
Faneuil Hall, 75, 110, 281
Farmers: and Am. Rev., 22, 68, 102, 103, 134; in backcountry, 22, 123, 134, 135, 188, 190; as bankers, 65; as clergy, 256, 258; as consumers, 102, 107, 109; and courts, 102, 117; and culture, 12, 19, 316; culture of, 103, 188; and debt, 11, 113, 117, 131, 145, 194, 297; in eastern Mass., 134; and economy, 102, 186; elites on, 311; and Federalists, 104–5, 111, 117; as Friends of Government, 124; grievances of, 7; imprisonment of, 297; and Maine, 19, 296; and Mass. government, 103, 117, 134; and merchants, 11, 12, 107, 109; Minot on, 197; and money, 61, 102–4, 110, 111, 115, 117; in N.H., 147; in Pelham, Mass., 14; and prices, 68, 69–72, 70, 74, 76; and property, 65, 102, 297; scholarship on, 101, 134; and Shays's Rebellion, 3, 102, 145; as social group, 188; stereotypes of, 303; and taxes, 102, 103, 117, 145; and trade, 74, 102; values of, 103; wealth of, 134, 190
Farming, 17
Farms, 16, 131, 165, 191–92
Fathers of the People, 159
Federalism, 11–12, 114, 117, 203, 258, 317
Federalist, The, 6, 104, 142–43, 167, 172
Federalists: and Annapolis convention, 114; and Antifederalists, 292, 294, 295; and Articles of Confederation, 114; and British, 105–6, 116, 117; and class, 157, 218; and commerce, 103; and Confederation, 181; and Congress, 116; and county conventions, 114; and courts, 103, 114, 117; and Daniel Shays, 179–80; and debt, 117; in drama, 318; and economy, 117; education of, 103; and farmers, 104–5, 111, 117; and federal government, 115; as Friends of Government, 152; ideology of, 115; in Maine, 157, 159, 283, 291, 295; and Mass. government, 103, 104, 117; and money,

Federalists (*continued*)
104, 111, 117; and newspapers, 111, 116; occupations of, 106, 113, 114, 118; organization of, 111; and political culture, 116, 157, 291; and property, 103, 104; and religion, 218; scholarship on, 240; and Shaysites, 104–5, 291; and Shays's Rebellion, 5, 12, 102, 104–6, 114–18, 179–80, 295; and taxes, 117; and towns, 103; and trade, 111, 113; and U.S. bill of rights, 293; and U.S. Constitution, 179–80, 291

Federal political theology. *See* Political theology

Feer, Robert, 85, 123, 206
Ferguson, E. James, 334 n. 12
Fessenden, John, 220
Finance, 58–59
Financiers, 114
First Baptist Church (Boston), 258
First Church (Amherst, Mass.), 251–52
First Church (Boston), 254
First Church (Templeton, Mass.), 276
First Parish (Rehoboth, Mass.), 275
First Presbyterian (Pelham, Mass.), 277
Fisher, Jabez, 277
Fiske, John, 161
Fitchburg, Mass., 235
Flagg, Samuel, 224, 225
Folklore, 299, 302
Forbush, Robert, 205
Forrest, Uriah, 180
Forward, Justus, 131
Foster, Dwight, 218
Foster, Joel, 277
Foster, John, 276
Foye, William, 64
France, 52, 67, 102, 111, 112, 300
Franchise, 22, 136
Franklin, Benjamin, 173, 188, 307–8
Franklin, Mass., 254
Fraud, 59, 84, 303–4
Freeholders, 145
Freeman, Samuel, 284
Freemasons, 209
French, Joseph, 148
French, 48, 52, 74, 213
French and Indian War, 67, 72
Friends of Government: and Am. Rev., 13; in Berkshire Co., Mass., 277; clergy as, 263, 266, 267, 277; and community, 223; conservative republicans as, 168; and Mass. Constitution of 1780, 223; creditors as, 16–17, 21, 22, 151–52, 218–21; debtors as, 17; as Federalists, 152; on Great Britain, 303; in Hampshire Co., Mass., 145, 263, 277; Henry Knox as, 157; local leaders as, 217, 220, 223; motives of, 20; in N.H., 145, 148–50; political culture of, 12–13, 274; and religion, 218–29, 240, 250, 255, 267; rioters as, 225; and Shaysites, 202, 303; wealth of, 214; in Worcester Co., Mass., 213–28, 245

Friends of the People, 15, 159
Fuller, Timothy, 252, 276

Gardner, Mass., 235
Garrick, David, 307
General Court (Mass.), 68; "Address to the People" of, 59, 135, 137, 265; and Am. Rev., 252; Antifederalists and, 284, 294; and backcountry, 103; and bankruptcy, 84; and banks, 61, 65; and bills of credit, 70, 72, 102; clergy and, 205; and Congress, 54–55, 74, 331 n. 52; and consumerism, 270; and creditors, 59; Daniel Shays and, 3; and debt, 22, 49, 59, 60, 73, 137; and East Pelham parish, 241; and economy, 69, 135; factions in, 103; farmers and, 103, 117, 134; Federalists and, 103, 116, 117; Friends of Government and, 13, 139; governors and, 127; and land claims, 159; and loans, 59, 63; location of, 125–26, 286; and Maine, 156, 158–60, 285–86, 288, 289–90, 294–95; and Mass. Constitution of 1778, 135–36, 200; merchants and, 9, 11, 61; and money supply, 102; and paper money, 9, 22, 53, 60, 67, 69, 265; and political theology, 69–70; and prices, 72; reform of, 125; and religion, 242, 246, 265–66; scholarship on, 98–99, 325 n. 8; and Shaysites, 132, 140–41, 146; and Shays's Rebellion, 134–35, 137–38, 139, 171, 297–98; and silver, 63, 66; and taxes, 8, 22, 48, 51, 53, 60, 72, 137; and tenor notes, 78; and trade, 52, 65; and treasury notes, 72; and veterans, 48, 72

Georgetown, Maine, 283
Gibbs, Jonas, 94
Gill, John, 259, 260
Gloucester, Mass., 261
Goffe, William, 299
Gold, 60, 62, 68, 217
Good, public, 59, 74, 134, 317
Gore, Christopher, 290
Gorham, Maine, 284

INDEX | 403

Goshen, Mass., 233
Gould, John, 220
Government, federal: and army, 292; conservatives and, 105; and credit, 56; and debt, 8, 55–56, 115; Federalists and, 115; and foreign powers, 55–56; and legislation, 292; merchants and, 11–12; and North, 54; politicians and, 11–12; and Shays's Rebellion, 4–6, 11–12, 19–20, 105, 115; and South, 54; and states, 8; and taxes, 56, 292; and trade, 11–12, 115, 292
Government, local, 21, 86, 94
Government, provisional (Mass.), 127
Government, republican, 55, 56, 99, 143, 166
Government, state, 19, 20, 21, 86, 105, 151
Government by the People, 161
Grafton, Mass., 235, 259, 262
Grafton Presbytery, 260
Graham, Richard Crouch, 243
Granby, Mass., 233
Granet, David, 324 n.6
Grant, Charles, 190–91, 192, 193
Granville, Mass., 233
Gray, Daniel, 198, 243–44, 245, 267
Great Awakening: Congregationalists and, 253, 254, 255–56; in Conn. Valley, 308; dissenters and, 213, 241, 256, 305–6; in Pelham, Mass., 243; and politics, 206; scholarship on, 206; and society, 304, 305–6
Great Barrington, Mass., 232, 254
Great Britain: clergy in, 261; consumerism in, 107; corruption in, 60; credit in, 54, 131; debt in, 60, 67; emigration from, 261; finance in, 9, 58, 59, 60, 80; Friends of Government on, 303; government of, 9, 14, 58, 60, 61, 65–66; and Mass., 9, 52, 64; merchants in, 131, 217; military expenses in, 60; money in, 63, 270–71; officials of, 63; religion in, 262; and R.I., 64; and Shays's Rebellion, 303; silver in, 67; trade with, 52, 60, 62, 106, 111, 283; wealth in, 60; and West Indies, 112
Great Proprietors: employees of, 154; Federalists and, 159; Henry Knox as, 157, 269, 288; and Mass. government, 156; and settlers, 146–7, 157, 159–60, 269, 288; and Waldo Patent, 269
Greenfield, Mass., 209, 233
Greenwich, Mass., 199, 200, 233, 276
Gross, Robert A., 190

Grosvenor, Daniel, 276
Grosvenor, Ebenezer, 275
Groton, Mass., 138, 252, 260, 275

Habeas corpus, 177, 267
Hadley, Mass., 190, 233
Half-Way Covenant, 222, 229, 254, 261, 275
Hall, Percival, 220
Hall, Stephen, 284
Hall, Van Beck, 206, 291
Hamilton, Alexander, 6, 167, 172, 173, 174
Hammond, John, 95
Hampshire Co., Mass., 213; and border disputes, 267; class in, 213; Congregationalists in, 209, 211, 227, 233–34, 248–50, 255, 257–60, 263, 305–6, 308; county conventions in, 125, 127, 137; courts in, 200; East Pelham parish in, 241; Freemasons in, 209; Friends of Government in, 277; officials of, 195; sects in, 209, 211, 233–34, 248, 257–63, 276–77; settlement of, 188; and Shaysites, 209, 266–67, 276–77, 308; Shays's Rebellion in, 71, 174, 187, 199, 244; and taxes, 329 n.43; towns in, 187, 213, 233–34
Hampstead, N.H., 148
Hancock, John, 138, 139, 177, 272–73
Hancock, Thomas, 66
Hancock, Mass., 232, 262
Handlin, Mary, 134, 136
Handlin, Oscar, 134, 136
Hanover, N.H., 260, 300, 301, 311, 312
Hardwick, Mass., 235, 247
Harlow, Ralph V., 133–34
Hartford, Conn., 76, 268
Harvard, Mass., 235, 263, 275
Harvard College, 94, 176, 245, 255, 301
Hatch, Nathan, 240
Hatfield, Mass., 125–26, 195, 233, 244, 266
Hawley, Joseph, 104
Hawley, Mass., 233
Hayden, Charles, 155
Heath, Mass., 233
Heimert, Alan, 206
Hemmenway, Moses, 265
Hemphill, Samuel, 307–8
Henry, Patrick, 175
Heywood, Daniel, Jr., 89
Higginson, Stephen, 116–17
Hill, Abraham, 252, 277
Hinds, Nehemiah, 244, 245
Hingham, Mass., 111
Historic Deerfield, Inc., 6
History of Augusta, 157

404 | INDEX

History of the Insurrections in Massachusetts, 104–5, 181
History of the Rise, Progress, and Termination of the American Revolution, 181–82
History of Western Massachusetts, 122
Holden, Mass., 205, 235
Holland, Josiah Gilbert, 122
Holland, Park, 129
Holland, 111
Holland, Mass., 233
Hood, Otis, 122
Hopkins, Samuel, 254, 259
House of Representatives (Mass.): and banks, 62; conservatives in, 103; Federalists in, 104; and Great Britain, 63; merchants in, 69; and money, 70, 92; and prices, 68, 70, 71, 74; and Shays's Rebellion, 139. *See also* General Court (Mass.)
Howard, Bezaleel, 255
Howard, Simeon, 265
Hubbardston, Mass., 129, 227, 235, 275
Hunt, Ebenezer, 189
Huntington, Joseph, 311–12
Hutchinson, Edward, 64
Hutchinson, Thomas, Jr., 65, 66, 333 n.8
Hutchinson, Thomas, Sr., 64
Hutchinson (family), 65
Hyde, Alvan, 277
Hyde, Ephraim, 275

Ideology: Am. Rev. and, 5–6, 20; in backcountry, 12–13; on bankers, 65; in Boston, 135; and class, 59; of clergy, 274; and commerce, 69; of community, 141; and conflict, 20; and consensus, 141; and credit, 58–59; and debt, 59; and economy, 62, 69; and Enlightenment, 299; Federalists and, 104, 115; and finance, 58–59; of Friends of Government, 21, 274; of merchants, 60, 61; and money, 58–63, 68–69, 74–75, 78; and political economy, 59; and prices, 58–59, 62, 74; and sectionalism, 133; of Shaysites, 21; and Shays's Rebellion, 133; Shays's Rebellion and, 104; and trade, 60, 62–63
Ilsley, Enoch, 284
Immigrants, 309
Immigration, 187–88, 191, 242, 260, 296
Imports, 59, 60, 70, 102, 106
Imposters, 308–11
Imposts, 48, 50, 52–53, 56, 103, 111, 113. *See also* Taxes
Imprisonment, 85

Indentured servitude, 84
Independence, republican, 208
Independent Chronicle, 164, 167, 329 n.43
Indians, 213, 303
Indians, White. *See* White Indians
Inflation, 58, 68–69, 72, 74–76, 92, 243. *See also* Economy
Ingalls, Elkanah, 262
Insolvency, 87, 91
Insurrections, 167. *See also* Protest, popular
Interest: concept of, 58; of debtors, 99; of General Court, 54; of merchants, 59, 111, 113; Minot on, 104–5; Shaysites and, 124
Interest (monetary): on consolidated notes, 53; on Continental notes, 77; on promissory notes, 83; on state debt, 49, 50; on treasury notes, 58, 67
Intolerable Acts, 135
Ireland, Shadrack, 210
Ireland, 187
Italy, Renaissance, 143
Ives, Jesse, 277

Jackson, Henry, 141–42
Jaffrey, N.H., 262
J. and J. Amory (import firm), 109–10
Jarvis, Charles, 138
Jay, John, 6, 173, 177
Jefferson, Thomas, 159, 171, 177, 180, 182, 298
Jefferson, Maine, 154
Jeffersonianism, 240
Jeffersonians, 15, 158, 159, 361 n.25. *See also* Republicans
Jennison, Nathaniel, 85, 97
Jennison, William, 96
Jensen, Merrill, 123
Johnson, Daniel, 275
Johnson, Henry, 155
Judd, Benjamin, 227, 267, 277
Judd, Jonathan, 196
Judges, 81, 91, 128, 220, 267, 283
Justices of the peace, 127, 132, 136, 137, 200

Karsky, Barbara, 123, 131, 186
Keith, John, 91
Kelly, Richard, 219
Kennebec Co., Maine, 156
Kennebec Proprietors, 288. *See also* Great Proprietors
Kennebec River, 153, 288
Kent, Conn., 190–91, 192, 193
Kenyon, Cecilia, 124

King, Richard, 151
King, Rufus, 111, 113
King George's War, 66
King's Falls, N.H., 148, 149
Kingston, N.H., 147
Knox, Henry: on economy, 169; as Great Proprietor, 157, 269, 288; on Maine statehood, 290; on political thought, 162; and Shays's Rebellion, 102, 117, 141–42, 167, 169; on U.S Constitution, 290
Kramnick, Isaac, 162

Laborers, 11, 58, 62, 70, 304
Lafayette, Marie Joseph Paul Yves Roch Gilbert du Motier, marquis de, 1, 2, 3, 129, 309, 318
Lake (family), 288 *See also* Great Proprietors
Lamb, Reubin, 225
Lamson, Ebenezer, 262
Lancaster, Mass., 235
Land, 146, 159, 304. *See also* Property
Landholders, 58, 65, 71, 73
Land speculation, 61, 65, 146, 284, 295
Lanesborough, Mass., 232, 272
Lathrop, Joseph, 308
Laws, 12; on bankruptcy, 84; on currency, 66; on debt, 60, 194; during Am. Rev., 133; and economy, 68; on land, 146, 159; and legal fees, 113; on legal tender, 11, 53, 92, 163, 288; and liberty, 59, 168; in Maine, 15; merchants and, 59; on paper money, 60, 62, 67–68, 79; Privy Council and, 84; and property, 59; scholarship on, 92; on specie, 68
Lawyers: in backcountry, 102; as bankers, 65; as conservatives, 114; and courts, 201; and creditors, 137; and debtors, 93, 113, 137; education of, 94; as elites, 113; and farmers, 113; as Federalists, 113, 114; fees of, 91, 94, 113; as Friends of Government, 148; imposters as, 309; increase in, 102; and legal appeals, 93; in Maine, 154, 156, 288; and merchants, 114; in N.H., 147, number of, 18; popular opinion on, 11, 94, 97–98, 113, 114; and prices, 71; Royall Tyler as, 301; Shaysites on, 125, 303; and Supreme Judicial Court, 219; as sureties, 92–93, 220; visibility of, 18; wealth of, 113; in Worcester Co., Mass , 94, 220
Lee, Ann, 210, 246, 247, 262
Lee, Henry, 129, 169, 177

Lee, Richard Henry, 169
Lee, Mass., 232, 277
Leicester, Mass., 95, 213–14, 220–22, 224, 235, 260
Leicester Academy, 223
Lenox, Mass., 232
Leominster, Mass., 235
Leverett, Mass., 199, 233, 276
Lexington, Battle of, 10, 130, 252
Lexington, Mass., 206
Leyden, Mass., 233, 276
Liberals. *See* Arminianism
Liberty: and Am. Rev., 4, 133; and currency finance, 334 n.12; definitions of, 168; in eastern Mass., 135; Friends of Government and, 4, 12, 21, 168; and laws, 168; in Maine, 159; protection of, 150–51; radical republicans on, 171; rulers and, 166; Samuel Ely on, 269; Shaysites and, 12, 21, 171
Liberty Men. *See* White Indians
Lincoln, Benjamin: army of, 13, 19, 21, 115, 130, 132; and Christopher Babbitt, 272; and Daniel Shays, 175; expedition of, 130, 132, 138, 139; and Mass. Constitution of 1780, 141; Mercy Otis Warren on, 181; in Petersham, Mass., 130; and Royall Tyler, 19, 301; Samuel Holden and, 126; and Shaysites, 139, 140–41
Lincoln, Levi, 92–94
Lincoln Co., Maine, 154, 156, 288, 291
Lincolnville, Maine, 269
Literature, 6, 7, 19–20, 297, 301
Lithgow, Arthur, 156, 157
Livermore, Jonathan, 91–92
Livestock, 225
Loans, 9, 58–59, 61–65, 76, 80
Locke, John, 165, 171, 209, 228
London, Eng.: banks in, 61; creditors in, 65; and Mass., 63, 64; and monetary policy, 66; religion in, 259, 271
Londonderry, N.H., 243, 260
Longmeadow, Mass., 233, 276
Louden, Mass , 232
Loyalists, 163; in backcountry, 199, 209, 246; as clergy, 246, 252–53, 263, 275, 276, 277; departure of, 18; Federalists and, 116; Friends of Government and, 124; in Groton, Mass., 263; in Hampshire Co., Mass., 195–96; in Maine, 283; merchants and, 106; on New Englanders, 318; property of, 106, 147, 308
Ludlow, Mass., 233, 276
Ludwig, Walter, 324 n.6

Lunenburg, Mass., 235
Luxuries, 107, 109
Luxury, 13, 60, 134, 137, 310, 315–17
Lyman, Joseph, 266–67, 271, 273
Lynde, Jonathan, 82

McCulloch, Henry, 131, 197, 198, 202, 299
McCulloch, Sarah, 197, 198, 299
McCusker, John J., 342 n.1
McDonald, Forrest, 161
McKendrick, Neil, 107
McLoughlin, William G., 206, 239, 240, 270
McMaster, John Bach, 161
Madison, James: and Annapolis convention, 114; on monarchy, 173; on private interests, 104; on republican government, 143; on Shays's Rebellion, 171, 177; and U.S. Constitution, 142–43; and Washington, 171, 177
Madison, James, Sr., 177
Magistrates: and farmers, 12; in Maine, 157; and merchants, 9; and petitioners, 165; and political culture, 13, 124; Shaysites on, 303; and Shays's Rebellion, 8, 12–13, 124
Maier, Pauline, 123
Main, Jackson Turner, 131, 161
Maine: agrarian resistance in, 14–16, 145–47; Am. Rev. in, 283–85, 292, 295; Antifederalists in, 281–83, 291–94; backcountry of, 154; British in, 283–84, class in, 19; clergy in, 269; constitution of, 19; county conventions in, 286–92, 291, 294, 296; courts in, 283, 296; debt in, 296; economy of, 295–96; farmers in, 296; Federalists in, 291, 295; Great Proprietors of, 146, 154, 156, 157, 159, 160; immigration to, 288, 296; land speculation in, 61; law in, 15; lawyers in, 288; legislature of, 15; Loyalists in, 283; and Mass. General Court, 145, 285–86, 295; merchants, 284; merchants and, 19; merchants in, 283, 288, 296; militia in, 283, 284; newspapers in, 284, 285; officeholders in, 288; paper money in, 288, 295; political culture in, 125, 146; political culture of, 157–60; property in, 137; reports of Shays's Rebellion in, 283, 285, 290; Shaysites in, 295, 296; statehood movement in, 19, 283, 284–92, 294–95, 296; trade with, 283, 285; and U.S. Constitution, 281–

82, 283, 290–94, 295; wealth in, 153, 288–89; "White Indians" in, 146–47, 153–58
Manchester, Eng., 262
Manufacturers, 111
Manufacturing, 61, 110
Marblehead, Mass., 69
Marini, Stephen, 206, 209
Markets, 6, 14, 16, 18, 59, 106–9
Marston, John, 110
Massachusetts, Commonwealth of, 163; agriculture in, 117; and backcountry, 7, 11, 13, 14, 22; Baptists and, 209; and Confederation, 54; and Congress, 8, 49–50, 51–52, 53, 73; credit in, 47, 49–50, 52, 57, 68, 73; critics of, 20–21, 138; currency in, 78; and Daniel Shays, 3; debt in, 7, 52, 79, 80; east of, 133–36, 186; economy of, 7, 117, 217; elections in, 70, 292–93; elites in, 8, 22; factions in, 6, 20; finances of, 53; fiscal policies of, 7–8; franchise in, 22; and Great Britain, 52; Jeffersonians and, 159; leaders of, 22; and Maine, 145, 159, 283–86, 294; and merchants, 9–10, 57, 58; militia of, 21, 115, 132, 138–41, 202, 205–6, 303; Minot on, 105; mobs in, 135; monetary policy of, 1; officials of, 49, 126, 177; paper money in, 9, 58, 78, 83; political culture of, 6, 124–25, 135; prices in, 57; and religion, 266; and Rev. War debt, 1, 47, 49, 50, 54, 83; scholarship on, 9–10, 186; and Shaysites, 21, 123, 124; and Shays's Rebellion, 2, 21, 121–23, 136–41, 173, 202; specie in, 49–50, 53, 57, 68, 78, 80; taxes in, 1, 7–9, 48–50, 53, 77, 83, 102; towns in, 133, 136; and trade, 52, 102, 117; and U.S. Constitution, 5, 6, 179, 281–82. *See also* Constitution of 1780 (Mass.)
Massachusetts, Province of: and Am. Rev., 9, 48, 54, 58, 73, 133, 135; banks in, 61, 62; and centralized authority, 49; charter of, 135, 222; credit in, 57, 58, 62, 64, 67, 68; currency in, 57; debt in, 67; economy of, 58; finance in, 9, 57, 58, 67; gold in, 60; governor of, 127; and Great Britain, 9, 64; land speculation in, 61; merchants in, 9, 57, 58, 64; military expenses of, 60; monetary policy in, 66; paper money in, 9, 47–48, 60, 64, 67–68, 73–77; prices in, 57, 60; silver in, 60, 64, 66;

specie in, 60, 61, 64, 67; sterling in, 60; taxes in, 9; trade with, 61, 64; treasury of, 60, 67
Massachusetts, western. *See* Backcountry
Massachusetts Centinel, 5, 135, 142, 177, 299, 310
Massachusetts Gazette, 163
Massachusetts Spy, 111
Mather, Cotton, 253
Mattoon, Ebenezer, 131, 202, 252
May, John, Jr., 86
Meacham, Joseph, 262
Medford, Mass., 307
Mediterranean (region), 112
Medway, Mass., 254
Memoirs of Stephen Burroughs, 301, 312, 315
Menard, Russell R., 342 n.1
Mendon, Mass., 235
Mercantilism, 110
"Merchantile Interest," 58, 60, 70, 78, 79. *See also* Merchants
Merchants: accounts of, 82; and advertising, 107–8; and Am. Rev., 9, 58, 67, 69, 71–72, 106; and artisans, 110–11, 113; and backcountry, 9, 12, 107, 190, 217; and banks, 61, 63, 64, 65–66, 80; and British, 111, 118; and British credit, 58, 60, 65–66, 109, 131, 160; and British factors, 11, 106, 110; and British government, 58, 61, 64; and Congress, 110; in Conn., 69; as conservatives, 105, 114; and Council, 61, 68, 69, 71; and credit, 71; as creditors, 10–11, 64, 82, 131, 217; and debtors, 11, 64, 131; and economy, 11, 18, 58, 72; as elites, 9, 124; and farmers, 11, 12, 107, 109; as Federalists, 11–12, 106, 111, 113–14, 118, 281; and fiscal policy, 57, 60, 80; in Great Britain, 131, 217; in Hingham, Mass., 111; ideology of, 60, 61; interests of, 57, 59–60, 75–76, 80, 113; Isaac Backus on, 271; and Maine, 19, 153, 283, 284; and manufacturers, 111; in Marblehead, Mass., 69; and Mass. government, 9, 11, 61, 64–65, 69, 71; and militia, 115, 138, 202; and monetary policy, 9, 57–58, 60–61, 67, 71–72, 75–76, 79–80; in Newburyport, Mass., 69; in N.H., 69; in Northampton, Mass., 189; as Patriots, 58, 118; and political culture, 59; and prices, 68, 69–72, 75; and R.I., 63, 64, 66, 69; in Salem, Mass., 111; and Shaysites, 124, 303; and Shays's Rebellion, 8, 12–13, 67, 76, 105; and social mobility, 65; and taxes, 58, 69, 76, 80; in towns, 217, 218; and trade, 18, 71, 109, 110–11, 112–13; wealth of, 10, 124, 301; in Worcester Co., Mass., 94, 131, 218
Merchants' money. *See* Notes, treasury
Meritocracy, 157, 309
Merrill, Nathaniel, 243, 277
Merrimack Valley, 260
Metz, William, 333 n.8
Micawber, Mr., 81, 90
Michener, Ronald, 338 n.29
Middleborough, Mass., 209, 257
Middlefield, Mass., 233
Middlesex Co., Mass.: clergy in, 250, 275; conventions in, 127; Friends of Government in, 133; and Gov. Bowdoin, 138; religion in, 263, 275; Shaysites in, 21, 139, 275
Middle States, 131
Middleton, Mass., 252
Milford, Mass., 235
Militias: and Am. Rev., 130, 284; captains of, 208, 210, 218–19; and Congress, 303; debtors in, 17; in Maine, 155, 156, 283, 284; merchants and, 202; in N.H., 148; officers of, 224; and religion, 221, 226; Shaysites and, 128, 131; and Shays's Rebellion, 132, 202, 205–6, 218–19, in Worcester Co., Mass., 213, 218, 221, 224
Millennialism, 240, 272
Minot, George Richards: on courts, 98–99; and Fisher Ames, 181; on Mass. Constitution of 1780, 143; on monetary policy, 92; on religion, 239; on Shaysites, 197; on Shays's Rebellion, 13, 79, 104–5, 117, 121–22, 142–143, 181; on U.S. Constitution, 181
Mississippi River, 112
Mobility, social, 18, 308–9
Monarchy, 142, 166, 173
Money, Continental, 49, 58, 68, 70–78
Money, hard. *See* Specie
Money, paper: Antifederalists on, 291; backcountry and, 9, 11; Congress and, 77, 101; conservatives and, 115; and consumer purchases, 107; county conventions on, 76, 126, 163; creditors and, 104; and debt, 60; in eastern Mass., 103; and economic development, 57–58; farmers and, 102, 103, 104, 110, 115, 117; Federalists and, 104, 117; Great Britain and, 63–65,

Money, paper (*continued*)
  270–71; and ideology, 57–59, 63, 68, 78; issues of, 69, 107, 109; laborers and, 62, 70; law on, 60, 62, 66, 67, 68; in Maine, 288, 295; Mass. General Court and, 22, 53, 60, 67, 69, 265; Mass. governors on, 65, 66; merchants and, 9, 58, 60, 67, 70–71, 75, 79; in N.H., 147; in N.Y., 107, 109; opponents of, 62, 78; redemption of, 67, 77; R.I. and, 62, 64, 65; Shaysites and, 127; and specie, 62; sale of, 83, 109; speculation in, 308; supporters of, 57–58, 61, 62–63; and taxes, 65, 66, 68, 77, 109; and trade, 60; and trader, 70; and trades, 74; value of, 60, 65, 67–68, 77, 126, 217. *See also* Currency finance; Law: on legal tender; Specie; *specific bills and notes*
Monson, Mass., 233, 277
Montague, Mass., 233
Montgomery, Mass., 233
Moore, William, 108
Moral economy, 207, 225
Moral philosophy, 62
Morris, Robert, 48, 113
Morse, Joshua, 257
Morse, Royall, 301
Morse, Samuel, 149
Moss, Reuben, 277
Mount Washington, Mass., 232
Murray, John, 261

National Endowment for the Humanities, 6
Nationalism, 111, 124
Nationalists, 5, 48, 113
New Ashford, Mass., 232, 277
New Braintree, Mass., 220, 224, 225, 235
Newbury, Mass., 68, 132
Newburyport, Mass., 68, 69, 94
New Divinity Evangelicalism, 254–55, 260
New England: community studies on, 190, 193, 203; ethnicity in, 196; farms in, 131; Federalists in, 157; merchants in, 112–13; political culture in, 195; and Robert Morris, 113; and sectionalism, 112; and South, 112, 114; and Spanish-American treaty, 112; and trade, 112–13, 114
New England Way, 16
New Gloucester, Maine, 281
New Hampshire, 109; clergy in, 260–61, 300, 311; courts in, 163; elites in, 218; and fiscal policy, 69, 71; newspapers in, 163; publication in, 301; religion in, 210, 243, 260–61, 262, 311; Shaysites in, 146; uprisings in, 55, 145, 146, 147–50, 151, 153; and U.S. Constitution, 282, 294
New Hampshire Mercury, 163
New-Haven Gazette, 178
New Jersey, 6
New Lebanon, N.Y., 262
New Lights: Eden Burroughs as, 311; and Jonathan Edwards, 259; in Pelham, Mass., 243; and political theology, 270; and property, 225; and Separate Baptists, 256, 259–60; and Shays's Rebellion, 272, 273; and Singing Controversy, 253
New Light Stir, 209–10, 247, 256, 257, 260, 261
New Marlborough, Mass., 232
Newport, R.I., 49, 64, 66, 215, 254
New Providence, Mass., 209, 232
New Salem, Mass., 233, 241, 258, 277
New Side Presbytery, 260
New York: Antifederalists in, 176; conservative republicans in, 172; Daniel Shays in, 1, 2; in drama, 317; frontiers of, 2; government of, 174; immigration to, 191; paper money in, 107, 109; prices in, 71; radical republicans in, 174; religion in, 210, 262; Shaysites in, 301; and Shays's Rebellion, 174; and U.S. Constitution, 6, 174, 180
New York City, 302, 316, 319
New York Evening Post, 2
Niskeyuna, N.Y., 210, 262
North, James W., 157
Northampton, Mass.: Am. Rev. in, 195–96; class in, 189, 195–96; courts in, 104, 267, 285, 297; Freemasons in, 209; Friends of Government in, 233; merchants in, 189; newspapers in, 103; religion in, 233, 243; Shaysites in, 209, 233; Shays's Rebellion in, 267; Stephen Burroughs in, 315; wealth in, 190
Northborough, Mass., 235
Northbridge, Mass., 235, 260
North Carolina, 188
Northfield, Mass., 209, 233
North Yarmouth, Maine, 288
Norwich, Mass., 233
Notes, army, 50, 52, 53
Notes, consolidated, 50, 52, 53, 79, 109
Notes, depreciation, 49, 50
Notes, merchants', 64, 65

INDEX | 409

Notes, promissory, 67, 73, 82–83
Notes, state, 107, 109
Notes, tenor, 78
Notes, treasurer's, 49, 58
Notes, treasury, 67, 69, 72–76, 79, 338 n.29
Nye, Ebenezer, 219
Nye, Timothy, 219

Oakham, Mass., 17, 213, 214, 218–20, 235, 275
Officeholding, 166, 208, 288, 292, 308
Officers, military, 103, 114, 132
Officers, militia, 132, 224
Offices, public, 125, 216, 227
Offices, religious, 207, 208
Old Lights, 255, 306
Onuf, Peter S., 325 n.13
Orange, Mass., 233
Order, social, 15, 59, 150, 306
Orders, treasurers, 109
Orders-in-council, 52
Orne, Azor, 69, 71, 75
Osborne, John, 64
Oxford, Mass., 225, 235, 262

Paine, Robert Treat, 71, 73, 130
Paine, Thomas, 55
Palmer, Mass., 234, 261
Parker, John, 82
Parker, Nehemiah, 275
Parliament, 51, 61, 66
Parmalee, Elisha, 277
Parrington, Vernon Louis, 123
Parsons, David, Sr., 251
Parsons, David, II, 251–52
Parsons, Eli, 129
Parsons, Samuel Holden, 126
Partisanship, 163–64
Partridgefield, Mass., 232
Patch, Nathan, 82, 90
Patriots, 118, 170, 246, 310
Patronage, 206
Paxton, Mass., 220, 235, 276
Paxton Boys, 188
Peace of Utrecht, 213
Peckham, Samuel, 246
Pejepscot Company, 288. See also Great Proprietors
Pelham, Mass., 4, 306, agriculture in, 192–93; and Am. Rev., 195–97, 305; class in, 193, 212; clergy in, 19, 212, 242–44, 300, 304–5; Congregationalists in, 234; and county conventions, 198; culture of, 14, 15; Daniel Shays in, 129, 185, 187, 195–97, 299, 301; economy of, 14, 193–94, 243; ethnicity in, 14, 187–88, 189; farms in, 191–92; Friends of Government in, 234; in literature, 301; and Mass. constitutions, 14, 200; political culture of, 13–14, 187, 195–97, 198, 199, Presbyterians in, 14, 187–89, 212, 242–45, 248, 260, 277, 304–5; Scots-Irish in, 304–5; sects in, 234; settlement of, 187–88, 190, 191; Shaysites in, 131, 187, 194, 202, 234, 267, 298–99, 313; and Shays's Rebellion, 187, 198, 302; and Stephen Burroughs, 19, 196, 212, 243–44, 299–30, 304–5, 308, 313–14; taxes in, 245; wealth in, 189, 191, 193
Peltason, J. W., 161
Pembroke, N.H., 148
Pennsylvania, 55, 127, 170, 180, 188, 316
Penobscot expedition, 49, 327 n.14
Pepperell, Mass., 275
Petersham, Mass., Am. Rev. in, 246; clergy in, 252; Friends of Government in, 235, 245; government troops in, 132; religion in, 235, 245–48, 252; Shaysites in, 132, 145, 150, 157, 235, 245; Shays's Rebellion in, 121, 130, 132, 245, 298
Petitioners, 166, 167
Petitions, 125, 165–66, 289–90, 294
Philadelphia, Pa., 291; currency in, 77; nationalists in, 113; Paxton Boys in, 188; regional conferences in, 76; religion in, 307–8; U.S. Constitutional Convention in, 4, 6, 56, 102, 161, 173, 179, 186, 292
Phillipston, Mass., 235
Pickering, John, 138
Pickering, Timothy, 106, 138
Pilgrim's Progress, The, 299
Pittsfield, Mass., 136, 232, 257–58, 262, 272, 277
Placemen, 165
Plagiarism, 307–8
Plainfield, Mass., 234
Plumer, William, 147–49, 151
Pluralism, 157, 222–23, 241, 274
Plymouth Co., Mass., 209, 215
Political culture: and Am. Rev., 18, 150, 199–200; of backcountry, 13, 15–16, 199–200, 203; change in, 162, 165; of community, 203, 207; and consensus, 141; elites and, 13, 151–52; Henry Knox on, 162; in New England, 195; of Pelham, Mass., 195–97, 198, 199; and political discourse, 165; and reform, 165; and religion, 206,

Political culture (*continued*)
225–29, 261; and resistance, 165; and revolution, 165; Shaysites and, 146, 150–51, 152; and Shays's Rebellion, 162, 202–3; in towns, 13; of White Indians, 146
Political economy, 7, 59, 62
Political science, 7
Political scientists, 12, 161–62
Political theology, 263–74
Politicians, 11–12, 22, 65
Politics, 162, 221–24, 240–41, 252–53, 255, 263–74
Polls, 53
Pope, Joseph, 227, 276
"Popular Party," 61
Populism, 22, 104
Populists, 57–58, 65
Porter, Nehemiah, 276
Portland, Maine, 284–85, 287, 288, 289, 295. *See also* Falmouth, Maine
Portsmouth, N.H., 148
Portugal, 112
Power, 18, 168
Pownalborough, Maine, 283
Presbyterianism, 260–61
Presbyterians: in Bristol Co., Mass., 275; clergy of, 307–8; divisions among, 276; in folklore, 189; in Groton, Mass., 260, 263; in Hampshire Co., Mass., 260, 263, 276–77; immigration by, 187–88; in Middlesex Co., Mass., 275; in N.H., 243, 311; in Pelham, Mass., 14, 187–89, 212, 242, 244–45, 248, 304–5; political culture of, 261; and revivals, 256; Shaysites as, 244; in Worcester Co., Mass., 187, 275
Presbytery of Boston, 243
Presbytery of Londonderry, N.H., 243
Prescott, Oliver, 138
Prices: and Am. Rev., 74; backcountry and, 13; in Commonwealth of Mass., 68; controls on, 58, 68, 69–77, 74, 75; decline in, 72; in farm communities, 68; and ideology, 58–59; 62; of silver, 60, 64, 65; in towns, 68
Princeton, Mass., 235, 252, 253, 260, 276
Privileges, 165
Privy Council (Great Britain), 84
Property, 165; clergy and, 242, 249; conservatives and, 104, 127; of creditors, 105; as debt payment, 84, 137, 194, 297, 344 n.6; of farmers, 102, 297; of Loyalists, 106, 147, 308; in Maine, 137, 159, 160; Mass. Senate and, 104; and officeholding, 292; protection of, 59, 150, 225; Shaysites and, 127, 130, 145; Shays's Rebellion and, 169; and taxes, 69, 137; value of, 160
Protection covenant, 15–16, 136, 146, 150, 152, 157–59
Protest, popular: and Am. Rev., 14, 124, 126–28, 151–52, 163, 165, 286; in backcountry, 14–16; clergy and, 269; conservative republicans/Friends of Government on, 167–68; decentralization of, 147; and economy, 169; elites and, 150–51, 152, and Hatfield convention, 125; liberals on, 4; in Maine, 14–15, 125, 146–47, 153–58; in N.H., 14–15; in Pelham, Mass., 14; and political discourse, 163–64; and protection covenant, 150–51; radical republicans/Shaysites on, 13, 115, 124, 162, 172; as rebellion, 143, 162, 171–74, 180–82, 291, 298; and religion, 264–65; and republicanism, 6, 124–25, 152; as resistance, 162, 164, 165–67, 170, 182, 195; as revolution, 12, 16, 20, 162, 165, 170–72, 182; scholarship on, 7, 123; and Shays's Rebellion, 174; in Va., 169; and wealth, 169
Protestantism, 205, 206, 242
Providence, R.I., 69, 71, 73
Providence resolves, 69–70
Pruitt, Bettye Hobbs, 192–93
Puritanism, 58–59, 207, 229, 242, 306
Puritans, 16, 17, 21, 299
Putnam, Rufus, 132, 303
Pynchon, William, 130

Quakers, 188, 256, 260, 262
Queen Anne's War, 57, 60, 61

Radical Sects of Revolutionary New England, 206
Rand, William, 306
Rathbun, Valentine, 257, 258
Rawson, Edward, 220
Rawson, Grindall, 308
Rawson, Timothy, 87–89, 90, 91, 93, 97, 99
Read, Samuel, Jr., 87
Reagan, Ronald W., 5
Reason, 167–68
Rebellion, agrarian. *See* Protest, popular
Recession. *See* Depression, economic
Reed, Solomon, 246
Reed, William, 275
Reeves, Ezra, 277

Reform, 69, 123, 162, 165, 175, 182
Reformation men, 225
Regulating acts, 70–71, 72, 76
Regulation. *See* Protest, Popular; Shays's Rebellion
Regulators (Mass.). *See* Shaysites
Regulators (N.C.), 188
Regulators (N.H.). *See* Shaysites
Rehoboth, Mass., 275
Religion. in Amherst, Mass., 251–52; and Am. Rev., 206, 208–10, 240, 242, 246, 249–50, 255–57, 264, 272–73; in Andover, Mass., 265; and Antifederalism, 206, 240; in backcountry, 16–18, 206, 210, 241, 255, 262, 272, 305, 312; in Bellingham, Mass., 258; in Berkshire Co., Mass., 209, 211, 248–49, 254, 257–58, 262–63, 277; in Billerica, Mass., 265; in Blackstone Valley, 225; in Boston, 243, 253–54, 258, 260–61, 265, 271; in Bristol Co., Mass., 257, 263, 275; change in, 17, 241, 245, 263; in Chileab, Mass., 258; and class, 213–21; and community, 207–8; in Concord, Mass., 255, 307; conflict in, 17–18; in Conn., 262, 267–68, 311–12; in Conn. Valley, 261, 308; Continental army and, 209, 210; and culture, 241, 258; Daniel Shays and, 244, 245; and economy, 251–52; elites and, 188; and ethnicity, 242, 245, 260; and Federalism, 218, 258; Friends of Government and, 218–29, 240, 250, 255; in Gloucester, Mass., 261; in Great Britain, 262, 271; in Hampshire Co., Mass., 209, 211–12, 227, 248–49, 252, 255, 257–59, 261–63, 306, 308; and Jeffersonianism, 158, 240; in Maine, 265; and Mass. constitutions, 217, 222, 241–42, 245, 247; Mass. government and, 242, 265–66; in Medford, Mass., 307; in Middlesex Co., Mass., 252, 263, 275; in N.H., 210, 243, 260–61, 262, 311; in N.Y., 210, 262; offices of, 207, 208, 244; in Palmer, Mass., 261; and parish system, 251–52; in Pelham, Mass., 300; in Philadelphia, 307–8; and pluralism, 241; and political culture, 206, 225–29, 259, 264–65; and politics, 221–23, 240–41, 252–53, 255, 263–74; in R.I., 256, 257; in Salem, Mass., 261; scholarship on, 7, 240, 248; Shaysites and, 207, 213–29, 244–45, 250, 255, 266–69, 274; and Shays's Rebellion, 6, 17, 20, 205–7, 210, 230–31, 239–40, 248–49, 263–74; in Shirley, Mass., 262; and society, 17, 253, 304; in Suffolk Co., Mass., 254; and taxes, 17, 20, 207, 217, 241–43, 245, 251, 257, 260, 263, 311; in towns, 261, 262; and U.S. Constitution, 258; in Va., 188; in Vt., 257; and wealth, 216, 263; women and, 253; in Worcester Co., Mass., 94, 187, 209, 211, 213–29, 245–49, 252–53, 255, 257, 259–63, 275, 311. *See also* Clergy; New Lights; Sects, evangelical; *specific denominations*
Religion and the American Mind from the Great Awakening to the Revolution, 206
Relly, James, 261
Republicanism: and anarchy, 316; Antifederalists and, 282–83; in backcountry, 12, 15, 135; and class, 3, 12, 15, 151, 157; conservative republicans and, 167; debtors and, 166; eastern Mass. and, 124, 133, 135; and factions, 169; Friends of Government and, 13, 14; in Maine, 157, 160, 282–83; Mass. government and, 22, 124–25; and popular protest, 124–25; rhetoric of, 308–9; scholarship on, 143; Shaysites and, 14, 124, 203; and Shays's Rebellion, 3, 6, 316; and social order, 124; and U.S. Constitution, 282. *See also* Political culture
Republicans, 3, 15, 162, 166–79, 203
Republics, 1, 4, 13, 142–43, 172, 317
Resistance. *See* Protest, popular: as resistance
Revenue, 52–53, 61, 111, 113
Revivals, 210, 246, 256, 257, 308
Revolution, American: achievements of, 47, 188; in Amherst, Mass., 209; anniversary of, 1, 2; army of, 128–29, 130, 132; backcountry and, 13–14, 20, 22, 133–35, 203; in Boston, 133; British sabotage of, 105–6, 116; and change, 18, 20, 102; clergy and, 205–6, 249–50, 252–53, 261, 298, 305, 307; and community, 186, 187; Congress and, 47–48, 74; conservative republicans on, 171; and county conventions, 104; and courts, 201; and credit, 51, 54, 58; and culture, 255, 319; Daniel Shays and, 1–3, 170, 212, 309; and debt, 47, 48, 55–56; and economy, 18, 22, 53, 58, 68, 74, 79, 133–35, 241, 243; elites and, 151; farmers and, 22, 102, 103, 134; and finance, 1, 47–48, 53, 58, 68–74,

77–78, 80; French and, 48; in Hampshire Co., Mass., 201, 209, 305; and ideology, 5–6, 20, 151; Isaac Backus on, 271; Lafayette and, 1; in Maine, 283–85, 292, 295; in Mass., 9, 133–35; in Mass. and, 54; and "Merchantile Interest," 58; merchants and, 9, 58, 67, 72, 106; militias in, 130; and money, 57, 67, 68–72, 79; in Pelham, Mass., 195–97; and political culture, 18, 143, 150, 163, 199–200, 241, 310; and popular protest, 124, 126–27, 128, 151–52, 165, 286; and religion, 206, 208–10, 240, 242, 246, 249–50, 255–57, 264, 272–73; Samuel Adams on, 170; Samuel Thompson and, 283–84, 292; Shaysites and, 124, 125, 129–30, 135–36, 150, 194, 227; Shaysites on, 170; Shays's Rebellion and, 3, 4, 7, 12–13, 186; and society, 18, 304, 308–9, 310; states and, 47, 48; and taxes, 54, 70; towns and, 133; veterans of, 2, 13, 103, 132, 165, 194, 227, 261, 284, 288; and wealth, 308; in Worcester Co., Mass., 209, 246, 247
Revolution, French, 182
Rhode Island: and Am. Rev., 49, 213; merchants in, 64, 66; and monetary policy, 61, 63, 64, 65, 66, 69; and prices, 71; reformation men in, 225; religion in, 256, 257
Rice, Samuel, 227
Rich, Caleb, 261–62
Richardson, Tilly, 86
Riche, John, 124
Richmond, Mass., 232
Richmond, N.H., 260, 262
Riot acts, 177, 205
Riots, 225, 228
Ripley, Ezra, 255
River Gods, 195, 212, 218, 310
Road, Daniel, 89, 91, 92
Robinson Crusoe, 299
Rochambeau, Donatien Marie Joseph de Vimeur, vicomte de, 49
Rockingham Co., N.H., 147
Rogerson, Robert, 275
Rothenberg, Winifred, 342 n.1
Rousseau, Jean-Jacques, 171
Rowe, John, 67
Rowe, Mass., 138–39, 233
Royalston, Mass., 235
Rulers, 165–66, 168–69
Russell, Benjamin, 5

Russell, Joseph, 276
Rutland, Mass., 107, 235, 244, 313, 314

Salem, Mass., 111, 138, 261
Salem Village, Mass., 17
Salisbury, Stephen, 83, 84, 85, 90, 95–97, 131
Salisbury (brother of Stephen Salisbury), 96
Sandisfield, Mass.; 232
S. and S. Salisbury (importers), 108
Sanford, David, 254
Sargent, Winthrop, 138
Savage, Samuel Phillips, 138
Scarborough, Maine, 151, 284, 288
Scots, 242, 261
Scots-Irish: and class, 189; and discrimination, 187, 196; in Hampshire Co., Mass., 14, 187–89, 196, 242, 245, 260, 301; in Middlesex Co., Mass., 260; and religion, 14, 242, 245, 260, 287–89; Stephen Burroughs and, 301, 304–5, 313, 314; in Worcester Co., Mass., 187
Seaports: and Am. Rev., 133–34; debtors in, 217–18; in Maine, 288–89; merchants in, 217–18; prices in, 70; religion in, 261; and Shays's Rebellion, 20; tax collectors in, 50; trade with, 70, 74
Second Church (Templeton, Mass.), 276
Second Parish (Rehoboth, Mass.), 275
Second Presbyterian (Pelham, Mass.), 277
Sectarianism, 207
Sectionalism, 113, 133
Sects, evangelical: in backcountry, 16, 17–18, 29, 305–6; in Berkshire Co., Mass., 209, 211, 232; and clergy, 264; Friends of Government and, 239; in Hampshire Co., Mass., 211, 233–34; in Plymouth Co., Mass., 209; proliferation of, 210; and revivals, 241, 256, Shaysites and, 212, 213, 214–16, 217, 239; in Worcester Co., Mass., 211, 212, 213, 214–16, 234–35. *See also* Religion; specific denominations
Securities, 109, 217, 325 n.8
Sedgwick, Theodore, 113
Sedition acts, 177
Selectmen, 70, 129, 208, 218–19, 223, 227
Sellon, John, 247
Senate (Mass.), 92, 104, 125, 127, 136, 139. *See also* General Court (Mass.)

INDEX | 413

Separates, 259, 267–69, 305, 311. *See also* Baptists, Separate
Separation movement (Maine), 284–92, 294–95, 296
Separatism, 19
Settling. *See* Clergy: employment of
Sewall, David, 291
Sewall, Samuel, Jr., 64
Sewall, Stephen, 84, 96–97
Shaftesbury, Vt., 257
Shaftesbury Baptist Association, 259, 260
Shakerism, 262
Shakers: in backcountry, 210; in Hampshire Co., Mass., 276; in Middlesex Co., Mass., 275; establishment of, 256, 261; and pacificism, 273; and public life, 18; in Rehoboth, Mass., 275; in Shaysite towns, 17; theology of, 270, 272, 274; in Worcester Co., Mass., 246–47, 275, 277
Shattuck, Job, 130, 178
Shaw, Peter, 126
Shays, Abigail, 244, 302
Shays, Daniel: and Am. Rev., 1–3, 129, 130, 170, 212, 251, 274, 309, 313; Antifederalists on, 176, 180, 181–82; at Springfield arsenal, 121, 126, 139; and Benjamin Lincoln, 175; birth of, 129; in Brookfield, Mass., 194; Commonwealth of Mass. on, 197; contemporaries on, 1–4, 129, 170, 178, 198, 273, 309; and county conventions, 198; as creditor, 129; in culture, 4, 178, 185, 318, 319; death of, 1, 2; as debtor, 194; defeat of, 174, 177; elites on, 309–10; and expansion, 20; as farmer, 129, 185; Federalists/conservative republicans and, 172–73, 179–80; as Freemasons, 209; as fugitive, 302; goals of, 126; and Lafayette, 1, 129, 309, 318; letters of, 166; as local leader, 198; in Mass., 1, 6; in N.Y., 1, 2; in Pelham, Mass., 129, 185, 187, 195–98, 299, 301; political thought of, 126, 166, 170; punishment of, 2, 3; and religion, 244, 245; Royall Tyler and, 319; scholarship on, 3, 130, 197–98; and Shays's Rebellion, 1–2, 115, 163, 175, 198–99, 201–2, 298–99, 303–4; in Vt., 2, 3, 180; wealth of, 1, 129, 181, 309
Shaysites: and Am. Rev., 60, 124, 125, 129–30, 131, 135–36, 150, 170, 194, 227; as armed force, 115, 125–27, 128–29, artisans as, 145; Benjamin Lincoln and, 140–41; in Berkshire Co., Mass., 211; casualties of, 121; characteristics of, 130–32, 149, 150, 194; and class, 217–21, 223; clergy as, 267–69; in Concord, Mass., 128; contemporaries on, 123, 131–32; and county conventions, 125, 127, 219–20, 244; and courts, 108–9, 125, 127–28, 145–46, 151; and creditors, 17, 194, 219–21; in culture, 297; culture of, 21–22; and debt, 16–17, 108–9, 123, 131, 145, 194, 219–21, 223–24; defeat of, 146, 152, 157; and elites, 130, 147–48, 156, 206, 303; farmers as, 145, 185; Federalists on, 101–2, 104–5, 291; as Freemasons, 209; and Friends of Government, 303; goals of, 123–28, 146, 151, 225; and Gov. Bowdoin, 124, 126, 127, 137, 140–41; grievances of, 125, 145, 186, 267; in Hampshire Co., Mass., 209, 210, 308; and Jeffersonians, 158; leaders of, 270, 303–4; and liquor, 197, 299; local leaders as, 208, 217, 219–21, 227, 228, 239; and Maine, 287, 288, 291, 295, 296; and Mass. Constitution of 1780, 125, 133, 135–36, 141; and Mass. General Court, 125, 132, 137–38, 140–41, 146; and merchants, 124; in Middlesex Co., Mass., 139; Minot on, 99; in N.H., 147–48, 151, 153; in N.Y., 301; organization of, 123; and paper money, 127; in Pelham, Mass., 131, 187, 194, 202, 267, 298–99, 313; and political culture, 124, 145–46, 150–51, 152, 157, 166, 203; and property, 127, 130–31, 145; punishment of, 121, 124, 126, 137, 139–41, 149, 152, 173, 177, 202, 267, 299; and religion, 205–7, 213–29, 239, 244–45, 250, 255, 266–69, 274; as Republicans, 203; rhetoric of, 170; and Royall Tyler, 301–3; scholarship on, 122–24, 197–98; in Springfield, Mass., 21, 150, 157, 267; and state government, 151; and taxes, 123, 127, 145, 158; and U.S. Constitutional Convention, 130; in Vt., 129, 267, 301, 302; wealth of, 131, 158, 214, 239, 313; in Worcester Co., Mass., 128, 130, 132, 150, 157, 206, 211, 213–28, 245
Shays's Rebellion: Adams on, 182, 193, 301; aftermath of, 176–79; and Am. Rev., 3, 4, 7, 12–13, 186; as anarchy, 177; Antifederalists and, 175–76, 180–

Shays's Rebellion (*continued*)
82; backcountry and, 12–13, 20, 200, 282; Barbara Karsky on, 123, 186; in Berkshire Co., Mass., 174, 199, 287; Boston and, 115, 124, 138; British and, 105–6, 116, 303; Cambridge, Mass., and, 115; casualties of, 121, 224; and change, 20, 21–22, 103; and class, 15, 20, 22, 79–82, 117, 123, 212–16; clergy and, 205–7, 210, 220, 224, 227, 264–65, 270; commemoration of, 5, 324 n.6; Commonwealth of Mass. and, 2–3, 102, 112–23, 163, 173, 197, 202; and community, 186–87, 207, 208, 212, 228, 248–49; Concord, Mass., and, 138; in Conn., 190; conservatives and, 115, 171, 177–78; contemporaries on, 2–5, 134–35, 138–39, 170; and county conventions, 114, 123, 127, 302; and courts, 2, 10–11, 81, 114, 122–23, 135, 139, 145, 151, 163, 199–202, 205–6, 213, 217, 224–25, 227, 285, 297–98, 302; creditors and, 16–17, 76, 117, 228; and culture, 103, 298, 315–19; Daniel Shays and, 1–2, 115, 163, 175, 298–99; David Szatmary on, 123, 161, 239; and debt, 55, 78; debtors and, 16–17, 76, 117, 228; and economy, 6–8, 79, 194–95, 208, 217, 241; elites and, 8, 22, 146, 152, 158; and factions, 104; farmers and, 76; and federal government, 105, 115; Federalists and, 101–2, 104–6, 114–18, 179–80, 295; in folklore, 122; Gordon Wood on, 123, 161; in Hampshire Co., Mass., 174, 199, 244, 267, 302; Henry Knox on, 117, 167, 169; Henry Lee on, 169; and ideology, 104, 133; James Warren on, 170; James Winthrop and, 176; Jeffersonians and, 361 n.25; Jefferson on, 171; John L. Brooke on, 239–40; Joseph Warren on, 122–23; leaders of, 197, 198, 208; Leftist historians on, 4, 80; and literature, 6, 12, 122, 297; Madison on, 171, 177; and Maine, 283, 285, 286–87, 290, 295; Marion Starkey on, 239; Mass. and, 5, 6, 13; and Mass. Constitution of 1780, 102; Mass. General Court and, 134–35, 137–39, 171, 297–98; merchants and, 8–9, 67, 76, 105, 115, 124; in Middlesex Co., Mass., 21; as military contest, 127, 133; and militia, 205–6, 218–19; Minot on, 13, 79, 104–5, 121–22, 142, 143; and monetary policy, 9, 67; nationalist historians on, 4, 8; in N.H., 13, 174; and N.Y., 174; organization of, 115; in Pelham, Mass., 244–45; Peter S. Onuf on, 325 n.13; and political culture, 105, 158, 162, 174, 197, 202–3, 207; political scientists on, 161–62; and politics, 224, 241; Progressive historians on, 7, 79–80, 123, 161; and property, 169; and public opinion, 116–17; radical republicans and, 169, 174; and reform, 123; and regionalism, 133, 189; and religion, 6, 17, 20, 205–7, 210, 230–31, 239–40, 248–49, 263–74; and republicanism, 143; results of, 22; Richard Brown on, 161; Robert Feer on, 123, 206; Robert J. Taylor on, 198; Ronald Reagan on, 5; and Rowe, Mass., 138–39; Royall Tyler and, 301–3, 315–19; Samuel Adams on, 169; scholarship on, 5–7, 51, 81, 101, 185–86, 299; scope of, 115, 174; Shakers and, 272; significance of, 6, 55, 123, 126, 143, 186; and society, 17, 20, 186, 298; in Springfield, Mass., 2, 103, 121, 123, 126, 129–30, 139, 150, 197, 201–2, 298; states and, 19; Stephen Burroughs on, 302, 314; Stephen Marini on, 206; suppression of, 55, 101–2, 121, 123–24, 145, 147–50, 174, 202; and taxes, 5, 7, 8, 55; towns and, 12–13, 20, 187; and U.S. Constitution, 3–5, 7, 102, 105, 161–62, 178–80, 185–86; Van Beck Hall, 206; and wealth, 105, 221; William G. McLoughlin on, 206, 239, 249; in Worcester Co., Mass., 199, 206, 213, 236–38, 245, 298

Sheffield, Mass., 232
Shelburne, Mass., 234
Shepherd, William, 129, 139–40
Sheridan, Richard, 302
Sherman, Asaph, 93
Sherman, David, 88
Shirley, William, 66
Shirley, Mass., 247, 275, 298
Shrewsbury, Mass., 235
Shurtleleff, James, 159
Shutesbury, Mass., 199, 209, 234, 252, 277
Sibley, Joseph, 88
Silver, 60, 62–68, 217
Singing Controversy, 253, 276
Singletary, Amos, 220
Smith, Ebenezer, Jr., 258

Smith, Ebenezer, Sr., 258
Smith, Jonathan, 101, 102
Smith, Melancton, 175–76
Smith, Nathan, 298
Snow, Seth, 220
Society. and Am. Rev., 304; in backcountry, 186; change in, 18, 20, 304, 308; and communitarianism, 124; and culture, 19; and debt, 82, 225; and economy, 304; elites and, 310; and land pressures, 304; and religion, 17, 253, 304; and republicanism, 124; and Shays's Rebellion, 17, 298; and taxes, 225
Solemn League and Covenant, 283
Somers, Conn., 267, 268, 269
Sons of Liberty, 124
Southampton, Mass., 196, 234
Southborough, Mass., 86, 235
South Brimfield, Mass., 234, 277
Southgage, Isaac, 224
South Hadley, Mass., 234, 308
South Leicester, Mass., 226
South Sea Bubble Act, 66
Southwick, Mass., 234
Spain, 111, 112
Sparhawk, Ebenezer, 276
Sparta, N.Y., 1
Specie: and Am. Rev., 74; availability of, 66, 109, 136, 111; in backcountry, 109; and banks, 61; Board of Trade on, 65; in cities, 109; Commonwealth of Mass. and, 1, 78; Congress and, 52; and credit, 82; creditors and, 50, 53, 78; and currency, 57; and debt, 86; debtors and, 82; and debt payments, 48, 52, 60; farmers and, 111; Federalists and, 111; Hutchinson on, 66; and ideology, 58–59, 60, 62–63, 74–75; issues of, 60, 137; and loans, 58; Mass. government and, 50, 51, 66, 68; merchants and, 9, 57, 60, 80; opposition to, 74–75, 92; and paper money, 52, 62, 65, 67; and paper money supporters, 62; Province of Mass. and, 60, 61, 64, 67; and taxes, 8, 50, 51, 52, 53; and trade, 82; value of, 48, 49, 62, 83
Speculation, 50–51, 308
Speculators, 73, 163
Spencer, Mass.: creditors in, 17, 214, 216, 219–20; debtors in, 214–15, 219, 220; elites in, 218, 219–20; Friends of Government in, 214–16, 219; religion in, 17, 214–16, 222, 227, 253, 276;

Shaysites in, 17, 213, 214–16, 218–20, 222, 227, 235, 253
Springfield, Mass.: Am. Rev. in, 201; artisans in, 103; clergy in, 255; counterfeiting in, 300; courts in, 201–2; culture of, 255; Friends of Government in, 234; newspapers in, 103, 107; regional conventions in, 71–72, 73; Shaysites in, 157; Shays's Rebellion in, 2, 21, 121, 123, 126, 129–32, 139, 145, 150, 201–2, 267, 298; Stephen Burroughs in, 300; wealth in, 190
Springfield resolutions, 72
Squatters, 14, 15, 19, 269, 288, 296
Stamp Act, 51, 106
Standing Order. *See* Congregationalism; Congregationalists; Religion
Standisfield, Mass., 257
Stanton, John, 224, 225
Starkey, Marion, 239
State of nature, 12, 127, 159, 171, 209, 222
Stearns, William Jennison, 89–90, 92, 94, 97
Stebbins, Daniel, 130, 315
Steele, Eliphalet, 267, 277
Sterling, 60, 62
Sterling, Mass., 86, 235
Steuben, Friedrich Wilhelm von, 130
Steward, Antipas, 276
Stiles, Ezra, 250, 305
Stillman, Samuel, 258
Stockbridge, Mass., 121, 128, 232, 254
Stoddard, Solomon, 195–96
Storer, Ebenezer, 107
Storrs, Richard, 276
Streeter, Adams, 262
Strickland, John, 275
Strong, Caleb, 113, 131
Sturbridge, Mass., 213, 214, 221, 222, 235
Suffolk Co., Mass., 68, 254, 329 n.43
Sullivan, James, 155, 156–57
Sullivan, John, 147–48, 149
Sunderland, Mass., 234, 306
Supreme Court of Judicature (Mass.): closings of, 122, 128; debt cases in, 10, 81, 87–90, 97, 219–20, 223; reform of, 97–98, 127
Sutton, Mass., 87, 235, 259, 261, 262
Swan, James, 327 n.16
Symmes, William, 265
System of Doctrines, 254
Szatmary, David: on Backus's *Address to the Inhabitants of New England . . .*, 270; on Commonwealth of Mass.,

416 | INDEX

Szatmary, David (*continued*)
  12; on rural debt, 193; on Shaysites, 123, 129, 130, 131, 239; on Shays's Rebellion, 186, 207, 248, 249

Taft, Aaron, Jr., 88
Taggart, Samuel, 276
Taxes: and Am. Rev., 54, 70; artisans and, 145; in backcountry, 14, 74, 135, 136; Concord convention and, 76; consumers and, 103; and credit, 69, 72; and creditors, 55; and debt, 60, 78, 125, 217; and debtors, 55; and depreciation, 69; Essex Co., Mass., and, 329 n.43; farmers and, 69, 102, 103, 117, 145; federal government and, 49, 56, 292; Federalists and, 117; Friends of Government and, 132; Hampshire Co., Mass., and, 329 n.43; on land, 69; and loan interest, 9; in Mass., 1, 7, 8; Mass. government and, 22, 49, 51, 60, 77, 102, 137, merchants and, 58, 69, 76, 80; in N.H., 147; officials of, 165; and paper money, 9, 49, 52, 58, 65–66, 68, 72, 77–78; payment of, 109, 137, 138, in Pelham, Mass., 245; on polls, 69; protests against, 19; relief from, 22; and religion, 17, 20, 207, 217, 241–43, 245, 251, 257, 260, 263, 311; and Rev. War debt, 1, 50; Shaysites and, 123, 125, 127, 145, 158; and Shays's Rebellion, 7, 8, 55; and society, 225; in Southborough, Mass., 86; and specie, 8, 51, 52; and state currencies, 72; Suffolk Co., Mass., and, 329 n.43; on towns, 53, 134; and trade, 52; types of, 48, 50, 56, 103; veterans and, 103, 132
Taylor, Robert J., 135, 198, 206, 325 n.8
Templeton, Mass., 235, 263, 276
Testimonies of Mother Ann Lee, 246
Thacher, Peter, 138
Thacher, Thomas, 180
Thatcher, Samuel, 154
Thayer, Alexander, 276
Thayer, David, 87–88
Thayer, Ezra, 277
Theater, 302, 315–19
Theology, 17, 241, 245, 251. *See also* Political theology
Thetford, Vermont, 129
Thompson, James, 277
Thompson, Samuel, 282–84, 288, 289, 292–93, 294–96
Thompson, Stephen, 198
Thoreau, Henry David, 319

Tilly, Charles, 212
Todd, Samuel, 277
Tomlinson, Daniel, 275
Topsham, Maine, 282, 284, 292, 294
Tories. *See* Loyalists
Towne, Col., 206
Town meetings, 1, 71, 220, 285
Towns: and Am. Rev., 130; assets of, 53; in backcountry, 16–17, 20, 70, 103–4, 187–88, 190; banks in, 65; in Berkshire Co., Mass., 213, 232; and Boston, 213; collectors in, 50; in Conn., 190–91; county conventions in, 104; culture of, 19, 299, and debt, 53, 72–73; and debtors, 85; in eastern Mass., 53, 136, 189; economy of, 190; farming in, 190; Federalism in, 117; Federalists in, 103; in Hampshire Co., Mass., 187, 213, 233–34; and ideology, 21; increase in, 130; interests of, 124; Jeffersonians in, 361 n.25; and Maine, 19, 153, 154; merchants in, 103; and paper money, 73; political culture of, 13; political power of, 53; and prices, 68, 70, 72; Revolutionary veterans in, 130, scholarship on, 186; and Shays's Rebellion, 12–13, 20, 187; and taxes, 73; trade with, 74; wealth in, 53, 190; in Worcester Co., Mass., 213, 234–35
Townsend, Mass., 275
Townshend acts, 106
Trade: and Am. Rev., 74; with backcountry, 22, 75, 106, 190; balance of, 52, 59, 60, 62–63, 82; with Boston, 74, 75, 96; British factors and, 116; with China, 112; Confederation and, 111; Congress and, 68, 110, 116, with Cuba, 49; elites and, 18; with Europe, 70, 75, 111, 112, 270; expansion of, 61; farmers and, 102; federal government and, 11, 115, 292; Federalists and, 111, 115; with France, 102, 111, 112; with Great Britain, 52, 60, 62, 106, 111, 283; with Holland, 111; ideology and, 62–63; with Maine, 285; with Mass., 49, 52, 61, 64; with Mediterranean, 112; and money, 60, 66–67, 82; with New England, 112–13; with Portugal, 112; protection of, 11, 52; regulation of, 22, 59, 102, 110, 112–16, 292; and revenue, 52; with R.I., 64, with South, 111, 112–13; with Spain, 111, 112; and taxes, 52; with towns, 74; with West Indies, 69, 75, 102, 106, 111–12, 270; with

Worcester Co., Mass., 96
Trade goods, 102–3, 106–9, 111, 134
Traders, 70, 87, 105, 110, 285
Tradesmen, 65, 74, 110–11
Trask, Nicholas, 93
Treaty of Paris (1763), 58
Treaty of Paris (1783), 112, 143, 270
True, Benjamin *See* Burroughs, Stephen
Tucker, Ebenezer, 276
Tucker, Samuel, 227
Turrell, Ebenezer, 307
Tyler, Lemuel, 131
Tyler, Royall, 19, 301–4, 315–19
Tyranny, 5, 152, 172, 174, 179, 264
Tyrants, 12, 166
Tyringham, Mass., 232, 277

Ulster, Ire., 187
United States, 1, 2, 3, 5, 8, 20
Universalism, 261–62
Universalists: and Am. Rev., 210, 305; and Baptists, 210, 217; in Charlton, Mass., 224, 311; confidence men as, 314; establishment of, 256; as Friends of Government, 223; as Shaysites, 225; in Shaysite towns, 17
University of Edinburgh, 243
Upton, Mass, 235
Uxbridge, Mass., 87, 225, 235, 260

Van Schaack, Henry, 128, 142
Vaughan, Charles, 154
Vaughan, Elliot G., 154–55
Vermont: clergy in, 269; Daniel Shays in, 2, 180; legislature of, 127; religion in, 257; Royall Tyler in, 302, 303, 319; Shaysites in, 129, 267, 301, 302
Virginia, 6, 169, 180, 188
Virtue: and Am. Rev., 133; and debt, 54, 60, 99; in eastern Mass., 133; Friends of Government and, 13; Mass. government and, 265; and money, 58–59, 68; republicanism, 309, Shaysites and, 170; and society, 124; and trade, 58–59
Voluntarism, 17, 228
Voluntary associations, 20, 223, 224

Wadsworth, Peleg, 284
Wait, Thomas, 284, 286–87, 289
Waldo Patent (Maine), 269
War bonds *See* Notes, treasury
Ward, Artemas, 124, 128
Ward, Mass, 225, 235, 276
Ware, Mass., 192, 227, 234, 263, 267, 277
Warner, Gen., 206

Warren, Daniel, 87
Warren, James, 70, 76, 170, 309
Warren, Joseph, 122–23, 127
Warren, Mercy Otis, 181–82
Warren, R.I , 257
Warren Baptist Association, 209, 213, 257, 258–59, 260
Warwick, Mass., 209, 234, 262
Washington, George: Antifederalists on, 293; and Daniel Shays, 178; and Henry Lee, 177; and Lafayette, 1; and Madison, 171, 177; as potential dictator, 173; regiments of, 129; and slavery, 293
Washington, Mass., 232
Watkins, John, 308
Watson, Oliver, 219
Watson (family), 219
Watts, Isaac, 253
Wealth: and Am. Rev., 18, 134, 308; in backcountry, 134, 190, 192, in Boston, 124; and class, 22, 150, 151; in Conn., 190–91; of creditors, 81; of Daniel Shays, 129, 181; in eastern Mass., 123, 134; and farm size, 192; and federal government, 105, of Friends of Government, 214; in Great Britain, 60; in Hampshire Co., Mass , 189, 190, 191, 193; of lawyers, 113; in Maine, 153, 288–89; in Mass., 192; of merchants, 124; and religion, 216, 259, 263; of Shaysites, 169, 214, 239, 313; and Shays's Rebellion, 105, 221; of Stephen Burroughs, 313; in Worcester Co , Mass., 187, 190, 216
Webster, Noah, 134
Wells, Rufus, 277
Wells, Samuel, 64
Wells, Maine, 288
Wendell, Jacob, 64
Wendell, Mass., 234
Werden, Peter, 257
Weson, John, Jr., 88–89
Weson, John, Sr., 89
West, Stephen, 254
Westborough, Mass., 235
West Church (Boston), 265
Western Massachusetts in Revolution, 198
Westfield, Mass., 234, 306
Westhampton, Mass., 234
West Indies, 69, 75, 102, 106, 111–12, 270
Westminster, Mass., 86, 235
Westminster Confession of Faith, 244
West Springfield, Mass., 129, 234, 308
West Stockbridge, Mass , 232, 277
Wetmore, Ephraim, 96

Whalley, Edward, 299
Whately, Mass., 234, 277
Wheeler, Adam, 126, 129, 168, 170–71, 227–28
Wheelock, Eleazar, 260–61
Whiggism, 165, 171
Whigs, 170, 196, 199, 283, 284
White, David, 247–48
White and Clap (store), 107
Whitefield, George, 261, 306–7
White Indians, 14, 146–47, 153–60
Whiteing, William, 130
White v. Trask, 91
Whitney, Aaron, 245–46, 252
Whitney, Phinehas, 275
Whittaker, James, 247, 262, 272
Widgery, William, 281, 282, 294
Wilbraham, Mass., 234
Wilkinson, Jemima, 210
Williams, Henry, 276
Williams, Israel, 195
Williams, Stephen, 276
Williamsburg, Mass., 234
Williamstown, Mass., 232
Winchendon, Mass., 235
Windsor, Mass., 232
Winslow, Jacob, 64
Winslow, Maine, 155
Winthrop, James, 176
Winthrop, John, 168
Wiscasset, Maine, 283
Wise, John, 62
Wiser, Joseph, 86
Wolves in Sheep's Clothing, 308
Women, 86, 108, 253
Wood, Aaron, 247
Wood, Gordon, 123, 124, 161
Wood, Joseph, 109
Woodbury, Jeremiah, 95

Worcester Co., Mass.: Baptists in, 221, 222–26, 275, 276; class in, 213; clergy in, 209, 211, 213, 248, 250, 255, 275; Congregationalists in, 187, 217–24, 226–29, 253, 255, 275; county conventions in, 127, 311; courts in, 10, 81, 213, 285; creditors in, 10, 214, 216, 218–21; debt cases in, 10, 81–82, 85–99, 217; debtors in, 10, 214–15, 217, 218–21; ethnicity in, 187; Friends of Government in, 214–16; immigration to, 187; Jeffersonians in, 361 n.25; justices in, 213; lawyers in, 220; and Maine, 286, 291; merchants in, 131; militia from, 213; newspaper in, 103; newspapers in, 107, 111; Presbyterians in, 187, 260; publishing in, 104; Quakers in, 260; religion in, 248–49, 275; scholarship on, 187; sects in, 211, 213–17, 220–26, 228–29, 263; Separate Baptists in, 213, 216, 257, 259; settlement of, 213; Shakers in, 275; Shaysites in, 122, 128, 130, 214–16, 275–76; Shays's Rebellion in, 187, 199, 206, 236–38; and taxes, 329 n.43; towns in, 213, 234–35; Universalists in, 223, 225, 261–62; wealth in, 187, 190, 216
Worcester Magazine, 131, 164, 168
Worthington, Mass., 234
Writs, 156, 157, 224
Wroth, L. Kinvin, 93

Yale College, 247, 250, 255, 267, 298, 311
Yankee, 298–320
York Co., Maine, 291
York, Maine, 265, 285, 288, 294

Zobel, Hiller, 93

www.ingramcontent.com/pod-product-compliance
Lightning Source LLC
Chambersburg PA
CBHW031958220426
43664CB00005B/65